WHAT THEY S...
THE JOBBANK

"If you are looking for a job...before you go to the newspapers and the help-wanted ads, listen to Bob Adams, editor of *The Metropolitan New York JobBank*."
→ -Tom Brokaw
NBC TELEVISION

"...A superior series of job hunt directories."
→ -Cornell University
Career Center
WHERE TO START

"Help on the job hunt...Anyone who is job-hunting in the New York area can find a lot of useful ideas in a new paperback called *The Metropolitan New York JobBank*..."
→ -Angela Taylor
THE NEW YORK TIMES

"A timely book for Chicago job hunters follows books from the same publisher that were well received in New York and Boston...A fine tool for job hunters..."
→ -Clarence Petersen
THE CHICAGO TRIBUNE

"Job hunting is never fun, but this book can ease the ordeal...[*The Los Angeles JobBank*] will help allay fears, build confidence, and avoid wheel-spinning."
→ -Robert W. Ross
THE LOS ANGELES TIMES

"This well-researched, well-edited job hunter's aid includes most major businesses and institutional entities in the New York metropolitan area...Highly recommended."
→ -Cheryl Gregory-Pindell
LIBRARY JOURNAL

"Here's the book for your job hunt...Trying to get a job in New York? I would recommend a good look through *The Metropolitan New York JobBank*..."
→ -Maxwell Norton
NEW YORK POST

"No longer can jobseekers feel secure about finding employment just through want ads. With the tough competition in the job market, particularly in the Boston area, they need much more help. For this reason, *The Boston JobBank* will have a wide and appreciative audience of new graduates, job changers, and people relocating to Boston. It provides a good place to start a search for entry-level professional positions."
→ -from a review in
THE JOURNAL OF
COLLEGE PLACEMENT

What makes the JobBank Series the nation's premier line of employment guides?

With vital employment information on thousands of employers across the nation, the JobBank Series is the most comprehensive and authoritative set of career directories available today.

Each book in the series provides information on **dozens of different industries** in a given city or area, with the primary employer listings providing contact information, telephone numbers, addresses, a thumbnail sketch of the firm's business, and in many cases descriptions of the firm's typical professional job categories, the principal educational backgrounds sought, and the fringe benefits offered.

In addition to the **detailed primary employer listings**, the new 1993 JobBank books--for the first time--also give contact information, telephone numbers, and addresses for hundreds of other large employers as well as for **thousands of smaller and medium-sized employers.**

All of the reference information in the JobBank Series is as up-to-date and accurate as possible. Every year, the entire database is thoroughly researched and verified, first by mail and then by telephone. Bob Adams Inc. publishes **more local JobBank books more often** than any other publisher of career directories.

In addition, the JobBank Series features important information about the local job scene--**forecasts on which industries are the hottest,** overviews of **local economic trends,** and even **lists of regional professional associations,** so you can get your job hunt started off right.

Hundreds of discussions with job hunters show they prefer information organized geographically, because most people look for jobs in specific areas. The JobBank Series offers **twenty regional titles,** from Minneapolis to Houston, and from Washington, D.C., to San Francisco. The future employee moving to a particular area can review the local employment data not only for information on the type of industry most common to that region, but also for names of specific employers.

A condensed, but thorough, review of the entire job search process is presented in the chapter **"The Basics of Job Winning"**, a feature which has received many compliments from career counselors. In addition, each JobBank directory is completed by a section on **resumes and cover letters** *The New York Times* has acclaimed as "excellent."

The JobBank Series gives job hunters the most comprehensive, most timely, and most accurate career information, organized and indexed to facilitate the job search. An entire career reference library, JobBank books are the consummate employment guides.

Published by Bob Adams, Inc.
260 Center Street, Holbrook MA 02343

Copyright ©1993 by Bob Adams, Inc. All rights reserved. No part of the material printed may be reproduced or utilized in any form or by any means, electronic or mechanical, including photo-copying, recording, or by any information storage retrieval system without written permission from the publisher.

The St. Louis JobBank and its cover design are trademarks of Bob Adams, Inc.

Brand name products mentioned in the employer listings are proprietary property of the applicable firm, subject to trademark protection, and registered with government offices.

While the publisher has made every reasonable attempt to obtain accurate information and to verify same, occasional errors are inevitable due to the magnitude of the data base. Should you discover an error, please write to the publisher so that corrections may be made in future editions.

The appearance of a listing anywhere in this book does not constitute an endorsement from the publisher.

Cover design by Peter Weiss.

ISBN:1-55850-266-1

The St. Louis JobBank
4th Edition

Managing Editor
Carter Smith

Associate Editor
Steven Graber

Editorial Assistants
Kenny Brooks
Keith Moore

Top career publications from Bob Adams, Inc:

THE JOBBANK SERIES:

The Atlanta JobBank ($15.95)
The Boston JobBank ($15.95)
The Carolina JobBank ($15.95)
The Chicago JobBank ($15.95)
The Dallas-Ft. Worth JobBank ($15.95)
The Denver JobBank ($15.95)
The Detroit JobBank ($15.95)
The Florida JobBank ($15.95)
The Houston JobBank ($15.95)
The Los Angeles JobBank ($15.95)
The Minneapolis-St. Paul JobBank ($15.95)
The New York JobBank ($15.95)
The Ohio JobBank ($15.95)
The Philadelphia JobBank ($15.95)
The Phoenix JobBank ($15.95)
The San Francisco Bay Area JobBank ($15.95)
The Seattle JobBank ($15.95)
The St. Louis JobBank ($15.95)
The Tennessee JobBank ($15.95)
The Washington DC JobBank ($15.95)

The National JobBank
 (Covers 50 states: $240.00)

The JobBank Guide to Employment Services
 (Covers 50 states: $140.00)

OTHER CAREER TITLES:

America's Fastest Growing Employers ($14.95)
Careers and the College Grad ($9.95)
Careers and the Engineer ($9.95)
Careers and the MBA ($9.95)
Cold Calling Techniques that Really Work ($7.95)
Cover Letters that Knock'em Dead ($7.95)
The Elements of Job Hunting ($4.95)
Harvard Guide to Careers in the Mass Media ($7.95)
High Impact Telephone Networking for Job Hunters ($6.95)
How to Become Successfully Self-Employed ($9.95)
How to Get a Job in Education ($6.95)
Job Search Handbook ($6.95)
Knock 'em Dead: The Ultimate Job Seeker's Handbook ($7.95)
The Minority Career Book ($9.95)
Resume Handbook ($5.95)
Resumes that Knock 'em Dead ($7.95)
300 New Ways to Get A Better Job ($7.95)

To order these books or additional copies of this book, send check or money order (including $3.75 for postage) to:

Bob Adams, Inc., 260 Center Street, Holbrook MA 02343

Ordering by credit card?
Just call 1-800/USA-JOBS
(In Massachusetts, call 617/767-8100)

HOW TO USE THIS BOOK

A copy of *The St. Louis JobBank* book is one of the most effective tools you can use in your professional job hunt. In this guide, you will find the most up-to-date information available on thousands of businesses throughout Greater St. Louis. This book will supply you with specific addresses, phone numbers, and personnel contact information--and often much more than that--for companies which employ over 50 people.

Separate yourself from the flock of candidates who rely on help-wanted advertisements as their main job hunting strategy. The method this book offers, direct employer contact, boasts twice the success rate of any other. Exploit it.

Read and use *The St. Louis JobBank* to uncover new opportunities. Here's how:

--Read the introductory economic overview in order to gain insights on what the overall trends are for the St. Louis economy.

--Map out your job-seeking strategy by reading the "Basics of Job Winning" section. This section gives a condensed version of the most effective job search methods.

--Write a winning resume and learn how to sell yourself most effectively on paper, using the "Resumes and Cover Letters" section.

--Within each industry you will find detailed information on "Primary St. Louis Employers." These primary listings give contact information, a telephone number, an address, a thumbnail sketch of the firm, and in many cases, descriptions of the firm's typical professional categories, the educational backgrounds sought, and the fringe benefits offered. Formulate a target list of the potential employers in your field by selecting appropriate companies from the "Primary St. Louis Employers" section of each industry. Use the detailed information provided in this section to supplement your own research on the major local employers in your area--so you'll be knowledgeable about each firm before your interview. Then expand your list of target employers by consulting the "Additional large employers" and the "Small to medium sized employers" section within each industry. These listings provide contact information, telephone numbers, and addresses.

--Increase your knowledge of your field, as well as your connections within it, by using our major professional and trade associations.

Whether you are just out of college and starting your first job search, looking for a new position in your current field, or entering an entirely new sector of the job market, *The St. Louis JobBank* will give you an idea of the range and diversity of employment possibilities throughout the metropolitan area. Your ultimate success will depend on how rigorously you use the information provided here. This one-of-a-kind employment guide can lead you to a company, and a job, that would otherwise have remained undiscovered. With a willingness to apply yourself, a positive attitude, and the research within these covers, you can attain your career objective.

TABLE OF CONTENTS

Introduction/11
A complete and informative economic overview designed to help you understand all of the forces shaping the St. Louis job market.

The Basics of Job Winning/15
A condensed review of the basic elements of a successful job search campaign. Includes advice on developing an effective strategy, time planning, preparing for interviews, interview techniques, etc.

Resumes and Cover Letters/29
Advice on creating a strong resume. Includes sample resumes and cover letters.

Primary St. Louis Employers/43
The St. Louis JobBank is organized according to industry. Many listings include the address and phone number of each major firm listed, along with a description of the company's basic product lines and services, and, in most cases, a contact name and other relevant hiring information. Also includes thousands of secondary listings providing addresses, numbers, and contact names for smaller and mid-sized firms.

Accounting and Auditing/43
Advertising, Marketing, & Public Relations/46
Aerospace/51
Amusement, Arts, and Recreation/54
Apparel and Textiles/60
Architecture, Construction, & Real Estate/66
Automotive/79
Banking/Savings and Loan/83
Book and Magazine Publishing/100
Broadcasting/103
Charitable, Non-Profit, Social Services/106
Chemical and Environmental/110
Colleges & Universities/Education/115
Communications/127

Computers/132
Electrical and Electronic/135
Energy, Mining, & Petroleum/145
Engineering & Design/151
Fabricated and Primary Metals/155
Financial Services/Management Consulting/170
Food & Beverages: Production/Distribution/177
General Merchandise: Retail/190
Government/217
Health Care and Pharmaceuticals/219
Hospitality: Hotels and Restaurants/241
Insurance/251
Legal Services/257
Manufacturing: Miscellaneous Consumer/259
Manufacturing: Miscellaneous Industrial/271
Miscellaneous Services/281
Newspaper Publishing/287
Paper & Packaging/Glass & Forest Products/290
Printing/Graphic Arts/298
Research and Development/305
Rubber and Plastics/306
Transportation/311
Utilities/322

Professional Employment Services /325
Includes the address, phone number, description of each company's services, contact name, and a list of positions commonly filled.

Executive Search Firms/330
Includes the address, phone number, description of each company's services, contact name, and a list of positions commonly filled.

Index/337
An alphabetical index of St. Louis' primary employer listings only. Due to space constraints, employers that fall under the headings "Large Employers", or "Small to Medium Sized Employers" are not indexed here.

INTRODUCTION

Overview

With a variety of international cultural centers, a multitude of well-respected educational institutions and a cost of living that remains lower than nearly all other large metro areas in the country, St. Louis is rebounding after a number of hard years. Recently cited by the Lomas Mortgage Company as possessing the most affordable housing in the nation, metropolitan St. Louis has clearly emerged as one of the most attractive and promising cities in the Midwest.

Nationally, the city scores high marks in several categories. The *Places Rated Almanac* currently ranks St. Louis in the top 10% of places to live out of the more than 300 metro areas in the country, while the St. Louis region as a whole falls well below the national average in both violent crime rates and the total crime index. In addition, state and local taxes in St. Louis are 10% lower than the average for other major American cities. Together, these statistics and accomplishments profile a city that is experiencing rapid change and growth. The current population in St. Louis stands close to 2.5 million people.

An Economic Overview

Economically, St. Louis is backed by its ever-developing diversity. The city's recent emergence in the fields of high technology, health care, services, distribution, and office facilities have helped prepare it for the 21st century, as well as to strengthen its role as a burgeoning Midwestern city. Some 570,000 people currently hold positions as professionals and managers, for example, while another 100,000 work in the field of high-tech (engineering, science, and computers). St. Louis also relies on its more traditional sectors of manufacturing, including the defense and auto industries.

St. Louis is a city of moderate growth, whose local economy tends to follow that of the nation. Since 1982, for example, the city's employment figures have grown 1.5% every year, which is just below the national average of 1.9%. Furthermore, the annual unemployment rate never reached higher than 0.8% above the national rate during that same ten-year period.

Employment Opportunities

The unemployment rate continues to drop in St. Louis. In October of 1992, for example, unemployment numbers fell from 5.9% to 5.3% from the previous month. Although job opportunities in manufacturing, particularly the transportation equipment manufacturing sector, remain stagnant, the service sector continues to improve. Overall growth and recovery have both been slow, however, with the area's labor force dropping some 7,700 jobs between October, 1991, and October, 1992.

Manufacturing

Losses in manufacturing have been a constant in St. Louis for several years. Heavy reliance on both the defense and auto industries have hurt the city's economic growth, with cuts in defense spending and the decline of the auto industry forcing several plants to shut down and many companies to layoff workers. Don't look for any drastic changes in the near future, either.

According to the Missouri Division of Employment Security, 5,000 jobs were lost in the manufacturing sector between October of 1991 and October of 1992, with the aerospace (-3,000 jobs) and the apparel (-1,200 jobs) industries suffering the biggest losses. Decreases in lumber, stone, and food were also reported.

The news wasn't all bad, however. The textile, chemical, and petroleum industries all saw increases over the course of the year, and employment in the auto industry for October, 1992, was up 500 jobs from October, 1991.

Non-Manufacturing

The overall outlook for employment opportunities in the non-manufacturing sector is much brighter. Some 3,400 non-manufacturing jobs were added between October of 1991 and October of 1992, with the largest improvements occurring in services, especially in apparel stores, furniture stores, and restaurants. As of October, 1992, seasonal losses were registered in the amusement and recreation industry.

Company Profiles

There are many large and small companies in Metropolitan St. Louis, several of which have designated the city home to their corporate headquarters. Of the top 100 industrial corporations compiled by *Forbes* magazine, for example, St. Louis places fifth, with five corporate headquarters in the metropolitan area. In addition, 29 St. Louis-based companies are ranked in either *Forbes, Business Week* or *Fortune*. Some of the largest companies in St. Louis include **Anheuser-Busch, Emerson Electric, May Department Stores, McDonnell Douglas, Monsanto, Ralston Purina** and **Southwestern Bell.**

Anheuser-Busch:

Founded in 1860, Anheuser-Busch is the largest brewer in the world and the second largest operator of theme parks. The company runs 12 breweries here in the United States, and operates nine theme parks across the country, including Busch Gardens in Tampa Bay, Florida, and Busch Garden's "The Old Country" in Williamsburg, Virginia. Plans to open a similar park in Barcelona, Spain are currently in the works.

With an increase in beer volume and higher beer prices, Anheuser-Busch experienced a 3.5% year-to-year, increase in sales for the six months ended June 30, 1992. Overall earnings for 1993 are projected to benefit from price and volume increases, and decreases in material and financing costs.

Anheuser-Busch is a giant corporation. Besides the major role it currently plays in the beer industry, the company also owns Campbell Taggart, the second largest commercial baker in the nation. Eagle Snacks, a subsidiary that produces peanuts, chips and crackers, currently ranks fifth nationally in salted snacks. The company's overall commercial base has also been strengthened by the success of the **St. Louis Cardinals** baseball team (purchased in 1953) and a recent venture into the real estate market.

Ralston Purina:

The largest producer of pet foods, bread, and batteries in America, Ralston Purina was founded in 1894. In addition to its businesses that include breakfast cereals and soy proteins, Ralston Purina also produces baby foods (it purchased Beech-Nut in 1989) and feeds for both livestock and poultry.

A 3.0% rise, year-to-year, was reported in sales for the six months ended March 31, 1992, although a less favorable product mix forced margins to narrow. Perhaps the biggest news for Ralston in 1992 came with its decision to acquire Ever Ready Limited, from Hanson, PLC for $230 million.

McDonnell Douglas:

The struggling defense industry has certainly affected America's number one defense contractor, McDonnell Douglas. Makers of fighter planes, helicopters, missiles, space systems and commercial jetliners, McDonnell Douglas prospered during the 1980s under Ronald Reagan, but the end of the cold war has meant a decline in orders for several of the company's products, including the C-17 transport.

McDonnell Douglas expected earnings losses for 1992 and reported a 1.8% decrease in revenues, year-to-year, in the first six months of that same year. The company also eliminated 17,000 jobs in July of 1990 in an effort to reduce costs. Recovery in 1993, of course, will depend on an increase in overall orders and a decrease in write-offs.

Conclusion

Backed by the presence of several large corporations, its excellent distribution facilities (the city has the second-largest port in the nation and is the third-largest rail hub), and a reputation as one of the most affordable cities in the nation, St. Louis has much to offer those in search of a job. Although the city certainly hasn't escaped unscathed by the recent national recession, there are signs of improvement. If the manufacturing sector can rebound and the non-manufacturing sector can maintain its overall stability, St. Louis should continue to emerge as one of the country's most important economic centers.

THE BASICS OF JOB WINNING: A CONDENSED REVIEW

The best way to obtain a better professional job is to contact the employer directly. Broad-based statistical studies by the Department of Labor show that job seekers find jobs more successfully by contacting employers directly than by using any other method.

However, given the diversity and the increasingly specialized nature of both industries and job tasks, in some situations other job seeking methods may also be successful. Three of the other most commonly used methods are: relying on personal contacts, using employment services, and following up help wanted advertisements. Many professionals have been successful in finding better jobs using one of these methods. However, the Direct Contact method boasts twice the success rate of any other method, and is used successfully by many more professionals. So unless you have specific reasons to believe that another method would work best for you, the Direct Contact method should form the foundation of your job search.

The Objective

With any business task, you must develop a strategy for meeting a goal. This is especially true when it comes to obtaining a better job. First you need to clearly define your objectives.

The first step in beginning your job search is to clearly define your objectives.

Setting your job objectives is better known as career planning (or life planning for those who wish to emphasize the importance of combining the two). Career planning has become a field of study in and of itself. Since many of our readers are probably well-entrenched in their career path, we will touch on career planning only briefly.

If you are thinking of choosing or switching careers, we particularly emphasize two things. First, choose a career where you will enjoy most of the day-to-day tasks. This sounds obvious, but most of us have at one point or another been attracted by a glamour industry or a prestigious sounding job without thinking of the most important consideration: Would we enjoy performing the everyday tasks the position entailed?

The second key consideration is that you are not merely choosing a career, but also a lifestyle. Career counselors indicate that one of the most common problems people encounter in job seeking is that they fail to consider how well-suited they are for a particular position or career. For example, some people, attracted to management consulting by good salaries, early responsibility, and high-level corporate exposure, do not adapt well to the long hours, heavy travel demands, and the constant pressure to produce. So be sure to ask yourself how you might adapt to not only the day-to-day duties and working environment that a specific position entails, but also how you might adapt to the demands of that career or industry choice as a whole.

The Strategy

Assuming that you've established your career objectives, the next step of the job search is to develop a strategy. If you don't take the time to develop a strategy and lay out a plan, you will find yourself going in circles after several weeks of random searching for opportunities that always seem just beyond your reach.

Your strategy can be thought of as having three simple elements:

1. Choosing a method of contacting employers.

2. Allocating your scarce resources. (In most job searches the key scarce resource will be time, but financial considerations will become important in some searches, too.)

3. Evaluating how the selected contact method is working and then considering adopting other methods.

We suggest you consider using the Direct Contact method exclusively. However, we realize it is human nature to avoid putting all your eggs in one basket. So if you prefer to use other methods as well, try to expend at least half your effort on the Direct Contact method, spending the rest on all of the other methods combined. Millions of other jobseekers have already proven that Direct Contact has been twice as effective in obtaining employment, so why not benefit from their effort?

With your strategy in mind, the next step is to work out the details. The most important detail is setting up a schedule. Of course, since job searches aren't something most people do regularly, it may be hard to estimate how long each step will take. Nonetheless, it is important to have a plan so that you can see yourself progressing.

When outlining your job search schedule, have a realistic time frame in mind. If you will be job searching full-time, your search will probably take at least two months. If you can only devote part-time effort, it will probably take four months.

You probably know a few people who seem to spend their whole lives searching for a better job in their spare time. Don't be one of them. Once you begin your job search on a part-time basis, give it your whole-hearted effort. If you don't feel like devoting a lot of energy to job seeking right now, then wait. Focus on enjoying your present position, performing your best on the job, and storing up energy for when you are really ready to begin your job search.

Those of you currently unemployed should remember that job hunting is tough work physically and emotionally. It is also intellectually demanding work that requires you to be at your best. So don't tire yourself out by working on your job campaign around the clock. At the same time, be sure to discipline yourself. The most logical way to manage your time while looking for a job is to keep your regular working hours.

Job hunting is intellectually demanding work that requires you to be at your best. So don't tire yourself out working around the clock.

For those of you who are still employed, job searching will be particularly tiring because it must be done in addition to your regular duties. So don't work yourself to the point where you show up to interviews looking exhausted and start to slip behind at your current job. On the other hand, don't be tempted to quit your current job! The long hours are worth it. Searching for a job while you have one puts you in a position of strength.

If you are searching full-time and have decided to choose several different contact methods, we recommend that you divide up each week allowing some time for each method. For instance, you might devote Mondays to following up newspaper ads because most of them appear in Sunday papers. Then you might devote Tuesdays, and Wednesday mornings to working and developing the personal contacts you have, in addition to trying a few employment services. Then you could devote the rest of the week to the Direct Contact method. This is just one plan that may succeed for you.

By trying several methods at once, job-searching will be more interesting, and you will be able to evaluate how promising each of the methods seems, altering your schedule accordingly. Be very careful in your evaluation, however, and don't judge the success of a particular method just by the sheer number of interviews you obtain. Positions advertised in the newspaper, for instance, are likely to generate many more interviews per opening than positions that are filled without being advertised.

If you are searching part-time and decide to try several different contact methods, we recommend that you try them sequentially. You simply won't have enough time to put a meaningful amount of effort into more than one method at once. So estimate the length of your job search, and then allocate so many weeks or months for each contact method you will use. (We suggest that you try Direct Contact first.)

If you're expected to be in your office during the business day, then you have an additional problem to deal with. How can you work interviews into the business day? And if you work in an open office, how can you even call to set up interviews? As much as possible you should keep up the effort and the appearances on your present job. So maximize your use of the lunch hour, early mornings and late afternoons for calling. If you keep trying you'll be surprised how often you will be able to reach the executive you are trying to contact during your out-of-office hours. Also you can catch people as early as 8 AM and as late as 6 PM on frequent occasions. Jot out a plan each night on how you will be using each minute of your precious lunch break.

Your inability to interview at any time other than lunch just might work to your advantage. If you can, try to set up as many interviews as possible for your lunch hour. This will go a long way to creating a relaxed rapport. (Who isn't happy when eating?) But be sure the interviews don't stray too far from the agenda on hand.

Try calling as early as 8 AM and as late as 6 PM. You'll be surprised how often you will be able to reach the executive you want during these times of the day.

Lunchtime interviews are much easier to obtain if you have substantial career experience. People with less experience will often find no alternative to taking time off for interviews. If you have to take time off, you have to take time off. But try to do this as little as possible. Try to take the whole day off in order to avoid being blatantly obvious about your job search. Try to schedule in two to three interviews for the same day. (It is very difficult to maintain an optimum level of energy at more than three interviews in one day.) Explain to the interviewer why you might have to juggle your interview schedule -- he/she should honor the respect you're showing your current employer by minimizing your days off and will probably appreciate the fact that another prospective employer is interested in you.

We want to stress that if you are searching for a job -- especially part-time -- get out there and do the necessary tasks to the best of your ability and get it over with. Don't let your job search drag on endlessly.

And remember that all schedules are meant to be broken. The purpose of a job search schedule is not to rush you to your goal but to help you map out the road ahead, and then to periodically evaluate how you're progressing.

The Direct Contact Method

Once you have scheduled your time, you are ready to begin your search in earnest. We'll limit discussion here to the Direct Contact method.

The first step in preparing for Direct Contact is to develop a check list for categorizing the types of firms for which you'd like to work. You might categorize firms by product line, size, customer-type (such as industrial or consumer), growth prospects, or, by geographical location. Your list of important criteria might be very short. If it is, good! The shorter it is, the easier it will be to locate the company that is right for you.

Consider where your skills might be in demand, the degree of competition for employment, and the employment outlook at each particular firm.

Next, try to decide at which firms you're most likely to be able to find a job. Try matching your skills with those that a specific job demands. Consider where your skills might be in demand, the degree of competition for employment, and the employment outlook at each particular firm.

Now you'll want to assemble your list of potential employers. Build up your list to at least 100 prospects. Then separate your prospect list into three groups. The first tier of around 25 firms will be your primary target group, the second tier of another 25 firms will be your secondary group, and the remaining names you can keep in reserve.

This book will help you greatly in developing your prospect list. Refer to our primary employers section. You'll notice that employer listings are arranged according to industry, beginning with "Accounting and Auditing", followed by "Advertising, Marketing, and Public Relations", and so on through to "Utilities."

If you know of a firm, but you're unsure of what industry it would be classified under, then refer to the alphabetical employer index at the rear of the book to find the page number that the firm's listing appears on.

After you form your prospect list begin work on your resume. Refer to the sample resumes included in the Resumes and Cover Letters section following this chapter in order to get ideas.

Once your resume is complete, begin researching your first batch of 25 prospective employers. You will want to determine whether you would be happy working at the firms you are researching and also get a better idea of what their employment needs might be. You also need to obtain enough information to sound highly informed about the company during phone conversations and in mail correspondence. But don't go all out on your research yet! At some of these firms you probably will not be able to arrange interviews, so save your big research effort until you start to arrange interviews. Nevertheless, you should plan to spend an average of three to four hours researching each firm. Do your research in batches to save time and energy. Use one resource at a time and find out what you can about each of the 25 firms in the batch. Start with the easiest resources to use (such as this book). Keep organized. Maintain a folder on each firm.

You should plan to spend an average of three or four hours researching each firm.

If you discover something that really disturbs you about the firm (they are about to close their only local office), or if you discover that your chances of getting a job there are practically nil (they have just instituted a hiring freeze), then cross them off your prospect list.

If possible, supplement your research efforts with contacts to individuals who know the firm well. Ideally you should make an informal contact with someone at the particular firm, but often a contact at a direct competitor, or a major supplier or customer will be able to supply you with just as much information. At the very least, try to obtain whatever printed information that the company has available, not just annual reports, but product brochures and any other printed material the firm may have to offer. The company might have printed information about career opportunities.

DEVELOPING YOUR CONTACTS

Some career counselors feel that the best route to a better job is through somebody you already know or through somebody to whom you can be introduced. The counselors recommend that you build your contact base beyond your current acquaintances by asking each one to introduce you, or refer you, to additional people in your field of interest.

The theory goes like this: You might start with 15 personal contacts, each of whom introduces you to three additional people, for a total of 45 additional contacts. Then each of these people introduces you to three additional people, which adds 135 additional contacts. Theoretically, you will soon know every person in the industry.

Of course, developing your personal contacts does not usually work quite as smoothly as the theory suggests because some people will not be able to introduce you to anyone. The further you stray from your initial contact base, the weaker your references may be. So, if you do try developing your own contacts, try to begin with as many people you know personally as you can. Dig into your personal phone book and your holiday greeting card list and locate old classmates from school. Be particularly sure to approach people who perform your personal business such as your lawyer, accountant, banker, doctor, stockbroker, and insurance agent. These people develop a very broad contact base due to the nature of their professions.

Getting The Interview

Now it is time to arrange an interview, time to make the Direct Contact. If you have read many books on job searching you may have noticed that most of these books tell you to avoid the personnel office like the plague. It is said that the personnel office never hires people, they just screen out candidates. Unfortunately, this is often the case, but there are other options available to you. If you can identify the appropriate manager with the authority to hire you, contact that person directly. This will take a lot of time in each case, and often you'll be bounced back to personnel despite your efforts. So we suggest that initially you begin your Direct Contact campaign through personnel offices. If it seems that the firms on your prospect list do little hiring through personnel, you might consider some alternative courses of action. The three obvious means of initiating Direct Contact are:

-Showing up unannounced
-Mail
-Phone calls

Cross out the first one right away. You should never show up to seek a professional position without an appointment. Even if you are somehow lucky enough to obtain an interview, you will appear so unprofessional that you will not be seriously considered.

Mail contact seems to be a good choice if you have not been in the job market for a while. You can take your time to prepare a letter, say exactly what you want, and of course include your resume. Remember that employers receive many resumes every day. Don't be surprised if you do not get a response to your inquiry, so don't spend weeks waiting for responses that may never come. If you do send a cover letter, follow it up (or precede it) with a phone call. This will increase your impact, and because of the initial research you did, will underscore both your familiarity and your interest in the firm.

Always include a cover letter with your resume even if you are not specifically asked to do so.

Another alternative is to make a "Cover Call." Your Cover Call should be just like your cover letter: concise. Your first sentence should interest the employer in you. Then try to subtly mention your familiarity with the firm. Don't be overbearing; keep your introduction to three sentences or less. Be pleasant, self-confident, and relaxed. This will greatly increase the chances of the person at the other end of the line developing the conversation. But don't press. When you are asked to follow up "with something in the mail", don't try to prolong the conversation once it has ended. Don't ask what they want to receive in the mail. Always send your resume and a highly personalized follow-up letter, reminding the addressee of the phone conversation. Always include a cover letter if you are requested to send a resume.

Unless you are in telephone sales, making smooth and relaxed cover calls will probably not come easily. Practice them on your own and then with your friends or relatives.

If you obtain an interview as a result of a telephone conversation, be sure to send a thank you note reiterating the points you made during the conversation. You will appear more professional and increase your impact.

However, unless specifically requested, don't mail your resume once an interview has been arranged. Take it with you to the interview instead.

Preparing For The Interview

Once the interview has been arranged, begin your in-depth research. You should arrive at an interview knowing the company upside down and inside out. You need to know the company's products, types of customers, subsidiaries, the parent company, principal locations, rank in the industry, sales and profit trends, type of ownership, size, current plans, and much more. By this time you have probably narrowed your job search to one industry. If you haven't then be familiar with the trends in the firm's industry, the firm's principal competitors and their relative performance, and the direction that the industry leaders are headed. Dig into every resource you can! Read the company literature, the trade press, the business press, and if the company is public, call your stockbroker (if you have one) and ask for additional information. If possible, speak to someone at the firm before the interview, or if not, speak to someone at a competing firm. The more time you spend, the better. Even if you feel extremely pressed for time, you should set aside at least 12 hours for pre-interview research.

You should arrive at an interview knowing the company upside down and inside out.

If you have been out of the job market for some time, don't be surprised if you find yourself tense during your first few interviews. It will probably happen every time you re-enter the market, not just when you seek your first job after getting out of school.

Tension is natural during an interview, but if you can be relaxed you will have an advantage. Knowing you have done a thorough research job should put you more at ease. Make a list of questions that you think might be asked in an interview. Think out your answers carefully; practice reviewing them with a friend. Tape record your responses to the problem questions. If you feel particularly unsure of your interviewing skills, arrange your first interviews at firms you are not as interested in. (But remember it is common courtesy to seem excited about the possibility of working for any firm at which you interview.) Practice again on your own after these first few interviews. Go over the difficult questions that you were asked.

DON'T BOTHER WITH MASS MAILINGS OR BARRAGES OF PHONE CALLS

Direct Contact does not mean burying every firm within a hundred miles with mail and phone calls. Mass mailings rarely work in the job hunt. This also applies to those letters that are personalized -- but dehumanized -- on an automatic typewriter. Don't waste your time or money on such a project; you will fool no one but yourself.

The worst part of sending out mass mailings or making unplanned phone calls is that you are likely to be remembered as someone with little genuine interest in the firm, who lacks sincerity, and as somebody that nobody wants to hire.

HELP WANTED ADVERTISEMENTS

Only a small fraction of professional job openings are advertised. Yet a majority of job seekers -- and a lot of people not in the job market -- spend a lot of time studying the help wanted ads. As a result, the competition for advertised openings is often very severe.

A moderate-sized Manhattan employer told us about an experience advertising in the help wanted section of a major Sunday newspaper:

It was a disaster. We had over 500 responses from this relatively small ad in just one week. We have only two phone lines in this office and one was totally knocked out. We'll never advertise for professional help again.

If you insist on following up on help wanted ads, then research a firm before you reply to an ad. Preliminary research might help to separate you from all of the other professionals responding to that ad, many of whom will only have a passing interest in the opportunity, and will give you insight about a particular firm to help you determine if it is potentially a good match. That said, your chances of obtaining a job through the want-ads are still much smaller than they are if you use the Direct Contact method.

How important is the proper dress for a job interview? Buying a complete wardrobe of Brooks Brothers pinstripes or Liz Claiborne suits, donning new wing tip shoes or pumps, and having your hair styled every morning is not enough to guarantee you a career position as an investment banker. But on the other hand, if you can't find a clean, conservative suit or a nice skirt and blouse, or won't take the time to wash your hair, then you are just wasting your time by interviewing at all.

The very beginning of the interview is the most important part because it determines the rapport for the rest of it.

Very rarely will the final selection of candidates for a job opening be determined by dress. So don't spend a fortune on a new wardrobe. But be sure that your clothes are adequate. Men applying for any professional position should wear a suit; women should either wear a dress or a suit (but not a pant suit). Your clothes should be at least as formal or slightly more formal and more conservative than the position would suggest.

Top personal grooming is more important than finding the perfect clothes for a job interview. Careful grooming indicates both a sense of thoroughness and self-confidence.

Be sure that your clothes fit well and that they are immaculate. Hair must be neat and clean. Shoes should be newly polished. Women need to avoid excessive jewelry and excessive makeup. Men should be freshly shaven, even if the interview is late in the day.

Be complete. Everyone needs a watch, a pen, and a notepad. Finally, a briefcase or a leather-bound folder (containing extra copies of your resume) will help complete the look of professionalism.

Sometimes the interviewer will be running behind schedule. Don't be upset, be sympathetic. There is often pressure to interview a lot of candidates and to quickly fill a demanding position. So be sure to come to your interview with good reading material to keep yourself occupied. This will help you to relax.

The Interview

The very beginning of the interview is the most important part because it determines the rapport for the rest of it. Those first few moments are especially crucial. Do you smile when you meet? Do you establish enough eye contact, but not too much? Do you walk into the office with a self-assured and confident stride? Do you shake hands firmly? Do you make small talk easily without being garrulous? It is human nature to judge people by that first impression, so make sure it is a good one. But most of all, try to be yourself.

SOME FAVORITE INTERVIEW QUESTIONS

Tell me about yourself...

Why did you leave your last job?

What excites you in your current job?

What are your career goals?

Where would you like to be in 5 years?

What are your greatest strengths?

What are your greatest weaknesses?

Why do you wish to work for this firm?

Where else are you seeking employment?

Why should we hire you?

Often the interviewer will begin, after the small talk, by telling you about the company, the division, the department, or perhaps, the position. Because of your detailed research, the information about the company should be repetitive for you and the interviewer would probably like nothing better than to avoid this regurgitation of the company biography. So if you can do so tactfully, indicate to the interviewer that you are very familiar with the firm. If he or she seems intent on providing you with background information, despite your hints, then acquiesce.

But be sure to remain attentive. If you can manage to generate a brief discussion of the company or the industry at this point, without being forceful, great. It will help to further build rapport, underscore your interests, and increase your impact.

Soon (if it didn't begin that way) the interviewer will begin the questions. This period of the interview falls into one of two categories (or somewhere in between): either a structured interview, where the interviewer has a prescribed set of questions to ask; or an unstructured interview, where the interviewer will ask only leading questions to get you to talk about yourself, your experiences and your goals. Try to sense as quickly as possible which direction the interviewer wishes to proceed. This will make the interviewer feel more relaxed and in control of the situation.

Many of the questions will be similar to the ones that you were expecting and have practiced. Remember to keep attuned to the interviewer and make the length of your answers appropriate to the situation. If you are really unsure as to how detailed a response the interviewer is seeking, then ask.

As the interview progresses, the interviewer will probably mention some of the most important responsibilities of the position. If applicable, draw parallels between your experience and the demands of the position as detailed by the interviewer. Describe your past experience in the same manner that you did on your resume: emphasizing results and achievements and not merely describing activities. If you listen carefully (listening is a very important part of the interviewing process) the interviewer might very well imply the skills needed for the position. Don't exaggerate. Be on the level about your abilities.

Try not to cover too much ground during the first interview. This interview is often the toughest, where many candidates are screened out. If you are interviewing for a very competitive position, you will have to make an impression that will last. Focus on a few of your greatest strengths that are relevant to the position. Develop these points carefully, state them again in other words, and then try to summarize them briefly at the end of the interview.

Often the interviewer will pause towards the end and ask if you have any questions. Particularly in a structured interview, this might be the one chance to really show your knowledge of and interest in the firm. Have a list prepared of specific questions that are of real interest to you. Let your questions subtly show your research and your knowledge of the firm's activities. It is wise to have an extensive list of questions, as several of them may be answered during the interview.

Do not turn your opportunity to ask questions into an interrogation. Avoid bringing your list of questions to the interview.

YOU'RE FIRED!!

You are not the first and will not be the last to go through this traumatic experience. Thousands of professionals are fired every week. Remember, being fired is not a reflection on you as a person. It is usually a reflection of your company's staffing needs and its perception of your recent job performance. Share the fact with your relatives and friends. Being fired is not something of which to be ashamed.

Don't start your job search with a flurry of unplanned activity. Start by choosing a strategy and working out a plan. Now is not the time for major changes in your life. If possible, remain in the same career and in the same geographical location, at least until you have been working again for a while. On the other hand, if the only industry for which you are trained is leaving, or is severely depressed in your area, then you should give prompt consideration to moving or switching careers.

Register for unemployment compensation immediately. A thorough job search could take months. After all, your employers have been contributing to unemployment insurance specifically for you ever since your first job. Don't be surprised to find other professionals collecting unemployment compensation as well. Unemployment compensation is for everybody who is between jobs.

Be prepared for the question, "Why were you fired?", during job interviews. Avoid mentioning you were fired while arranging interviews. Try especially hard not to speak negatively of your past employer and not to sound particularly worried about your status of being temporarily unemployed. But don't spend much time reflecting on why you were fired or how you might have avoided it. Learn from your mistakes and then look ahead. Think positively. And be sure to follow a careful plan during your job search.

Ask questions that you are fairly certain the interviewer can answer (remember how you feel when you cannot answer a question during an interview).

Even if you are unable to determine the salary range beforehand, do not ask about it during the first interview. You can always ask about it later. Above all, don't ask about fringe benefits until you have been offered a position. (Then be sure to get all the details.) You should be able to determine the company's policy on fringe benefits relatively easily before the interview.

Try not to be negative about anything during the interview. (Particularly any past employer or any previous job.) Be cheerful. Everyone likes to work with someone who seems to be happy.

Don't let a tough question throw you off base. If you don't know the answer to a question, say so simply -- do not apologize. Just smile. Nobody can answer every question -- particularly some of the questions that are asked in job interviews.

Before your first interview, you may be able to determine how many interviews there usually are for positions at your level. (Of course it may differ quite a bit even within the different levels of one firm.) Usually you can count on attending at least three or four interviews, although some firms, such as some of the professional partnerships, are well-known to give a minimum of six interviews for all professional positions. While you should be more relaxed as you return for subsequent interviews, the pressure will be on. The more prepared you are, the better.

Depending on what information you are able to obtain, you might want to vary your strategy quite a bit from interview to interview. For instance, if the first interview is a screening interview, then be sure a few of your strengths really stand out. On the other hand, if later interviews are primarily with people who are in a position to veto your hiring, but not to push it forward (and few people are weeded out at these stages), then you should primarily focus on building rapport as opposed to reiterating and developing your key strengths.

If it looks as though your skills and background do not match the position your interviewer was hoping to fill, ask him or her if there is another division or subsidiary that perhaps could profit from your talents.

After The Interview

Write a follow-up letter immediately after the interview, while it is still fresh in the interviewer's mind. Then, if you have not heard from the interviewer within seven days, call to stress your continued interest in the firm, and the position, and request a second interview.

A parting word of advice. Again and again during your job search you will be rejected. You will be rejected when you apply for interviews. You will be rejected after interviews. For every job you finally receive, you will have probably been rejected a multitude of times. Don't let rejections slow you down. Keep reminding yourself that the sooner you go out and get started on your job search, and get those rejections flowing in, the closer you will be to obtaining the job you want.

RESUMES AND COVER LETTERS

RESUMES/OVERVIEW

When filling a position, a recruiter will often have 100 plus applicants, but time to interview only the 5 or 10 most promising ones. So he or she will have to reject most applicants after a brief skimming of their resume.

Unless you have phoned and talked to the recruiter -- which you should do whenever you can -- you will be chosen or rejected for an interview entirely on the basis of your resume and cover letter. So your resume must be outstanding. (But remember -- a resume is no substitute for a job search campaign. YOU must seek a job. Your resume is only one tool.)

RESUME PREPARATION

One page, usually

Unless you have an unusually strong background with many years of experience and a large diversity of outstanding achievements, prepare a one page resume. Recruiters dislike long resumes.

8 1/2 x 11 Size

Recruiters often get resumes in batches of hundreds. If your resume is on small sized paper it is likely to get lost in the pile. If oversized, it is likely to get crumpled at the edges, and won't fit in their files.

Typesetting

Modern photocomposition typesetting gives you the clearest, sharpest image, a wide variety of type styles and effects such as italics, bold facing, and book-like justified margins. Typesetting is the best resume preparation process, but is also the most expensive.

Word Processing

The most flexible way to get your resume typed is on a good quality word processor. With word processing, you can make changes almost instantly because your resume will be stored on a magnetic disk and the computer will do all the re-typing automatically. A word processing service will usually offer you a variety of type styles in both regular and proportional spacing. You can have bold facing for emphasis, justified margins, and clear, sharp copies.

Typing

Household typewriters and office typewriters with nylon or other cloth ribbons are NOT good for typing the resume you will have printed. If you can't get word processing or typesetting, hire a professional who uses a high quality office typewriter with a plastic ribbon (usually called a "carbon ribbon").

Printing

Find the best quality offset printing process available. DO NOT make your copies on an office photocopier. Only the personnel office may see the resume you mail. Everyone else may see only a copy of it. Copies of copies quickly become unreadable. Some professionally maintained, extra-high-quality photocopiers are of adequate quality, if you are in a rush. But top quality offset printing is best.

Proofread your resume

Whether you typed it yourself or had it written, typed, or typeset, mistakes on resumes can be embarrassing, particularly when something obvious such as your name is misspelled. No matter how much you paid someone else to type or write or typeset your resume, YOU lose if there is a mistake. So proofread it as carefully as possible. Get a friend to help you. Read your draft aloud as your friend checks the proof copy. Then have your friend read aloud while you check. Next, read it letter by letter to check spelling and punctuation.

If you are having it typed or typeset by a resume service or a printer, and you can't bring a friend or take the time during the day to proof it, pay for it and take it home. Proof it there and bring it back later to get it corrected and printed.

RESUME FORMAT (See samples)

Basic data

Your name, phone number, and a complete address should be at the top of your resume. (If you are a university student, you should also show your home address and phone number.)

Functional Resume
(Prepared on a Word Processor and Letter-Quality Printer.)

Michelle Hughes
430 Miller's Crossing
Essex Junction, VT 05452
802/555-9354

Solid background in plate making, separations, color matching, background definition, printing, mechanicals, color corrections, and supervision of personnel. A highly motivated manager and effective communicator. Proven ability to:

- **Create Commercial Graphics**
- **Produce Embossing Drawings**
- **Color Separate**
- **Analyze Consumer Acceptance**
- **Meet Graphic Deadlines**
- **Control Quality**
- **Resolve Printing Problems**
- **Expedite Printing Operations**

Qualifications

Printing: Black and white and color. Can judge acceptability of color reproduction by comparing it with original. Can make four or five color corrections on all media. Have long developed ability to restyle already reproduced four-color artwork. Can create perfect tone for black and white match fill-ins for resume cover letters.

Customer Relations: Work with customers to assure specifications are met and customers are satisfied. Can guide work through entire production process and strike a balance between technical printing capabilities and need for customer approval.

Management: Schedule work to meet deadlines. Direct staff in production procedures. Maintain quality control from inception of project through final approval for printing.

Specialties: Make silk screen overlays for a multitude of processes. Velo bind, GBC bind, perfect bind. Have knowledge to prepare posters, flyers, and personalized stationery.

Personnel Supervision: Foster an atmosphere that encourages highly talented artists to balance high level creativity with a maximum of production. Meet or beat production deadlines. Am continually instructing new employees, apprentices and students in both artistry and technical operations.

Experience

Professor of Graphic Arts, University of Vermont, Burlington, VT (1977-present).
Assistant Production Manager, Artsign Digraphics, Burlington, VT (1981-present) Part time.

Education

Massachusetts Conservatory of Art, PhD 1977
University of Massachusetts, B.A. 1974

Separate your education and work experience

In general, list your experience first. If you have recently graduated, list your education first, unless your experience is more important than your education. (For example, if you have just graduated from a teaching school, have some business experience and are applying for a job in business you would list your business experience first.) If you have two or more years of college, you don't need to list high schools.

Reverse chronological order

To a recruiter your last job and your latest schooling are the most important. So put the last first and list the rest going back in time.

Show dates and locations

Put the dates of your employment and education on the left of the page. Put the names of the companies you worked for and the schools you attended a few spaces to the right of the dates. Put the city and state, or the city and country where you studied or worked to the right of the page.

Avoid sentences and large blocks of type

Your resume will be scanned, not read. Short, concise phrases are much more effective than long-winded sentences. Keep everything easy to find. Avoid paragraphs longer than six lines. Never go ten or more lines in a paragraph. If you have more than six lines of information about one job or school, put it in two or more paragraphs.

RESUME CONTENT

Be factual

In many companies, inaccurate information on a resume or other application material will get you fired as soon as the inaccuracy is discovered. Protect yourself.

Be positive

You are selling your skills and accomplishments in your resume. If you achieved something, say so. Put it in the best possible light. Don't hold back or be modest, no one else will. But don't exaggerate to the point of misrepresentation.

Chronological Resume
(Prepared on a Word Processor and Laser Printer.)

WALLACE R. RECTORIAN
412 Maple Court
Seattle, WA 98404
206/555-6584

EXPERIENCE

1984-present   THE CENTER COMPANY, Seattle, WA
Systems Analyst, design systems for the manufacturing unit. Specifically, physical inventory, program specifications, studies of lease buy decisions, selection of hardware the outside contractors and inside users. Wrote On-Site Computer Terminal Operators Manual. Adapted product mix problems to the LASPSP (Logistical Alternative Product Synthesis Program).

As *Industrial Engineer* from February 1984 to February 1986, computerized system design. Evaluated manufacturing operations operator efficiency productivity index and budget allocations. Analyzed material waste and recommended solutions.

ADDITIONAL EXPERIENCE

1980-1984   *Graduate Research Assistant* at New York State Institute of Technology.

1978-1980   *Graduate Teaching Assistant* at Salem State University.

EDUCATION

1982-1984   NEW YORK STATE INSTITUTE OF TECHNOLOGY, Albany, NY
M.S. in Operations Research. GPA: 3.6. Graduate courses included Advanced Location and Queueing Theories, Forecasting, Inventory and Material Flow Systems, Linear and Nonlinear Determination Models, Engineering Economics and Integer Programming.

1980-1982   M.S. in Information and Computer Sciences. GPA: 3.8
Curriculum included Digital Computer Organization & Programming. Information Structure & Process. Mathematical Logic, Computer Systems, Logic Design and Switching Theory.

1976-1980   SALEM STATE UNIVERSITY, Salem, OR
B.A. in Mathematics. GPA: 3.6.

AFFILIATIONS

Member of the American Institute of Computer Programmers, Association for Computing Machinery and the Operations Research Society of America.

PERSONAL

Married, three dependents, able to relocate.

Be brief

Write down the important (and pertinent) things you have done, but do it in as few words as possible. The shorter your resume is, the more carefully it will be examined.

Work experience

Emphasize continued experience in a particular type of function or continued interest in a particular industry. De-emphasize irrelevant positions. Delete positions that you held for less than four months. (Unless you are a very recent college grad or still in school.)

Stress your results

Elaborate on how you contributed to your past employers. Did you increase sales, reduce costs, improve a product, implement a new program? Were you promoted?

Mention relevant skills and responsibilities

Be specific. Slant your past accomplishments toward the type of position that you hope to obtain. Example: Do you hope to supervise people? Then state how many people, performing what function, you have supervised.

Education

Keep it brief if you have more than two years of career experience. Elaborate more if you have less experience. Mention degrees received and any honors or special awards. Note individual courses or research projects that might be relevant for employers. For instance, if you are a liberal arts major, be sure to mention courses in such areas as: accounting, statistics, computer programming, or mathematics.

Job objective

Leave it out. Even if you are certain of exactly the type of job that you desire, the inclusion of a job objective might eliminate you from consideration for other positions that a recruiter feels are a better match for your qualifications.

Personal data

Keep it very brief. Two lines maximum. A one-word mention of commonly practiced activities such as golf, skiing, sailing, chess, bridge, tennis, etc., can prove to be good way to open up a conversation during an interview. Do not include your age, weight, height, etc.

Chronological Resume
(Prepared on an Office-Quality Typewriter.)

Lorraine Avakian
70 Monback Avenue
Oshkosh, WI 54901
Phone: 414/555-4629

Business Experience

1984-1991 **NATIONAL PACKAGING PRODUCTS**, Princeton, WI

1989-1991 **District Sales Manager.** Improved 28-member sales group from a company rank in the bottom thirty percent to the top twenty percent. Complete responsibility for personnel, including recruiting, hiring and training. Developed a comprehensive sales improvement program and advised its implementation in eight additional sales districts.

1986-1988 **Marketing Associate.** Responsible for research, analysis, and presentation of marketing issues related to long-term corporate strategy. Developed marketing perspective for capital investment opportunities and acquisition candidates, which was instrumental in finalizing decisions to make two major acquisitions and to construct a $35 million canning plant.

1984-1986 **Salesperson, Paper Division.** Responsible for a four-county territory in central Wisconsin. Increased sales from $700,000 to over $1,050,000 annually in a 15 month period. Developed six new accounts with incremental sales potential of $800,000. Only internal candidate selected for new marketing program.

AMERICAN PAPER PRODUCTS, INC., Oshkosh, WI
1983-1984 **Sales Trainee.** Completed the intensive six month training program and was promoted to salesperson status. Received the President's Award for superior performance in the sales training program.

HENDUKKAR SPORTING GOODS, INC., Oshkosh, WI
1983 **Assistant Store Manager.** Supervised six employees on the evening shift. Handled accounts receivable.

Education
1977-1982 **BELOIT COLLEGE**, Beloit, WI
Received Bachelor of Science Degree in Business Administration in June 1982. Varsity Volleyball. Financed 50% of educational costs through part-time and co-op program employment.

Personal Background
Able to relocate; Excellent health; Active in community activities.

SHOULD YOU HIRE A RESUME WRITER?

If you write reasonably well, there are some advantages to writing your resume yourself. To write it well, you will have to review your experience and figure out how to explain your accomplishments in clear, brief phrases. This will help you when you explain your work to interviewers.

If you write your resume, everything in it will be in your own words -- it will sound like you. It will say what you want it to say. And you will be much more familiar with the contents. If you are a good writer, know yourself well, and have a good idea of what parts of your background employers are looking for, you may be able to write your own resume better than anyone else can. If you write your resume yourself, you should have someone who can be objective (preferably not a close relative) review it with you.

When should you have your resume professionally written?

If you have difficulty writing in "resume style" (which is quite unlike normal written language), if you are unsure of which parts of your background you should emphasize, or if you think your resume would make your case better if it did not follow the standard form outlined here or in a book on resumes, then you should have it professionally written.

There are two reasons even some professional resume writers we know have had their resumes written with the help of fellow professionals. First, when they need the help of someone who can be objective about their background, and second, when they want an experienced sounding board to help focus their thoughts.

If you decide to hire a resume writer

The best way to choose a writer is by reputation -- the recommendation of a friend, a personnel director, your school placement officer or someone else knowledgeable in the field.

You should ask, "If I'm not satisfied with what you write, will you go over it with me and change it?"

You should ask, "How long has the person who will write my resume been writing resumes?"

There is no sure relation between price and quality, except that you are unlikely to get a good writer for less than $50 for an uncomplicated resume and you shouldn't have to pay more than $300 unless your experience is very extensive or complicated. There will be additional charges for printing.

Few resume services will give you a firm price over the phone, simply because some people's resumes are too complicated and take too long to do at any predetermined price. Some services will quote you a price that applies to almost all of their customers. Be sure to do some comparative shopping. Obtain a firm price before you engage their services and find out how expensive minor changes will be.

Chronological Resume
(Prepared on a Word Processor and Laser Printer.)

Melvin Winter
43 Aspen Wall Lane
Wheaton, IL 60512
312/555-6923 (home)
312/555-3000 (work)

RELATED EXPERIENCE
1982-Present GREAT LAKES PUBLISHING COMPANY, Chicago, IL
Operations Supervisor (1986-present)
in the Engineering Division of this major trade publishing house, responsible for maintaining on line computerized customer files, title files, accounts receivable, inventory and sales files.

Organize department activities, establish priorities and train personnel. Provide corporate accounting with monthly reports of sales, earned income from journals, samples, inventory levels/value and sales and tax data. Divisional sales average $3 million annually.

Senior Customer Service Representative (1984-1986)
in the Construction Division. Answered customer service inquiries regarding orders and accounts receivable, issued return and shortage credits and expedited special sales orders for direct mail and sales to trade schools.

Customer Service Representative (1982-1983)
in the International Division. Same duties as for construction division except that sales were to retail stores and universities in Europe.

1980-1982 B. DALTON, BOOKSELLER, Salt Lake City, UT
Assistant Manager of this retail branch of a major domestic book seller, maintained all paperback inventories at necessary levels, deposited receipts daily and created window displays.

EDUCATION
1976-1980 UNIVERSITY OF MAINE, Orono, ME
Awarded a degree of Bachelor of Arts in French Literature.

LANGUAGES
Fluent in French. Able to write in French, German and Spanish.

PERSONAL
Willing to travel and relocate, particularly in Europe.

References available upon request.

Chronological Resume
(Prepared on a Word Processor and Laser Printer.)

DAMIEN W. PINCKNEY

U.S. Address:
15606 Center Street
Bottineau, ND 58777
701/555-9320

Jamaican Address:
Oskarrataan Building, Room 1234
Hedonism II
Negril, Jamaica
809/555-6634

Experience

1984-present   **HEDONISM II**, Negril, Jamaica
Resident Engineer for this publicly owned resort with main offices in Kingston. Responsibilities include:

Maintaining electrical generating and distribution equipment.

Supervising an eight-member staff in maintenance of refrigeration equipment, power and light generators, water purification plant, and general construction machinery.

1982-1984   **NEGRIL BEACH HOTEL**, Negril Beach, Jamaica
Resident Engineer for a privately held resort, assigned total responsibility for facility generating equipment.

Directed maintenance, operation and repair of diesel generating equipment.

1980-1982   Directed overhaul of turbo generating equipment in two Mid-Western localities and assisted in overhaul of a turbo generating unit in Mexico.

1975-1980   **CAPITAL CITY ELECTRIC**, Washington, DC
Service Engineer for the power generation service division of this regional power company, supervised the overhaul, maintenance and repair of large generators and associated auxiliary equipment.

Education

1972-1975   **FRANKLIN INSTITUTE**, Baltimore, MD
Awarded a degree of Associate of Engineering. Concentration in Mechanical Power Engineering Technology.

Personal

Willing to travel and relocate.
Interested in sailing, scuba diving, deep sea fishing.

References available upon request.

COVER LETTERS

Always mail a cover letter with your resume. In a cover letter you can show an interest in the company that you can't show in a resume. You can point out one or two skills or accomplishments the company can put to good use.

Make it personal

The more personal you can get, the better. If someone known to the person you are writing has recommended that you contact the company, get permission to include his/her name in the letter. If you have the name of a person to send the letter to, make sure you have the name spelled correctly and address it directly to that person. Be sure to put the person's name and title on both the letter and envelope. This will ensure that your letter will get through to the proper person, even if a new person now occupies this position. But even if you are addressing it to the "Personnel Director" or the "Hiring Partner", send a letter.

Type cover letters in full. Don't try the cheap and easy ways like photocopying the body of your letter and typing in the inside address and salutation. You will give the impression that you are mailing to a multitude of companies and have no particular interest in any one. Have your letters fully typed and signed with a pen.

Phone

Precede or follow your mailing with a phone call.

Bring extra copies of your resume to the interview

If the person interviewing you doesn't have your resume, be prepared. Carry copies of your own. Even if you have already forwarded your resume, be sure to take extra copies to the interview, as someone other than the interviewer(s) might now have the first copy you sent.

General Model for a Cover Letter

```
                                                    Your Address
                                                    Date

Contact Person Name
Title
Company
Address



Dear Mr./Ms._____:


Immediately explain why your background makes you the best candidate
for the position that you are applying for. Keep the first paragraph
short and hard-hitting.

Detail what you could contribute to this company. Show how your
qualifications will benefit this firm. Remember to keep this letter
short; few recruiters will read a cover letter longer than half a
page.

Describe your interest in the corporation. Subtly emphasize your
knowledge about this firm (the result of your research effort) and
your familiarity with the industry. It is common courtesy to act ex-
tremely eager to work for any company that you interview.

In the closing paragraph you should specifically request an inter-
view. Include your phone number and the hours when you can be
reached. Alternatively, you might prefer to mention that you will
follow up with a phone call (to arrange an interview at a mutually
convenient time within the next several days).




                                                    Sincerely,

                                                    (signature)

                                                    Your full name (typed)
```

Cover Letter

49 Chinwick Circle
Houston, TX 77031
October 5, 1993

Ms. Ruth Herman-George
V.P./Director of Personnel
Holly Rock Fire Insurance Group
444 Rolling Cloud Lane, Suite 24
Houston, TX 77035

Dear Ms. Herman-George:

I am a career-oriented individual who can successfully provide technical direction and training to pension analysts in connection with FKLE system.

My major and most recent background is directly involved in the administration of pension and profit sharing plans with TRMZ. Furthermore, my extensive experience both as a Group Pension Pre-Scale Underwriter and as a Pension Underwriter involves data processing knowledge and overall pension administration.

A prime function of mine is decision making with reference to group pension business. You specifically seek an idividual who can recommend changes and/or new procedures of plan administration and maintenance plus assistance in development of pension administration kits for use by the field force at Holly Rock. I feel that I possess the ability to fulfill your need dramatically.

I would welcome the practical opportunity to work directly with general agents and plan trustees in qualifying, revising and requalifying pension and profit sharing plans required by TRMZ. You will note in my resume my background in working with others in both an advisory and shirt-sleeve capacity.

I look forward to hearing from you.

Sincerely,

Henry Washington

ACCOUNTING AND AUDITING

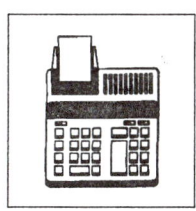

Demand for accounting, auditing, and bookkeeping services is on the rise, which will result in higher industry receipts and employment. In times of recession, the accounting industry can actually benefit. Bankruptcies, for example, have more than doubled in the past decade, all of which means more business for accountants.

ARTHUR ANDERSEN AND COMPANY
1010 Market St., Suite 1100, St. Louis MO 63101. 314/621-6767. **Contact:** Personnel Department. **Description:** One of the six largest certified public accounting firms in the world. Organized in 1913, with offices in forty countries. **Operates in the following divisions:** Audit (offering assignments in all types of businesses and industries); Tax (offering assignments involving consultation and compliance in all areas of taxation, including income, real estate, trust, and gift taxation); and Management Information Consulting (offering opportunities for both entry-level and experienced personnel in providing professional systems and consulting services to clients in a wide-range of businesses and industries). **Corporate headquarters:** Chicago, IL. **Employees (St. Louis office):** 200+.

COOPERS AND LYBRAND
One Metropolitan Square, Suite 2200, St. Louis MO 63102-2737. 314/436-3200. **Contact:** Debbie Diamant, Personnel Assistant. **Description:** An international certified public accounting firm. **Employees:** 100.

DELOITTE & TOUCHE
One City Center, St. Louis MO 63101. 314/231-3110. **Contact:** Donna Nolan, Office Manager. **Description:** One of the largest certified public accounting organizations in the world. Provides accounting, auditing, management consultation, tax, and actuarial services to clients through a wide network of offices throughout the world.

PEAT MARWICK
1010 Market Street, St. Louis MO 63101. 314/444-1400. **Contact:** Judy Akin, Personnel Director. **Description:** A St. Louis office of the well known national certified public accountants firm. One of the Big Six certified public accounting firms, with offices throughout the United States and the world (approximately 400 international locations in 115 countries). Provides auditing, accounting, management consulting, and tax services. Over 1700 partners and principals in the United States in approximately 100 offices.

Additional large employers: 250+

ACCOUNTING, AUDITING AND BOOKKEEPING SERVICES

Ernst & Young
701 Market, St. Louis MO 63101-1850. 314/231-7700. Employs: 250-499.

Price Waterhouse & Co
1 Centerre Pl, St. Louis MO 63101-2602. 314/425-0500. Employs: 250-499.

Small to medium sized employers: 50-249

ACCOUNTING, AUDITING AND BOOKKEEPING SERVICES

Landmark Services
11692 Wilburn Park Rd, St. Louis MO 63105. 314/569-1303. Employs: 100-249.

Control Data Business Mgmt Svc
425 N New Ballas Rd, St. Louis MO 63141-6814. 314/872-2200. Employs: 50-99.

For more information on career opportunities in accounting and auditing:

Associations

AMERICAN ACCOUNTING ASSOCIATION
5717 Bessie Drive, Sarasota FL 34233. 813/921-7747.

AMERICAN INSTITUTE OF CERTIFIED PUBLIC ACCOUNTANTS
1211 Avenue of the Americas, New York NY 10036. 212/575-6200.

ASSOCIATION OF GOVERNMENT ACCOUNTANTS
2000 Mount Vernon Avenue, Alexandria VA 22301. 703/684-6931.

THE EDP AUDITORS FOUNDATION
455 Kehoe Boulevard, Suite 106, Carol Stream IL 60188. 708/682-1200.

INSTITUTE OF INTERNAL AUDITORS
P.O. Box 140099, Orlando FL 32889. 407/830-7600.

INTERNATIONAL CREDIT ASSOCIATION
Education Department, Box 419057, St. Louis MO 63141-1757. 314/991-3030.

INSTITUTE OF MANAGEMENT ACCOUNTING
10 Paragon Drive, Box 433, Montvale NJ 07645. 201/573-9000.

NATIONAL ASSOCIATION OF TAX CONSULTORS
454 North 13th Street, San Jose CA 92112. 408/298-1458.

NATIONAL ASSOCIATION OF TAX PRACTITIONERS
720 Association Drive, Appleton WI 54914. 414/749-1040.

NATIONAL SOCIETY OF PUBLIC ACCOUNTANTS
1010 North Fairfax Street, Alexandria VA 22314. 703/549-6400.

Directories

AICPA SURVEYS
American Institute of Certified Public Accountants, 1211 Avenue of the Americas, New York NY 10036. 212/575-6200.

ACCOUNTING FIRMS AND PRACTITIONERS
American Institute of Certified Public Accountants, 1211 Avenue of the Americas, New York NY 10036. 212/575-6200.

Magazines

ACCOUNTING NEWS
Warren, Gorham, and Lamont, Inc., 210 South Street, Boston MA 02111. 617/423-2020.

CPA JOURNAL
200 Park Avenue, New York NY 10166. 212/973-8300.

CPA LETTER
American Institute of Certified Public Accountants, 1211 Avenue of the Americas, New York NY 10036. 212/575-6200.

CORPORATE ACCOUNTING
Warren, Gorham, and Lamont, Inc., 210 South Street, Boston MA 02111. 617/423-2020.

JOURNAL OF ACCOUNTANCY
American Institute of Certified Public Accountants, 1211 Avenue of the Americas, New York NY 10036. 212/575-6200.

MANAGEMENT ACCOUNTING
Institute of Management Accounting, 10 Paragon Drive, Box 433, Montvale NJ 07645. 201/573-9000.

NATIONAL PUBLIC ACCOUNTANT
National Society of Public Accountants, 1010 North Fairfax Street, Alexandria VA 22314. 703/549-6400.

ADVERTISING, MARKETING AND PUBLIC RELATIONS

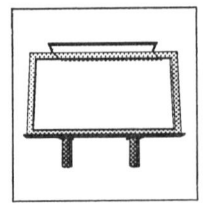

The long recession has put a continued damper on the advertising industry, as client companies put tighter reigns on their advertising budgets. Throughout the past ten years, mergers have played a major role, with advertising giants like Saatchi and Saatchi buying up competitors.
Another trend has been the emergence of in-house agencies, which means that more advertising jobs will be available in addition to the traditional advertising agencies. Overall, however, job prospects remain weak as many companies continue layoffs and job competition grows even fiercer.

CLAYTON-DAVIS & ASSOCIATES
8229 Maryland, St. Louis MO 63105. 314/862-7800. **Contact:** Steven Pezold, Vice President. **Description:** A St. Louis full-service advertising and public relations firm.

CLIFF KELLEY INC.
2850 South Jefferson Street, St. Louis MO 63118. 314/664-0023. **Contact:** Vic Wamsley, General Manager. **Description:** A St. Louis company engaged in direct mail/printing services.

D'ARCY MASIUS BENTON & BOWLES
One Memorial Drive, St. Louis MO 63102. 314/342-8600. **Contact:** Jerome B. Sexton, Senior V.P./Director of H.R. and Administration. **Description:** An office of an international advertising agency, DMB&B/St. Louis is the 10th largest agency in the Midwest. **Common positions:** Advertising Worker; Media Planner; Media Buyer. **Educational backgrounds sought:** Art/Design; Business Administration; Liberal Arts; Marketing. **Benefits:** medical insurance; dental insurance; pension plan; life insurance; tuition assistance; disability coverage; employee discounts; savings plan. **Corporate headquarters:** New York, NY. **Other U.S. locations:** Chicago, Bloomfield Hills, Los Angeles. **Parent company:** DMB&B, Inc. **Employees:** 250. **Projected hires for the next 12 months:** 12.

DIMAC DIRECT
One Corporate Woods Drive, Bridgeton MO 63044. 314/344-1220. **Contact:** Doreen M. Nersesian, Manager, Employee Relations. **Description:** Creators and producers of direct mail advertising and sales promotion programs. **Common positions:** Accountant; Advertising Worker; Commercial Artist; Computer Programmer; Customer Service Representative; Operations/Production Manager; Marketing Specialist; Public Relations Specialist; Quality Controller; Sales Representative; Direct Mail Professionals. **Educational backgrounds sought:** Accounting; Art/Design; Business Administration; Communications; Computer Science; Liberal Arts; Marketing. **Special programs:** Training programs and internships. **Benefits:** medical insurance; dental insurance; life

insurance; tuition assistance; disability coverage; 401(K); credit union. **Other U.S. locations:** San Francisco, Boston. **Parent company:** DIMAC Corporation. **Operations at this facility include:** Service. **Employees:** 600 nationally, 450 in St. Louis.

GANNETT OUTDOOR COMPANY OF ST. LOUIS
6767 N. Hanley Road, P.O. Box 5868, St. Louis MO 63134. 314/524-0800. **Contact:** Mary Jane Raniszeski, Personnel Representative. **Description:** A St. Louis agency engaged in outdoor advertising services. **Common positions:** Accountant; Branch Manager; Department Manager; Operations/Production Manager; Sales Representative. **Educational backgrounds sought:** Accounting; Art/Design; Business Administration; Marketing. **Benefits:** medical insurance; dental insurance; pension plan; life insurance; tuition assistance; disability coverage; savings plan. **Parent company:** Gannett Co., Inc. (Washington, DC). **Employees:** 65-70.

JEROME HIRSCH & ASSOCIATES
#18 South Kings Highway, St. Louis MO 63108. 314/367-7081. **Contact:** Jerry Hirsch, President. **Description:** A St. Louis advertising agency.

GEORGE JOHNSON ADVERTISING
13523 Barrett Parkway, Suite 221, Ballwin MO 63021-3800. 314/822-0553. **Contact:** Mrs. Jabet Wilkins, Vice President and General Manager. **Description:** A St. Louis advertising agency and publisher of newsletters and association magazines. Services also include marketing planning and business management workshops. **Common positions:** Advertising Worker; Marketing Specialist; Sales Representative. **Educational backgrounds sought:** Art/Design; Marketing. **Benefits:** medical insurance. **Corporate headquarters:** This location. **Parent company:** Communications Management. **Operations at this facility include:** research and development; administration; service; sales.

KRUPNICK & ASSOCIATES INC.
135 North Meramec, St. Louis MO 63105. 314/862-9393. **Contact:** Personnel Director. **Description:** A full-service advertising agency.

KUPPER PARKER COMMUNICATIONS
6900 Delmar Boulevard, St. Louis MO 61130. 314/727-4000. **Contact:** Margaret Russell, Director of Personnel. **Description:** A St. Louis advertising agency.

LANG & SMITH GROUP INC.
14220 Ladue Road, Chesterfield MO 63017. 314/878-2115. **Contact:** Personnel Department. **Description:** A St. Louis advertising agency.

NATIONWIDE ADVERTISING SERVICE INC.
605 Old Dallas Road, Suite 204, St. Louis MO 63141. 314/432-3221. **Contact:** Amy Walton, Manager. **Description:** A St. Louis advertising agency.

48/The St. Louis JobBank

RALSTON PURINA
One Checkerboard Square, St. Louis MO 63164. 314/982-3355. **Contact:** Barb Cant, Personnel Director. **Description:** Engaged in the placement of advertising in various media outlets for the Ralston Purina Company.

ROSS ADVERTISING, INC.
311 North Lindbergh Blvd., St. Louis MO 63141. 314/567-5200. **Contact:** Ellen F. Ross, Corporate Secretary/VP-Human Resources. **Description:** St. Louis advertising agency. **Common positions:** Advertising Worker; Marketing Specialist; Commercial Artist; Public Relations Specialist. **Educational backgrounds sought:** Art/Design; Marketing; Business Administration. **Special programs:** Training programs; Internships. **Benefits:** medical and dental insurance; tuition assistance; disability coverage; profit sharing; savings plan; vision plan. **Operations at this facility:** service; sales; administration. **Revenues (1991):** $20 million. **Employees:** 58. **Projected hires for the next 12 months:** 6. **Corporate headquarters:** This location.

TBWA ADVERTISING INC.
1000 St. Louis Union Station, Suite 300, St. Louis MO 63103. 314/241-4656. **Contact:** Donna Pfieffer, Personnel Department. **Description:** A full-service advertising agency. **Common positions:** Advertising Worker. **Educational backgrounds sought:** Art/Design; Business Administration; Communications; Liberal Arts; Marketing. **Benefits:** medical, dental and life insurance; vision insurance. **Corporate headquarters location:** New York, NY.

Large employers: 250+

ADVERTISING AGENCIES

Gardner Advertising Co
10 Broadway, St. Louis MO 63102. 314/444-2000. Employs: 250-499.

Small to medium sized employers: 50-249

ADVERTISING AGENCIES

Ross Advertising Inc
130 S Bemiston Av, St. Louis MO 63105-1913. 314/863-1201. Employs: 50-99.

Advanswers Media Programming
10 Broadway, St. Louis MO 63102. 314/444-2100. Employs: 50-99.

RADIO, TELEVISION AND PUBLISHERS' ADVERTISING REPRESENTATIVES

KDNL Inc
1215 Cole St, St. Louis MO 63106-3818. 314/436-3030. Employs: 50-99.

K-USA
10155 Corporate Square Dr, St. Louis MO 63132-2905. 314/997-5594. Employs: 50-99.

Cable Advertising Network Greater St. Louis
2029 Woodland Pkwy, St. Louis MO 63146-4247. 314/997-3800. Employs: 50-99.

DIRECT MAIL ADVERTISING SERVICES

Market Dev Co Div Metromail
41 Kimler Dr, Maryland Hts MO 63043-3702. 314/878-4212.
Employs: 50-99.

COMMERCIAL ECONOMIC, SOCIOLOGICAL AND EDUCATIONAL RESEARCH

Economic Conversion Project
438 N Skinker Blvd, St. Louis MO 63130-4834. 314/726-6406.
Employs: 50-99.

Micro Economics Ltd
7728 W Biltmore Dr, St. Louis MO 63105-2608. 314/725-3773.
Employs: 50-99.

Warren & Associates
473 N Kirkwood Rd, St. Louis MO 63122-3911. 314/821-8585.
Employs: 50-99.

Global Information Services
1605 S Big Bend Blvd, St. Louis MO 63117-2207. 314/647-0081.
Employs: 50-99.

St Louis Inter Fth Committee
438 N Skinker Blvd, St. Louis MO 63130-4834. 314/721-2977.
Employs: 50-99.

PUBLIC RELATIONS SERVICES

Amertech
11960 Westline Industrial Dr, St. Louis MO 63146. 314/434-5070.
Employs: 50-99.

Arron D Cushman & Assoc Inc
7777 Bonhomme Ave, St. Louis MO 63105-1911. 314/725-6400.
Employs: 50-99.

For more information on career opportunities in advertising, marketing, and public relations:

Associations

ACADEMY OF MARKETING SCIENCE
School of Business Administration, University of Miami, Coral Gables FL 33124. 305/284-6673.

ADVERTISING RESEARCH FOUNDATION
Three East 54th Street, 15th Floor, New York NY 10022. 212/751-5656.

AFFILIATED ADVERTISING AGENCIES INTERNATIONAL
2280 South Xanadu Way, Suite 300 Aurora CO 80014. 303/671-8551.

AMERICAN ADVERTISING FEDERATION
1400 K Street NW, Suite 1000, Washington DC 20005. 202/898-0089.

AMERICAN ASSOCIATION OF ADVERTISING AGENCIES
666 Third Avenue, New York NY 10017. 212/682-2500.

AMERICAN MARKETING ASSOCIATION
250 South Wacker Drive, Suite 200, Chicago IL 60606. 312/648-0536.

BUSINESS-PROFESSIONAL ADVERTISING ASSOCIATION
901 N. Washington Street, Suite 206, Alexandria VA 22314. 703/683-2722.

DIRECT MARKETING ASSOCIATION
1101 17th St. NW, Washington DC 20036. 202/347-1222.

INTERNATIONAL ADVERTISING ASSOCIATION
342 Madison Avenue, Suite 2000, New York NY 10173-0073. 212/557-1133.

INTERNATIONAL MARKETING INSTITUTE
314 Hammond Street, Chestnut Hill MA 02167. 617/552-8690.

LEAGUE OF ADVERTISING AGENCIES
2 South End Avenue #4C, New York NY 10280. 212/945-4991.

MARKETING RESEARCH ASSOCIATION
2189 Silas Deane Highway, Suite #5, Rocky Hill CT 06067. 203/257-4008.

PUBLIC RELATIONS SOCIETY OF AMERICA
33 Irving Place, New York NY 10003. 212/995-2230.

TELEVISION BUREAU OF ADVERTISING
477 Madison Avenue, 10th Floor, New York NY 10022-5892. 212/486-1111.

Directories

AAAA ROSTER AND ORGANIZATION
American Association of Advertising Agencies, 666 Third Avenue, New York NY 10017. 212/682-2500.

DIRECTORY OF MINORITY PUBLIC RELATIONS PROFESSIONALS
Public Relations Society of America, 33 Irving Place, New York NY 10003. 212/995-2230.

O'DWYER'S DIRECTORY OF PUBLIC RELATIONS FIRMS
J. R. O'Dwyer Co., 271 Madison Avenue, New York NY 10016. 212/679-2471.

PUBLIC RELATIONS CONSULTANTS DIRECTORY
American Business Directories, Division of American Business Lists, 5707 South 86th Circle, Omaha NE 68127. 402/331-7169.

PUBLIC RELATIONS JOURNAL REGISTER ISSUE
Public Relations Society of America, 33 Irving Place, New York NY 10003. 212/995-2230.

STANDARD DIRECTORY OF ADVERTISING AGENCIES
National Register Publishing Company, 3004 Glenview Road, Wilmette IL 60091. 708/256-6067.

Magazines

ADVERTISING AGE
Crain Communications, 740 North Rush Street, Chicago IL 60611. 312/649-5316.

ADWEEK
49 E. 21st Street, New York NY 10010. 212/529-5500.

BUSINESS MARKETING
Crain Communications, 740 Rush Street, Chicago IL 60611. 312/649-5260.

JOURNAL OF MARKETING
American Marketing Association, 250 South Wacker Drive, Suite 200, Chicago IL 60606. 312/648-0536.

THE MARKETING NEWS
American Marketing Association, 250 South Wacker Drive, Suite 200, Chicago IL 60606. 312/648-0536.

PR REPORTER
PR Publishing Co., P.O. Box 600, Exeter NH 03833. 603/778-0514.

PUBLIC RELATIONS JOURNAL
Public Relations Society of America, 33 Irving Place, New York NY 10003. 212/995-2230.

PUBLIC RELATIONS NEWS
Phillips Publishing Inc., 7811 Montrose Road, Potomac MD 20854. 301/340-2100.

AEROSPACE

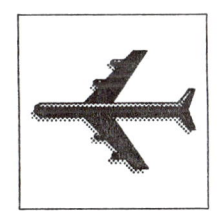

Most analysts believe that while the commercial aerospace industry will continue to be hurt by the recession, the industry is well-poised for solid growth in the long run. Throughout the decade, air traffic is expected to rise rapidly, increasing the demand for new planes. That's good news for jobseekers, especially those with training in aerospace engineering.

ENGINEERED AIR SYSTEMS INC.
1270 North Price Road, St. Louis MO 63132. 314/993-5885, ext. 303. **Contact:** Mrs. Aurora D. Lane, Director/Human Resources. **Description:** Manufacture ground support equipment for military-air conditioning/ heating portable units, environmental control systems, containers. **Common positions:** Accountant; Attorney; Blue-Collar Worker Supervisor; Buyer; Computer Programmer; Draftsperson; Electrical Engineer; Industrial Engineer; Mechanical Engineer; Metallurgical Engineer; Financial Analyst; Personnel and Labor Relations Specialist; Purchasing Agent; Quality Control Supervisor; Systems Analyst; Technical Writer/Editor. **Educational backgrounds sought:** Accounting; Business Administration; Computer Science; Engineering; Finance; Liberal Arts; Marketing. **Benefits:** medical, dental, and life insurance; pension plan-hourly workforce; tuition assistance; disability coverage; ESOP for salaried workforce. **Corporate headquarters:** This location. **Operations at this facility:** regional headquarters; divisional headquarters; manufacturing; research and development; administration; service; sales. **Listed on:** New York Stock Exchange.

ESSEX INDUSTRIES INC.
7700 Gravois Avenue, St. Louis MO 63123. 314/832-4500. **Contact:** Mr. Jay Hotaling, Personnel Director. **Description:** Designs, develops and manufactures aircraft systems and components (quick disconnect couplings, check valves, relief and drain valves, pressure switches, regulators, pressure vessels, cryogenics oxygen systems) solenoids and rain repellant systems, screw machine products. **Common positions:** Accountant; Blue-Collar Worker

Supervisor; Computer Programmer; Draftsperson; Mechanical Engineer; Quality Controller. **Educational backgrounds sought:** Accounting; Business Administration; Computer Science; Engineering. **Special programs:** Training programs. **Benefits:** medical, dental and life insurance; tuition assistance; disability coverage; profit sharing; employee discounts; savings plan. **Other U.S. locations:** Illinois, Maryland, Ohio, North Carolina, Pennsylvania. **Operations at this facility:** manufacturing; administration; sales. **Employees:** 450.

GARRETT GENERAL AVIATION SERVICES DIVISION
P.O. Box 2177, Springfield IL 62705. 217/544-3431. **Contact:** Jay Davis, Manager Human Resources. **Description:** Provides a comprehensive group of services to the aircraft industry. Parent company, Allied Signal Corporation, serves a broad spectrum of industries through its more than 40 strategic businesses, which are grouped into three sectors: Aerospace, Automotive, and Engineered Materials. Allied Signal is one of the nation's largest industrial organizations, and has 115,000 employees in over 30 countries. **Common positions:** Accountant; Administrator; Customer Service Representative; Operations/Production Manager; Personnel and Labor Relations Specialist; Purchasing Agent; Quality Control Supervisor; Blue-Collar Worker Supervisor; Computer Programmer; Department Manager; A&P Mechanics; Structural Sheet Metal Trim and Upholsters; Cabinet Makers. **Educational backgrounds sought:** Aviation Applied Sciences; Aviation Management; Aviation Maintenance; Accounting; Liberal Arts; Business Administration; Computer Science; Marketing. **Benefits:** medical, dental, and life insurance; pension plan; tuition assistance; disability coverage; profit sharing; savings plan; paid vacation. **Corporate headquarters:** Morristown, NJ. **Parent company:** Allied Signal Inc. **Listed on:** New York Stock Exchange.

McDONNELL DOUGLAS CORPORATION
P.O. Box 516, St. Louis MO 63166. Mailed inquiries only. **Contact:** Section Manager of Employee Relations. **Description:** Engaged in the research, development, and manufacture of aircraft, spacecraft, missiles, and data processing systems. **Corporate headquarters:** This location.

McDONNELL DOUGLAS ELECTRONICS COMPANY
P.O. Box 426, St. Charles MO 63302. 314/925-4000. **Contact:** Personnel Department. **Description:** Corporate headquarters location of an internationally recognized company engaged in the development and application of aerospace technology and the supply of information related products and services. Major product lines include combat aircraft, transport aircraft, space systems and missiles, and information systems. The company is also active in commercial financing and leasing and energy systems. Company ranks 42nd in sales among U.S. industrial corporations, second in defense contract awards, eighth in value of exports and 16th among U.S.-based suppliers of information systems. **Other facilities are located in:** California, Florida, Oklahoma, and Ontario, Canada.

SABRELINER CORPORATION
18118 Chesterfield Airport Road, Chesterfield MO 63005-1121. 314/537-3660. **Contact:** Janet Gaines, Personnel Manager. **Description:** A retailer of aircraft sales and service.

Additional large employers: 250+

AIRCRAFT

Advanced Aircraft Inc
18421 Edison Ave, Chesterfield MO 63005-3632. 314/537-2333. Employs: 500-999.

Bell Helicopter Textron
4411 Woodson Rd, St. Louis MO 63134-3701. 314/427-4987. Employs: 500-999.

British Aerospace Inc
5995 McDonnell Blvd, St. Louis MO 63134-2028. 314/731-1360. Employs: 500-999.

AIRCRAFT PARTS AND AUXILIARY EQUIPMENT

Alco Controls Div
Box 12700, St. Louis MO 63141. 314/569-4500. Employs: 1,000+.

GUIDED MISSILES AND SPACE VEHICLES

Aerospace Avionics Inc
1065 Executive Parkway Dr, St. Louis MO 63141-6326. 314/469-8977. Employs: 500-999.

Aerospace Assocs Division Kenneth
4650 W Florissant Ave, St. Louis MO 63115-2233. 314/381-0038. Employs: 1,000+.

Beech Aerospace Svcs Inc
Scott AFB, Scott AFB IL 62225. 618/744-0760. Employs: 500-999.

GEC Avionics
13801 Riverport Dr, Maryland Hts MO 63043-4810. 314/298-7722. Employs: 500-999.

Grumman Corporation
500 Northwest Plz, Saint Ann MO 63074-2209. 314/291-4146. Employs: 500-999.

Martin Marietta Corporation
10801 Pear Tree Ln, Saint Ann MO 63074-1450. 314/429-1500. Employs: 500-999.

Rockwell International
500 Northwest Plz, Saint Ann MO 63074-2209. 314/298-3423. Employs: 500-999.

Smiths Industries
500 Northwest Plz, Saint Ann MO 63074-2209. 314/298-8009. Employs: 500-999.

Western Gear Corp
500 Northwest Plz, Saint Ann MO 63074-2209. 314/298-0092. Employs: 500-999.

GUIDED MISSILE AND SPACE VEHICLE PARTS AND AUXILIARY EQUIPMENT

Mc Donnell Douglas Flexs Systs
2600 N 3rd St, Saint Charles MO 63301-0060. 314/925-4708. Employs: 1,000+.

Additional small to medium sized employers: 50-249

AIRCRAFT PARTS AND AUXILIARY EQUIPMENT

Essex Cryogenics Of Mo
8007 Chivvis Dr, St. Louis MO 63123-2333. 314/832-8077.
Employs: 50-99.

Precision Engineering Co
10182 Natural Bridge Rd, St. Louis MO 63134-3301. 314/428-1388.
Employs: 50-99.

For more information on career opportunities in aerospace:

Associations

AIR TRANSPORT ASSOCIATION OF AMERICA
1301 Pennsylvania Avenue NW, Suite 1100, Washington DC 20004. 202/626-4000.

AMERICAN INSTITUTE OF AERONAUTICS AND ASTRONAUTICS
555 West 57th Street, New York NY 10019. 212/247-6500.

AVIATION MAINTENANCE FOUNDATION
P.O. Box 2826, Redmond WA 98073. 206/828-3917.

FUTURE AVIATION PROFESSIONALS OF AMERICA
4959 Massachusetts Boulevard, Atlanta GA 30337. 404/997-8097.

NATIONAL AERONAUTIC ASSOCIATION OF USA
1815 North Fort Meyer Drive, Suite 700, Arlington VA 22209. 703/527-0226.

PROFESSIONAL AVIATION MAINTENANCE ASSOCIATION
500 NW Plaza, Suite 809, St. Ann MO 63074. 314/739-2580.

AMUSEMENT, ARTS AND RECREATION

During the past few years, the entertainment industry has been hit by a wave of major buy outs. For jobseekers, the competition is as fierce as in any other industry. The jobs are there but tough to get. Right now, the music industry is in a stronger position than the film industry.

FAIRMONT RACE TRACK/ OGDEN FAIRMONT INC.
Route 40, Collinsville IL 62234. 618/345-4300. **Contact:** Brian Zander, General Manager. **Description:** An area race track specializing in horse racing. **Employees:** 400+.

MISSOURI ATHLETIC CLUB
405 Washington Avenue, St. Louis MO 63102. 314/231-7220. **Contact:** Dave Miller, Director of Operational Services. **Description:** An exclusive downtown, private club offering a full gymnasium, heated swimming pool and solarium, multiple private dining rooms and ala carte outlets, a pro shop and hotel rooms. **Common positions:** Accountant; Hotel Manager/Assistant Manager; Personnel and Labor Relations Specialist; Purchasing Agent; Chefs; Cooks; Food Servers. **Educational backgrounds sought:** Hotel/Restaurant Management. **Special programs:** Training programs and internships. **Benefits:** medical, dental, and life insurance; pension plan; disability coverage; employee discounts; savings plan. **Corporate headquarters:** This location. **Operations at this facility:** service. **Employees:** 265. **Projected number of hires for the next 12 months:** 80.

MISSOURI BOTANICAL GARDEN
2345 Tower Grove Avenue, St. Louis MO 63110. 314/577-5100. **Contact:** Sue L. Wilkerson, Director, Human Resource Management. **Description:** A nonprofit cultural organization. Primary functions are education, display (horticulture), and research (botanical). The Garden has a visitor center, research library, historical house, and gift shop. **Common positions:** Accounting/Financial Staff (Payroll, Grants and Contracts; Accounts Payable); Administrator; Manager; Computer Programmer; Data Processor; Customer Service (Visitors Desk Worker, Tour Guide, Salesperson); Public Relations; Fund Raiser; Membership Staff; Publications Staff; Horticulturist; Biologist; Botanist; Researcher; Curator; Housekeeper; Custodian; Receiving; Human Resource Management; Instructor/Trainer; Teacher; Library Staff; Maintenance; Security Staff. **Educational backgrounds sought:** Accounting; Biology; Botany; Business Administration; Communications; Computer Science; Liberal Arts; Marketing. **Special programs:** Training programs; Internships. **Benefits:** Medical, Dental, and Life Insurance; Pension Plan; Disability Coverage; Child Care Referral Program; Flexible Benefit Dependent Care Program; Tax Deferred Annuity Plan; Employee Assistance Program; Garden Membership; Employee Discounts. **Employees:** 350.

MUNICIPAL THEATRE ASSOC. OF ST. LOUIS
Forest Park, St. Louis MO 63112. 314/361-1900. **Contact:** Barbara Boland, Assistant to the General Manager and CEO. **Description:** A St. Louis theatrical productions company. **Common positions:** Accountant; Advertising Worker; Customer Service Representative; Department Manager; Operations/Production Manager; Marketing Specialist; Public Relations Specialist; Development. **Educational backgrounds sought:** Accounting; Art/Design; Business Administration; Communications; Finance; Liberal Arts; Marketing. **Special programs:** Internships. **Benefits:** medical and dental insurance (salaried employee only). **Corporate headquarters:** This location. **Operations at this facility:** sales. **Revenues (1991):** Non-profit. **Employees:** 20. **Projected hires for the next 12 months:** 0-2.

SIX FLAGS OVER MID-AMERICA
P.O. Box 60, Eureka MO 63025. 314/938-5300. **Contact:** Cheryl Heitzler, Human Resources Manager. **Description:** Engaged in the entertainment, theme park industry. **Common positions:** Accountant; Administrator; Buyer; Personnel and Labor Relations Specialist; Public Relations Specialist;

Purchasing Agent; Sales Representative. **Educational backgrounds sought:** Accounting; Business Administration; Communications; Computer Science; Finance; Liberal Arts; Marketing. **Special programs:** Internships. **Benefits:** medical, dental and life insurance; pension plan; tuition assistance; disability coverage; daycare assistance; employee discounts; savings plan. **Corporate headquarters:** Parsippany, NJ. **Parent company:** Six Flags Theme Parks. **Operations at this facility:** sales; divisional headquarters.

ST. LOUIS SYMPHONY SOCIETY
718 North Grand Boulevard, St. Louis MO 63103. 314/533-2500. **Contact:** Personnel Director. **Description:** Offices of the St. Louis Symphony Orchestra.

Additional large employers: 250+

PUBLIC GOLF COURSES

Breckenridge Hotels Corp
900 S Hwy Dr, Fenton MO 63026-2042. 314/349-5255. Employs: 1,000+.

AMUSEMENT PARKS

Chesterfield Billiards
1676 Clarkson Rd, Chesterfield MO 63017-4601. 314/537-9229. Employs: 250-499.

Fun-N-Games
872 Chesterfield Village Pkwy, Chesterfield MO 63017. 314/536-2454. Employs: 250-499.

Le Mans Family Fun Center
616 Westport Plz, St. Louis MO 63146-3106. 314/576-3856. Employs: 250-499.

Meramec Skate Park
400 Meramec Station Rd, Valley Park MO 63088-1331. 314/225-0067. Employs: 250-499.

Tilt 76
Northwest Plaza, Saint Ann MO 63074. 314/298-3440. Employs: 250-499.

Wet Willy's Water Slide
313 Highway 141, Valley Park MO 63088. 314/225-4240. Employs: 250-499.

Additional small to medium sized employers: 50-249

MOTION PICTURE AND VIDEO TAPE PRODUCTION

Technisonic Studios
500 S Ewing Ave, St. Louis MO 63103-2933. 314/533-1777. Employs: 50-99.

Videonine Productions
6996 Millbrook Blvd, St. Louis MO 63130-4433. 314/725-2460. Employs: 50-99.

MOTION PICTURE THEATERS, EXCEPT DRIVE-IN

B A C Theatres Inc
100 S Charles St, Belleville IL 62220-2212. 618/233-5210. Employs: 100-249.

DANCE STUDIOS, SCHOOLS AND HALLS

Corvette Disco
6900 N Illinois St, E St. Louis IL 62208-1313. 618/632-4747. Employs: 50-99.

PROFESSIONAL SPORTS CLUBS AND PROMOTERS

Busch Memorial Stadium
250 Stadium Pl, St. Louis MO 63102-1722. 314/421-3060. Employs: 100-249.

AMUSEMENT PARKS

Busch Entertainment Corp
One Busch Pl, St. Louis MO 63118-1849. 314/577-4702. Employs: 50-99.

Meramec Caverns
Hwy W, Stanton MO 63079. 314/468-3166. Employs: 50-99.

MUSEUMS AND ART GALLERIES

Mid-America Aquacenter
4020 Pontoon Rd, Granite City IL 62040-7200. 618/797-2782. Employs: 50-99.

For more information on career opportunities in amusement, arts, and recreation:

Associations

ACTOR'S EQUITY ASSOCIATION
165 West 47th Street, New York NY 10036. 212/869-8530.

AFFILIATE ARTISTS
37 West 65th Street, 6th Floor, New York NY 10023. 212/580-2000.

AMERICAN ALLIANCE FOR THEATRE AND EDUCATION
Division of Performing Arts, Virginia Tech, Blacksburg VA 24061-0141. 703/231-5335.

AMERICAN ASSOCIATION OF MUSEUMS
1225 I Street NW, Washington DC 20005. 202/289-1818.

AMERICAN ASSOCIATION OF ZOOLOGICAL PARKS & AQUARIUMS
Oglebay Park, Wheeling WV 26003. 304/242-2160.

AMERICAN COUNCIL FOR THE ARTS
1 E. 53rd Street, New York NY 10022. 212/245-4510.

AMERICAN CRAFTS COUNCIL
72 Spring Street, New York NY 10012. 212/274-0630.

AMERICAN DANCE GUILD
33 West 21st Street, New York NY 10010. 212/627-3790.

AMERICAN FEDERATION OF MUSICIANS
1501 Broadway, Suite 600, New York NY 10036. 212/869-1330.

AMERICAN FEDERATION OF TELEVISION AND RADIO ARTISTS
260 Madison Avenue, New York NY 10016. 212/532-0800.

AMERICAN FILM INSTITUTE
John F. Kennedy Center for the Performing Arts, Washington DC 20566. 202/828-4000.

AMERICAN GUILD OF MUSICAL ARTISTS
1727 Broadway, New York NY 10019-5284. 212/265-3687.

AMERICAN MUSIC CENTER
30 West 26th Street, Suite 1001, New York NY 10010. 212/366-5260.

AMERICAN SOCIETY OF COMPOSERS, AUTHORS, AND PUBLISHERS
1 Lincoln Plaza, New York NY 10023. 212/595-3050.

AMERICAN SYMPHONY ORCHESTRA LEAGUE
777 14th Street NW, Suite 500, Washington DC 20005. 202/628-0099.

ASSOCIATION OF INDEPENDENT VIDEO AND FILMMAKERS
625 Broadway, 9th Floor, New York NY 10012. 212/473-3400.

BUSINESS COMMITTEE FOR THE ARTS
1775 Broadway, Suite 510, New York NY 10019-1942. 212/664-0600.

DANCE THEATER WORKSHOP
219 West 19th Street, New York NY 10011. 212/691-6500.

DANCE USA
777 14th Street NW, Suite 540, Washington DC 20005. 202/628-0144.

INTERNATIONAL SOCIETY OF PERFORMING ARTS ADMINISTRATORS
6065 Pickerel, Rockford MI 49341. 616/874-6200.

NATIONAL ARTISTS' EQUITY ASSOCIATION
P.O. Box 28068, Central Station, Washington DC 20038-8068. 202/628-9633.

NATIONAL DANCE ASSOCIATION
1900 Association Drive, Reston VA 22091. 703/476-3436.

NATIONAL ENDOWMENT FOR THE ARTS
1100 Pennsylvania Avenue NW, Washington DC 20506. 202/682-5400.

NATIONAL FOUNDATION FOR ADVANCEMENT IN THE ARTS
3915 Biscayne Boulevard, Miami FL 33137. 305/573-0490.

NATIONAL ORGANIZATION FOR HUMAN SERVICE EDUCATION
Fitchburg State College, 160 Pearl Street, Fitchburg MA 01420. 508/345-2151.

NATIONAL RECREATION AND PARK ASSOCIATION
2775 S. Quincy Street, Suite 300, Arlington VA 22206. 703/820-4940.

PROFESSIONAL ARTS MANAGEMENT INSTITUTE
408 West 57th Street, New York NY 10019. 212/245-3850.

PRODUCERS GUILD OF AMERICA
400 S. Beverly Drive, Suite 211, Beverly Hills CA 90212. 310/557-0807.

SCREEN ACTORS GUILD
7065 Hollywood Boulevard, Hollywood CA 90028. 213/465-4600.

SOCIETY OF MOTION PICTURE AND TELEVISION ENGINEERS
595 West Hartsdale Avenue, White Plains NY 10607. 914/761-1100.

THEATRE COMMUNICATIONS GROUP
355 Lexington Avenue, New York NY 10017. 212/697-5230.

WOMEN'S CAUCUS FOR ART
Moore College of Art, 20th & The Parkway, Philadelphia PA 19103. 215/854-0922.

Directories

THE ACADEMY PLAYERS DIRECTORIES
The Academy of Motion Picture Arts and Sciences, 8949 Wilshire Boulevard, Beverly Hills CA 90211. 310/247-3000.

ARTIST'S MARKET
Writer's Digest Books, 1507 Dana Avenue, Cincinnati OH 45207. 513/531-2222.

CREATIVE BLACK BOOK
115 5th Avenue, New York NY 10003. 212/254-1330.

PLAYERS GUIDE
165 West 46th Street, New York NY 10036. 212/869-3570.

ROSS REPORTS TELEVISION
Television Index, Inc., 40-29 27th Street, Long Island City NY 11101. 718/937-3990.

Magazines

AMERICAN ARTIST
One Astor Place, New York NY 10036. 212/764-7300.

AMERICAN CINEMATOGRAPHER
American Society of Cinematographers, 1782 North Orange Drive, Los Angeles CA 90028. 213/876-7107.

ART BUSINESS NEWS
Myers Publishing Co., 777 Summer Street, Stamford CT 06901. 203/356-1745.

ART DIRECTION
10 East 39th Street, 6th Floor, New York NY 10016. 212/889-6500.

ARTFORUM
65 Bleecker Street, New York NY 10012. 212/475-4000.

ARTWEEK
12 S. First Street, Suite 520, San Jose CA 95113. 408/279-2293.

AVISO
American Association of Museums, 1225 I Street NW, Washington DC 20005. 202/289-1818.

BACK STAGE
330 West 42nd Street, New York NY 10036. 212/947-0020.

BILLBOARD
Billboard Publications, Inc., 1515 Broadway, New York NY 10036. 212/764-7300.

CASHBOX
157 West 57th Street, Suite 503, New York NY 10019. 212/586-2640.

CRAFTS REPORT
700 Orange Street, Wilmington DE 19801. 302/656-2209.

DRAMA-LOGUE
P.O. Box 38771, Los Angeles CA 90038. 213/464-5079.

HOLLYWOOD REPORTER
6715 Sunset Boulevard, Hollywood
CA 90028. 213/464-7411.

VARIETY
475 Park Avenue South, New York
NY 10016. 212/779-1100.

WOMEN ARTIST NEWS
300 Riverside Drive, New York
NY 10025. 212/666-6990.

APPAREL AND TEXTILES

After employment gains for four straight years in the late '80s, layoffs hit the industry hard as the '90s opened. The worst appears to be over and employment should rise. New jobs will not consist of old-style production line work; automation has changed the industry's make-up, and those with technical and computer backgrounds have a distinct advantage.

ANGELICA CORPORATION
10176 Corporate Square Drive, St. Louis MO 63132. 314/854-3800. **Contact:** Human Resources. **Description:** Manufacturers and retailers of industrial, professional and vocational washable service garments. Also wholesalers of apparel, textile rental and laundry service to hospitals. **Employees:** 8000+. **Common positions:** Accountant; Credit Manager; Customer Service Representative; Industrial Designer; Operations/Production Manager; Marketing Specialist; Quality Control Supervisor; Sales Representative; Systems Analyst. **Educational backgrounds sought:** Accounting; Art/Design; Business Administration; Computer Science; Liberal Arts; Marketing. **Benefits:** medical, dental, and life insurance; pension plan; tuition assistance; disability coverage; employee discounts; savings plan. **Corporate headquarters:** This location. **Operations at this facility:** manufacturing; administration; service; sales. **Listed on:** New York Stock Exchange.

ARTEX INTERNATIONAL INC.
1405 S. Walnut Street, Highland IL 62249. 618/654-2114. **Contact:** Personnel Department. **Description:** An area apparel company, specializing in the manufacture of dyed and imprinted tablecloths and napkins. **Employees:** 100+.

BELLEVILLE SHOE MANUFACTURING COMPANY
P.O. Box 508, Belleville IL 62222. 618/233-5600. **Contact:** Bill Tripp, Plant Manager. **Description:** Manufacturers of men's and boy's shoes. **Employees:** 300+.

THE BILTWELL COMPANY INC.
2005 Walton Road, St. Louis MO 63114. 314/426-3850. **Contact:** Executive Vice-President. **Description:** Engaged in apparel manufacturing. Parent company, Interco, is a broadly based manufacturer and retailer of consumer

products and services with operations in apparel manufacturing, retailing, footwear manufacturing, and furniture and home furnishings.

CENTRAL STATES WIPING MATERIALS CO.
420 East De Soto Street, St. Louis MO 63147. 314/421-4487. **Contact:** Personnel Director. **Description:** Manufacturer of wiping and polishing cloths, and cotton and wool waste products.

ELDER MANUFACTURING COMPANY
12747 Olive Street, Suite 300, St. Louis MO 63141. 314/469-1120. **Contact:** Greg Beile, Manager of Customer Service. **Description:** Manufacturers of boys' clothing and furnishings and men's shirts. **Employees:** 100+.

JOHANSEN BROTHERS SHOE COMPANY INC.
710 North Tucker Boulevard, Suite 705, St. Louis MO 63101. 314/231-0700. **Contact:** Manager. **Description:** Manufacturers of women's dress shoes. **Common positions:** Accountant; Administrator; Buyer; Credit Manager; Purchasing Agent; Sales Representative. **Benefits:** medical and life insurance; savings plan. **Corporate headquarters:** This location. **Operations at this facility:** regional headquarters.

MELBOURNE MANUFACTURING COMPANY
1708 Delmar Boulevard, St. Louis MO 63103. 314/231-7123. **Contact:** Joann Marr, Office Manager. **Description:** A St. Louis company engaged in the manufacture of women's handbags and purses.

MISS ELAINE
1717 Olive St., St. Louis MO 63103. 314/421-3312. **Contact:** Mrs. Adele Branz, Personnel. **Description:** Manufacturers of a variety of sleep and lounge wear.

NORWOOD SHOE CORPORATION
1 Penaljo Drive, Box 75D, De Soto MO 63020. 314/586-0770. **Contact:** James C. Bauer, CFO. **Description:** Manufacturers of ladies' shoes. **Employees:** 215. **Common positions:** Accountant; Credit Manager; Customer Service Representative; Operations and Production Manager; Purchasing Agent; Sales Representative. **Educational backgrounds sought:** Accounting; Business Administration; Computer Science; Finance. **Benefits:** Medical, Dental, and Life Insurance; Profit Sharing. **Corporate headquarters:** This location. **Operations at this facility:** Manufacturing; Administration; Service; Sales. **Revenues (1991):** $8 million. **Projected hires for the next 12 months:** 10.

PRINCE GARDNER
6245 Lemay Ferry Road, St. Louis MO 63129. 314/487-3100. **Contact:** Joan DeGeare, Personnel Human Resources Manager. **Description:** Manufacturer of a variety of personal leather goods.

TOBER INDUSTRIES INC.
1520 Washington Avenue, St. Louis MO 63103. 314/421-2030. **Contact:** Elizabeth Stoley, Personnel Director. **Description:** Wholesaler of a popular line of women's shoes.

WESTERN TEXTILE PRODUCTS COMPANY
P.O. Box 7139, St. Louis MO 63177. 314/225-9400. **Contact:** Linda Miller, Personnel Director. **Description:** A manufacturer of extruded plastic construction products, apparel and industrial textile products, shoe industry textile products, textile finishing, and cutting and slitting.

Additional large employers: 250+

MEN'S AND BOYS' CLOTHING

California Manufacturing Co
2270 Weldon Pkwy, St. Louis MO 63146-3206. 314/567-4404.
Employs: 250-499.

WOMEN'S, MISSES' AND JUNIORS' SUITS, SKIRTS AND COATS

Grove Co Inc
8300 Manchester Rd, St. Louis MO 63144-2806. 314/961-2345.
Employs: 250-499.

WOMEN'S, MISSES', CHILDREN'S AND INFANTS' UNDERWEAR AND NIGHTWEAR

Kellwood Co
600 Kellwood Pkwy, Chesterfield MO 63017-5800. 314/576-3100.
Employs: 1,000+.

LEATHER TANNING AND FINISHING

Brown Shoe Co Inc
510 S Mc Kinley, Union MO 63084-2228. 314/583-2533.
Employs: 250-499.

MEN'S FOOTWEAR, EXCEPT ATHLETIC

Brown Shoe Co
8300 Maryland Ave, St. Louis MO 63105-3645. 314/854-4000.
Employs: 1,000+.

PERSONAL LEATHER GOODS, EXCEPT WOMEN'S HANDBAGS AND PURSES

Hazel Inc
1200 S Stafford St, Washington MO 63090-4231. 314/239-2781.
Employs: 250-499.

Additional small to medium sized employers: 50-249

NARROW FABRIC AND OTHER SMALLWARES MILLS: COTTON, WOOL, SILK AND MANMADE FIBER

St Louis Braid Co
2035 Lucas Ave, St. Louis MO 63103-1621. 314/231-0540.
Employs: 50-99.

St Louis Trimming Inc
5040 Arsenal St, St. Louis MO 63139-1012. 314/771-8388.
Employs: 100-249.

MEN'S AND BOYS' SUITS, COATS AND OVERCOATS

De Moulin Bros & Co
1025 S 4th St, Greenville IL 62246-2168. 618/664-2000.
Employs: 100-249.

MEN'S AND BOYS' SHIRTS, EXCEPT WORK SHIRTS

H T I Corp
400 S Lindell St, Vandalia MO 63382-1763. 314/594-6418. Employs: 100-249.

MEN'S AND BOYS' NECKWEAR

Meyer-Mueller-Goodman Co
1717 Olive St, St. Louis MO 63103-1724. 314/421-2182. Employs: 100-249.

MEN'S AND BOYS' WORK CLOTHING

Gale-Sobel Co
1209 Washington Ave, St. Louis MO 63103-1934. 314/436-1440. Employs: 50-99.

Todd Uniform Inc
3668 S Geyer Rd, St. Louis MO 63127-1243. 314/984-0365. Employs: 100-249.

WOMEN'S, MISSES' AND JUNIORS' DRESSES

Bridal Originals Inc
401 E 4th St, Sparta IL 62286. 618/443-3732. Employs: 100-249.

Bridal Originals Inc
701 S 3rd St, Belleville IL 62220-2525. 618/233-4800. Employs: 100-249.

Bridal Originals Inc
1700 St Louis Rd, Collinsville IL 62234-1802. 618/345-2345. Employs: 100-249.

Bridal Originals Inc
101 S 7th St, Bowling Green MO 63334. 314/324-2268. Employs: 100-249.

WOMEN'S, MISSES', AND JUNIORS' OUTERWEAR

Inter Style Inc
1136 Washington Av, St. Louis MO 63101-1158. 314/231-2350. Employs: 100-249.

WOMEN'S, MISSES', CHILDREN'S AND INFANTS' UNDERWEAR AND NIGHTWEAR

Wonder Maid Inc
801 Terry Ln, Washington MO 63090-3543. 314/239-3696. Employs: 100-249.

HATS, CAPS AND MILLINERY

Henschel Mfg Co
1706 Olive St, St. Louis MO 63103-1721. 314/421-0009. Employs: 50-99.

International Hat Co Inc
101 S Hanley Rd Ste 1900, St. Louis MO 63105-3493. 314/771-8800. Employs: 50-99.

Langenberg Hat Co
R R 2 1018 Maupin, New Haven MO 63068-9576. 314/237-2166. Employs: 50-99.

Langenberg Hat Co
200 Rosalie St, Berger MO 63014. 314/834-5241. Employs: 50-99.

Paramount Cap Mfg Co
Hwy H, Gerald MO 63037. 314/764-3351. Employs: 100-249.

Premier Headwear Co
2705 Olive St, St. Louis MO 63103-1425. 314/371-7272. Employs: 100-249.

Stylemaster Apparel Inc
1 Stylemaster Dr, Union MO 63084. 314/583-8383. Employs: 50-99.

Sylvia Inc
1110 Washington Ave, St. Louis MO 63101-1157. 314/231-7565. Employs: 50-99.

APPAREL AND ACCESSORIES

Wee Ones Inc
33 Cherokee Dr, Saint Peters MO 63376-3927. 314/441-6301. Employs: 100-249.

Weissmans Theatrical Splys Inc
1600 Macklind Ave, St. Louis MO 63110-2006. 314/773-9000. Employs: 50-99.

CURTAINS AND DRAPERIES

Midwest Window Art Inc
703 N 13th St, St. Louis MO 63103-1930. 314/241-0334. Employs: 50-99.

HOUSEFURNISHINGS, EXCEPT CURTAINS AND DRAPERIES

Roho Incorporated
100 Florida Av, Belleville IL 62221-5429. 618/277-9150. Employs: 100-249.

TEXTILE BAGS

Eagle Inds Unltd Inc
400 Biltmore Dr #530, Fenton MO 63026-4641. 314/343-7547. Employs: 50-99.

LEATHER TANNING AND FINISHING

Hermann Oak Leather Co
4050 N First St, St. Louis MO 63147-3427. 314/421-1173. Employs: 50-99.

BOOT AND SHOE CUT STOCK AND FINDINGS

Jones & Vining
815 E Cherry St, Troy MO 63379-1415. 314/528-7041. Employs: 50-99.

MEN'S FOOTWEAR, EXCEPT ATHLETIC

JD's Boots & Western Shop
5765 Godfrey Rd, Godfrey IL 62035-2425. 618/466-9070. Employs: 100-249.

WOMEN'S FOOTWEAR, EXCEPT ATHLETIC

Beacon Shoe Co Inc
Lions Estates Dr, Jonesburg MO 63351. 314/488-5444. Employs: 100-249.

Brown Shoe Co Inc
1211 N Jefferson Ave, St. Louis MO 63106-2132. 314/371-2400. Employs: 100-249.

PERSONAL LEATHER GOODS, EXCEPT WOMEN'S HANDBAGS AND PURSES

Foster Pond Inds Inc
503 W Moredock St, Valmeyer IL 62295-2425. 618/935-2100. Employs: 100-249.

MINERAL WOOL

Louisiana-Pacific Corp
2001 Hitzert Ct, Fenton MO 63026-2506. 314/343-9103. Employs: 50-99.

For more information on career opportunities in the apparel and textile industries:

Associations

AFFILIATED DRESS MANUFACTURERS
1440 Broadway, New York NY 10018. 212/398-9797.

AMERICAN APPAREL MANUFACTURERS ASSOCIATION
2500 Wilson Boulevard, Suite 301, Arlington VA 22201. 703/524-1864.

AMERICAN CLOAK AND SUIT MANUFACTURERS ASSOCIATION
450 Seventh Avenue, New York NY 10123. 212/244-7300.

AMERICAN TEXTILE MANUFACTURERS INSTITUTE
1801 K Street NW, Suite 900, Washington DC 20006. 202/862-0500.

CLOTHING MANUFACTURERS ASSOCIATION OF THE USA
1290 Avenue of the Americas, New York NY 10104. 212/757-6664.

COUNCIL OF FASHION DESIGNERS OF AMERICA
1412 Broadway, Suite 1714, New York NY 10018. 212/302-1821.

THE FASHION GROUP
9 Rockefeller Plaza, Suite 1722, New York NY 10020. 212/247-3940.

INTERNATIONAL ASSOCIATION OF CLOTHING DESIGNERS
240 Madison Avenue, New York NY 10016. 212/685-6602.

MEN'S FASHION ASSOCIATION OF AMERICA
240 Madison Avenue, New York NY 10016. 212/683-5665.

NORTHERN TEXTILE ASSOCIATION
230 Congress Street, Boston MA 02110. 617/542-8220.

TEXTILE RESEARCH INSTITUTE
Box 625, Princeton NJ 08540. 609/924-3150.

Directories

AAMA DIRECTORY
American Apparel Manufacturers Association, 2500 Wilson Boulevard, Suite 301, Arlington VA 22201. 703/524-1864.

APPAREL TRADES BOOK
Dun & Bradstreet Inc., 1 Diamond Hill Road, Murray Hill NJ 07974. 908/665-5000.

FAIRCHILD'S MARKET DIRECTORY OF WOMEN'S AND CHILDREN'S APPAREL
Fairchild Publications, 7 West 34th Street, New York NY 10001. 212/630-4000.

Magazines

AMERICA'S TEXTILES
Billiam Publishing, 211 Century Drive, Suite 208-A, Greenville SC 29607. 803/242-5300.

APPAREL INDUSTRY MAGAZINE
Shore Communications Inc., 180 Allen Road NE, Suite 300-N, Atlanta GA 30328-4893. 404/252-8831.

BOBBIN
Bobbin Publications, P.O. Box 1986, 1110 Shop Road, Columbia SC 29202. 803/771-7500.

ACCESSORIES
Business Journals, 50 Day Street, P.O. Box 5550, Norwalk CT 06856. 203/853-6015.

WOMEN'S WEAR DAILY (WWD)
Fairchild Publications, 7 West 34th Street, New York NY 10001. 212/630-4000.

ARCHITECTURE, CONSTRUCTION AND REAL ESTATE

In the construction industry, home building is expected to stabilize, but commercial real estate construction - especially office buildings and hotels - will continue to decline. Home improvement, hospitals, schools, water supply buildings, and public service buildings construction should offer the best opportunities.

J.S. ALBERICI CONSTRUCTION CO.
2150 Kienlen Avenue, St. Louis MO 63121. 314/261-2611. **Contact:** Jack Bartnett, Personnel Administrator. **Description:** A St. Louis general contracting firm. **Employees:** 100+.

ARROW GROUP INDUSTRIES
1101 North 4th Street, Breese IL 62230. 618/526-4546. **Contact:** Patty Sellers, Director, Personnel. **Description:** Manufacturers of utility storage buildings. **Employees:** 200+.

ASSOCIATED GROCERS' COMPANY OF ST. LOUIS
1130 East Road, St. Louis MO 63110. 314/647-4630. **Contact:** Personnel. **Description:** Real estate holding company. **Employees:** 100+.

BSI CONSTRUCTORS INC.
6767 Southwest Avenue, St. Louis MO 63143. 314/781-7820. **Contact:** Joseph M. Kaiser, Executive Vice-President. **Description:** A St. Louis-area general contracting and construction management firm. **Employees:** 100+. **Common positions:** Civil Engineer; Construction Management. **Educational backgrounds sought:** Engineering; Construction Management. **Benefits:** medical, dental, and life insurance; pension plan; tuition assistance; disability coverage; profit sharing. **Corporate headquarters:** This location.

BANGERT BROTHERS CONSTRUCTION COMPANY
8510 Eager Road, St. Louis MO 63144. 314/968-1414. **Contact:** Personnel Department. **Description:** A St. Louis construction firm specializing in road and heavy general contracting. **Employees:** 100+.

EDWARD L. BLAKEWELL, INC.
REALTOR
7716 Forsyth Boulevard, St. Louis MO 63105. 314/721-5555. **Contact:** Jane Dempsey, Personnel. **Description:** A St. Louis real estate agency. **Employees:** 100+.

CLIMATE ENGINEERING CORPORATION
152 East Kirkham, St. Louis MO 63119. 314/968-8400. **Contact:** Cindy Moser, Personnel Director. **Description:** A company engaged in a variety of contracting services including plumbing, heating, and air conditioning. **Employees:** 100+.

COLDWELL BANKER
7711 Bonhomme Avenue, St. Louis MO 63105. 314/725-9880. **Contact:** Jim Dohr, Director of Finance. **Description:** A St. Louis real estate agency. **Employees:** 800+.

CONDAIRE INC.
1141 Reco, P.O. Box 8658, St. Louis MO 63126. 314/821-8388. **Contact:** Malcolm J. Sweet, President. **Description:** A St. Louis mechanical contracting firm engaged in a variety of heating, ventilating, air conditioning, plumbing and industrial piping services. **Employees:** 100+.

CORRIGAN COMPANY
3545 Gratiot Street, St. Louis MO 63103. 314/771-6200. **Contact:** Personnel Director. **Description:** A St. Louis mechanical contracting company. **Employees:** 500+.

EQUITABLE REAL ESTATE INVESTMENT MANAGEMENT, INC.
One Boatman's Plaza, Suite 2100, St. Louis MO 63101. 314/421-5900. **Contact:** Karen L. Poole, Administrative Assistant. **Description:** Subsidiary of a life insurance company dealing with commercial real estate investment and management, as well as servicing mortgage portfolios. **Common positions:** Asset/Portfolio Managers. **Educational backgrounds sought:** Real Estate. **Benefits:** medical insurance; dental insurance; pension plan; life insurance; tuition assistance; disability coverage; savings plan. **Corporate headquarters:** Atlanta, GA. **Other U.S. locations:** New York, Chicago, Philadelphia, Dallas, San Francisco, Irvine CA, Washington DC. **Parent company:** The Equitable Life Assurance Society of the United States. **Operations at this facility:** Administration. **Employees:** 200+.

1st FINANCIAL BUILDING CORP.
13537 Barrett Parkway Drive #215, Manchester MO 63021. 314/821-2265. **Contact:** Betty Krentz, Supervisor, Human Resources. **Description:** National design/building firm which also operates in consulting and planning. **Common positions:** Accountant; Architect; Buyer; Draftsperson; Electrical Engineer; Mechanical Engineer; Purchasing Agent. **Educational backgrounds sought:**

Accounting; Business Administration; Economics; Engineering; Finance; Liberal Arts; Architecture. **Benefits:** medical, dental, and life insurance. **Operations at this facility:** regional headquarters; administration.

FOLLMAN PROPERTIES
ONCOR INTERNATIONAL
165 North Meramec, St. Louis MO 63105-3798. 314/721-3444. **Contact:** G.A. Follman, Executive Vice President. **Description:** Full-service, commercial real estate services firm. Part of Oncor International, serving office, industrial, retail, and investment brokerage requirements. Also involved in asset and property management; consulting; appraisal; and information services. The company maintains a full professional brokerage and asset management staff, including five CPMs.

FRU-CON CONSTRUCTION CORPORATION
15933 Clayton Road, Ballwin MO 63011. 314/391-4510. **Contact:** James Coleman, Director of Personnel. **Description:** A national construction/engineering firm. **Employees:** 1,000. **Common positions:** Civil Engineer; Electrical Engineer; Mechanical Engineer. **Educational backgrounds sought:** Accounting; Business Administration; Engineering; Finance. **Benefits:** medical, dental, and life insurance; pension plan; tuition assistance; disability coverage; savings plan. **Corporate headquarters:** This location.

GENERAL INSTALLATION COMPANY
2500 Drilling Service Drive, Maryland Heights MO 63043. 314/291-5330. **Contact:** Lori O'Toole, Office Manager. **Description:** Mechanical contractors for piping, equipment erection, heating, cooling and power plants. **Employees:** 100.

GROSS MECHANICAL COMPANY
7379 Pagedale Industrial Court, St. Louis MO 63133. 314/727-3688. **Contact:** Personnel Department. **Description:** A heating, air conditioning and industrial piping contracting firm.

H.B.D. CONTRACTING INC.
5517 Manchester Avenue, St. Louis MO 63110. 314/781-8000. **Contact:** Brian Kowert, Treasurer. **Description:** A St. Louis general contracting firm specializing in commercial work. **Common positions:** Civil Engineer. **Educational backgrounds sought:** Engineering. **Special programs:** Training programs. **Benefits:** medical, dental, and life insurance; pension plan; disability coverage; profit sharing. **Corporate headquarters:** This location. **Operations at this facility:** administration. **Employees:** 100.

HBE CORPORATION
11330 Olive Street Road, P.O. Box 419039, St. Louis MO 63141. 314/567-9000. **Contact:** Mike Herndon, Director of Operations. **Description:** One of the nation's largest companies specializing in the design and building of hospitals, financial institutions, and hotels. HBE Corporation also operates and manages hotels. **Common positions:** Accountant; Architect; Credit Manager; Draftsperson; Civil Engineer; Electrical Engineer; Mechanical Engineer; Hotel Manager/Assistant Manager; General Manager; Personnel and Labor Relations Specialist; Purchasing Agent; Sales Representative. **Educational backgrounds**

sought: Accounting; Art/Design; Engineering. **Benefits:** medical, dental, and life insurance; tuition assistance; disability coverage; employee discounts; savings plan. **Corporate headquarters:** This location. **Operations at this facility:** divisional headquarters.

HALL, H.H. CONSTRUCTION COMPANY
211 South 15th Street, P.O. Box 2439, East St. Louis IL 62202. 618/274-2500. **Contact:** Personnel Department. **Description:** An area contracting firm engaged in industrial and commercial construction work. Also manufactures ready mix concrete.

HARTMAN-WALSH CORPORATION
7144 North Market Street, St. Louis MO 63133. 314/863-1800. **Contact:** Personnel Department. **Description:** A St. Louis contracting company specializing in painting and waterproofing services.

JAY HENGES ENTERPRISES, INC.
4133 Shoreline Drive, Earth City MO 63045. 314/291-6600. **Contact:** Joyce Fix, Personnel Director. **Description:** A company engaged in the installation of carpet, wood, and vinyl floors; insulation and acoustical ceiling work; and the manufacture of portable buildings. **Corporate headquarters:** This location.

KLOSTER COMPANY INC.
4245 Bi-State Industrial Drive, St. Louis MO 63128. 314/894-8888. **Contact:** Rick Grebel, President. **Description:** A St. Louis general contracting company specializing in industrial work.

MFG ASSOCIATED INC.
SUBSIDIARY OF THE HANLEY GROUP
4101 Clayton Avenue, St. Louis MO 63110. 314/647-8750. **Contact:** Ralph Wagner, V.P./Operations. **Description:** St. Louis office of a construction corporation engaged in a variety of services, including insulation, hard board for industrial buildings; also material sales of industrial doors, daylighting, wall systems, sealants, insulation, adhesives, waterproofing, steel and ornamental iron erection.

McBRIDE & SON
#11 McBride & Son Corporate Center Drive, Chesterfield MO 63005. 314/537-2000. **Contact:** Faye Peats, Legal Coordinator. **Description:** A St. Louis construction company, engaged in concrete foundation work, carpentry work, home building, general contracting, real estate sales, property management, and remodeling. **Common positions:** Accountant; Sales Representative. **Educational backgrounds sought:** Accounting; Business Administration. **Benefits:** medical insurance; dental insurance; life insurance; pension plan; tuition assistance; disability coverage; daycare assistance. **Corporate headquarters:** This location. **Operations at this facility:** regional headquarters.

THE MICHELSON ORGANIZATION
7701 Forsyth Boulevard, Suite 900, St. Louis MO 63105. 314/862-7080. **Contact:** Beth Bean, Personnel Director. **Description:** A St. Louis organization of real estate agents and property managers. **Common positions:** Accountant;

Financial Analyst; Property Manager. **Benefits:** medical, dental, and life insurance; savings plan. **Corporate headquarters:** This location. **Revenues (1991):** $2 million. **Employees:** 37. **Projected hires for the next 12 months:** 2-4.

NIEHAUS CONSTRUCTION SERVICES INC.
4151 Sarpy Avenue, St. Louis MO 63110. 314/533-8434. **Contact:** Dory Pollard, Director of Personnel. **Description:** A St. Louis company engaged in terrazzo, tile, marble and mosaic work.

NOONEY KROMBACH COMPANY
7701 Forsyth Boulevard, Suite 300, Clayton MO 63105. 314/863-7700. **Contact:** Annette Maul, Assistant Vice President. **Description:** A St. Louis real estate investment, management and developing company. **Benefits:** medical insurance; dental insurance; pension plan; life insurance; tuition assistance; disability coverage. **Corporate headquarters:** This location.

C. RALLO CONTRACTING COMPANY INC.
5000 Kemper Avenue, St. Louis MO 63139. 314/664-2900. **Contact:** Peter Rowell, Personnel Director. **Description:** A St Louis general contracting company.

RICHARDS BRICK COMPANY
234 Springer Avenue, Box 407, Edwardsville IL 62025. 618/656-0230. **Contact:** John Motley, Plant Superintendent. **Description:** A manufacturer of building bricks.

STRUCTURAL SYSTEMS INC.
816 South Kirkwood Road, Kirkwood MO 63122. 314/966-5920. **Contact:** Mike Ortmann, Personnel Director. **Description:** A St. Louis-area architecture and construction firm, specializing in fabricated buildings, general contracting and design/build contracting.

SUBSURFACE CONSTRUCTORS
110 Angelica Street, St. Louis MO 63147. 314/421-2460. **Contact:** Clark Uline, Personnel Director. **Description:** A foundation contracting firm which provides piledriving and core drilling services.

SVERDRUP CORPORATION CENTRAL GROUP
801 North Eleventh Street, St. Louis MO 63101. 314/436-7600. **Contact:** John S. Busker, Manager/Professional Employment. **Description:** An engineering/architectural/construction firm that provides consulting, design, construction management, construction, and operations management to a diverse clientele. Offices located in St. Louis. **Common positions:** Architect; Civil Engineer; Electrical Engineer; Mechanical Engineer; Process Engineer; Construction Manager; Environmental Engineer; Chemical Engineer. **Educational backgrounds sought:** Engineering: Chemical, Civil, Environmental, Mechanical, and Electrical. **Benefits:** medical insurance; pension plan; tuition assistance; disability coverage; savings plan. **Operations at this facility:** regional headquarters; administration; service; sales. **Employees:** 850.

TARLTON CORPORATION
5500 West Park Avenue, St. Louis MO 63110-1898. 314/647-6000. **Contact:** Patricia Allers, Personnel Manager. **Description:** A general contractor and construction company. **Common positions:** Accountant; Civil Engineer; Mechanical Engineer; Department Manager; Marketing Specialist. **Educational backgrounds sought:** Accounting; Business Administration; Engineering; Marketing. **Special programs:** Training programs and internships. **Benefits:** medical, dental, and life insurance; tuition assistance; disability coverage; profit sharing; 401(K) plan. **Corporate headquarters:** This location. **Operations at this facility:** administration. **Revenues (1991):** $40 million. **Employees:** 43.

TURLEY-MARTIN COMPANY
700 Corporate Park Drive, Suite 150, Clayton MO 63105. 314/231-7100. **Contact:** Sandy Tate, Personnel. **Description:** A real estate and office building management firm.

CHARLES F. VATTEROTT & CO.
10449 St. Charles Rock Road, St. Ann MO 63074. 314/427-4000. **Contact:** Roni Finkbeiner, Personnel Department. **Description:** An eastern Missouri construction firm specializing in residential construction work.

FRED WEBER INC.
2320 Creve Core Mill Road, Maryland Heights MO 63043. 314/344-0070. **Contact:** Personnel Department. **Description:** A Missouri contractor specializing in highway construction, stone quarries, asphalt plants, sand plants, and commercial construction.

THOMAS J. WHITE COMPANY
940 Westport Plaza, Suite 264, St. Louis MO 63146. 314/878-0400. **Contact:** Virginia Mansfield, Personnel Department. **Description:** A real estate company specializing in the management of non-residential building operators.

WINCO VENTILATOR COMPANY
6200 Maple Avenue, P.O. Box 3221, St. Louis MO 63130. 314/725-8088. **Contact:** Personnel Department. **Description:** Manufacturer of aluminum windows and curtain walls.

YOUNG SALES CORPORATION
1054 Central Industrial Drive, St. Louis MO 63110. 314/771-3080. **Contact:** Joseph N. Bacino, CEO. **Description:** A sheet metal contractor, sheet metal and plate fabricator, national roofing contractor, insulation and asbestos abatement contractor, building restoration and water proofing and industrial siding contractor. **Common positions:** Accountant; Administrator; Blue-Collar Worker Supervisor; Draftsperson; Branch Manager; General Manager. **Educational backgrounds sought:** Accounting; Engineering; Liberal Arts; Marketing. **Benefits:** medical insurance; pension plan; life insurance; profit sharing. **Corporate headquarters:** This location. **Operations at this facility:** manufacturing; administration; sales.

Additional large employers: 250+

GENERAL CONTRACTORS-SINGLE-FAMILY HOUSES

Hoeffken Bros Inc
222 W B St, Belleville IL 62220-1332. 618/233-0268. Employs: 250-499.

Luhr Bros Inc
250 W Sand Bank Rd, Columbia IL 62236-1044. 618/281-4106. Employs: 500-999.

GENERAL CONTRACTORS-INDUSTRIAL BUILDINGS AND WAREHOUSES

Millstone Constr Inc
8510 Eager Rd, St. Louis MO 63144-1414. 314/961-8500. Employs: 250-499.

PLUMBING, HEATING AND AIR-CONDITIONING

Murphy Co Mech Contr & Engineers
1340 N Price Rd, St. Louis MO 63132-2306. 314/997-6600. Employs: 500-999.

ELECTRICAL WORK

Flex-O-Lite Inc
P O Box 4366, St. Louis MO 63123-0866. 314/351-4450. Employs: 250-499.

Sachs Holdings Inc
16300 Justus Post Rd, Chesterfield MO 63017-4608. 314/532-2000. Employs: 250-499.

STRUCTURAL STEEL ERECTION

Canam Steel Corp
2000 W Main St, Washington MO 63090-1008. 314/239-6716. Employs: 250-499.

OPERATORS OF APARTMENT BUILDINGS

Lutheran Apartments For Elderly
S Broadway & Gasconade, St. Louis MO 63147. 314/388-2867. Employs: 250-499.

Additional small to medium sized employers: 50-249

GENERAL CONTRACTORS-SINGLE-FAMILY HOUSES

Korte Construction Co
7 Industrial Ct, Highland IL 62249-1131. 618/654-8611. Employs: 100-249.

Morrissey Construction Co
705 Southmoor Dr, Godfrey IL 62035-1871. 618/466-3112. Employs: 50-99.

Opel Construction Co
1427 Ladd Av, Edwardsville IL 62025-1352. 618/656-8886. Employs: 50-99.

Richard P Norden
2180 First Capitol Dr, Saint Charles MO 63301-5804. 314/947-1500. Employs: 50-99.

Goodwin Bros Construction Co
1766 Highway 61-67, Crystal City MO 63019. 314/296-3720. Employs: 100-249.

Wefelmeyer Construction Co
11656 Lilburn Park Rd, St. Louis MO 63146-3535. 314/432-6802. Employs: 50-99.

Fischer & Frichtel Inc
7 The Pines Ct, St. Louis MO 63141. 314/576-0500. Employs: 50-99.

GENERAL CONTRACTORS-RESIDENTIAL BUILDINGS, OTHER THAN SINGLE-FAMILY

Casco
5850 Delor St, St. Louis MO 63109-3107. 314/832-2814. Employs: 50-99.

Woermann Construction Co
7120 Manchester Ave, St. Louis MO 63143-2534. 314/647-5400. Employs: 100-249.

GENERAL CONTRACTORS-INDUSTRIAL BUILDINGS AND WAREHOUSES

Associated Crafts Inc
N Service Rd W, Sullivan MO 63080. 314/468-5111. Employs: 50-99.

GENERAL CONTRACTORS-NONRESIDENTIAL BUILDINGS, OTHER THAN INDUSTRIAL BUILDINGS AND WAREHOUSES

Aviston Lumber Co
101 S Clement St, Aviston IL 62216. 618/228-7247. Employs: 50-99.

Bank Building & Equipment Southwest Div
3630 S Geyer Rd, St. Louis MO 63127-1230. 314/690-3434. Employs: 100-249.

HIGHWAY AND STREET CONSTRUCTION, EXCEPT ELEVATED HIGHWAYS

Magruder Construction Co Inc
PO Box 8, Eolia MO 63344-0008. 314/485-2161. Employs: 50-99.

Capcom Construction Inc
731 N Bluff Rd, Collinsville IL 62234-3718. 618/345-2158. Employs: 50-99.

BRIDGE, TUNNEL AND ELEVATED HIGHWAY CONSTRUCTION

Affholder Inc
17988 Edison Ave, Chesterfield MO 63005-3700. 314/532-2622. Employs: 50-99.

WATER, SEWER, PIPELINE, COMMUNICATIONS AND POWER LINE CONSTRUCTION

Insituform Mid-America Inc
18022 Edison Ave Box 1026, Chesterfield MO 63005. 314/532-6137. Employs: 100-249.

Pulrler Connon Schult
PO Box 117, Old Monroe MO 63369-0117. 314/665-5282. Employs: 50-99.

John Fabick Tractor Co
1 Fabick Dr, Fenton MO 63026-2928. 314/343-5900. Employs: 100-249.

HEAVY CONSTRUCTION

Dave Kolb Grading Inc
5733 Westwood Dr, Saint Charles MO 63304-7650. 314/441-0200. Employs: 50-99.

PLUMBING, HEATING AND AIR-CONDITIONING

The Rust Company Inc
920 West A St, Belleville IL
62220-1154. 618/233-3260.
Employs: 100-249.

PAINTING AND PAPER HANGING

Clark Painting Co
9921 Saint Charles Rock Rd, Saint Ann MO 63074-2019. 314/427-1114. Employs: 100-249.

Pandjiris Inc
5151 Northrup Ave, St. Louis MO 63110-2031. 314/776-6893. Employs: 50-99.

ELECTRICAL WORK

Aschinger Electric Co
877 Horan Dr Box B, Fenton MO 63026-2405. 314/343-1211. Employs: 50-99.

Kaiser Electric Inc
904 Hanley Industrial Ct, St. Louis MO 63144-1431. 314/968-3700. Employs: 50-99.

Butler Electrical Constructing Co Inc
200 N Central Ave, Eureka MO 63025-1824. 314/587-3456. Employs: 50-99.

MASONRY, STONE SETTING AND OTHER STONE WORK

C J Milligan Inc
12564 Glencroft Dr, St. Louis MO 63128-2513. 314/849-1004. Employs: 50-99.

PLASTERING, DRYWALL, ACOUSTICAL AND INSULATION WORK

Henges Interiors
4133 Shoreline Dr, Earth City MO 63045-1211. 314/291-6600. Employs: 100-249.

Woodard Contract
9308 Manchester Rd, St. Louis MO 63119-1449. 314/961-8484. Employs: 50-99.

ROOFING, SIDING AND SHEET METAL WORK

Allen Roofing & Supply Co
17418 Manchester Rd, Glencoe MO 63038-1905. 314/458-3700. Employs: 50-99.

CONCRETE WORK

C Sansone Concrete Contractors
1560 Fairview, St. Louis MO 63132-1302. 314/426-3322. Employs: 100-249.

STRUCTURAL STEEL ERECTION

Federal Steel & Erection Co
200 E Alton Ave, East Alton IL 62024-1464. 618/254-0106. Employs: 50-99.

WRECKING AND DEMOLITION WORK

Jay Vee Cement Constructing Co Inc
8053 Chivvis Dr, St. Louis MO 63123-2333. 314/351-3366. Employs: 50-99.

SPECIAL TRADE CONTRACTORS

The Western Group
1637 N Warson Rd, St. Louis MO 63132-1027. 314/427-6733. Employs: 50-99.

CEMENT, HYDRAULIC

Holman Inc
Hwy 79, Clarksville MO 63336. 314/242-3571. Employs: 100-249.

River Cement Co
500 Cedar Plaza Pkwy, St. Louis MO 63128. 314/849-6980. Employs: 100-249.

River Cement Co/Selma Plt
I-55 & Hwy 61, Festus MO 63028. 314/937-7601. Employs: 100-249.

BRICK AND STRUCTURAL CLAY TILE

Hydraulic-Press Brick Co
705 Olive St, St. Louis MO 63101-2234. 314/621-9306. Employs: 50-99.

Richards Brick Co
234 Springer Ave, Edwardsville IL 62025-1806. 618/656-0230. Employs: 100-249.

CONCRETE PRODUCTS, EXCEPT BLOCK AND BRICK

Beco Concrete Products
4855 Baumgartner Rd, St. Louis MO 63129-2819. 314/892-7400. Employs: 50-99.

Inventory Sales Co
3140 Park Ave, St. Louis MO 63104-1436. 314/776-6200. Employs: 50-99.

READY-MIXED CONCRETE

Kienstra Inc
301 W Ferguson Ave, Wood River IL 62095-1410. 618/254-4366. Employs: 100-249.

MORTGAGE BANKERS AND LOAN CORRESPONDENTS

A A A Funding
6005 Lemay Ferry Rd, St. Louis MO 63129-2216. 314/892-7808. Employs: 50-99.

Affiliated Financial Svc Co
744 Office Pkwy, St. Louis MO 63141-7128. 314/569-0035. Employs: 50-99.

Associate Mortgage Loan
9369 Olive Blvd, St. Louis MO 63132-3217. 314/432-0506. Employs: 50-99.

Associates Equity Svc Mo Inc
11885 Lackland Rd, St. Louis MO 63146-4236. 314/993-7077. Employs: 50-99.

Beechwood Investment Co
1503 S Rock Hill Rd, St. Louis MO 63119-4608. 314/961-2535. Employs: 50-99.

Boatmen's Mortgage Corporation
5353 S Lindbergh Blvd, St. Louis MO 63126-3520. 314/525-7001. Employs: 50-99.

Clayton Mortgage Assocs Inc
7 N Brentwood Blvd, St. Louis MO 63105-3757. 314/727-2666. Employs: 50-99.

Consumer Investment & Financial Svc Inc
8119 Airport Rd, St. Louis MO 63134-1907. 314/521-3121. Employs: 50-99.

Creve Coeur Mortgage Assocs
795 Office Pkwy, St. Louis MO 63141-7137. 314/997-4646. Employs: 50-99.

Delmar Mortgage and Financial Co
120 S Central Ave, St. Louis MO 63105-1705. 314/726-5577. Employs: 100-249.

E Thomas Burch & Associates
950 Francis Pl, St. Louis MO 63105-2465. 314/423-9720. Employs: 50-99.

Equality Savings & Loan Assn
1281 S Laclede Station Rd S, St. Louis MO 63119-5327. 314/962-9688. Employs: 50-99.

Farm & Home Savings Assn
7801 Forsyth Blvd, St. Louis MO 63105-3307. 314/863-5800. Employs: 50-99.

Firemans Fund Mortgage Corp
1001 Craig Rd, St. Louis MO 63146-5277. 314/567-9055. Employs: 50-99.

First Bank A Savings Bank
11 E Lockwood Ave, St. Louis MO 63119-3019. 314/961-8415. Employs: 50-99.

Fleet Finance Inc
9666 Olive Blvd, St. Louis MO 63132-3013. 314/997-4037. Employs: 50-99.

Franklin Mortgage & Investment
8515 Delmar Blvd, St. Louis MO 63124-2168. 314/993-1926. Employs: 50-99.

George C Doering Inc
11041 Lin Valle Dr, St. Louis MO 63123-7214. 314/892-5555. Employs: 50-99.

Grashoff Financial Co Inc
231 S Bemiston Ave, St. Louis MO 63105-1914. 314/725-6783. Employs: 50-99.

Great Financial Mortgage
11720 Borman Dr, St. Louis MO 63146-4129. 314/432-0012. Employs: 50-99.

Knutson Mortgage Co
1215 Fern Ridge Pkwy, St. Louis MO 63141-4401. 314/878-3777. Employs: 50-99.

Magnum Mortgage Co
12125 Woodcrest Executive Dr, St. Louis MO 63141-5001. 314/469-6800. Employs: 50-99.

Mid Amer Mrtg Svc St Louis Inc
1031 Executive Parkway Dr, St. Louis MO 63141-6339. 314/434-6227. Employs: 50-99.

Mid-America Financial Group
9952 Edmil Ave, St. Louis MO 63114-1301. 314/423-1541. Employs: 50-99.

Missouri Savings Assn
11100 Larimore Rd, St. Louis MO 63138-2041. 314/355-4600. Employs: 50-99.

Missouri Savings Assn
2041 Union Rd, St. Louis MO 63125-3054. 314/544-3400. Employs: 50-99.

Missouri Savings Assn
5433 Telegraph Rd, St. Louis MO 63129-3555. 314/894-2100. Employs: 50-99.

Murphy Real Estate
9469 Dielman Rock Island Dr, St. Louis MO 63132-2101. 314/994-9960. Employs: 50-99.

Northland Financial Company
12935 North Forty Drive, St. Louis MO 63141. 314/469-1666. Employs: 50-99.

People's Mortgage
9378 Olive Blvd, St. Louis MO 63132-3215. 314/991-5005. Employs: 50-99.

Prudential Home Mortgage Co
8000 Maryland Ave, St. Louis MO 63105-3752. 314/726-3900. Employs: 50-99.

Roosevelt Bank
900 Roosevelt Pkwy, Chesterfield MO 63017-2064. 314/532-6200. Employs: 100-249.

Town & Country Mortgage
8301 Maryland Ave, St. Louis MO 63105-3644. 314/727-5144. Employs: 50-99.

Transcoastal Mortgage Corp
12747 Olive Blvd, St. Louis MO 63141-6269. 314/434-3775. Employs: 50-99.

Union Mortgage Comp Inc
721 Emerson Rd, St. Louis MO 63141-6748. 314/567-6999. Employs: 50-99.

United Companies Lending Corp
2200 Westport Plaza Dr, St. Louis MO 63146-3211. 314/878-2929. Employs: 50-99.

United Mortgage Inc
9191 W Florissant Ave, St. Louis MO 63136-1424. 314/521-5700. Employs: 50-99.

OPERATORS OF NONRESIDENTIAL BUILDINGS

Southern Real Estate
705 Olive St, St. Louis MO 63101-2234. 314/241-6294. Employs: 50-99.

American Legion Rock Memorial Post 283
Montebello Rd, Imperial MO 63052. 314/464-9608. Employs: 100-249.

OPERATORS OF APARTMENT BUILDINGS

Retirement Care Associates Inc
212 N Kirkwood Rd, St. Louis MO 63122-4030. 314/822-8383. Employs: 100-249.

Tesson Heights Retirement Ctr
12335 W Bend Dr, St. Louis MO 63128-2160. 314/849-1366. Employs: 50-99.

REAL ESTATE AGENTS AND MANAGERS

Gundaker Realtors
1622 Country Club Plaza, Saint Charles MO 63303-3887. 314/946-6455. Employs: 50-99.

Shockley Realtors
501 1st Capitol Dr, Saint Charles MO 63301-2768. 314/946-9753. Employs: 50-99.

Deutsch Partnership
10920 Schuetz Rd, St. Louis MO 63146-5704. 314/432-4000. Employs: 100-249.

L K Wood Realty
5600 Hampton Ave, St. Louis MO 63109-3434. 314/352-7400. Employs: 50-99.

Laura McCarthy Inc Realtors
124 Gay Ave, St. Louis MO 63105-3620. 314/721-1774. Employs: 50-99.

Love Real Estate Company
515 Olive St, St. Louis MO 63101-1849. 314/621-1200. Employs: 100-249.

Carr Square Tenant Management
1521 Carr Dr, St. Louis MO 63106-3621. 314/241-0883. Employs: 50-99.

Gannon Management Co
12541 Bennington Pl, St. Louis MO 63146-2710. 314/434-3440. Employs: 50-99.

Trammell Crow Co
8000 Maryland Ave, St. Louis MO 63105-3752. 314/727-5700. Employs: 100-249.

Gundaker Realtors Betr Homes
68 Charleston Sq, Saint Charles MO 63304-8571. 314/441-1360. Employs: 50-99.

Trans Union
408 Olive St, St. Louis MO 63102-2729. 314/241-4333. Employs: 50-99.

TITLE ABSTRACT OFFICES

Commonwealth Land Title Ins Co
910 N 11th St, St. Louis MO 63101-2914. 314/241-1312. Employs: 50-99.

First American Title Ins Co
7600 Forsyth Blvd, St. Louis MO 63105-3404. 314/727-8131. Employs: 50-99.

Missouri Title Co
St Louis City Hall, St. Louis MO 63103. 314/241-0403. Employs: 50-99.

LAND SUBDIVIDERS AND DEVELOPERS, EXCEPT CEMETERIES

The Lockwood Group
17 W Lockwood Ave, St. Louis MO 63119-2931. 314/968-2205. Employs: 50-99.

ARCHITECTURAL SERVICES

Booker Associates Inc
1139 Olive St, St. Louis MO 63101-1946. 314/421-1476. Employs: 100-249.

Casco Corporation
10877 Watson Rd, St. Louis MO 63127-1032. 314/821-1100. Employs: 50-99.

Jonesmayer Inc
2190 S Mason Rd, St. Louis MO 63131-1637. 314/965-3400. Employs: 50-99.

SURVEYING SERVICES

Y & A Group Inc
777 Craig Rd, St. Louis MO 63141-7114. 314/993-1650. Employs: 100-249.

For more information on career opportunities in architecture, construction, and real estate:

<u>Associations</u>

APARTMENT OWNERS AND MANAGERS ASSOCIATION
65 Cherry Plaza, Watertown CT 06795. 203/274-2589.

BUILDING OWNERS AND MANAGERS ASSOCIATION
1521 Ritchie Highway, P.O. Box 9709, Arnold MD 21012. 301/261-2882.

INSTITUTE OF REAL ESTATE MANAGEMENT
430 North Michigan Avenue, Chicago IL 60611. 312/661-1930.

INTERNATIONAL ASSOCIATION OF CORPORATE REAL ESTATE EXECUTIVES
440 Columbia Drive, Suite 100, West Palm Beach FL 33409. 407/683-8111.

INTERNATIONAL REAL ESTATE INSTITUTE
8383 East Evans Road, Scottsdale AZ 85260. 602/998-8267.

NATIONAL ASSOCIATION OF REAL ESTATE INVESTMENT TRUSTS
1129 20th Street NW, Suite 705, Washington DC 20036. 202/785-8717.

NATIONAL ASSOCIATION OF REALTORS
430 North Michigan Avenue, Chicago IL 60611. 312/329-8200.

Magazines

JOURNAL OF PROPERTY MANAGEMENT
Institute of Real Estate Management, 430 North Michigan Avenue, Chicago IL 60611. 312/661-1930.

NATIONAL REAL ESTATE INVESTOR
6255 Barfield, Atlanta GA 30328. 404/256-9800.

REAL ESTATE FORUM
12 West 37th Street, New York NY 10018. 212/563-6460.

REAL ESTATE NEWS
2600 W. Peterson, Suite 100, Chicago IL 60659. 312/465-5151.

AUTOMOTIVE

Industry insiders are counting on a healthier overall economy and the easing of regulatory burdens to revive the long-slumping auto industry. In the meantime, auto manufacturers are slashing costs by reducing production schedules, offering higher price-incentives to buyers, and laying off workers. On a brighter note, sales of American vans and trucks rose during 1992.

AAA-AUTO CLUB OF MISSOURI
12901 North Forty Drive, St. Louis MO 63141. 314/523-7350. **Contact:** Jack Dunning, Personnel Manager. **Description:** Headquarters location for AAA-Affiliate in the four-state Midwest area (MO, IL, AR, KS). Provides travel and other services for motorists. **Employees:** 700. **Common positions:** Claim Representative; Customer Service Representative; Insurance Agent/Broker; Sales Representative; Underwriter; Computer Programmer; Counselor. **Educational backgrounds sought:** Business Administration; Computer Science; Liberal Arts; Economics; Marketing; Mathematics. **Benefits:** medical, dental, and life insurance; pension plan; tuition assistance; disability coverage; employee discounts; 401(K) profit-sharing plan. **Corporate headquarters:** This location. **Operations at this facility:** administration. **Other U.S. locations:** 42 branch offices in MO, IL, AR, KS. **Employees:** 750. **Projected hires for the next 12 months:** 125.

CARTER AUTOMOTIVE CO. INC.
A FEDERAL MOGUL COMPANY
2841 North Spring Avenue, St. Louis MO 63107. 314/289-7500. **Contact:** Christine Riegler, Employee Relations Manager. **Description:** St. Louis manufacturer of motor vehicle parts-fuel systems.

CHRYSLER CORPORATION/ST. LOUIS ASSEMBLY COMPLEX
1050 Dodge Drive, St. Louis MO 63026. 314/349-4040. **Contact:** Jim Crouse, Personnel Manager. **Description:** A St. Louis-area assembly plant for the manufacture of automobiles. **Employees:** 5,000+.

GENERAL MOTORS CORPORATION/
GENERAL MOTORS ASSEMBLY DIVISION WENTZVILLE
1500 East Route A, Wentzville MO 63385. 314/327-2143. **Contact:** Tom Pilkington, Personnel Director. **Description:** Manufacture and assembly of automobiles. Parent company, General Motors, is a producer of cars, trucks, and buses sold worldwide; the firm has 152 facilities operating in 26 states and 93 cities in the United States and 13 plants in Canada, and also has assembly, manufacturing, distribution, sales or warehousing operations in 37 other countries. **Employees:** 3,000+.

KRIBS FORD INC.
10700 Page Boulevard, St. Louis MO 63132. 314/429-4455. **Contact:** Personnel Director. **Description:** A St. Louis dealer of new and used automobiles.

MOOG AUTOMOTIVE INC.
P.O. Box 7224, St. Louis MO 63177. 314/385-3400. **Contact:** Sally Flood, Personnel Director. **Description:** A St. Louis company engaged in the manufacture of motor vehicle replacement parts.

ORCHELN COMPANY
P.O. Box 280, Moberly MO 65270. **Contact:** Jeff Schulte, Human Resources Specialist. **Description:** A manufacturer of brake cable and lever assemblies for the automotive industry. **Common positions:** Accountant; Blue-Collar Worker Supervisor; Buyer; Computer Programmer; Draftsperson; Industrial Engineer; Mechanical Engineer; Financial Analyst; Industrial Manager; Mechanical Engineer; Financial Analyst; Industrial Designer; Operations/Production Manager; Personnel and Labor Relations Specialist; Purchasing Agent; Quality Control Supervisor; Sales Representative; Statistician. **Educational backgrounds sought:** Accounting; Business Administration; Engineering; Finance; Mathematics. **Benefits:** medical and life insurance; tuition assistance; disability coverage; savings plan-401(K); credit union; fitness center. **Corporate headquarters:** This location. **Operations at this facility:** regional headquarters; divisional headquarters; manufacturing; research and development; administration; sales.

Additional large employers: 250+

MOTOR VEHICLES AND PASSENGER CAR BODIES

Chrysler Motors
1001 N Highway Dr, Fenton MO 63026-1907. 314/343-2500. Employs: 1,000+.

Ford Motor Co
6250 N Lindbergh Blvd, Hazelwood MO 63042-2818. 314/731-6429. Employs: 1,000+.

GM Wentzville Assembly Center
Plant Operator, Wentzville MO 63385. 314/327-5711. Employs: 500-999.

GMAC Financial Services
721 Emerson Rd, St. Louis MO 63141-6748. 314/993-7800. Employs: 500-999.

MOTOR VEHICLE PARTS AND ACCESSORIES

A O Smith Automotive Products Co
3101 Hwy 3, Granite City IL 62040. 618/452-2100. Employs: 250-499.

Binkley Co
Main & Elm, Warrenton MO 63383. 314/456-3455. Employs: 500-999.

Inland Seat
831 Lone Star Dr, O Fallon MO 63366-1902. 314/272-0412. Employs: 250-499.

Nascote Inds
R R 1 Enterprise Ave, Nashville IL 62263-9801. 618/327-4381. Employs: 500-999.

Additional small to medium sized employers: 50-249

MOTOR VEHICLE PARTS AND ACCESSORIES

Brake Rebuilders Inc
835 Texas Ct, O Fallon MO 63366-1930. 314/755-1085. Employs: 50-99.

Craftsmen Inds Inc
1413 Howard St, St. Louis MO 63106-4112. 314/241-1300. Employs: 50-99.

Ligma Corp
1 Enterprise Ave, Nashville IL 62263-1619. 618/327-4416. Employs: 100-249.

Pacer Inds
1901 W Main St, Washington MO 63090-1005. 314/239-6731. Employs: 100-249.

Tomco Inc
1435 Woodson Rd, St. Louis MO 63132-2506. 314/567-4520. Employs: 50-99.

Unique Automotive Rebuilders
R R 1 Box 17, Jonesburg MO 63351-9705. 314/488-5242. Employs: 50-99.

United Technologies
300 Enterprise Way, Troy MO 63379-2712. 314/528-8220. Employs: 50-99.

PASSENGER CAR RENTAL

Weber Chevrolet Company
12015 Olive Blvd & I-270, St. Louis MO 63141-6721. 314/567-3300. Employs: 100-249.

AUTOMOBILE PARKING

Central Park Syst St Louis Inc
120 S Central Ave, St. Louis MO 63105-1705. 314/721-5089. Employs: 50-99.

TOP, BODY AND UPHOLSTERY REPAIR SHOPS AND PAINT SHOPS

Counts Brothers Ford
Church & Pine, Union MO 63084. 314/583-2229. Employs: 50-99.

Modern Auto Co
8 Jefferson St, Washington MO 63090-2508. 314/239-6777. Employs: 50-99.

AUTOMOTIVE TRANSMISSION REPAIR SHOPS

Midwest Rebuilders Inc
Smith & Laura Truesdale, Warrenton MO 63383. 314/456-3415. Employs: 50-99.

GENERAL AUTOMOTIVE REPAIR SHOPS

Autotire Car Care Centers
3840 Adie Road, Maryland Hts MO 63043. 314/291-0711. Employs: 50-99.

National Engines & Parts Co
4216 W Martin Luther King Dr, St. Louis MO 63113. 314/533-8484. Employs: 100-249.

AUTOMOTIVE REPAIR SHOPS

Auto Air Company
1175 S Kingshighway Blvd, St. Louis MO 63110-1556. 314/534-8080. Employs: 50-99.

AUTOMOTIVE SERVICES, EXCEPT REPAIR AND CARWASHES

Al Lang Towing
403 S Main St, Smithton IL 62285-1803. 618/234-7144. Employs: 50-99.

Rick's Auto Body Inc
By Pass 54, Louisiana MO 63353. 314/754-5055. Employs: 50-99.

For more information on career opportunities in the automotive industry:

Associations

ASSOCIATION OF INTERNATIONAL AUTOMOBILE MANUFACTURERS
1001 19th Street North, Suite 1200, Arlington VA 22209. 703/525-7788.

AUTOMOTIVE AFFILIATED REPRESENTATIVES
25 Northwest Point Boulevard, Elk Grove Village IL 60007. 708/228-1310.

AUTOMOTIVE ELECTRIC ASSOCIATION
25 Northwest Point Boulevard, Suite 425, Elk Grove Village IL 60007. 708/228-1310.

AUTOMOTIVE SERVICE ASSOCIATION
1901 Airport Freeway, Suite 100, Bedford TX 76021-0929. 817/283-6205.

AUTOMOTIVE SERVICE INDUSTRY ASSOCIATION
25 Northwest Point Boulevard, Elk Grove Village IL 60007. 708/228-1310.

MOTOR VEHICLE MANUFACTURERS ASSOCIATION
7430 2nd Avenue, Suite 300, Detroit MI 48202. 313/872-4311.

NATIONAL AUTOMOTIVE PARTS ASSOCIATION
2999 Circle 75 Parkway, Atlanta GA 30339. 404/956-2200.

NATIONAL INSTITUTE FOR AUTOMOTIVE SERVICE EXCELLENCE
13505 Dulles Technology Drive, Herndon VA 22071. 703/713-3800.

SOCIETY OF AUTOMOTIVE ENGINEERS
400 Commonwealth Drive, Warrendale PA 15096. 412/776-4841.

Directories

AUTOMOTIVE NEWS MARKET DATA BOOK
Automotive News, 1400 Woodbridge Avenue, Detroit MI 48207. 313/446-6000.

WARD'S AUTOMOTIVE YEARBOOK
Ward's Communications, 28 West Adams Street, Detroit MI 48226. 313/962-4433.

Magazines

AUTOMOTIVE INDUSTRIES
Chilton Book Co., Chilton Way, Radnor PA 19089. 800/695-1214.

AUTOMOTIVE NEWS
1400 Woodbridge Avenue, Detroit MI 48207. 313/446-6000.

WARD'S AUTO WORLD
Ward's Communications, Inc., 28 West Adams Street, Detroit MI 48226. 313/962-4433.

WARD'S AUTOMOTIVE REPORTS
Ward's Communications, Inc., 28 West Adams Street, Detroit MI 48226. 313/962-4433.

BANKING/SAVINGS AND LOAN

Heading into 1993, the banking industry continues to evolve. The industry began the decade with a series of mega-mergers aimed at solidifying its strongest institutions, resulting in a series of major layoffs. Increasingly, banks are facing new competition from mutual funds and other financial services that are not faced with the same regulatory burdens. As a result, short-term job prospects in the banking industry are fairly weak, and the competition is heavy.

BOATMEN'S NATIONAL BANK OF BELLEVILLE
23 Public Square, Belleville IL 62220. 618/233-6600. **Contact:** Personnel Officer. **Description:** A full-service St. Louis-area bank. **Employees:** 100. **Corporate headquarters:** St. Louis, MO. **Parent company:** Boatmen's

Bancshares, Inc. **Common positions:** Bank Office/Manager; Customer Service Representative; Branch Manager; Department Manager. **Educational backgrounds sought:** Accounting; Business Administration; Finance. **Benefits:** medical, dental, and life insurance; pension plan; tuition assistance; disability coverage; employee discounts; savings plan.

COMMERCE BANK OF ST. LOUIS
8000 Forsyth Street, 9th Floor, Clayton MO 63105. 314/854-7369. **Contact:** Roland Ranson, Personnel Manager. **Description:** A commercial banking institution with 34 locations in the St. Louis area; member FDIC. **Employees:** 800+.

FEDERAL RESERVE BANK OF ST. LOUIS
411 Locust Street, St. Louis MO 63102. 314/444-8444. **Contact:** Martha Perine, Vice President/Human Resources. **Description:** Regional office of the St. Louis federal reserve banking system. **Employees:** 800+.

FIRST BANK AND SAVINGS BANK
11550 Olive Street, Crevecoeur MO 63141. 314/995-5148. **Contact:** Marcia L. Heberle, Human Resources Officer. **Description:** A St. Louis-area state-insured savings and loan association. **Employees:** 100+. **Common positions:** Accountant; Administrator; Bank Officer; Computer Programmer; Customer Service Representative; Insurance Agent; Branch Manager; Department Manager; Operations/Production Manager; Marketing Specialist; Personnel and Labor Relations Specialist; Purchasing Agent; Sales Representative; Systems Analyst. **Educational backgrounds sought:** Business Administration; Finance; Liberal Arts. **Benefits:** medical insurance; dental insurance; pension plan; life insurance; tuition assistance; disability coverage; employee discounts; savings plan. **Corporate headquarters:** This location.

FIRST FINANCIAL BANK, FSB
6550 North Illinois, Fairview Heights IL 62208. 618/632-7421, ext. 203. **Contact:** Bill Bright, Employee Relations Manager. **Description:** First Financial is a federal savings bank. 95 branches throughout Wisconsin and Illinois. **Common positions:** Bank Officer/Manager; Customer Service Representative; Branch Manager; Operations/Production Manager; Personnel and Labor Relations Specialist; Securities Broker. **Educational backgrounds sought:** Business Administration; Finance. **Special programs:** Training programs. **Benefits:** medical, dental, and life insurance; pension plan; tuition assistance; disability coverage; employee discounts; savings plan; stock options. **Operations at this facility:** service; sales. **Employees:** 250 in Illinois. **Projected number of hires for the next 12 months:** 20.

FIRST NATIONAL BANK OF BELLEVILLE
19 Public Square, Belleville IL 62220. 618/234-0020. **Contact:** Carolyn Buxton, Personnel Director. **Description:** A St. Louis-area national banking institution. **Employees:** 300+.

HOME FEDERAL SAVINGS AND LOAN ASSOCIATION
12680 Olive Boulevard, St. Louis MO 63141. 314/576-4500. **Contact:** Personnel Department. **Description:** A St. Louis federal savings and loan association.

JEFFERSON SAVINGS & LOAN ASSOCIATION
14915 Manchester Road, P.O. Box 17, St. Louis MO 63022-0017. 314/227-3000. **Contact:** Ellen Stanko, Personnel Director. **Description:** A St. Louis state savings and loan institution.

LEMAY BANK & TRUST COMPANY
152 Lemay Ferry Road, St. Louis MO 63125. 314/631-5500. **Contact:** Marlene Lutzenberger, Personnel Director. **Description:** A St. Louis banking institution. Member of the Federal Reserve.

LINDELL TRUST COMPANY
2745 North Grant, St. Louis MO 63106. 314/652-6600. **Contact:** Personnel Director. **Description:** A St. Louis bank. Member of the Federal Reserve.

MAGNA BANK
1223 Broadway, P.O. Box 70, Highland IL 62249. 618/654-4511. **Contact:** Ruth Ann Kehrer, Personnel Director. **Description:** Bank holding company; national member of Federal Reserve System. **Employees:** 100+.

MAGNABANK BRENTWOOD CENTER
1401 South Brentwood Boulevard, St. Louis MO 63144. 314/963-2600. **Contact:** Ruth Pothoff at NW Plaza Center, P.O. Box 1097, St. Ann MO 63074. **Description:** A St. Louis national banking institution. Member of the Federal Reserve.

MARK TWAIN BANCSHARES INC.
7745 Carondelet, Suite 308, Clayton MO 63105. 314/863-7577. **Contact:** Laura Asher, Recruiting Manager. Call 314/863-6360 for 24 hour job line. **Description:** Mark Twain Bancshares, Inc., a 27-year-old bank holding company, operates 28 locations: 18 throughout St. Louis, St. Louis County and St. Charles County; as well as five in Kansas City, MO. Mark Twain also operates 43 brokerage locations in six states. Related financial services include: Mark Twain Bond Department; Mark Twain Brokerage Services, Inc.; Infinet Securities, Inc.; Mark Twain Commercial Finance Division; Mark Twain International; Mark Twain Leasing Co.; Mark Twain Mortgage Co.; and Mark Twain Trust Division. Mark Twain stock is traded over the counter under the NASDAQ symbol MTWN. **Common positions:** Accountant; Bank Officer/Manager; Computer Programmer; Customer Service Representative; Financial Analyst; Branch Manager; Sales Representative; Consumer Banking Representative; Teller; Secretary; Data Entry Operator. **Educational backgrounds sought:** Accounting; Business Administration; Communications; Computer Science; Economics; Finance; Liberal Arts; Marketing; Mathematics. **Special programs:** Training programs. **Benefits:** medical insurance; dental insurance; pension plan; life insurance; tuition assistance; disability coverage; employee discounts; savings plan; flex plan.

MERCANTILE BANCORPORATION INC.
P.O. Box 524, St. Louis MO 63166. 314/425-3990. **Contact:** College Relations Manager. **Description:** A bank serving as a member of the Federal Reserve. **Common positions:** Accountant; Bank Officer/Manager; Computer Programmer; Credit Manager; Customer Service Representative; Management Trainee. **Educational backgrounds sought:** Accounting; Finance. **Special programs:** Training programs and internships. **Benefits:** medical, dental, and life insurance; pension plan; tuition assistance; disability coverage; daycare assistance; profit sharing; employee discounts; savings plan. **Corporate headquarters:** This location. **Listed on:** NASDAQ.

MERCANTILE BANK OF ST. LOUIS
8301 Gravois Ave., St. Louis MO 63123. 314/352-6300. **Contact:** Ms. Mossie Schallon, Branch Manager. **Description:** A St. Louis state banking institution. Member of the Federal Reserve system. **Employees:** 100+.

ROOSEVELT BANK
A FEDERAL SAVINGS BANK
900 Roosevelt Parkway, Chesterfield MO 63017. 314/532-6200. **Contact:** Tim Teachout, Personnel Director. **Description:** A St. Louis-area financial institution. **Common positions:** Accountant; Bank Officer/Manager; Computer Programmer; Customer Service Representative; Financial Analyst; Insurance Agent/Broker; Branch Manager; Department Manager; Management Trainee; Marketing Specialist; Systems Analyst. **Educational backgrounds sought:** Accounting; Business Administration; Computer Science; Finance; Marketing. **Benefits:** medical insurance; dental insurance; pension plan; life insurance; tuition assistance; savings plan. **Corporate headquarters:** This location. **Listed on:** American Stock Exchange.

SOUTHSIDE NATIONAL BANK IN ST. LOUIS
3606 Gravois Avenue, St. Louis MO 63116. 314/776-7000. **Contact:** Joan Mungavin, Personnel Director. **Description:** A St. Louis national bank. Member of the Federal Reserve system.

SOUTHWEST BANK OF ST. LOUIS
2301 South Kingshighway Boulevard, St. Louis MO 63110. 314/776-5200. **Contact:** Donna Flanigan, Vice President. **Description:** A St. Louis financial institution. **Common positions:** Customer Service Representative; Management Trainee; Teller; General Office Worker. **Educational backgrounds sought:** Accounting; Business Administration; Communications; Economics; Finance. **Special programs:** Internships. **Benefits:** medical insurance; dental insurance; pension plan; life insurance; tuition assistance; disability coverage; savings plan. **Corporate headquarters:** This location. **Operations at this facility:** service. **Employees:** 180. **Projected hires for the next 12 months:** 5.

ST. JOHN'S BANK & TRUST COMPANY
11965 St. Charles Rock Road, Bridgeton MO 63044. **Contact:** Mark Wells, Senior V.P./Director of Human Resources. **Description:** A St. Louis state banking institution.

UNITED MISSOURI BANK
#6 South Broadway, St. Louis MO 63102. 314/621-1000. **Contact:** Human Resources Department. **Description:** A St. Louis national bank. Member of the Federal Reserve.

UNITED POSTAL SAVINGS ASSOCIATION
10015 Manchester Road, St. Louis MO 63122. 314/966-2530. **Contact:** Personnel Department. **Description:** A regional federal savings and loan association.

Additional large employers: 250+

BANKS, NATIONAL COMMERCIAL

Boatmen's Bancshares Inc
800 Market St, St. Louis MO 63101-2506. 314/466-7720. Employs: 1,000+.

Cass Commercial Corp
1015 Locust, St. Louis MO 63101. 314/621-2220. Employs: 250-499.

Farm Credit Bank Of St Louis
1415 Olive St, St. Louis MO 63103-2334. 314/342-3200. Employs: 250-499.

Magna Bank
19 Public Sq Box 308, Belleville IL 62220-1624. 618/234-0020. Employs: 1,000+.

Mark Twain Bancshares Inc
8820 Ladue Rd, St. Louis MO 63124-2056. 314/727-1000. Employs: 250-499.

Mercantile Bank St Louis N A
7th & Washington St, St. Louis MO 63101. 314/425-2525. Employs: 1,000+.

BANKS, STATE COMMERCIAL

A G Edwards Trust Company
No 1 N Jefferson, St. Louis MO 63103-2205. 314/289-4200. Employs: 1,000+.

Boatmens Nat Bank St Louis
100 N Broadway Box 63166, St. Louis MO 63166. 314/425-7500. Employs: 500-999.

Landmark Bank
1401 S Brentwood, St. Louis MO 63144-1440. 314/889-1600. Employs: 1,000+.

SAVINGS INSTITUTIONS, FEDERALLY CHARTERED

Germania Bank FSB
701 Market St, St. Louis MO 63101-1850. 314/241-8656. Employs: 250-499.

CREDIT UNIONS, FEDERALLY CHARTERED

Continental Credit Union
7140 N Broadway, St. Louis MO 63147-2708. 314/381-6622. Employs: 250-499.

NONDEPOSIT TRUST FACILITIES

Boatmens Trust Co
510 Locust St, St. Louis MO 63101-1845. 314/231-9300. Employs: 250-499.

Additional small to medium sized employers: 50-249

BANKS, NATIONAL COMMERCIAL

Alton Mercantile N Alton Office
2421 State St, Alton IL 62002-5108. 618/466-8333. Employs: 50-99.

American Bank
RR 4, Highland IL 62249-9101. 618/654-1111. Employs: 50-99.

Banc Star Inc
12300 Old Tesson Rd, St. Louis MO 63128-2228. 314/842-5290. Employs: 50-99.

Bankcenter One
1500 Country Club Plaza Dr, Saint Charles MO 63303-3858. 314/947-1155. Employs: 50-99.

Bethalto National Motor Bank
1 Terminal Dr, Bethalto IL 62010. 618/377-9165. Employs: 50-99.

Boatmen's National Bank
23 Public Sq Boxc 367, Belleville IL 62220-1627. 618/233-6600. Employs: 50-99.

Boatmens National Bank St Louis
Perc Administrative Center, Florissant MO 63031. 314/645-7372. Employs: 50-99.

Boatmens National Bank St Louis
2621 Dunn Rd, St. Louis MO 63136-4627. 314/355-5904. Employs: 50-99.

Central Bank
3601 Hwy 159 S, Edwardsville IL 62025. 618/288-6101. Employs: 50-99.

Commerce Bank
1319 N Truman Blvd, Crystal City MO 63019-1334. 314/937-9191. Employs: 50-99.

Commerce Bank
1699 Clarkson Rd, Chesterfield MO 63017-4616. 314/530-5005. Employs: 50-99.

Commerce Bank St Charles Cty
435 Mid Rivers Mall Dr Bx700, Saint Peters MO 63376-1578. 314/279-2800. Employs: 50-99.

Ctzns Natl Bank Greater St Louis
7305 Manchester, St. Louis MO 63143-3109. 314/645-0666. Employs: 50-99.

Drive-Up Facilities
1210 Jefferson St, Carlyle IL 62231-1323. 618/594-3741. Employs: 50-99.

Egl Bank & Trst Co Jefferson
4675 Gravois Rd, House Springs MO 63051-1377. 314/671-3373. Employs: 50-99.

Egl Bank & Trst Co Jefferson Co
S Mill St & Veterans Blvd, Festus MO 63028. 314/933-3660. Employs: 50-99.

First Bank
5720 W North Belt St, Belleville IL 62223. 618/277-6850. Employs: 50-99.

First Financial Bank
100 E Washington St, Belleville IL 62220-2206. 618/233-5656. Employs: 50-99.

First National Bank
319 W Broadway Box 97, Steeleville IL 62288-1416. 618/965-3441. Employs: 50-99.

First National Bank
203 E Walnut St Box 128, Okawville IL 62271-0128. 618/243-5500. Employs: 50-99.

First National Bank
324 N State St Box 450, Litchfield IL 62056-2003. 217/324-2105. Employs: 50-99.

First National Bank In Worden
200 W Wall St, Worden IL 62097-1238. 618/459-7211. Employs: 50-99.

First National Bank Steeleville
306 W Pine, Steeleville IL 62288. 618/497-8361. Employs: 50-99.

First Natl Bank St Louis Cnty
7707 Forsyth Blvd, St. Louis MO 63105-1809. 314/862-8300. Employs: 100-249.

Forbes 1st Financial Corp
8011 Clayton Rd, St. Louis MO 63117-1156. 314/726-1199. Employs: 50-99.

Germania Bank
501 E Broadway St, Alton IL 62002-6304. 618/465-5543. Employs: 50-99.

Germania Bank
201 E Center Dr, Alton IL 62002-5931. 618/465-8305. Employs: 50-99.

Germania Bank/A Fed Svgs Bank
6201 W Main St, Belleville IL 62223-4411. 618/398-6850. Employs: 50-99.

Green County National Bank
600 N Main St Box 270, Carrollton IL 62016-1029. 217/942-5454. Employs: 50-99.

Heartland Savings Bank Fsb
1532 Jeffco Blvd, Arnold MO 63010-2159. 314/296-5200. Employs: 50-99.

Heartland Savings Bank Fsb
10275 Clayton Rd, St. Louis MO 63124-1115. 314/997-8905. Employs: 50-99.

Heartland Savings Bank Fsb
10233 Manchester Rd, St. Louis MO 63122-1532. 314/822-3665. Employs: 50-99.

Heartland Savings Bank Fsb
8798 Manchester Rd, St. Louis MO 63144-2724. 314/968-1822. Employs: 50-99.

Heartland Savings Bank Fsb
Frndshp Vlge 12503 Vlge Cir Dr, St. Louis MO 63127. 314/842-4144. Employs: 50-99.

Heritage National Bank
7435 Watson Rd Box 13153, St. Louis MO 63119-4403. 314/968-7900. Employs: 50-99.

Home Federal Savings Bank
8890 Lackland Rd, St. Louis MO 63114-5707. 314/429-5000. Employs: 50-99.

Home Federal Savings Bank
15337 Manchester Rd, Ballwin MO 63011-3026. 314/394-7767. Employs: 50-99.

Home Federal Savings Bank
244 Mayfair Plaza Shopping Ctr, Florissant MO 63033-8009. 314/355-7200. Employs: 50-99.

Home Federal Savings Bank
3800 McKelvey Rd, Bridgeton MO 63044-2003. 314/291-4106. Employs: 50-99.

Illinois State Bank
821 Homer M Adams Pkwy, Godfrey IL 62035-3336. 618/466-2166. Employs: 50-99.

Laddonia State Bank
110 W State St, Vandalia MO 63382-1737. 314/594-6121. Employs: 50-99.

Landmark Bancshares Of Il Inc
10950 Lincoln Trail, E St. Louis IL 62208-2027. 618/397-9178. Employs: 100-249.

Landmark Bank
4633 World Parkway Cir, St. Louis MO 63134-3115. 314/253-5500. Employs: 50-99.

Landmark Bank Of O'Fallon
1201 Highway K, O Fallon MO 63366-2999. 314/281-2282. Employs: 50-99.

Magna Bank
4800 W Main St, Belleville IL 62223-4723. 618/234-3014. Employs: 50-99.

Magna Bank
202 S State St, Freeburg IL 62243-1441. 618/539-5554. Employs: 50-99.

Magna Bank Long Acre Facility
5901 N Illinois St, E St. Louis IL 62208-2710. 618/233-0022. Employs: 50-99.

Magna Bank Of Columbia
100 Columbia Ctr, Columbia IL 62236-2537. 618/281-5172. Employs: 50-99.

Magna Bank Of Madison County
3206 Nameoki Rd, Granite City IL 62040-5014. 618/451-5490. Employs: 50-99.

Magna Bank Of Madison County
20th & Edison, Granite City IL 62040. 618/451-5400. Employs: 100-249.

Magna Bank Of St Clair Cnty
2665 N Illinois St, Belleville IL 62221-2302. 618/233-8333. Employs: 50-99.

Magna Colonial Bank
2400 Pontoon Rd, Granite City IL 62040-4103. 618/451-5505. Employs: 50-99.

Magna Plex
1 Betty La, O Fallon IL 62269-2234. 618/632-9222. Employs: 50-99.

Magna Trust Co
222 E Main St, Belleville IL 62220-1608. 618/233-2120. Employs: 50-99.

Mark Twain Bank Of O'Fallon
201 Highway 175, O Fallon MO 63366. 314/272-8800. Employs: 50-99.

Mark Twain Bank 21
Tesson Ferry & I-270, St. Louis MO 63128. 314/849-6200. Employs: 50-99.

Mega Bank Of St Ann
10449 St Charles Rock Rd, Saint Ann MO 63074-1832. 314/426-6900. Employs: 50-99.

Meramec State Bank Of Gray Smt
2105 Highway 100, Gray Summit MO 63039. 314/742-0062. Employs: 50-99.

Mercantile Bank Of Il N
1050 Camp Jackson Rd, E St. Louis IL 62206-2228. 618/337-1555. Employs: 50-99.

Mercantile Bank Of Illinois
1 Plaza Dr, Bethalto IL 62010.
618/377-2121. Employs: 50-99.

Metropolitan Insurance Company
13001 Tesson Ferry Rd, St. Louis MO 63128-3407. 314/842-1177. Employs: 50-99.

National Bank
Rt 3 & Valmeyer Rd Box 130, Columbia IL 62236-9803. 618/281-7101. Employs: 50-99.

Pacific National Bank
2001 Old Highway 66 W Bx 447, Pacific MO 63069-0447. 314/257-3926. Employs: 50-99.

Public Service Bank Fsb
840 Meramec Station Rd, Valley Park MO 63088-1146. 314/225-3355. Employs: 50-99.

Pulaski Bank
11330 Gravois Rd, St. Louis MO 63126-3608. 314/842-6400. Employs: 50-99.

Pulaski Bank
4255 Bayless Ave, St. Louis MO 63123-7513. 314/638-2000. Employs: 50-99.

Ramsey National Bank
231 S Superior St Box 476, Ramsey IL 62080-0476. 217/423-2396. Employs: 50-99.

Roosevelt Bank
Downtown 119 N Broadway, St. Louis MO 63102. 314/231-5300. Employs: 100-249.

Royal Banks Of Missouri
9990 Manchester Rd, St. Louis MO 63122-1923. 314/966-6630. Employs: 50-99.

State Bank Of Aviston
18101 Saint Rose Rd, Breese IL 62230-2557. 618/526-2230. Employs: 50-99.

The Magna Bank Of Wood River
100 N Wood River Av, Wood River IL 62095-1939. 618/254-7700. Employs: 50-99.

Union Bank
200 Collinsbill Ave, E St. Louis IL 62201. 618/271-1000. Employs: 50-99.

Union Bank Of Illinois
4387 N Illinois Av, Belleville IL 62221-1836. 618/233-3100. Employs: 50-99.

United Federal Bank
104 Homer M Adams Pkwy, Alton IL 62002-5924. 618/465-4422. Employs: 50-99.

US National Bank Clayton
8151 Clayton Rd, St. Louis MO 63117-1103. 314/863-2274. Employs: 50-99.

BANKS, STATE COMMERCIAL

Allegiant Bank
PO Box 771910, St. Louis MO 63177-1910. 314/534-3000. Employs: 100-249.

Alton Banking & Trust Co
4365 N Alby St Rd, Alton IL 62002-5914. 618/463-4365. Employs: 50-99.

Alton Banking & Trust Co
620 E Broadway, Alton IL 62002-6305. 618/463-4200. Employs: 50-99.

American Bank Of St Louis
12275 Olive St Rd, St. Louis MO 63141-6600. 314/878-1311. Employs: 50-99.

American Bank Of St Louis
4666 Lansdowne Ave, St. Louis
MO 63116-1523. 314/421-3200.
Employs: 100-249.

American Bank Of St Louis
1731 S Broadway, St. Louis MO
63104-4050. 314/421-3200.
Employs: 50-99.

Bank Of Edwardsville
330 W Vandalia St, Edwardsville
IL 62025-1911. 618/656-0057.
Employs: 50-99.

Bank Of Edwardsville
120 W Market, Troy IL 62294-
1419. 618/667-6702. Employs: 50-
99.

Boatmen's Mortgage Corp
7800 Forsyth Blvd, St. Louis MO
63105-3311. 314/889-7333.
Employs: 50-99.

Boatmen's National Bank
400 S Kingshighway, St. Louis MO
63110-1014. 314/367-4700.
Employs: 100-249.

Boatmen's National Bank
55 W Moody, St. Louis MO 63119-
2313. 314/961-2400. Employs: 50-
99.

Boatmen's National Bank
8944 T Charles Rock Road, St.
Louis MO 63114. 314/428-5500.
Employs: 50-99.

Boatmen's National Bank
1200 Fern Ridge Pkwy, St. Louis
MO 63141-4451. 314/576-7600.
Employs: 50-99.

Boatmen's National Bank
2200 W Port Plaza Dr, St. Louis
MO 63146-3211. 314/434-9600.
Employs: 50-99.

Boatmen's National Bank
130 River Rds Shop Ctr, St. Louis
MO 63136-5046. 314/868-1142.
Employs: 50-99.

Boatmen's National Bank
4495 Lemay Ferry Road, St. Louis
MO 63129-1757. 314/892-5511.
Employs: 50-99.

Boatmen's National Bank
Skinker & Lindell, St. Louis MO
63130. 314/889-7156. Employs:
50-99.

Boatmen's National Bank
9629 Olive St Rd, St. Louis MO
63132-3022. 314/994-9100.
Employs: 50-99.

Boatmen's National Bank
910 W Hwy 50, O Fallon IL 62269.
618/632-5500. Employs: 50-99.

Boatmen's National Bank
714 N Second Street, St. Louis MO
63102-2519. 314/466-3626.
Employs: 100-249.

Boatmen's National Bank
720 Olive Street, St. Louis MO
63101-2338. 314/466-5700.
Employs: 100-249.

Boatmen's National Bank
510 Locust Street, St. Louis MO
63101-1845. 314/466-3000.
Employs: 100-249.

Boatmen's National Bank
9075 Goodfellow, St. Louis MO
63147-1401. 314/866-8600.
Employs: 100-249.

Boatmen's National Bank
4301 Hampton Ave, St. Louis MO
63109-2231. 314/352-4700.
Employs: 50-99.

Central Bank
3303 Namecki Rd, Granite City IL
62040-3708. 618/451-6600.
Employs: 50-99.

Community First Bank
4600 N Illinois Box 1983, E St. Louis IL 62208-0183. 618/234-9500. Employs: 50-99.

Daiwa Bank
200 North Broadway Ste 1920, St. Louis MO 63102-2757. 314/241-0373. Employs: 100-249.

First Bank
2516 Lemay Ferry Rd, St. Louis MO 63125-3131. 314/892-1694. Employs: 50-99.

First Bank Of Illinois
105 N Main St, O Fallon IL 62269-2970. 618/624-4343. Employs: 50-99.

First Excanghe Bank St Louis
1 North Brentwood, St. Louis MO 63105-3709. 314/725-1633. Employs: 50-99.

First Exchange Bank
8917 Riverview Dr, St. Louis MO 63137-2404. 314/868-8450. Employs: 50-99.

First Exchange Bank St Louis
4226 Bayless Ave, St. Louis MO 63123-7514. 314/638-5750. Employs: 50-99.

First Financial Bank
3803 S Broadway Box 1810, St. Louis MO 63118-4607. 314/664-6250. Employs: 50-99.

First Financial Bank
6100 W Main, Belleville IL 62223-1101. 618/233-5656. Employs: 50-99.

First Financial Bank
No 1 Junction Dr W, Glen Carbon IL 62034. 618/288-7412. Employs: 50-99.

First National Bank
9645 Clayton Rd, St. Louis MO 63124-1501. 314/997-2484. Employs: 50-99.

Guaranty Trust Company
7701 Forsyth Blvd Ste 1200, St. Louis MO 63105-1818. 314/725-9055. Employs: 50-99.

Heritage National Bank
10900 Manchester Rd, St. Louis MO 63122-1200. 314/821-4600. Employs: 50-99.

Illinois State Bank & Trust
251 E Airline Dr, East Alton IL 62024-1706. 618/259-1300. Employs: 50-99.

Jefferson Bank & Trust Co
12501 Olive Blvd, St. Louis MO 63141-6311. 314/576-5505. Employs: 50-99.

Landmark Bank
12395 Olive Blvd, St. Louis MO 63141-6401. 314/576-7733. Employs: 50-99.

Landmark Bank
9269 Lewis & Clark Blvd, St. Louis MO 63136. 314/869-1300. Employs: 50-99.

Landmark Bank
1944 Redman Rd, St. Louis MO 63138-1104. 314/355-8433. Employs: 50-99.

Landmark Bank
8866 Ladue Rd, St. Louis MO 63124-2046. 314/862-2127. Employs: 50-99.

Landmark Bank
7205 Watson Rd, St. Louis MO 63119-4401. 314/481-4480. Employs: 50-99.

Landmark Bank
10722 Sunset Hills Plaza, St. Louis MO 63127. 314/821-6444. Employs: 50-99.

Landmark Bank
5505 Telegraph Rd, St. Louis MO 63129-3557. 314/487-2200. Employs: 50-99.

Landmark Bank
6313 Dr M L King Dr, St. Louis MO 63133. 314/381-3000. Employs: 50-99.

Landmark Bank
100 McDonald Dr, Troy IL 62294-1375. 618/667-7800. Employs: 50-99

Landmark Bank
701 Olive St, St. Louis MO 63101-2202. 314/231-3333. Employs: 100-249.

Landmark Bank Of Illinois
400 E 8th St, O Fallon IL 62269-2705. 618/624-9000. Employs: 50-99.

Landmark Bank Of Illinois
8740 State St, E St. Louis IL 62203-2056. 618/271-2122. Employs: 50-99.

Magna Bank
655 Carlyle Ave, Belleville IL 62221-6224. 618/234-7985. Employs: 50-99.

Magna Bank
210 E Washington St, Belleville IL 62220-2208. 618/234-3374. Employs: 50-99.

Magna Trust Co
20th & Edison Aves, Granite City IL 62040. 618/451-5421. Employs: 50-99.

Mark Twain Bank
15839 Manchester Rd, Ballwin MO 63011-2224. 314/391-1335. Employs: 50-99.

Mark Twain Bank
Florissant & Lucas Hunt Rd, St. Louis MO 63136. 314/383-2000. Employs: 50-99.

Mark Twain Bank
12140 Woodcrest Executive Dr, St. Louis MO 63141-5048. 314/878-2000. Employs: 50-99.

Mega Bank Of St Louis County
4545 Lemay Ferry Rd, St. Louis MO 63129-1646. 314/894-7151. Employs: 50-99.

Mercantile Bank
2885 Netherton Dr, St. Louis MO 63136-4674. 314/741-9100. Employs: 50-99.

Mercantile Bank
304 Bargraves Blvd, Troy IL 62294-2304. 618/667-7020. Employs: 50-99.

Mercantile Bank
POB 30, High Ridge MO 63049-0030. 314/376-6600. Employs: 50-99.

Mercantile Bank Of St Louis
1050 Woods Mill Rd, Chesterfield MO 63017. 314/391-4200. Employs: 100-249.

Mercantile Bank Of St Louis
Olive & Mason Rds, St. Louis MO 63141. 314/878-9300. Employs: 50-99.

Mercantile Bank Of St Louis
12935 N Outer Forty R, St. Louis MO 63141. 314/391-4290. Employs: 50-99.

Mercantile Bank Of St Louis
11781 Manchester Rd, St. Louis
MO 63131-4618. 314/391-4240.
Employs: 50-99.

Midamerica Bank
8740 State St, E St. Louis IL
62203-2056. 618/271-2121.
Employs: 50-99.

Pioneer Bank & Trust Co
2211 S Big Bend Blvd, St. Louis
MO 63117-2407. 314/644-6600.
Employs: 50-99.

Roosevelt Bank
5807 Murdoch Ave, St. Louis MO
63109-2723. 314/532-6200.
Employs: 100-249.

Royal Banks Of Missouri
9895 Watson Rd, St. Louis MO
63126-1824. 314/821-9007.
Employs: 50-99.

Southwest Bank Of St. Louis
700 Corporate Plaza Dr, St. Louis
MO 63105-4209. 314/727-7070.
Employs: 50-99.

UMB First National Bank
101 N High St, Belleville IL
62220-1422. 618/277-7100.
Employs: 50-99.

UMB First National Bank
2601 N Illinois, Belleville IL
62221-2302. 618/236-2233.
Employs: 50-99.

United Illinois Bank
100 E Market St, Troy IL 62294-1510. 618/667-6755. Employs: 50-99.

United Missouri Bank
312 North Eight St, St. Louis MO
63101. 314/421-6868. Employs: 100-249.

United Missouri Bank
7911 Forsyth Blvd, St. Louis MO
63105-3860. 314/725-6000.
Employs: 50-99.

United Missouri Bank
426 N Kirkwood Rd, St. Louis MO
63122-3912. 314/966-4000.
Employs: 50-99.

West Pointe Bank & Trust Co
6100 W Main St Box 1228,
Belleville IL 62223-4404. 618/234-5700. Employs: 50-99.

Omni Bank
5111 Hwy 11 Box 8006, Granite
City IL 62040-8006. 618/797-5111.
Employs: 50-99.

First Collisville Bank
800 Beltline Rd Box 809,
Collinsville IL 62234-4413.
618/346-9000. Employs: 50-99.

Bank Of South County
9100 Gravois Ave, St. Louis MO
63123-4524. 314/544-9100.
Employs: 50-99.

Southern Commercial Bank
5515 S Grand Blvd, St. Louis MO
63111-1807. 314/481-6800.
Employs: 50-99.

Cass Bank & Trust Company
3636 So Geyer Rd, St. Louis MO
63127-1237. 314/821-1500.
Employs: 50-99.

SAVINGS INSTITUTIONS, FEDERALLY CHARTERED

American Home S & L Assn
12855 Tesson Ferry Rd, St. Louis
MO 63128-2912. 314/849-2311.
Employs: 50-99.

American Home S & L Assn
2909 Telegraph Rd, St. Louis MO
63125-4062. 314/487-7810.
Employs: 50-99.

American Home S & L Assn
8575 Watson Rd, St. Louis MO
63119-5218. 314/968-9998.
Employs: 50-99.

Amerimac Savings Bank Fsb
Box 357, Hillsboro IL 62049-0357.
217/532-9431. Employs: 50-99.

Clayton S & L Assn
135 N Meramec Ave, St. Louis MO
63105-3751. 314/862-6900.
Employs: 50-99.

Cmnty Fed S & L Mid Cnty
8637 Delmar Blvd, St. Louis MO
63124-1906. 314/993-5588.
Employs: 50-99.

Collinsville B & L Assn
701 E Belt Line, Collinsville IL
62234-4412. 618/344-3172.
Employs: 50-99.

Conservative Bank/A F S B
12400 Tesson Ferry Rd, St. Louis
MO 63128-2702. 314/849-3020.
Employs: 50-99.

Farm & Home Savings Assn
110 W Lockwood Ave, St. Louis
MO 63119-2916. 314/968-3083.
Employs: 50-99.

Fidelity Fed Svgs & Ln Assn
801 Lincoln Hwy, E St. Louis IL
62208-2216. 618/632-7480.
Employs: 50-99.

First Granite City S & L Assn
1529 Johnson Rd, Granite City IL
62040-3831. 618/452-3700.
Employs: 50-99.

Germania Bank
220 E Center Dr, Alton IL 62002-5900. 618/465-2371. Employs: 50-99.

Greater St Louis S & L
744 Office Pky, St. Louis MO
63141-7128. 314/997-6070.
Employs: 50-99.

Home Federal Savings
243 Alton Sq, Alton IL 62002-5920. 618/462-8866. Employs: 50-99.

Jefferson Savings & Loan Assn
5600 S Lindbergh Blvd, St. Louis
MO 63123-6924. 314/849-5700.
Employs: 50-99.

Jefferson Savings & Loan Assn
9994 Manchester Rd, St. Louis MO
63122-1923. 314/821-9004.
Employs: 50-99.

Jefferson Savings & Loan Assn
5533 Oakville Shopping Ctr, St.
Louis MO 63129-3554. 314/892-0700. Employs: 50-99.

Public Service Bank Fsb
9936 Kennerly Rd, St. Louis MO
63128-2704. 314/849-3355.
Employs: 50-99.

Roosevelt Bank
1299 Reavis Barracks Rd, St. Louis
MO 63125-3260. 314/487-3717.
Employs: 50-99.

Roosevelt Bank
6969 S Lindbergh Blvd, St. Louis
MO 63125-4220. 314/487-9669.
Employs: 50-99.

Roosevelt Bank
200 River Roads Shopping Ctr, St.
Louis MO 63136-5047. 314/868-3115. Employs: 50-99.

Savings Of America
10067 Bellefontaine Rd, St. Louis
MO 63137-1921. 314/868-1414.
Employs: 50-99.

Savings Of America
201 N Florissant Rd, St. Louis MO
63135-1949. 314/524-0500.
Employs: 50-99.

Savings Of America
10101 Gravois Rd, St. Louis MO
63123-4025. 314/638-2800.
Employs: 50-99.

Savings Of America
9841 Clayton Rd, St. Louis MO
63124-1603. 314/569-3760.
Employs: 50-99.

Savings Of America
1859 Craig Rd, St. Louis MO
63146-4711. 314/576-6951.
Employs: 50-99.

South Side National Bank
8440 Morganford Rd, St. Louis
MO 63123-6851. 314/631-1900.
Employs: 50-99.

St Louis Financial Svc Corp
470 N Kirkwood Rd, St. Louis MO
63122-3912. 314/966-6626.
Employs: 50-99.

United Postal Savings Assn
470 N Kirkwood Rd, St. Louis MO
63122-3912. 314/822-9044.
Employs: 50-99.

United Postal Savings Assn
1400 S Big Bend Blvd, St. Louis
MO 63117-2204. 314/645-2422.
Employs: 50-99.

United Postal Savings Assn
12117 Bellefontaine Rd, St. Louis
MO 63138-1906. 314/741-5505.
Employs: 50-99.

United Postal Savings Assn
669 N New Ballas Rd, St. Louis
MO 63141-6713. 314/432-1900.
Employs: 50-99.

United Postal Savings Assn
107 Concord Plaza Shopping Ctr,
St. Louis MO 63128-1307.
314/842-6111. Employs: 50-99.

United Postal Savings Assn
52 S Central Ave, St. Louis MO
63105-1710. 314/726-0333.
Employs: 50-99.

St Louis Fed S & L Assn
9666 Olive Blvd Ste 600, St. Louis
MO 63132-3026. 314/726-2800.
Employs: 50-99.

Frontier Fed Savings Bank
401 S Illinois St, Belleville IL
62220-2135. 618/233-0538.
Employs: 50-99.

Reliance Fed S & L Assn
8930 Gravois Ave, St. Louis MO
63123-4624. 314/631-7500.
Employs: 50-99.

Home Federal Savings
Box 160, Alton IL 62002-0160.
618/466-7700. Employs: 50-99.

Metro Savings Fsb
1301 Edwardsville Rd, Wood River
IL 62095-1831. 618/259-5030.
Employs: 50-99.

St Louis County Fed S & L Assn
10385 W Florissant, St. Louis MO
63136-2107. 314/524-6500.
Employs: 50-99.

Missouri Savings Assn Fa
10 N Hanley, St. Louis MO 63105-
3426. 314/862-3300. Employs: 50-
99.

**CREDIT UNIONS,
FEDERALLY CHARTERED**

EDS Financial Services Divsn
12747 Olive Blvd, St. Louis MO
63141-6269. 314/878-2100.
Employs: 100-249.

NONDEPOSIT TRUST FACILITIES

Carrollton Bank & Trust Co The
315 W Public Sq, Carrollton IL 62016. 217/942-5408. Employs: 100-249.

Ultra Life Inc
2010 Franklin St, Carlyle IL 62231-1608. 618/594-7711. Employs: 100-249.

FUNCTIONS RELATED TO DEPOSITORY BANKING

Mercantile Bank Of St Louis Na
5375 Southwest Ave, St. Louis MO 63139-1445. 314/772-8700. Employs: 50-99.

Missouri Savings Assn
5418 Hampton Ave, St. Louis MO 63109-3105. 314/832-6600. Employs: 50-99.

Missouri Savings Assn
3590 Lindell Blvd, St. Louis MO 63103-1021. 314/533-4900. Employs: 50-99.

B B Exchange Co
4962 Union Blvd, St. Louis MO 63115-1317. 314/383-4685. Employs: 50-99.

Checks 4 Cash
4300 Natural Bridge Ave, St. Louis MO 63115-2846. 314/652-4060. Employs: 50-99.

Delmar & Union Curr Exch Inc
5215 Delmar Blvd, St. Louis MO 63108-1027. 314/454-3007. Employs: 50-99.

Delmar Sta & Hodiamont Curr
5982 Delmar Blvd, St. Louis MO 63112-2054. 314/725-1841. Employs: 50-99.

P-X Stores
7842 N Broadway, St. Louis MO 63147-2531. 314/383-0439. Employs: 50-99.

Escrow Consultants Inc
10853 Indian Head Industrial B, St. Louis MO 63132-1103. 314/428-0818. Employs: 50-99.

Land Title Ins Co St Louis
12th & Market, St. Louis MO 63102. 314/241-2204. Employs: 50-99.

Missouri Title Co
904 Chestnut St, St. Louis MO 63101-1411. 314/241-5891. Employs: 50-99.

Community Check Exchange
3825 S Kingshighway Blvd, St. Louis MO 63109-1818. 314/353-7445. Employs: 50-99.

National Money Order Service
4938 Natural Bridge Ave, St. Louis MO 63115-2009. 314/389-1505. Employs: 50-99.

OFFICES OF BANK HOLDING COMPANIES

Central Banc System Inc
One Central Bank Bldg, E St. Louis IL 62208. 618/451-6600. Employs: 100-249.

For more information on career opportunities in the banking/savings and loan industry:

Associations

AMERICAN BANKERS ASSOCIATION
1120 Connecticut Avenue NW, Washington DC 20036. 202/663-5221.

BANK ADMINISTRATION INSTITUTE
1 North Franklin, Chicago IL 60606. 800/323-8552.

BANK MARKETING ASSOCIATION
309 West Washington Street, Chicago IL 60606. 312/782-1442.

INDEPENDENT BANKERS ASSOCIATION OF AMERICA
One Thomas Circle NW, Suite 950, Washington DC 20005. 202/659-8111.

INSTITUTE OF FINANCIAL EDUCATION
111 East Wacker Drive, 9th Floor, Chicago IL 60601. 312/946-8800.

NATIONAL COUNCIL OF SAVINGS INSTITUTIONS
1101 15th Street NW, Suite 400, Washington DC 20005. 202/857-3100.

U.S. LEAGUE OF SAVINGS AND LOAN INSTITUTIONS
111 East Wacker Drive, Chicago IL 60601. 312/644-3100.

Directories

AMERICAN BANK DIRECTORY
McFadden Business Publications, 6195 Crooked Creek Road, Norcross GA 30092. 404/448-1011.

AMERICAN BANKER DIRECTORY OF U.S. BANKING EXECUTIVES
American Banker, Inc., 1 State Street Plaza, New York NY 10004. 212/943-6700.

AMERICAN BANKER YEARBOOK
American Banker, Inc., 1 State Street Plaza, New York NY 10004. 212/943-6700.

AMERICAN SAVINGS DIRECTORY
McFadden Business Publications, 6195 Crooked Creek Road, Norcross GA 30092. 404/448-1011.

BUSINESS WEEK/TOP 200 BANKING INSTITUTIONS ISSUE
McGraw-Hill, Inc., 1221 Avenue of the Americas, 39th Floor, New York NY 10020. 212/512-4776.

MOODY'S BANK AND FINANCE MANUAL
Moody's Investors Service, Inc., 99 Church Street, New York NY 10007. 212/553-0300.

POLK'S BANK DIRECTORY
R.L. Polk & Co., 2001 Elm Hill Pike, Nashville TN 37210. 615/889-3350.

Magazines

ABA BANKING JOURNAL
American Bankers Association, 1120 Connecticut Avenue NW, Washington DC 20036. 202/663-5221.

BANK ADMINISTRATION
1 North Franklin, Chicago IL 60606. 800/323-8552.

BANKERS MAGAZINE
Warren, Gorham & Lamont, 210 South Street, Boston MA 02111. 617/423-2020.

JOURNAL OF COMMERCIAL BANK LENDING
Robert Morris Associates, 1 Liberty Place, 1650 Market Street, Suite 2300, Philadelphia PA 19103. 215/851-9100.

BOOK AND MAGAZINE PUBLISHING

The continuing recession has hit the book and magazine industries hard. In fact, between 1989 and 1990 alone, over 2,600 book publishing workers lost their jobs. Despite cost containment efforts, most major houses have failed to prevent profits from shrinking further since that time. Higher postal rates and tighter school and library budgets have exacerbated the problem. Gradually, as the economy recovers and disposable income increases, sales in adult trade books should climb. The expanding 5-14 year-old age group should prompt a rise in sales of juvenile books. These forces should help boost job prospects by about 2,000 new positions annually. In the magazine sector, where much of the revenues are derived from advertising sales, the recession has severely affected bottom lines, and ad pages have declined. An ongoing trend is specialty and niche magazines aimed at increasingly specific audiences.

CBP PRESS
1316 Convention Plaza, St. Louis MO 63103. 314/231-8500. **Contact:** Melvin Carr, Personnel Director. **Description:** A St. Louis book and magazine publisher that specializes in religious material.

CONCORDIA PUBLISHING HOUSE
3558 South Jefferson Avenue, St. Louis MO 63118. 314/268-1252. **Contact:** Richard Talley, Personnel Manager. **Description:** Publishers of religious curriculum, periodicals, books, pamphlets, and Bibles. **Employees:** 335. **Common positions:** Accountant; Advertising Worker; Blue-Collar Worker Supervisor; Buyer; Commercial Artist; Computer Programmer; Credit Manager; Customer Service Representative; Financial Analyst; Industrial Manager; Department Manager; General Manager; Management Trainee; Operations/Production Manager; Marketing Specialist; Personnel and Labor Relations Specialist; Purchasing Agent; Sales Representative. **Educational backgrounds sought:** Accounting; Art/Design; Business Administration; Communications; Finance; Marketing. **Benefits:** medical insurance; dental insurance; pension plan; life insurance; tuition assistance; disability coverage; employee discounts. **Corporate headquarters:** This location. **Operations at this facility:** administration; service; sales. **Revenues (1991):** $32.7 million. **Employees:** 335. **Projected hires for the next 12 months:** 15.

WARREN H. GREEN INC.
8356 Olive Boulevard, St. Louis MO 63132. 314/991-1335. **Contact:** Dr. Warren Green, Ph.D., President. FAX: 314/997-1788. **Description:** A St. Louis book publisher specializing in the field of medicine. **Common positions:** Accountant; Credit Manager; Customer Service Representative; Marketing Specialist; Purchasing Agent; Quality Controller; Reporter/Editor. **Educational backgrounds sought:** Accounting; Communications; Computer Science; Marketing. **Special programs:** Internships. **Benefits:** medical insurance; life insurance; disability coverage. **Corporate headquarters:** This location. **Operations at this facility:** research and development; administration; service; sales. **Revenues (1991):** $1.5 million. **Employees:** 10. **Projected number of hires for the next 12 months:** 4.

IEA INC.
716 Hanley Industrial Court, St. Louis MO 63144. 314/644-4322. **Contact:** Mrs. Satoko Kimzey, Office Manager. **Description:** Publishing company specializing in medical and dental books.

MOSBY-YEAR BOOK, INC.
11830 Westline Industrial Drive, St. Louis MO 63146. 314/453-4248. **Contact:** Ms. Lucy Morgan, Employment Manager. **Description:** A St. Louis publisher of books and periodicals in the health sciences. **Common positions:** Accountant; Commercial Artist; Computer Programmer; Customer Service Representative; Marketing Specialist; Editorial Assistant; Sales Representative; Systems Analyst; Editor. **Educational backgrounds sought:** English; Art/Design; Biology; Communications; Journalism; Liberal Arts; Marketing. **Benefits:** medical, dental, and life insurance; pension plan; tuition assistance; disability coverage; employee discounts; savings plan. **Corporate headquarters:** This location. **Parent company:** Times Mirror. **Revenues (1991):** $100 million. **Employees:** 900. **Projected number of hires for the next 12 months:** 100.

Additional large employers: 250+

BOOKS: PUBLISHING, OR PUBLISHING AND PRINTING

John S Swift Co Inc
1248 Research Blvd, St. Louis MO 63132-1714. 314/991-4300.
Employs: 250-499.

McGraw-Hill Inc
13955 Manchester Rd, Ballwin MO 63011-4505. 314/256-2213.
Employs: 250-499.

Additional small to medium sized employers: 50-249

PERIODICALS: PUBLISHING OR PUBLISHING AND PRINTING

North American Eqpt Dealers
10877 Watson Rd, St. Louis MO 63127-1032. 314/821-7220.
Employs: 50-99.

BOOKS: PUBLISHING OR PUBLISHING AND PRINTING

Christian Board Of Publication
1316 Convention Plaza, St. Louis MO 63103-1908. 314/231-8500. Employs: 50-99.

Liguori Publications
1 Liguori Dr, Liguori MO 63057-9999. 314/464-2500. Employs: 50-99.

Pentecostal Publishing House
8855 Dunn Rd, Hazelwood MO 63042-2212. 314/837-7300. Employs: 100-249.

MISCELLANEOUS PUBLISHING

Liturgical Publications
160 Old State Rd, Ballwin MO 63021-5915. 314/394-7000. Employs: 50-99.

Officeplus
111 Westport Plz, St. Louis MO 63146-3011. 314/542-3000. Employs: 50-99.

For more information on career opportunities in book and magazine publishing:

Special Programs

THE NEW YORK UNIVERSITY SUMMER PUBLISHING PROGRAM
48 Cooper Square, Room 108, New York NY 10003. 212/998-7219.

THE RADCLIFFE PUBLISHING COURSE
77 Brattle Street, Cambridge MA 02138. 617/495-8678.

RICE UNIVERSITY PUBLISHING PROGRAM
Office of Continuing Studies, P.O. Box 1892, Houston TX 77001. 713/520-6022.

UNIVERSITY OF DENVER PUBLISHING PROGRAM
2199 South University Boulevard, Denver CO 80208. 303/871-2570.

Associations

AMERICAN BOOKSELLERS ASSOCIATION
560 White Plains Road, Tarrytown NY 10591. 914/631-7800.

ASSOCIATION OF AMERICAN PUBLISHERS
220 East 23rd Street, New York NY 10010. 212/689-8920.

MAGAZINE PUBLISHERS ASSOCIATION
575 Lexington Avenue, Suite 540, New York NY 10022. 212/752-0055.

WRITERS GUILD OF AMERICA EAST
555 West 57th Street, Suite 1230, New York NY 10019. 212/767-7800.

WRITERS GUILD OF AMERICA WEST
8955 Beverly Boulevard, Los Angeles CA 90048. 310/550-1000.

BROADCASTING

Across the board, a very tough field to break into - whether it's TV, radio, or cable. Many analysts look to local broadcast outlets for the most job opportunities, and local all-news cable stations are the newest trend on the dial.

INTERNATIONAL LUTHERAN LAYMEN'S LEAGUE
2185 Hampton Avenue, St. Louis MO 63139. 314/647-4900. **Contact:** Neva Sprung, Manager of Human Resources. **Description:** The International Lutheran Laymen's League produces the radio program The Lutheran Hour and other religious media products. **Common positions:** Clerical; Secretary. **Educational backgrounds sought:** Liberal Arts; Secretarial. **Benefits:** medical, dental and life insurance; pension plan; tuition assistance; disability coverage; employee discounts; savings plan. **Corporate headquarters:** This location. **Operations at this facility:** research and development; administration.

KMOX-RADIO/TV
CBS TELEVISION CHANNEL 4
One Memorial Drive, St. Louis MO 63102. 314/621-4444. **Contact:** Helen Campbell, Director of Personnel. **Description:** St. Louis radio and television broadcasting station.

KPLR-TV/
CHANNEL 11
4935 Lindell Boulevard, St. Louis MO 63108. 314/367-7211. **Contact:** Business Office. **Description:** A St. Louis television broadcasting station.

KSDK-TV/MULTIMEDIA INC.
MULTIMEDIA INC.
1000 Market Street, St. Louis MO 63101. 314/421-5055. **Contact:** Warren Canull, Personnel Director. **Description:** A St. Louis television broadcasting station.

KTVI-TV/
CHANNEL 2
5915 Berthold Avenue, St. Louis MO 63110. 314/647-2222. **Contact:** Diane Abernathy, Asst. to V.P./Gen. Manager. **Description:** A St. Louis television broadcasting station.

MIDWEST TELEVISION, INC.
509 South Neil Street, P.O. Box 777, Champaign IL 61824-0777. 217/356-8333. **Contact:** department of interest. **Description:** A television and radio broadcasting company.

Small to medium sized employers: 50-249

RADIO BROADCASTING STATIONS

Contemporary Media Bdcstg Gp
222 Indacom Dr, Saint Peters MO 63376-2433. 314/947-0600. Employs: 50-99.

KLOU 103 Fm
1 S Memorial Dr, St. Louis MO 63102-2425. 314/621-2345. Employs: 50-99.

TELEVISION BROADCASTING STATIONS

KMOV-TV
8 Executive Park Dr Rm 160E, E St. Louis IL 62208-1345. 618/632-6397. Employs: 50-99.

Koplar Communications Inc
4935 Lindell Blvd, St. Louis MO 63108-1523. 314/454-6300. Employs: 100-249.

Lloyd's Rentals & Sales Inc
6601 W Main St, Belleville IL 62223-3025. 618/398-0500. Employs: 50-99.

Catholic Family TV Channel 69
9705 Watson Rd, St. Louis MO 63126-1853. 314/822-9699. Employs: 50-99.

Channel Nine Viewer Info
6996 Millbrook Blvd, St. Louis MO 63130-4433. 314/726-9900. Employs: 50-99.

KNLC Channel 24
1411 Locust St, St. Louis MO 63103-2332. 314/436-2424. Employs: 100-249.

Pulitzer Broadcast Co
516 N 6th St, St. Louis MO 63101-1808. 314/231-5950. Employs: 100-249.

CABLE AND OTHER PAY TELEVISION SERVICES

Aim Inc
5621 Delmar Blvd, St. Louis MO 63112-2656. 314/361-4404. Employs: 50-99.

American Cablevision-St Louis
9231 W Florissant Ave, St. Louis MO 63136-1422. 314/524-6880. Employs: 50-99.

Capital Cable
150 N Meramec Ave, St. Louis MO 63105-3753. 314/726-0099. Employs: 50-99.

Cencom Cable Television
200 W Divsn, Maryville IL 62062. 618/345-8121. Employs: 50-99.

Continental Cablevision
7053 Emma Ave, St. Louis MO 63136-1049. 314/389-0808. Employs: 50-99.

Continental Cablevision
11838 Borman Dr, St. Louis MO 63146-4113. 314/569-2111. Employs: 50-99.

Continental Cablevision
1000 Des Peres, St. Louis MO 63131. 314/821-4909. Employs: 50-99.

Excel Communications Inc
7211 Olive Blvd, St. Louis MO 63130-2320. 314/725-8400. Employs: 50-99.

Higher Education Channel
6996 Millbrook Blvd, St. Louis MO 63130-4433. 314/725-3712. Employs: 50-99.

Mega Hertz Sales
1515 N Warson Rd, St. Louis MO 63132-1111. 314/429-3600. Employs: 50-99.

North Area Community Accss Brd
200 Church St, St. Louis MO 63135-2413. 314/521-9303. Employs: 50-99.

St Louis City Communications
1408 N Kingshighway Blvd, St. Louis MO 63113-1400. 314/361-1284. Employs: 50-99.

STL Cablevision
4940 Delmar Blvd, St. Louis MO 63108-1615. 314/361-3616. Employs: 50-99.

For more information on career opportunities in broadcasting:

Associations

ACADEMY OF TELEVISION ARTS & SCIENCES
5220 Lankershim Boulevard, North Hollywood CA 91601. 818/754-2800.

BROADCAST EDUCATION ASSOCIATION
1771 N Street NW, Washington DC 20036. 202/429-5355.

BROADCAST PROMOTION AND MARKETING EXECUTIVES
6225 Sunset Boulevard, Suite 624, Los Angeles CA 90028. 213/465-3777.

INTERNATIONAL RADIO AND TV SOCIETY
420 Lexington Avenue, Suite 1714, New York NY 10170. 212/867-6650.

INTERNATIONAL TELEVISION ASSOCIATION
6311 North O'Connor Road, LB51, Irving TX 75039. 214/869-1112.

NATIONAL ACADEMY OF TELEVISION ARTS & SCIENCES
111 West 57th Street, Suite 1020, New York NY 10019. 212/586-8424.

NATIONAL ASSOCIATION OF BROADCASTERS
1771 N Street NW, Washington DC 20036. 202/429-5300.

NATIONAL ASSOCIATION OF BUSINESS AND EDUCATIONAL RADIO
1501 Duke Street, Suite 200, Alexandria VA 22314. 703/739-0300.

NATIONAL ASSOCIATION OF PUBLIC TELEVISION STATIONS
1350 Connecticut Avenue NW, Suite 200
Washington DC 20036. 202/887-1700.

NATIONAL CABLE TELEVISION ASSOCIATION
1724 Massachusetts Avenue NW, Washington DC 20036. 202/775-3550.

TELEVISION BUREAU OF ADVERTISING
477 Madison Avenue, New York NY 10022-5892. 212/486-1111.

WOMEN IN RADIO AND TV, INC.
1101 Connecticut Avenue NW, Suite 700, Washington DC 20036. 202/429-5102.

Magazines

BROADCAST MANAGEMENT/ ENGINEERING
295 Madison Avenue, New York NY 10017. 212/685-5320.

BROADCASTING
Broadcasting Publications Inc., 1735 DeSales Street NW, Washington DC 20036. 202/638-1022.

ELECTRONIC MEDIA
Crain Communications, 220 East 42nd Street, New York NY 10017. 212/210-0100.

TELEVISION RADIO AGE
Television Editorial Corporation, 1270 Avenue of the Americas, New York NY 10020. 212/757-8400.

CHARITABLE, NON-PROFIT, SOCIAL SERVICES

The outlook for social services workers is better than average. In fact, opportunities for qualified applicants are expected to be excellent, partly due to the rapid turnover in the industry, the growing number of older citizens, and an increased awareness of the needs of the mentally and physically handicapped.

HUMANE SOCIETY OF MISSOURI
1210 Macklind Avenue, St. Louis MO 63110. 314/647-8800. **Contact:** Diana Rigley, Director of Personnel. **Description:** The fourth largest and fifth oldest Humane Society in the U.S., providing emergency field services in St. Louis County and city. The organization investigates cruelty and neglect to animals statewide and operates two animal shelters and two veterinary clinics. Provides public relations and educational programs and operates a rehabilitation farm for large animals. **Common positions:** Accountant; Administrator; Branch Manager; General Manager; Kennel Worker; Sectretarial; Humane Officer; Development Director; Animal Health Technician; Veterinarian. **Educational backgrounds sought:** Accounting; Business Administration; Management; Animal Health; Veterinary Medicine. **Special programs:** Training programs and internships. **Benefits:** medical, dental, and life insurance; pension plan; tuition assistance; disability coverage; employee discounts. **Corporate headquarters:** This location. **Operations at this facility:** service.

JEWISH COMMUNITY CENTERS ASSOCIATION
#2 Millstone Campus Drive, St. Louis MO 63146. 314/432-5700. **Contact:** Eunice Reichman, Director of Personnel. **Description:** St. Louis office of the social service agency.

LUTHERAN ALTENHEIM SOCIETY OF MISSOURI
1265 McLaran, St. Louis MO 63147. 314/388-2867. **Contact:** David Piehl, Personnel Director. **Description:** A St. Louis non-profit home and service agency for the aged.

MISSOURI GOODWILL INDUSTRIES INC.
4140 Forest Park Boulevard, St. Louis MO 63108. 314/371-6320, ext. 212. **Contact:** Ms. Sheila N. Bouie-Sledge, Human Resources Director. **Description:** Provides vocational rehabilitation services for cleints needing evaluation, work adjustment, business career training, computer training and placement services. **Employees:** 300+. **Common positions:** Counselor (Vocational Rehabilitation); Instructor/Trainer/Teacher; Case Manager; Textile/Processing Manager; Retail Store Manager. **Educational background sought:** Social Services. **Special programs:** Training programs and internships. **Benefits:** medical, dental, and life insurance; tuition assistance; disability coverage; employee discounts; savings plan. **Corporate headquarters:** This location.

YMCA OF GREATER ST. LOUIS
1528 Locust Street, St. Louis MO 63103. 314/436-1177. **Contact:** Jean Hubler, Director of Personnel. **Description:** One of the nation's largest and most comprehensive service organizations. The YMCA provides health and fitness; social and personal development; sports and recreation; education and career development; and camps and conferences to children, youths, adults, the elderly, families, the disabled, refugees and foreign nationals, YMCA residents, and community residents through a broad range of specific programs. An equal opportunity employer. **Corporate headquarters:** Chicago, IL. International. **Common positions:** Branch Manager; Program Director; Child Care Directors; Physical Education Director. **Educational backgrounds sought:** Liberal Arts; Recreational Education; Physical Education; Health/Fitness; Psychology; Education; Child Development; Sociology; Business Administration. **Benefits:** medical insurance; dental insurance; pension plan; life insurance; tuition assistance; disability coverage. **Operations at this facility:** administration.

Additional large employers: 250+

INDIVIDUAL AND FAMILY SOCIAL SERVICES

Maritz Inc
1375 N Highway Dr, Fenton MO 63099-0001. 314/827-4000. Employs: 1,000+.

Depaul Health Center Rehab
12303 De Paul Dr, Bridgeton MO 63044-2512. 314/344-6460. Employs: 500-999.

American Red Cross
10195 Corporate Square Dr, St. Louis MO 63132-2990. 314/658-2000. Employs: 250-499.

Salvation Army
3949 Forest Park Ave, St. Louis MO 63108-3211. 314/535-0057. Employs: 500-999.

JOB TRAINING AND VOCATIONAL REHABILITATION SERVICES

Industrial Aid Inc
4417 Oleatha Ave, St. Louis MO 63116-1717. 314/773-3200.
Employs: 250-499.

Project Workshop Inc
6301 Manchester Ave, St. Louis MO 63139-3034. 314/647-3300.
Employs: 250-499.

RELIGIOUS ORGANIZATIONS

Ball World Missions
8955 Lemay Ferry Rd, Hillsboro MO 63050. 314/789-4368.
Employs: 250-499.

Small to medium sized employers: 50-249

LIBRARIES

Maplewood Public Library
7601 Manchester Rd, St. Louis MO 63143-2811. 314/781-2174.
Employs: 50-99.

INDIVIDUAL AND FAMILY SOCIAL SERVICES

Clayton House Healthcare
13995 Clayton Rd, Ballwin MO 63011-2918. 314/227-5070.
Employs: 100-249.

Psychc Inst At Luth Medl Ctr
2639 Miami St, St. Louis MO 63118-3929. 314/577-5774.
Employs: 50-99.

Jordan Ranken Child Rehab Ctr
10621 Ladue Rd, St. Louis MO 63141-8406. 314/993-1207.
Employs: 50-99.

Pike County Memorial Hospital
2305 Georgia St, Louisiana MO 63353-2559. 314/754-5531.
Employs: 100-249.

Miriam Foundation
501 Bacon Ave, St. Louis MO 63119-1512. 314/962-6059.
Employs: 50-99.

JOB TRAINING AND VOCATIONAL REHABILITATION SERVICES

Boone Center Inc
927 E Terra Ln, O Fallon MO 63366-2748. 314/272-6079.
Employs: 100-249.

Boone Center Workshop
1913 N 2nd St, Saint Charles MO 63301-2163. 314/946-3161.
Employs: 50-99.

Canterbury Entrprs Inc
9359 Watson Indl Pk, St. Louis MO 63126. 314/961-2949.
Employs: 50-99.

Florissant Vly Sheltered Wshp
210 St Francois St, Florissant MO 63031-5014. 314/839-1406.
Employs: 100-249.

Goodwill Inds
4140 Forest Pk Ave, St. Louis MO 63108-2809. 314/371-6320.
Employs: 100-249.

I T E Inc
4621 World Parkway Cir, St. Louis MO 63134-3115. 314/429-0866.
Employs: 100-249.

Jeffco Subcontracting Inc
2065 Pomme Rd, Arnold MO
63010-2435. 314/296-6211.
Employs: 50-99.

Lafayette Inds
179 Gaywood Dr, Ballwin MO
63021-5421. 314/227-5666.
Employs: 100-249.

Lighthouse For The Blind
10440 Trenton Ave, St. Louis MO
63132-1223. 314/423-4333.
Employs: 50-99.

Metro Employment and Rehab Svc
1727 Locust St, St. Louis MO
63103-1703. 314/241-3464.
Employs: 100-249.

Metro Employment and Rehab Svc
2545 S Hanley Rd, St. Louis MO
63144-2503. 314/647-7453.
Employs: 50-99.

Temco Inc
Rfd 2 Box 187, Marthasville MO
63357-9624. 314/433-2335.
Employs: 50-99.

Universal Sheltered Workshop
6912 W Florissant Ave, St. Louis
MO 63136-3639. 314/389-7072.
Employs: 50-99.

W A C Industries Inc
8520 Mac Kenzie Rd, St. Louis
MO 63123-3433. 314/631-8300.
Employs: 100-249.

Worth Inds Inc
3501 N Broadway, St. Louis MO
63147-3415. 314/231-6600.
Employs: 50-99.

Barnard Career Mgmt Assocs
2300 Westport Plaza Dr, St. Louis
MO 63146-3213. 314/469-3030.
Employs: 50-99.

Career Dimensions Inc
7777 Bonhomme Ave, St. Louis
MO 63105-1911. 314/725-3818.
Employs: 50-99.

Interview Workshop
PO Box 31542, St. Louis MO
63131-0542. 314/569-1169.
Employs: 50-99.

Network Career Development
201 S Central Ave, St. Louis MO
63105-3517. 314/721-1143.
Employs: 50-99.

Florissant Vly Sheltered
10746 Trenton Ave, St. Louis MO
63132-1026. 314/428-2222.
Employs: 100-249.

Lighthouse For The Blind
10616 Trenton Ave, St. Louis MO
63132-1209. 314/423-7955.
Employs: 50-99.

CHILD DAY CARE SERVICES

Patterson Schls Tree Hvn Day
363 Jungermann Rd, Saint Peters
MO 63376-5351. 314/447-2611.
Employs: 50-99.

RESIDENTIAL CARE

Memorial Home
3625 Magnolia Ave, St. Louis MO
63110-4048. 314/771-2990.
Employs: 50-99.

Sunset Nursing and Retirement Homes
400 W Park Ave, Union MO
63084-1140. 314/583-2252.
Employs: 50-99.

North American Healthcare Ctr
620 W Bridgeport St, White Hall
IL 62092-1001. 217/374-2144.
Employs: 50-99.

Randolph County Nursing Home
310 W Belmont St, Sparta IL
62286-1709. 618/443-4351.
Employs: 50-99.

St Louis Altenheim
5408 S Broadway, St. Louis MO
63111-2023. 314/353-7225.
Employs: 50-99.

SOCIAL SERVICES

Sheltered Workshops Inc
1902 W Main St, Washington MO
63090-1006. 314/239-2744.
Employs: 50-99.

Specialized Services Inc
110 Northgate Indus Dr, Granite City IL 62040. 618/876-4145.
Employs: 100-249.

BUSINESS ASSOCIATIONS

American Optometric Assn
243 N Lindbergh Blvd, St. Louis MO 63141-7851. 314/991-4100.
Employs: 100-249.

CIVIC, SOCIAL AND FRATERNAL ASSOCIATIONS

American Soybean Assn
777 Craig Rd, St. Louis MO
63141-7114. 314/432-1600.
Employs: 50-99.

RELIGIOUS ORGANIZATIONS

Il S Conf United Chch Christ
1312 Broadway, Highland IL
62249-1942. 618/654-2125.
Employs: 100-249.

Missionary Assoc Mary
15 S 59th St, Belleville IL 62223-4647. 618/233-2238. Employs: 50-99.

Archdiocese St Louis Cath Ctr
4445 Lindell Blvd, St. Louis MO
63108-2403. 314/533-1887.
Employs: 100-249.

Shrine Of Our Lady Of Snows
9500 W Illinois Highway 15,
Belleville IL 62223. 618/397-6700.
Employs: 50-99.

CHEMICAL AND ENVIRONMENTAL

Historically, the chemicals industry has been a cyclical one and is currently on the low end of its cycle. In response, the industry has diversified, imposed tight cost controls, and streamlined operations. Look for a growing number of firms to move into the environmental field. Jobseekers with chemical engineering experience will benefit from the current shortage of workers in the industry.

AMERICAN INGREDIENTS COMPANY
3947 Broadway, Kansas City MO 64111. 816/561-9050. **Contact:** Mary Barnett, Personnel. **Description:** A manufacturer and processor of specialty chemicals and food ingredients. **Corporate headquarters:** This location.

Common positions: Accountant; Chemist; Computer Programmer; Credit Manager; Customer Service Representative; Chemical Engineer; Industrial Engineer; Financial Analyst; Food Technologist; General Manager; Operations/ Production Manager; Marketing Specialist; Quality Control Supervisor; Sales Representative; Systems Analyst. **Educational backgrounds sought:** Accounting; Business Administration; Chemistry; Computer Science; Finance; Marketing. **Benefits:** medical insurance; pension plan; life insurance; tuition assistance; disability coverage; savings plan. **Operations at this facility:** research and development; administration; sales

BROD-DUGAN COMPANY
2145 Schuetz Road, St. Louis MO 63146. 314/567-1111. **Contact:** Dale Hahn, Controller/Office Manager. **Description:** Manufacturers and retailers of paints, varnish, wallpaper, and allied products. **Employees:** 100+.

DOW CHEMICAL USA
12647 Olive Boulevard, St. Louis MO 63141. **Contact:** Personnel. For employment information contact 2020 Dow Center, Midland, MI 48674. **Description:** Wholesalers of chemicals and allied products as part of the international chemicals and manufacturing firm. **Corporate headquarters:** Midland, MI. **Listed on:** New York Stock Exchange. **Employees:** 100+.

GROW GROUP INC.
U.S. PAINT DIVISION
831 South 21st Street, St. Louis MO 63103. 314/621-0525. **Contact:** Personnel Department. **Description:** Manufacturers of a wide variety of industrial finishes.

HARCROS PIGMENTS INC.
2001 Lynch Avenue, East St. Louis IL 62205. 618/271-4700. **Contact:** Dave Goeddel, Personnel Director. **Description:** Manufacture synthetic, natural and magnetic iron oxides, colors, extender pigments, and barytes.

LAROUCHE INDUSTRIES, INC.
P.O. Box 140, Crystal City MO 63019. 314/937-1100. **Contact:** Personnel Department. **Description:** Manufacturers of both solid and liquid nitrogen fertilizers.

LEVER BROTHERS COMPANY
1400 North Pennsylvania Avenue, St. Louis MO 63133. 314/863-5655. **Contact:** Beth Senn, Personnel Director. **Description:** A St. Louis manufacturer of soaps and detergents.

MONSANTO
800 North Lindbergh Boulevard, St. Louis MO 63167. 314/694-1000. **Contact:** Milton Wade, Personnel Director. **Description:** A St. Louis company engaged in the manufacture of chemicals, plastics, agricultural products, man-made fibers, specialized electronic materials and process control systems. **Corporate headquarters:** This location. **Employees:** 10,000 managers and professionals throughout the United States. **Common positions:** Accountant; Attorney; Biochemist; Biologist; Chemist; Computer Programmer; Agricultural Engineer; Biomedical Engineer; Chemical Engineer; Electrical Engineer; Industrial Engineer; Mechanical Engineer; Financial Analyst; Food Technologist;

Technologist; Personnel and Labor Relations Specialist; Physicist; Sales Representative; Systems Analyst; Genetic Engineer; Micro Biologist. **Educational backgrounds sought:** Accounting; Biology; Business Administration; Chemistry; Computer Science; Economics; Engineering; Finance; Liberal Arts; Marketing; Plant Physiology. **Benefits:** medical, dental, and life insurance; pension plan; tuition assistance; disability coverage; profit sharing; savings plan. **Operations at this facility:** regional headquarters; divisional headquarters; administration. **Listed on:** New York Stock Exchange.

BENJAMIN MOORE & COMPANY
P.O. Box 13290, Soulard Station, St. Louis MO 63157. 314/231-4060. **Contact:** Personnel Department. **Description:** A St. Louis company engaged in the manufacture of paints and allied products.

PETROLITE CORPORATION
369 Marshall Avenue, St. Louis MO 63119. 314/961-3500. **Contact:** Personnel Department. **Description:** Manufactures demulsifying, desalting, corrosion and fouling preventive chemicals.

QUAKER STATE CORPORATION
AND FREEDOM FREIGHTWAYS INC.
9060 Latty Avenue, St. Louis MO 63134. 314/521-3900. **Contact:** Marge Ritchie, Personnel Director. **Description:** Manufacturers of lubricants, chemicals and additives. Wholesaler and distributor of lubricants, additives and accessories for the automotive aftermarket.

SIGMA CHEMICAL COMPANY
P.O. Box 14508, St. Louis MO 63178. 314/771-5765. **Contact:** Don Zundel, Personnel. **Description:** Manufacture biochemicals, clinical laboratory reagents, and organic chemicals.

U.S. PAINT CORP.
831 South 21st Street, St. Louis MO 63103. 314/621-0525. **Contact:** Mary Rabbitt Smith, Executive Administrator. **Description:** Manufacturers of a wide variety of industrial finishes.

Additional large employers: 250+

INDUSTRIAL INORGANIC CHEMICALS

Monsanto Chemical Co
8201 Idaho Ave, St. Louis MO 63111-4039. 314/577-1600. Employs: 250-499.

Monsanto Enviro Chem Syst Inc
145225 S Outer Rd Box 1454, St. Louis MO 63188-1454. 314/275-5744. Employs: 500-999.

INDUSTRIAL ORGANIC CHEMICALS

Mallinckrodt Specialty Chem Co
675 McDonnell Blvd, St. Louis MO 63134. 314/895-2000. Employs: 1,000+.

Monsanto Co
500 Monsanto Ave, E St. Louis IL 62206-1137. 618/271-5835. Employs: 500-999.

Monsanto Co/J F Queeny Plt
1700 S 2nd St, St. Louis MO
63104-4610. 314/622-1400.
Employs: 250-499.

Petrolite Corp
100 N Broadway, St. Louis MO
63102-2728. 314/241-8370.
Employs: 500-999.

CHEMICALS AND CHEMICAL PREPARATIONS

Ethyl Petroleum Additives Inc
Monsanto Ave, E St. Louis IL
62201. 618/274-4000. Employs: 250-499.

Storz Instrument Company
3365 Tree Court Industrial Pk, St. Louis MO 63122-6615. 314/225-7600. Employs: 500-999.

Additional small to medium sized employers: 50-249

ALKALIES AND CHLORINE

Chemtech Inds Inc
1655 Des Peres, St. Louis MO
63131-1832. 314/966-9900.
Employs: 100-249.

INDUSTRIAL GASES

Acetylene Gas Co
3500 Bernard, St. Louis MO
63103. 314/533-3100. Employs: 50-99.

INORGANIC PIGMENTS

Columbian Chemicals Co
303 E Hoffmeister Ave, St. Louis MO 63125-2100. 314/544-1400.
Employs: 50-99.

Columbian Chemicals Co
433 E Arlee Av, St. Louis MO
63125-2809. 404/951-5570.
Employs: 50-99.

Rheox Inc
5548 Manchester Ave, St. Louis MO 63110-1919. 314/644-9840.
Employs: 50-99.

INDUSTRIAL INORGANIC CHEMICALS

Ireco
Hwy 79 & Cnty D, Louisiana MO
63353. 314/754-4501. Employs: 50-99.

PAINTS, VARNISHES, LACQUERS, ENAMELS AND ALLIED PRODUCTS

Dennis Chemical Co
2700 Papin St, St. Louis MO
63103-3042. 314/771-1800.
Employs: 50-99.

L H B Industries
8833 Fleischer Pl, St. Louis MO
63134-1000. 314/522-3141.
Employs: 50-99.

Masterchem Inds
3135 Hwy M, Imperial MO 63052-2834. 314/942-2510. Employs: 50-99.

Sherwin-Williams Paints
3020 Madison Av, Granite City IL
62040-3618. 618/452-6008.
Employs: 50-99.

St Louis Paint Mfg Co
2500 Ohio Ave, St. Louis MO
63104-2310. 314/776-7600.
Employs: 50-99.

INDUSTRIAL ORGANIC CHEMICALS

Aqualon Co
Hwy 79 At Cnty Rd, Louisiana MO 63353. 314/754-6211. Employs: 100-249.

PESTICIDES AND AGRICULTURAL CHEMICALS

Whitmire Research Labs Inc
3568 Tree Ct Indl Blvd, St. Louis MO 63122-6620. 314/225-5371. Employs: 50-99.

ADHESIVES AND SEALANTS

Carboline Company
350 Hanley Ind Ct, St. Louis MO 63144-1510. 314/644-1000. Employs: 100-249.

Eschem Incorporated
8 Farish St, Granite City IL 62040. 618/452-5550. Employs: 50-99.

United Technologies
1218 Central Indl Dr, St. Louis MO 63110. 314/577-1100. Employs: 100-249.

PRINTING INK

CZ Inks
4150 Carr Lane Ct, St. Louis MO 63119-2128. 314/645-3333. Employs: 50-99.

Midland Color
5215 Manchester Ave, St. Louis MO 63110-2015. 314/647-4850. Employs: 50-99.

CHEMICALS AND CHEMICAL PREPARATIONS

A B B Combustion Engrg Nuclear
Hwy P, Hematite MO 63047. 314/937-4691. Employs: 100-249.

Applause Academic & Fine Arts
225 S High St, Belleville IL 62220-2114. 618/233-0499. Employs: 50-99.

Bondex International Inc
3616 Scarlet Oak Blvd, St. Louis MO 63122-6606. 314/225-5001. Employs: 50-99.

Ethyl Petroleum Additive Inc
20 S 4th St, St. Louis MO 63102-1809. 314/421-3930. Employs: 50-99.

Western Lithotech
3433 Tree Court Indl Blvd, St. Louis MO 63122. 314/225-5031. Employs: 100-249.

For more information on career opportunities in the chemical and environmental industries:

Associations

AMERICAN CHEMICAL SOCIETY
Career Services, 1155 16th Street NW, Washington DC 20036. 202/872-4600.

AMERICAN INSTITUTE OF CHEMICAL ENGINEERING
345 East 47th Street, New York NY 10017. 212/705-7338.

AMERICAN INSTITUTE OF CHEMISTS
7315 Wisconsin Avenue, Bethesda MD 20814. 301/652-2447.

ASSOCIATION OF STATE & INTERSTATE WATER POLLUTION CONTROL ADMINISTRATORS
750 First Street NE, Suite 910, Washington DC 20002. 202/898-0905.

CHEMICAL MANUFACTURERS ASSOCIATION
2501 M Street, Washington DC 20037. 202/887-1100.

CHEMICAL MARKETING RESEARCH ASSOCIATION
60 Bay Street, Staten Island NY 10301. 718/876-8800.

WATER POLLUTION CONTROL FEDERATION
601 Wythe Street, Alexandria VA 22314. 703/684-2400.

Directories

CHEMICAL INDUSTRY DIRECTORY
State Mutual Book and Periodical Service, 521 Fifth Avenue, New York NY 10175. 212/682-5844.

COLLEGES AND UNIVERSITIES/EDUCATION

Job prospects for college faculty will increase at average speed during the '90s. Most openings will result from retirements. The best prospects are in business, engineering, health sciences, physical sciences, and mathematics. Among kindergarten and elementary school teachers, the best opportunities await those with training in special education. Among high school teachers, opportunities will increase rapidly. Increased teacher involvement and higher salaries will attract new applicants.

BELLEVILLE AREA COLLEGE
2500 Carlyle Road, Belleville IL 62221. 618/235-2700, ext. 255. **Contact:** Larry Friederich, Director of Personnel. **Description:** A public, two-year community college located in the St. Louis area. **Benefits:** medical insurance; pension plan; life insurance, tuition assistance; disability coverage; daycare assistance; employee discounts; savings plan. **Corporate headquarters:** This location.

CENTRAL INSTITUTE FOR THE DEAF
818 South Euclid, St. Louis MO 63110. 314/652-3200. **Contact:** Al Farron, Facilities Manager. **Description:** A specialized educational agency. **Operations at this facility:** An elementary school for the deaf, speech and hearing clinics, and research. **Employees:** 100.

CENTRAL MISSOURI STATE UNIVERSITY
Human Resources Office, Administration 190, Warrensburg MO 64093. 816/543-4255. **Contact:** Human Resources Department. **Description:** A state university.

CONCORDIA SEMINARY
801 DeMun Avenue, St. Louis MO 63105. 314/721-5934. **Contact:** Mr. Marvin Miller, V.P. for Business Services. **Description:** A four-year St. Louis seminary college which also offers a variety of graduate programs in the field of religion.

COVENANT THEOLOGICAL SEMINARY
12330 Conway Road, St. Louis MO 63141. 314/434-4044. **Contact:** Richard Green, Comptroller. **Description:** A St. Louis institute of religious training.

EAST CENTRAL COLLEGE
P.O. Box 529, Union MO 63084. 314/583-5193. **Contact:** Richard Bertrees, Dean of Financial Affairs. **Description:** A St. Louis-area junior college. **Employees:** 100+.

EASTERN ILLINOIS UNIVERSITY
Room 205, Old Main Building, Charleston IL 61920. 217/581-3463. **Contact:** Personnel Department. **Description:** A university.

FONTBONNE COLLEGE
6800 Wydown Boulevard, St. Louis MO 63105. 314/862-3456. **Contact:** Denise Keller, Personnel Department. **Description:** A four-year liberal arts college. **Employees:** 200.

JEFFERSON COUNTY JUNIOR COLLEGE DISTRICT
1000 Viking Drive, Hillsboro MO 63050. 314/789-3951. **Contact:** President's Office. **Description:** A two-year junior college.

KENRICK GLENNON SEMINARY
5200 Glennon Drive, St. Louis MO 63119. 314/644-0266. **Contact:** Mr. W. Matula, Personnel. **Description:** A men's seminary specializing a in four-year college program and a five-year graduate program towards priesthood.

LEWIS & CLARK COMMUNITY COLLEGE
5800 Godfrey Road, Godfrey IL 62035. 618/466-3411. **Contact:** Dr. Dale Chapman, V.P. of Administration and Finance. **Description:** A two-year junior college.

LINDENWOOD COLLEGE
209 South Kingshighway, St. Charles MO 63301. 314/949-2000. **Contact:** Adranna Stapleton, Personnel Director. **Description:** A St. Louis-area institution of higher learning. **Common positions:** Accountant; Administrator; Student Services Worker; Blue-Collar Worker/Supervisor; Computer Programmer; Purchasing Agent. **Educational backgrounds sought:** Accounting; Business Administration; Communications. **Benefits:** medical, dental, and life insurance; pension plan; tuition assistance; disability coverage; employee discounts; savings plan. **Corporate headquarters:** This location. **Operations at this facility:** education.

MARYVILLE UNIVERSITY
13550 Conway Road, St. Louis MO 63141-7299. 314/576-9300. **Contact:** Diana Dierberg, Director of Human Resources. **Description:** A four-year St. Louis college with 47 fields of study and two masters programs.

McKENDREE COLLEGE
701 College Road, Lebanon IL 62254. 618/537-4481. **Contact:** Mary Ann Newcomb, Personnel Director. **Description:** A St. Louis educational institution with 28 academic majors and an enrollment of over 1,000.

MISSOURI BAPTIST COLLEGE
12542 Conway Road, St. Louis MO 63141. 314/434-1115. **Contact:** Ken Revenaugh, Business Manager. **Description:** A four-year St. Louis Baptist institution of learning with an enrollment of approximately 1,000.

NORTHWEST MISSOURI STATE UNIVERSITY
800 University Dr., Maryville MO 64468. 816/562-1212. **Contact:** Personnel Department. **Description:** A state university.

SOUTHEAST MISSOURI STATE UNIVERSITY
1 University Plaza, Cape Girardeau MO 63701. 314/651-2206. **Contact:** Personnel Services. **Description:** A state university.

SOUTHERN ILLINOIS UNIVERSITY AT CARBONDALE
Carbondale IL 62901. 618/453-2121. **Contact:** Personnel Services. **Description:** A university.

SOUTHERN ILLINOIS UNIVERSITY AT EDWARDSVILLE
Box 1222, Edwardsville IL 62026. 618/692-2000. **Contact:** Personnel Services. **Description:** A state university offering several graduate programs as well as a four-year bachelor's degree program.

SOUTHERN MISSOURI STATE UNIVERSITY
901 South National Avenue, Springfield MO 65804. 417/836-5000. **Contact:** Personnel Department. **Description:** A state university.

ST. LOUIS CHRISTIAN COLLEGE
1360 Grandview Drive, Florissant MO 63033. 314/837-6777. **Contact:** Personnel Department. **Description:** A St. Louis institution of higher learning.

ST. LOUIS COLLEGE OF PHARMACY
4588 Parkview Place, St. Louis MO 63110. 314/367-8700. **Contact:** College Dean for faculty appointments, or Personnel Director for staff appointments. **Description:** A St. Louis college of pharmaceutical study. Founded in 1864. Degrees offered are Bachelor of Science in Pharmacy, Doctor of Pharmacy, and Master of Science in Pharmacy Administration. **Common positions:** College Professors and Instructors. **Educational backgrounds sought:** Biology; Chemistry; Communications; Liberal Arts; Mathematics; Physics; Pharmacy. **Benefits:** medical insurance; life insurance; disability coverage; fully vested retirement plan; tuition remission. This is a private independent college.

ST. LOUIS COMMUNITY COLLEGE
300 South Broadway, St. Louis MO 63102. 314/539-5000. **Contact:** Personnel Director. **Description:** Central offices of the St. Louis junior college system. Area campuses include: Forest Park; Meramec; Florissant Valley.

ST. LOUIS CONSERVATORY & SCHOOLS FOR THE ARTS
560 Trinity, St. Louis MO 63130. 314/863-3033. **Contact:** Susan Hagens, Personnel Director. **Description:** A St. Louis educational institution, with an emphasis on the study of music and all performing arts. **Common positions:** Accountant; Administrator. **Educational backgrounds sought:** Liberal Arts.

UNIVERSITY OF MISSOURI-COLUMBIA
201 South 7th Street, 130 Heinkel Building, Columbia MO 65211. 314/882-7976. **Contact:** Jamie Baker, Manager, Human Resources. **Description:** A university. **Common positions:** Accountant; Architect; Biochemist; Computer Programmer; Architectural Engineer; Department Manager; Marketing Specialist; Personnel and Labor Relations Specialist; Public Relations Specialist; Statistician; Systems Analyst; Technical Writer/Editor. **Educational backgrounds sought:** Accounting; Biology; Chemistry; Computer Science; Finance; Marketing. **Special programs:** Internships. **Benefits:** medical insurance; dental insurance; pension plan; life insurance; tuition assistance; disability coverage; employee discounts. **Corporate headquarters:** This location. **Operations at this facility:** research and development; administration; service. **Employees:** 11,000 full and part-time (approximately). **Projected hires for the next 12 months:** 200-300.

UNIVERSITY OF MISSOURI/ST. LOUIS
8001 Natural Bridge Road, St. Louis MO 63121. 314/553-5804. **Contact:** Personnel Department. **Description:** A university.

WASHINGTON UNIVERSITY
One Brookings Drive, St. Louis MO 63130. 314/935-5990. **Contact:** Personnel Director. **Description:** A university.

WEBSTER UNIVERSITY
470 East Lockwood Avenue, St. Louis MO 63119. 314/968-6960. **Contact:** Personnel Department. **Description:** A St. Louis university.

Additional large employers: 250+

ELEMENTARY AND SECONDARY SCHOOLS

Cahokia School District 187
1700 Jerome Lane, E St. Louis IL 62206-2329. 618/332-3700.
Employs: 250-499.

Washington School District
PO Box 357, Washington MO 63090-0357. 314/239-2727.
Employs: 250-499.

Pattonville School District R3
115 Harding Ave, Maryland Hts MO 63043-2644. 314/298-4502.
Employs: 250-499.

COLLEGES, UNIVERSITIES AND PROFESSIONAL SCHOOLS

Cardinal Glennon College
5200 Glennon Dr, St. Louis MO 63119-4330. 314/644-0266.
Employs: 250-499.

Parks College Of St Louis University
Falling Springs Rd, E St. Louis IL 62206. 618/337-7500. Employs: 250-499.

Deaconess Col Of Nursing
6150 Oakland Avenue, St. Louis MO 63139-3215. 314/768-3044. Employs: 250-499.

Greenville College
315 East College, Greenville IL 62246-1145. 618/664-1840. Employs: 250-499.

Jewish Hosp School Med Tech
216 S King's Highway, St. Louis MO 63110. 314/454-7188. Employs: 250-499.

St Louis Col Of Pharmacy
4588 Parkview Place, St. Louis MO 63110-1029. 314/367-8700. Employs: 250-499.

St Louis Rabbinical College
1004 Wild Cherry Ln, St. Louis MO 63130-2725. 314/727-1379. Employs: 250-499.

St Louis University
221 North Grand Boulevard, St. Louis MO 63103-2006. 314/658-2222. Employs: 250-499.

JUNIOR COLLEGES AND TECHNICAL INSTITUTES

Acad Of Beauty Inc
5400 W Main Street, Belleville IL 62223-4735. 618/234-4398. Employs: 250-499.

Barnes Hosp School Of Nursing
416 South Kingshighway, St. Louis MO 63110-1014. 314/3625225. Employs: 250-499.

Basic Inst Of Tech
4455 Chippewa, St. Louis MO 63116-1608. 314/771-1200. Employs: 250-499.

Belleville Area College
2500 Carlyle Road, Belleville IL 62221-7104. 618/235-2700. Employs: 250-499.

Florissant Valley Comm College
3400 Pershall Rd, St. Louis MO 63135-1408. 314/595-4200. Employs: 500-999.

Forest Park Community College
5600 Oakland Ave, St. Louis MO 63110-1316. 314/644-9100. Employs: 250-499.

Jefferson College
P O Box 1000, Hillsboro MO 63050-1000. 314/789-3951. Employs: 250-499.

Jewish Hosp School Of Nursing
306 South Kingshighway Blvd, St. Louis MO 63110-1028. 314/454-8686. Employs: 250-499.

Mo Baptist Hosp School Of Nursing
3015 N Ballas Road, St. Louis MO 63131-2317. 314/569-5193. Employs: 250-499.

Ranken Tech Inst
4431 Finney Avenue, St. Louis MO 63113-2811. 314/371-0236. Employs: 250-499.

St Louis Community College-Meramec
11333 Big Bend Blvd, St. Louis MO 63122-5720. 314/966-7500. Employs: 250-499.

St Louis Comm Col Forest Park
5600 Oakland Avenue, St. Louis MO 63110-1316. 314/539-5300. Employs: 250-499.

State Comm Col East St Louis
601 James R Thompson Blvd, E St. Louis IL 62201-1129. 618/274-6666. Employs: 250-499.

Vatterott Ed Ctrs
39-25 39 Industrial Drive, Saint Ann MO 63074. 314/428-5900. Employs: 250-499.

Additional small to medium sized employers: 50-249

ELEMENTARY AND SECONDARY SCHOOLS

Althoff Catholic High School
5401 W Main St, Belleville IL 62223-4734. 618/235-1100. Employs: 50-99.

Alton Senior High Sch
2200 College Av, Alton IL 62002-4602. 618/474-2700. Employs: 100-249.

E Alton Wood Riv Cmty High
777 N Wood River Av, Wood River IL 62095-1227. 618/254-3151. Employs: 50-99.

Edwardsville High School
145 West St, Edwardsville IL 62025-1467. 618/656-7100. Employs: 100-249.

Granite Cy Senior High School
3101 Madison Av, Granite City IL 62040-3620. 618/451-2666. Employs: 100-249.

Highland High School
1500 Troxler La Rt 1, Highland IL 62249-9801. 618/654-2106. Employs: 50-99.

Jefferson Middle Sch
2660 Zumbehl Rd, Saint Charles MO 63301-1134. 314/723-4934. Employs: 50-99.

North Middle School
210 Virgil St, O Fallon MO 63366-2644. 314/272-6620. Employs: 50-99.

Saint Charles High School
725 N Kingshighway, Saint Charles MO 63301-1722. 314/724-3940. Employs: 50-99.

St Charles W High School Library
3601 Droste Rd, Saint Charles MO 63301-1125. 314/723-7900. Employs: 50-99.

T L Hardin Middle School
1950 Elm St, Saint Charles MO 63301-1754. 314/724-7217. Employs: 50-99.

Bishop Dubourg High School
5850 Eichelberger St, St. Louis MO 63109-3454. 314/832-3030. Employs: 50-99.

Chaminade College Prep School
425 S Lindbergh Blvd, St. Louis MO 63131-2729. 314/993-4400. Employs: 50-99.

Christian Brothers College High School
6501 Clayton Rd, St. Louis MO 63117-1705. 314/721-1200. Employs: 50-99.

St Joseph Academy School
2307 S Lindbergh Blvd, St. Louis MO 63131-3505. 314/965-7205. Employs: 50-99.

St Thomas Aquinas Mercy High
845 Dunn Rd, Florissant MO 63031-8203. 314/837-1144. Employs: 50-99.

Vianney High School
1311 S Kirkwood Rd, St. Louis MO 63122-7226. 314/965-4853. Employs: 50-99.

The Principia School
13201 Clayton Rd, St. Louis MO 63131-1002. 314/434-2100. Employs: 50-99.

Ashland Elementary School
3921 N Newstead Ave, St. Louis MO 63115-2748. 314/385-4767. Employs: 50-99.

Becky-David Primary School
1155 Jungs Station Rd, Saint Charles MO 63303. 314/447-4232. Employs: 50-99.

Central Elementary School
4525 Central School Rd, Saint Charles MO 63304-7113. 314/447-5888. Employs: 50-99.

Hawthorn Elementary School
166 Boone Hills Dr, Saint Peters MO 63376-2431. 314/447-7595. Employs: 50-99.

Sixth Street Elementary School
533 N 6th St, Mascoutah IL 62258-1169. 618/566-2152. Employs: 50-99.

Vineland Elementary School
650 Vineland Rd, De Soto MO 63020. 314/586-8311. Employs: 50-99.

Wren Hollow Elementary School
655 Wren Ave, Ballwin MO 63021-6663. 314/227-0453. Employs: 50-99.

Brittany Woods Junior High School
8125 Groby Rd, St. Louis MO 63130-2017. 314/997-6570. Employs: 50-99.

Central Junior High School
471 N Woods Mill Rd, Chesterfield MO 63017-3327. 314/851-8265. Employs: 50-99.

Crestview Junior High School
16025 Clayton Rd, Ballwin MO 63011-2162. 314/227-3220. Employs: 50-99.

King Junior High School
70th & Ridge, E St. Louis IL 62203. 618/398-3166. Employs: 50-99.

Ladue Junior High School
9701 Conway Rd, St. Louis MO 63124-1646. 314/993-3900. Employs: 50-99.

Pattonville Hts Middle School
195 Fee Fee Rd, Maryland Hts MO 63043-2709. 314/298-4440. Employs: 50-99.

Riverview Gardens Middle School
9800 Schoolview Drive, St. Louis MO 63137. 314/869-2505. Employs: 50-99.

Robert H Sperreng Middle School
12111 Tesson Ferry Rd, St. Louis MO 63128-1728. 314/849 0123. Employs: 50-99.

Robert W Barnwell Junior High School
1035 Jungs Station Rd, Saint Charles MO 63303. 314/447-3340. Employs: 50-99.

South Middle School
300 Knaust Rd, Saint Peters MO 63376-1716. 314/272-6620. Employs: 50-99.

West Junior High School
2312 Baxter Rd, Chesterfield MO 63017-7721. 314/391-4750. Employs: 50-99.

Affton Senior High School
8309 MacKenzie Rd, St. Louis MO 63123-3455. 314/638-6330. Employs: 50-99.

Clayton High School
1 Mark Twain Cir, St. Louis MO 63105-1613. 314/726-2575. Employs: 50-99.

De Soto Senior High School
731 Amvets Dr, De Soto MO 63020-1013. 314/586-3347. Employs: 50-99.

East Lincoln Senior High School
1211 Bond Ave, E St. Louis IL 62201-2713. 618/583-8405. Employs: 50-99.

East St Louis Senior High School
4901 State St, E St. Louis IL 62205-1356. 618/583-8400. Employs: 100-249.

Eureka Senior High School
829 Hwy 109, Eureka MO 63025. 314/938-5350. Employs: 50-99.

Hazelwood Central High School
15875 New Halls Ferry Rd, Florissant MO 63031-1225. 314/831-7100. Employs: 100-249.

Hazelwood East High School
11300 Dunn Rd, St. Louis MO 63138-1047. 314/355-6800. Employs: 100-249.

Hillsboro Senior High School
PO Box 500, Hillsboro MO 63050. 314/789-3554. Employs: 50-99.

Horton Watkins Senior High School
1201 S Warson Rd, St. Louis MO 63124-1266. 314/993-6447. Employs: 50-99.

Jersey Community High School
801 N State St, Jerseyville IL 62052-1107. 618/498-5521. Employs: 50-99.

Lindbergh Senior High School
4900 S Lindbergh Blvd, St. Louis MO 63126-3235. 314/849-2000. Employs: 100-249.

McCluer Senior High School
1896 S New Florissant Rd, Florissant MO 63031-8311. 314/521-7432. Employs: 50-99.

Mehlville Senior High School
3200 Lemay Ferry Rd, St. Louis MO 63125-4418. 314/892-5000. Employs: 100-249.

Normandy High School
6701 Saint Charles Rock Rd, St. Louis MO 63133-1705. 314/389-8006. Employs: 100-249.

Northwest High School
2156 Russell Blvd, St. Louis MO 63104-2694. 314/385-0300. Employs: 50-99.

Oakville Senior High School
5557 Milburn Rd, St. Louis MO 63129-3514. 314/892-8800. Employs: 50-99.

Pacific Senior High School
RR 4, Pacific MO 63069-9804. 314/257-2449. Employs: 50-99.

Parkway South Senior High School
801 Hanna Rd, Ballwin MO 63021-6771. 314/394-8300. Employs: 100-249.

Pattonville High School
2497 Creve Coeur Mill Rd, Maryland Hts MO 63043-1172. 314/739-0776. Employs: 100-249.

Southwest High School
3125 S Kingshighway Blvd, St. Louis MO 63139-1107. 314/771-9906. Employs: 50-99.

Sumner High School
4248 Cottage Avenue, St. Louis MO 63113. 314/371-1048. Employs: 50-99.

Triad High School
RR 1, Saint Jacob IL 62281-9801. 618/644-5511. Employs: 50-99.

Vashon High School
3405 Bell Ave, St. Louis MO 63106-1604. 314/533-9487. Employs: 50-99.

Washington Senior High School
600 E 11th St, Washington MO 63090-4542. 314/239-4717. Employs: 50-99.

Webster Groves High School
100 Selma Ave, St. Louis MO 63119-3107. 314/961-1233. Employs: 50-99.

West Senior High School
75 W Clayton Rd, Ballwin MO 63011. 314/391-4700. Employs: 100-249.

South County Technical School
12721 W Watson Rd, St. Louis MO 63127-1324. 314/822-6604. Employs: 50-99.

Villa Duchesne Junior-Senior High School
801 S Spoede Rd, St. Louis MO 63131-2606. 314/432-2021. Employs: 50-99.

De Smet Jesuit High School
233 N New Ballas Rd, St. Louis MO 63141-7530. 314/567-3500. Employs: 50-99.

St Louis Univ High School
4970 Oakland Ave, St. Louis MO 63110-1402. 314/5310330. Employs: 50-99.

Mary Institute & Beasley School
101 N Warson Rd, St. Louis MO 63124-1326. 314/993-0472. Employs: 100-249.

St Louis Country Day School
425 N Warson Rd, St. Louis MO 63124-1332. 314/993-5100. Employs: 50-99.

Andrew's Academy
888 N Mason Rd, St. Louis MO 63141-6306. 314/878-1883. Employs: 50-99.

John Burroughs School
755 S Price Rd, St. Louis MO 63124-1866. 314/993-4040. Employs: 50-99.

United Cerebral Palsy Center
8645 Old Bonhomme Rd, St. Louis MO 63132-3901. 314/994-1600. Employs: 50-99.

Dunbar Elementary School
1415 N Garrison Ave, St. Louis MO 63106-1506. 314/533-2526. Employs: 50-99.

St Peters Elementary School
400 McMenamy Rd, Saint Peters MO 63376-1510. 314/2783211. Employs: 50-99.

Festus Elementary School
1500 Midmeadow Ln, Festus MO 63020-1544. 314/937-5720. Employs: 50-99.

Lewis & Clark Elementary School
460 McMenamy Rd, Saint Peters MO 63376-1510. 314/2783111. Employs: 50-99.

Trautwein Elementary School
5011 Ambs Rd, St. Louis MO
63128-2919. 314/892-2250.
Employs: 50-99.

Fairmount Elementary School
1725 Thoele Rd, Saint Peters MO
63376-3254. 314/447-4965.
Employs: 100-249.

Cross Keys Middle School
14205 Cougar Dr, Florissant MO
63033-1415. 314/831-2700.
Employs: 50-99.

East Junior High School
181 Coeur De Ville Dr, St. Louis
MO 63141-6602. 314/878-6414.
Employs: 50-99.

Ferguson Middle School
701 January Ave, St. Louis MO
63135-1807. 314/521-5792.
Employs: 50-99.

Hazelwood Junior High School
1605 Shackelford Rd, Florissant
MO 63031-3530. 314/837-5252.
Employs: 50-99.

Hoech Middle School
3312 Ashby Rd, Saint Ann MO
63074-3529. 314/429-3500.
Employs: 50-99.

Holman Middle School
11055 Saint Charles Rock Rd,
Saint Ann MO 63074-1509.
314/298-4438. Employs: 50-99.

Kirby Junior High School
1865 Dunn Rd, St. Louis MO
63138-1017. 314/741-4400.
Employs: 50-99.

Normandy Junior High School
7855 Natural Bridge Rd, St. Louis
MO 63121-4625. 314/389-0066.
Employs: 50-99.

South Junior High School
760 Woods Mill Rd, Ballwin MO
63011-3654. 314/227-0382.
Employs: 50-99.

Stowe Middle School
5750 Lotus Ave, St. Louis MO
63112-4020. 314/3827310.
Employs: 100-249.

Fred Hollenbeck Junior High School
4555 Central School Rd, Saint
Charles MO 63304-7113. 314/447-5605. Employs: 50-99.

Cleveland Junior Naval Academy
4352 Louisiana Ave, St. Louis MO
63111-1046. 314/832-0933.
Employs: 50-99.

Beaumont High School
2156 Russell Blvd, St. Louis MO
63104-2607. 314/771-0431.
Employs: 50-99.

Civic Memorial High School
200 School St, Bethalto IL 62010-1046. 618/377-7220. Employs: 50-99.

Mascoutah High School
1313 W Main St, Mascoutah IL
62258-1065. 618/566-8523.
Employs: 50-99.

Cahokia High School
800 Range Ln, E St. Louis IL
62206-2022. 618/332-3730.
Employs: 50-99.

Howell North High School
2549 Hackmann Rd, Saint Charles
MO 63303. 314/447-4450.
Employs: 50-99.

Riverview Gardens Senior High School
1218 Shepley Dr, St. Louis MO
63137-3505. 314/869-4700.
Employs: 50-99.

Roosevelt High School
3230 Hartford St, St. Louis MO
63118-2106. 314/776-6040.
Employs: 100-249.

Central Senior High School
369 N Woods Mill Rd, Chesterfield
MO 63017-3329. 314/851-8220.
Employs: 100-249.

Fox Senior High School
745 Jeffco Blvd, Arnold MO
63010-1432. 314/296-5210.
Employs: 50-99.

Hazelwood West Junior-Senior High School
6249 Howdershell Rd, Hazelwood
MO 63042-1119. 314/731-3333.
Employs: 100-249.

Howell High School
7001 S Hwy 94, Saint Charles MO
63304. 314/447-1122. Employs:
100-249.

Kirkwood Senior High School
801 W Essex Ave, St. Louis MO
63122-3608. 314/966-5700.
Employs: 50-99.

Lafayette Senior High School
17050 Clayton Rd, Ballwin MO
63011-1792. 314/458-0400.
Employs: 100-249.

McCluer North Senior High School
705 Waterford Dr, Florissant MO
63033-3647. 314/831-6600.
Employs: 50-99.

North Senior High School
12860 Fee Fee Rd, St. Louis MO
63146-4431. 314/851-8300.
Employs: 100-249.

South High School
650 W Mexico Rd, Saint Peters
MO 63376-1119. 314/281-1212.
Employs: 100-249.

North County Technical School
1700 Derhake Rd, Florissant MO
63033-6419. 314/839-6104.
Employs: 50-99.

Community Unit School District 007
510 W Elm St, Gillespie IL 62033-1167. 217/839-2464. Employs: 50-99.

Hillsboro School District 3
1311 Vandalia Rd, Hillsboro IL
62049-2034. 217/532-2942.
Employs: 100-249.

Litchfield Comm United District 12
1702 N State St, Litchfield IL
62056-1114. 217/324-2157.
Employs: 100-249.

Bethalto School District 8
322 East Central Street, Bethalto IL
62010-1303. 618/377-7200.
Employs: 100-249.

Meramec Valley School District R3
126 N Payne St, Pacific MO
63069-1224. 314/257-2438.
Employs: 100-249.

Belleville School District 118
105 W A St, Belleville IL 62220-1326. 618/233-2830. Employs:
100-249.

Bond County School District 2
1008 N Hena St, Greenville IL
62246-1378. 618/664-0170.
Employs: 50-99.

Carlyle Comm Unit School District 1
1701 12th St, Carlyle IL 62231-1254. 618/594-2455. Employs: 50-99.

De Soto School District 73
PO Box 579, De Soto MO 63020-0579. 314/586-8811. Employs: 100-249.

Jerseyville Comm Unit District 100
119 E Exchange St, Jerseyville IL 62052-1708. 618/498-5561. Employs: 100-249.

O'Fallon High School District 203
600 S Smiley St, O Fallon IL 62269-2316. 618/632-3507. Employs: 50-99.

Red Bud School District 132
815 Locust St, Red Bud IL 62278-1210. 618/282-3507. Employs: 50-99.

Windsor School District C 1
6208 Highway 61-67, Imperial MO 63052. 314/464-1100. Employs: 100-249.

COLLEGES, UNIVERSITIES AND PROFESSIONAL SCHOOLS

Saint Mary's College
200 N Main St, O Fallon MO 63366-2203. 314/272-6171. Employs: 100-249.

So Il Univ Of Dental
2800 College Av, Alton IL 62002-4742. 618/463-3821. Employs: 50-99.

JUNIOR COLLEGES AND TECHNICAL INSTITUTES

St Charles City Comm College
102L Compass Point Drive, Saint Charles MO 63301-4414. 314/723-1220. Employs: 100-249.

VOCATIONAL SCHOOLS

G & S Chicken Products
211 W Church St, Bowling Green MO 63334-1524. 314/324-2140. Employs: 50-99.

For more information on career opportunities in colleges and universities, and education:

Associations

AMERICAN ASSOCIATION OF SCHOOL ADMINISTRATORS
1801 North Moore Street, Arlington VA 22209. 703/528-0700.

AMERICAN FEDERATION OF TEACHERS
555 New Jersey Avenue NW, Washington DC 20001. 202/879-4400.

ASSOCIATION OF AMERICAN UNIVERSITIES
One Dupont Circle NW, Suite 730, Washington DC 20036. 202/466-5030.

COLLEGE AND UNIVERSITY PERSONNEL ASSOCIATION
1233 20th Street NW, Suite 503, Washington DC 20036. 202/429-0311.

NATIONAL ASSOCIATION OF BIOLOGY TEACHERS
11250 Roger Bacon Drive, #19, Reston VA 22090. 703/471-1134.

COMMUNICATIONS

Revenues in the domestic communications industry are expected to increase as the economy improves. Over the next few years, the globalization of private networks, innovations in broadband and radio technologies, and a steady march toward liberalized regulations will improve the prospects for the industry greatly. The short-term outlook for telecommunications equipment makers is fairly stable, with small 2-3 percent increases expected through the middle of the decade.
Unfortunately, employment in the equipment industry continues to decline due to continued mergers, new technology, and improved productivity.

AT&T NETWORK SYSTEMS
1111 Woods Mill Road, Baldwin MO 63011. 314/891-2000. **Contact:** Personnel Department. **Description:** Parent company, AT&T Communications, owns research, development, and manufacturing facilities to provide long distance telecommunications services, and to market a broad range of telecommunications and information management products in the United States and abroad. Having divested itself of its 22 local telephone companies, the firm now owns a small number of communications-related businesses that serve a worldwide marketplace. AT&T operates through two primary management sectors that support the company's operations: AT&T Communications, which provides long distance services throughout the United States and to most of the rest of the world; and AT&T Technologies, engaged in activities through a variety of susidiaries (such as AT&T Bell Laboratories and Western Electric) that offer such products as business information systems and computers, as well as a variety of consumer-oriented telephone equipment. With more than $34 billion in assets and over 370,000 employees, the firm remains one of the largest corporations in America. **Corporate headquarters:** New York, NY. **Listed on:** New York Stock Exchange. **Employees:** 2,000.

ALLTEL ILLINOIS, INC.
300 North Maplewood Street, Rantoul IL 61866. 217/892-9661. **Contact:** Julie Blodgett, Director of Personnel. **Description:** Provides telephone communications. A subsidiary of Alltel Communication.

ILLINOIS CONSOLIDATED TELEPHONE COMPANY
121 South 17th Street, Mattoon IL 61938. 217/235-3311. **Contact:** Carol O'Neill, Personnel. **Description:** Provides telephone communications.

MCI TELECOMMUNICATIONS
100 South 4th Street, St. Louis MO 63102. 314/342-8151. **Contact:** Manager/Employment. **Description:** Divisional office of a national telecommunications company. **Common positions:** Accountant; Sales Representative; Sales Manager. **Educational backgrounds sought:** Accounting; Business Administration; Economics; Finance; Marketing. **Special programs:** Training programs and internships. **Benefits:** medical, dental, and

life insurance; pension plan; tuition assistance; disability coverage; profit sharing; $25 of long-distance free. **Corporate headquarters:** Washington DC. **Parent company:** MCI Communications. **Operations at this facility:** headquarters. **Listed on:** New York Stock Exchange.

SOUTHWESTERN BELL CORPORATION
One Bell Center, Room 224, St. Louis MO 63101. 314/235-5494. **Contact:** Corporate Recruiting Manager. **Description:** SBC is a family of growing companies offering communications services and products to customers in regional, national and international markets. The corporate office is headquartered in St. Louis, Missouri, and has six principal subsidiaries, several smaller subsidiaries and corporate offices with a combined total of over 61,000 employees. **Common positions:** Computer Programmer; Analyst. **Educational backgrounds sought:** Computer Science. **Benefits:** medical, dental and life insurance; pension plan; tuition assistance; disability coverage; savings plan.

Additional large employers: 250+

TELEPHONE COMMUNICATIONS, EXCEPT RADIOTELEPHONE

AT&T
424 S Woods Mill Rd, Chesterfield MO 63017-3462. 314/275-3000. Employs: 250-499.

Southwestern Bell Telephone Co
1010 Pine St, St. Louis MO 63101-2015. 314/235-9800. Employs: 1,000+.

TELEGRAPH AND OTHER MESSAGE COMMUNICATIONS

Western Union Central Bur
13022 Hollenberg Dr, Bridgeton MO 63044-2409. 314/291-1010. Employs: 250-499.

Additional small to medium sized employers: 50-249

RADIOTELEPHONE COMMUNICATIONS

Cybertel Paging
100 Ludwig Dr, E St. Louis IL 62208-1333. 618/398-7700. Employs: 100-249.

TELEPHONE COMMUNICATIONS, EXCEPT RADIOTELEPHONE

AT&T Information Systems
400 Woods Mill Rd, Chesterfield MO 63017. 314/275-1400. Employs: 50-99.

General Telephone Co
815 Deal St, Highland IL 62249-1312. 618/654-4372. Employs: 50-99.

Illinois Bell Telephone Co
203 Goethe St, Collinsville IL 62234-3356. 618/346-6498. Employs: 50-99.

Illinois Bell Telephone Co
213 E 3D St, Alton IL 62002-6240. 618/465-9963. Employs: 50-99.

Illinois Bell Telephone Co
1805 Washington Av, Alton IL
62002-4626. 618/465-9950.
Employs: 50-99.

Allnet Communication Svc Inc
317 N 11th St, St. Louis MO
63101-1945. 314/436-4321.
Employs: 100-249.

Alton Cellular Inc
RR 1, Jerseyville IL 62052-9801.
618/498-4260. Employs: 50-99.

American Telephone Service
4251 Lindell Blvd, St. Louis MO
63108-2915. 314/533-2811.
Employs: 100-249.

Bi-State Telecommunications
4120 Geraldine Ave, St. Louis MO
63115-1209. 314/423-5776.
Employs: 100-249.

Cable and Wireless Communications Inc
101 S 11th St, St. Louis MO
63102-1100. 314/621-6100.
Employs: 100-249.

Cyber Tel Corporation
1935 Belt Way Dr, St. Louis MO
63114-5825. 314/423-6500.
Employs: 100-249.

Egyptian Telephone Co-Op Assn
1010 W Broadway, Steeleville IL
62288-1312. 618/965-3481.
Employs: 50-99.

GTE Government Systems Corp
333 Salem Pl, E St. Louis IL
62208-1341. 618/624-2013.
Employs: 100-249.

Hillsboro Telephone Company
10718 Highway 21, Hillsboro MO
63050. 314/789-5100. Employs:
50-99.

Metro Net
3308 Mayfield Ave, Alton IL
62002-3022. 618/463-4900.
Employs: 50-99.

Orchard Farm Tel Co
5065 N Hwy 94, Saint Charles MO
63301. 314/258-4450. Employs:
100-249.

Southwestern Bell
Tele Bud, Sullivan MO 63080.
314/468-3131. Employs: 50-99.

SP Telecom
400 Chesterfield Ctr, Chesterfield
MO 63017-4800. 314/537-7815.
Employs: 100-249.

Unitel Communications
263-C Lamp and Lantern Village,
Chesterfield MO 63017. 314/394-
7959. Employs: 100-249.

AT&T Company
701 Market St, St. Louis MO
63101-1850. 314/436-8900.
Employs: 100-249.

Allnet Communication Svc Inc
900 Walnut St, St. Louis MO
63102-1137. 314/421-0964.
Employs: 100-249.

Amer-I-Net Services Corp
121 N 1st St, Pacific MO 63069-
1501. 314/257-6695. Employs: 50-
99.

Comtech Network Systems Group Inc
460 Sovereign Ct # A, Ballwin MO
63011-4432. 314/256-8268.
Employs: 100-249.

ITT-USTS
720 Olive St, St. Louis MO 63101-
2338. 314/231-6300. Employs:
100-249.

LDDS
635 Maryville Centre Dr, St. Louis MO 63141-5817. 314/275-7200. Employs: 100-249.

MidAmerican Long Distance Co
11970 Borman Dr, St. Louis MO 63146-4137. 314/469-1230. Employs: 100-249.

Network Business Communications Inc
102 E Vandalia St, Edwardsville IL 62025-1782. 618/692-9372. Employs: 50-99.

US Sprint
1801 Park 270 Dr, St. Louis MO 63146-4020. 314/542-9000. Employs: 100-249.

Boston Technology Inc
1611 Des Peres Rd # 208, St. Louis MO 63131-1849. 314/436-7754. Employs: 100-249.

Nu Fone Corp
2708 Mary Ave, St. Louis MO 63144-2726. 314/963-1257. Employs: 100-249.

Access America Telemanagement
18040 Edison Ave, Chesterfield MO 63005-3702. 314/530-9500. Employs: 100-249.

Canada Wire & Cable Ltd
1515 N Warson Rd, St. Louis MO 63132-1111. 314/428-1550. Employs: 100-249.

CEI Communications
18102-P Chesterfield Airport Rd, Chesterfield MO 63005-1117. 314/532-2111. Employs: 100-249.

Circulation Development Inc
118 Centre On The Lake, Lake St Louis MO 63367. 314/625-2315. Employs: 100-249.

Communications General International
1000 Lake St Louis Blvd, Lake St Louis MO 63367. 314/625-8866. Employs: 100-249.

Datel Services Inc
126 Asilomar Ct, Ballwin MO 63021-6567. 314/391-4118. Employs: 100-249.

GTE Customer Networks
4284 N Rider Trl, Earth City MO 63045-1105. 314/298-7797. Employs: 100-249.

L & R Enterprises
8444 Florissant Rd, St. Louis MO 63121-1900. 314/521-7755. Employs: 100-249.

Lan Communications
166 Primrose Ln, Fenton MO 63026-5645. 314/349-2447. Employs: 100-249.

MCI Telecommunications Corp
9666 Olive Blvd, St. Louis MO 63132-3013. 314/872-1300. Employs: 100-249.

Octel Communications Inc
3300 S Rider Trl, Earth City MO 63045-1338. 314/344-0200. Employs: 100-249.

Republic Telcom Systems
5113 Vadil Ct, St. Louis MO 63129-3216. 314/845-2262. Employs: 100-249.

Rockwell International Telecom
720 Olive St, St. Louis MO 63101-2338. 314/621-4007. Employs: 100-249.

Rodata
Meremonte Rd, Warrenton MO 63383. 314/456-3196. Employs: 50-99.

Telecommunications Systems
93 Centre Pt, Saint Charles MO 63304. 314/441-6100. Employs: 100-249.

Telecommunications Today Inc
3930 S Old State Route 94, Saint Charles MO 63304-2836. 314/926-0060. Employs: 100-249.

Telesciences Co Systems Inc
758 Stump Ct, St. Louis MO 63131-2140. 314/966-5735. Employs: 100-249.

US Sprint Communications Co
1001 Craig Rd, St. Louis MO 63146-5277. 314/567-5336. Employs: 100-249.

Video Telecom
15477 Long Castle Forest Ct, Chesterfield MO 63017-7447. 314/530-0200. Employs: 100-249.

Videoconferencin Tech Inc
12120 Bridgeton Sq, Bridgeton MO 63044-2607. 314/344-0040. Employs: 100-249.

TELEGRAPH AND OTHER MESSAGE COMMUNICATIONS

WUI Service Corporation
314 N Broadway, St. Louis MO 63102-2035. 314/231-2492. Employs: 50-99.

COMMUNICATION SERVICES

Bush Communication Svcs
5441 Gutermuth Rd, Saint Charles MO 63304-7613. 314/949-5533. Employs: 50-99.

L & R Communications Limited
105 Boone Hills Dr, Saint Peters MO 63376-2432. 314/441-5570. Employs: 50-99.

For more information on career opportunities in communications:

Associations

COMMUNICATIONS WORKERS OF AMERICA
501 3rd Street NW, Washington DC 20001-2797. 202/434-1100.

UNITED STATES TELEPHONE ASSOCIATION
900 19th Street NW, Suite 800, Washington DC 20006. 202/835-3100.

COMPUTERS

Computer Services: Industry revenues for computer services, systems integration, consulting, and training services have been on the rise. Mergers and acquisitions of computer services firms have been an ongoing trend, and should continue. In the long-term, look for computer services firms to expand overseas, especially into Western Europe. *Equipment and Software:* The continuing effects of the long national recession have put the equipment and software industries on a bumpy road over the past few years. Layoffs at large companies like IBM, Apple, and Compaq grabbed big headlines. The biggest growth areas for U.S. firms will be in systems design, systems integration, software, and after-sales service. Over the long-term, the computer industry promises to be one of the best bets for jobseekers.

AUTOMATIC DATA PROCESSING INC.
9735 Landmark Parkway, St. Louis MO 63127. Mailed inquiries only. **Contact:** Personnel Department. **Description:** Regional office of a billion-dollar plus computer services firm providing Employer Services (payroll, tax preparation, and unemployment compensation management).

DIGITAL EQUIPMENT CORPORATION
721 Emerson Road, St. Louis MO 63141. 314/991-6400. **Contact:** Gloria Clayter, Personnel Director. **Description:** A wholesaler of commercial business equipment. Parent company designs, manufactures, sells, and services computers and associated peripheral equipment and related software and supplies. Applications and programs include: scientific research, computation, communications, education, data analysis, industrial control, time sharing, commercial data processing, graphic arts, word processing, health care, instrumentation, engineering, and simulation. **Employees:** 63,000 people in the United States and 37 foreign countries. **Corporate headquarters:** Maynard, MA. **Listed on:** New York Stock Exchange. **Employees:** 100 at this location.

NCR CORPORATION
9811 South Forty Drive, St. Louis MO 63124. 314/991-5511. **Contact:** Personnel Department. **Description:** Regional office of the national company that develops, manufactures, markets, installs and services business information processing systems for worldwide markets. Generally, company's products and services may be grouped in the following categories: general purpose computer systems, which range from small business systems to large mainframe processors; industry-specific occupational workstations, which include word-processing workstations, as well as application-specific workstations for retail, financial, manufacturing, and other markets; general purpose workstations; software at both the software and application levels; support services, which include hardware and software maintenance, consulting services, customer training, and documentation; data processing and telecommunications services, including a worldwide network of data processing centers; components,

including semiconductor products and component sub-assemblies marketed to other manufacturers; and business forms and supplies, marketed to both NCR and non-NCR users. Operates through the following divisions: Direct Marketing and Customer Support; Systemedia Group; Office Systems Division; Independent Marketing Organization; Development and Production Group; NCR Comten, Inc.; and Applied Digital Data Systems, Inc. **Corporate headquarters:** Dayton, OH. **Listed on:** New York Stock Exchange. International.

WANG LABORATORIES
1633 Des Peres Road, St. Louis MO 63131. 314/966-1200. **Contact:** Personnel Department. **Description:** A worldwide supplier of computer-based integrated information processing systems, including word, data, voice, and image processing, as well as telecommunications and networking products. Founded in 1951, the company ranks number 151 among the Fortune 500. **Corporate headquarters:** Lowell, MA. **Listed on:** American Stock Exchange.

Additional large employers: 250+

COMPUTER PERIPHERAL EQUIPMENT

General Dynamics Corp
Pierre Laclede Center, St. Louis MO 63105. 314/889-8200.
Employs: 1,000+.

COMPUTERS AND COMPUTER PERIPHERAL EQUIPMENT AND SOFTWARE

IBM Corp
1 Boatmens Plz, St. Louis MO 63101-2602. 314/554-9400.
Employs: 500-999.

Small to medium sized employers: 50-249

COMPUTER PERIPHERAL EQUIPMENT

Interface Technology Inc
1850 Borman Ct, St. Louis MO 63146-4126. 314/426-6880.
Employs: 50-99.

COMPUTERS AND COMPUTER PERIPHERAL EQUIPMENT AND SOFTWARE

Affinitec Corp
11737 Administration Dr, St. Louis MO 63146-3405. 314/569-3450.
Employs: 50-99.

Memorex Telex
11605 Lilburn Park Rd, St. Louis MO 63146-3535. 314/432-9500.
Employs: 50-99.

Hewlett-Packard Company
530 Maryville Centre Dr, St. Louis MO 63141-5825. 314/542-1500.
Employs: 100-249.

COMPUTER PROCESSING AND DATA PREPARATION AND PROCESSING SERVICES

Magna Data Service
1 S Church St Fl 2, Belleville IL 62220-2237. 618/235-6059.
Employs: 50-99.

Automated Information Inc
2628 S Big Bend Blvd, St. Louis MO 63143-2104. 314/644-4050. Employs: 100-249.

Bell Atlantic Bus Systems Svc
1880 Craigshire Rd, St. Louis MO 63146-4006. 314/434-7392. Employs: 100-249.

BT Tymnet Inc
680 Craig Rd, St. Louis MO 63141-7120. 314/569-3400. Employs: 50-99.

EKI Incorporated
145 Weldon Pkwy, Maryland Ht MO 63043-3106. 314/567-1780. Employs: 50-99.

For more information on career opportunities in the computer industry:

<u>Associations</u>

INFORMATION AND TECHNOLOGY ASSOCIATION OF AMERICA
1300 North 17th Street, Suite 300, Arlington VA 22209. 703/522-5055.

ASSOCIATION FOR COMPUTER SCIENCE
P.O. Box 19027, Sacramento CA 95819. 916/421-9149.

ASSOCIATION FOR COMPUTING MACHINERY
1515 Broadway, 17th Floor, New York NY 10036. 212/869-7440.

COMPUTER AND BUSINESS EQUIPMENT MANUFACTURERS ASSOCIATION
1250 Eye Street NW, Suite 200, Washington DC 20005. 202/737-8888.

COMPUTER AND COMMUNICATIONS INDUSTRY ASSOCIATION
666 11th Street NW, Suite 600, Washington DC 20001. 202/783-0070.

COMPUTER SOCIETY OF THE INSTITUTE OF ELECTRICAL & ELECTRONICS ENGINEERS
1730 Massachusetts Avenue NW, Washington DC 20036. 202/371-0101.

COMPUTER-AIDED MANUFACTURING INTERNATIONAL
1250 E. Copeland Road, Suite 500, Arlington TX 76011. 817/860-1654.

IEEE COMPUTER SOCIETY
1730 Massachusetts Avenue NW, Washington DC 20036-1903. 202/371-0101.

INFORMATION INDUSTRY ASSOCIATION
555 New Jersey Avenue NW, Washington DC 20001. 202/639-8260.

SEMICONDUCTOR INDUSTRY ASSOCIATION
4300 Stevens Creek Boulevard, Suite 271, San Jose CA 95129. 408/973-9973.

ELECTRICAL AND ELECTRONIC

Electrical component industry shipments are expected to grow at an annual rate of 5-7 percent through the mid-'90s. Suppliers will face a constant demand for higher performance products. The increased complexity of packaging and the interconnection of high-performance systems places a premium on compatibility among components. Jobseekers should seek out companies that can anticipate which technologies and product variants will be among industry standards.

ASCHINGER ELECTRIC COMPANY
877 Horan Drive, P.O. Box 26322, Fenton MO 63026. 314/343-1211. **Contact:** Steve Snow, Controller. **Description:** A St. Louis-area electrical contracting firm. **Employees:** over 100.

BALDOR ELECTRIC COMPANY
3560 Scarlet Oak Boulevard, St. Louis MO 63122. 314/225-5022. **Contact:** Royce Sykes, Personnel Director. **Description:** A manufacturer of electric motors and grinders. **Employees:** 300.

BALLMAN ENGINEERING
DIVISION OF MOTOR APPLIANCE
601 International Avenue, Washington MO 63090. 314/239-2772. **Contact:** Karen Bierbaum, Payroll. **Description:** St. Louis-area manufacturers of fractional horsepower electric motor equipment. **Employees:** 100.

BASLER ELECTRIC
Route 143, P.O. Box 269, Highland IL 62249. 618/654-2341. **Contact:** Marilyn A. Frey, Personnel Manager. **Description:** Manufacturers of transformers and electronic equipment. **Common positions:** Electrical Engineer; Sales Representative. **Educational backgrounds sought:** Engineering. **Special programs:** Training programs. **Benefits:** pension plan; life insurance; tuition assistance; disability coverage; Section 125 plan. **Other U.S. locations:** Corning, AR; Conway, AR; Huntingdon, TN; Taylor, TX. **Operations at this facility:** manufacturing; research and development; administration; service; sales. **Employees:** 1500.

BRASCH MANUFACTURING COMPANY INC.
11880 Dorsett Road, Maryland Heights MO 63043. 314/291-0440. **Contact:** Personnel Manager/Executive Secretary. **Description:** Manufacturers of electric duct heaters, remote control panels, electric and water steam boilers, electric storage water heaters, electrical enclosure boxes, electric unit heaters and baseboard heaters, and ASME pressure vessels. **Employees:** 100+.

BUSSMAN DIVISION/COOPER INDUSTRIES
P.O. Box 14460, St. Louis MO 63178-4460. 314/394-2877. **Contact:** Nancy Parker, Manager, Employee Relations. **Description:** A St. Louis manufacturer of electrical fuses and fuseholders. **Employees:** 2,000.

CONNECTOR CASTINGS INC.
2110 Howard Street, St. Louis MO 63106. Mailed inquiries only. **Contact:** Lisa Welborn, Personnel. **Description:** Manufactures non-ferrous grounding equipment, electrical hardware, non-ferrous castings, and non-current-carrying wiring devices.

DATAPAGE TECHNOLOGIES INTERNATIONAL INC.
222 Turners Boulevard, St. Peters MO 63376-1079. 314/278-8888. **Contact:** Patricia G. Schacher, Vice President of Human Resources. Fax: 314/278-2180. **Description:** An electronic typesetting, data processing services bureau and manufacturer of pressure sensitive bar code labels. **Common positions:** Computer Programmer; Customer Service Representative; Financial Analyst; Quality Control Supervisor; Systems Analyst. **Educational backgrounds sought:** Accounting; Business Administration; Computer Science; Marketing. **Benefits:** medical, dental, and life insurance; profit sharing; 401K; tuition assistance; disability coverage; savings plan.

EG&G VACTEC
10900 Page Boulevard, St. Louis MO 63132. 314/423-4900. **Contact:** Shirley Sweeney, Personnel Department. **Description:** A manufacturer of photocells, phototransistors, photodiodes, opto-isolators, and infra-red interrupter switches, and retro-reflective switches.

EMERSON ELECTRIC COMPANY
ALCO CONTROLS DIVISION
P.O. Box 411400, St. Louis MO 63141. 314/569-4500. **Contact:** Don Eichberger, Director/Human Resources. **Description:** Manufacturers of environmental and building systems, tools and service equipment, commercial control systems and components; industrial automation, process control and electronic systems. **Employees:** 400.

EMERSON ELECTRIC COMPANY
WORLD HEADQUARTERS
8000 West Florisant Avenue, P.O. Box 4100, St. Louis MO 63136. 314/553-2000. **Contact:** Personnel Manager. **Description:** Manufacturers of environmental and building systems, tools and service equipment, commercial control systems and components; industrial automation, process control and electronic systems. **Employees:** 5,000.

EMERSON ELECTRIC COMPANY
ELECTRONICS AND SPACE DIVISION
8100 West Florissant Avenue, St. Louis MO 63136. **Contact:** Personnel. **Description:** The Government and Defense Group (Electronics and Space Division) is engaged in the design and manufacture of electro-mechanical armaments for aircraft, ships and ground vehicles; automatic test equipment and electronic warfare equipment. Subsidiary of Emerson Electric Co., the

worldwide electronics and manufacturing firm (same location). Divisional headquarters location. **Operations at this facility:** manufacturing. **Common positions:** Accountant; Computer Programmer; Engineer; Electrical Engineer; Programmer; Systems Analyst; Technical Writer/Editor. **Educational background sought:** Engineering. **Benefits:** medical, dental, and life insurance; pension plan; tuition assistance; disability coverage; employee discounts; savings plan.

GENERAL ELECTRIC COMPANY
LIGHTING DIVISION
6251 Etzel Avenue, St. Louis MO 63133. 314/726-9159. **Contact:** Personnel Department. **Description:** A division of the electric-products company engaged in the sales and service of electrical apparatus, appliances, electrical components and defense products. **Employees:** 1,000.

GLASCO ELECTRIC COMPANY
24 Worthington Drive, Maryland Heights MO 63043. 314/469-2233. **Contact:** Scott Walker, Operations Manager. **Description:** Wholesalers and distributors of electrical products. **Employees:** 100. **Common positions:** Accountant; Buyer; Credit Manager; Customer Service Representative; Electrical Engineer; Branch Manager; Department Manager; Operations/Production Manager; Purchasing Agent; Sales Representative. **Educational backgrounds sought:** Accounting; Business Administration. **Special programs:** Training programs. **Benefits:** medical, dental, and life insurance; tuition assistance; disability coverage; employee discounts; savings plan. **Corporate headquarters:** Dallas, TX. **Parent company:** Summers Group, Inc. **Operations at this facility:** divisional headquarters; administration; sales.

GRAYBAR ELECTRIC COMPANY INC.
P.O. Box 7231, St. Louis MO 63177. 314/727-3900. **Contact:** Uraina Evans, Personnel Manager. **Description:** Distributors of electrical supplies and telecommunications products. **Employees:** 4,600. **Common positions:** Accountant; Computer Programmer; Customer Service Representative; Personnel and Labor Relations Specialist. **Educational backgrounds sought:** Accounting; Business Administration; Computer Science. **Benefits:** medical, dental, and life insurance; pension plan; tuition assistance; disability coverage; profit sharing; employee discounts. **Corporate headquarters:** This location.

H-R ELECTRONICS
P.O. Box 196, High Ridge MO 63049. 314/677-3377. **Contact:** Betty Logsden, Personnel Manager. **Description:** Manufacturers of electronic controls for coin changers.

INDUSTRIAL ENGINEERING
AND EQUIPMENT COMPANY
425 Hanley Industrial Court, St. Louis MO 63144. 314/644-4300. **Contact:** Barbara Cloward, Personnel Director. **Description:** Design and manufacture custom electric heating equipment for industrial and commercial applications.

KAISER ELECTRIC INC.
904 Hanley Industrial Court, St. Louis MO 63144. 314/968-3700. **Contact:** Personnel Director. **Description:** A St. Louis electrical contracting firm.

KILLARK ELECTRIC MANUFACTURING COMPANY
3940 Martin Luther King Drive, St. Louis MO 63113. 314/531-0460. **Contact:** Frank Chanblin, Director of Employee Relations. Mr. Chanblin can be contacted at P.O. Box 5325, St. Louis MO 63115. **Description:** Manufacture conduit fittings, lighting fixtures and control housings.

MACK ELECTRIC COMPANY
9832 Reavis Road, Box 4360, St. Louis MO 63123. 314/638-7000. **Contact:** Robert Schroell, Controller. **Description:** A St. Louis-area electrical contracting company.

PAUWELS TRANSFORMERS INC.
P.O. Box 189, Washington MO 63090. 314/239-6783. **Contact:** Mary Shofner, Personnel Director. **Description:** A manufacturer of transformers for the electric utility industry. **Common positions:** Accountant; Blue-Collar Worker Supervisor; Buyer; Draftsperson; Electrical Engineer; Industrial Engineer; Mechanical Engineer; Operations/Production Manager; Purchasing Agent; Quality Control Supervisor. **Educational backgrounds sought:** Engineering; Marketing. **Benefits:** medical, dental, and life insurance; pension plan; tuition assistance; disability coverage; savings plan. **Corporate headquarters:** Mechelen, Belgium. **Parent company:** Pauwels International. **Operations at this facility:** divisional headquarters; manufacturing; service; sales.

POTTER ELECTRIC SIGNAL COMPANY
2081 Craig Road, St. Louis MO 63146. 314/878-4321. **Contact:** Delores Hale, Personnel Director. **Description:** Manufacturers of alarm equipment for central station and local systems.

RCA SERVICE COMPANY/ ST. LOUIS AREA
1355 Warson Road North, St. Louis MO 63132. 314/993-6200. **Contact:** Personnel Department. **Description:** Two factory service branches of the national electronics corporation.

SACHS ELECTRIC COMPANY
P.O. Box 96, St. Louis MO 63166. 314/532-2000. **Contact:** Chris Butler, Personnel Director. **Description:** A St. Louis-area electrical contractor.

SYLVANIA LIGHTING DIVISION U.S.
5656 Campus Parkway, Hazelwood MO 63042. 314/821-4780. **Contact:** Mr. Robert Wiehe, Distribution/Service Manager. **Description:** Wholesale distributors of a wide variety of electrical equipment and supplies. **Employees:** 100.

WATLOW ELECTRIC MANUFACTURING CO.
12001 Lackland, St. Louis MO 63146. 314/878-4600. **Contact:** Personnel Department. **Description:** Manufactures industrial electric heating elements and other electric apparatus.

WESTINGHOUSE ELECTRIC CORPORATION

P.O. Box 28540, St. Louis MO 63146. 314/991-9600. **Contact:** District Manager. **Description:** Engaged principally in the manufacture, sale, and service of equipment and components for the generation, transmission, distribution, utilization, and control of electricity. Its businesses also include a wide range of products and services which are unrelated to electrical manufacturing, such as broadcasting and cable television operations, land development, bottling and distribution of beverage products, transport refrigeration, and financial services. Operates in four segments: Power Systems; Industry Products; Public Systems; and Broadcasting and Cable. **Corporate headquarters:** Pittsburgh, PA. **Listed on:** New York Stock Exchange. International.

XEROX CORPORATION

11885 Lackland Road, St. Louis MO 63146. 314/872-1600. **Contact:** Personnel Department. **Description:** A worldwide manufacturer of business machines, copiers, computer systems, and word processors. Also publishes educational materials through various subsidiaries, and manufactures other products such as aerospace systems and components, electrostatic printers, microfiche printers, and many other related products and services. Also provides international communications services and systems. Subsidiaries of parent corporation include: Xerox Publishing Group, R.R. Bowker, Diablo Systems, Rank Xerox Business Equipment, and many others. **Corporate headquarters:** Stamford, CT. **Listed on:** New York Stock Exchange.

Additional large employers: 250+

SWITCHGEAR AND SWITCH BOARD APPARATUS

Guarantee Electrical Co
3405 Bent Ave, St. Louis MO 63116-2601. 314/772-5400. Employs: 500-999.

MOTORS AND GENERATORS

Von Weise Gear Co
St Clair Indl Pk, Saint Clair MO 63077. 314/629-1010. Employs: 250-499.

RELAYS AND INDUSTRIAL CONTROLS

Alco Controls
11911 Adie Rd, Maryland Hts MO 63043-3215. 314/569-4500. Employs: 500-999.

HOUSEHOLD COOKING EQUIPMENT

Crunden Martin Mfg Co
760 S 2nd, St. Louis MO 63102-1647. 314/421-2992. Employs: 250-499.

HOUSEHOLD APPLIANCES

Nordyne Inc
1801 Park 270 Dr Box 4691, St. Louis MO 63146-4020. 314/878-6200. Employs: 500-999.

ELECTRIC LAMP BULBS AND TUBES

St Louis Lamp Plant
6251 Etzel Ave, St. Louis MO 63133-1901. 314/726-9101. Employs: 250-499.

NONCURRENT-CARRYING WIRING DEVICES

E M Wiegmann & Co Inc
501 Douglas Rd, Freeburg IL 62243. 618/539-3193. Employs: 250-499.

SEMICONDUCTORS AND RELATED DEVICES

Olin Electronic Materials Corp
427 Shamrock St, East Alton IL 62024-1174. 618/258-2000. Employs: 1,000+.

ELECTRONIC COILS, TRANSFORMERS AND OTHER INDUCTORS

A B B Power T & D Co Inc
4350 Semple Ave, St. Louis MO 63120-2241. 314/382-2100. Employs: 250-499.

ELECTRONIC CONNECTORS

Labarge Inc
707 N 2nd St, St. Louis MO 63102-2545. 314/231-5960. Employs: 500-999.

ELECTRONIC COMPONENTS

Atlas/Soundolier
1859 Intertech Dr, Fenton MO 63026-1926. 314/349-3110. Employs: 250-499.

Memc Electronic Materials Inc
501 Pearl Dr, Saint Peters MO 63376-1071. 314/279-5000. Employs: 1,000+.

MAGNETIC AND OPTICAL RECORDING MEDIA

Weber Fred Inc
2320 Creve Coeur Mill Rd, Maryland Hts MO 63043-4207. 314/344-0070. Employs: 500-999.

Additional small to medium sized employers: 50-249

SWITCHGEAR AND SWITCHBOARD APPARATUS

Ronk Electrical Industries Inc
106 E State St, Nokomis IL 62075-1340. 217/563-8333. Employs: 50-99.

Turner Electric Corp
9510 St Clair Ave, E St. Louis IL 62208-1639. 618/397-1865. Employs: 50-99.

MOTORS AND GENERATORS

Hutchinson Foundry Products
4131 Alby St, Alton IL 62002-4479. 618/465-5521. Employs: 50-99.

Magnetek
1881 Pine St, St. Louis MO 63103-2264. 314/342-2500. Employs: 100-249.

Marlo Coil/Nuclear Cooling Inc
6060 Hwy Pp, High Ridge MO 63049-2909. 314/677-6600. Employs: 100-249.

Motor Appl Corp Ballman Div
601 International Av, Washington MO 63090-3535. 314/239-2772. Employs: 50-99.

RELAYS AND INDUSTRIAL CONTROLS

Beta Raven Inc
4372 Green Ash Dr, Earth City MO 63045-1219. 314/291-4504. Employs: 100-249.

Bussmann Mfg Div McGraw Ed
PO Box 14460, St. Louis MO
63178-4460. 314/394-2877.
Employs: 100-249.

ELECTRICAL INDUSTRIAL APPARATUS

Associated Eqpt Corp
5043 Farlin Ave, St. Louis MO
63115-1204. 314/385-5178.
Employs: 100-249.

Bitrode Corp
1642 Manufacturers Dr, Fenton
MO 63026-2839. 314/343-6112.
Employs: 50-99.

Ferro Magnetics Corp
4328 Bridgeton Indl Dr, Bridgeton
MO 63044. 314/739-1414.
Employs: 100-249.

Pacific Heater Corp
115 Flier Dr, Pacific MO 63069-3465. 314/257-6166. Employs: 50-99.

HOUSEHOLD COOKING EQUIPMENT

Roesch Incorporated
100 N 24th St, Belleville IL 62223-6659. 618/233-2760. Employs: 100-249.

HOUSEHOLD LAUNDRY EQUIPMENT

Ever Ready Appliance Mfg Co
5727 W Park Ave, St. Louis MO
63110-1834. 314/645-1441.
Employs: 50-99.

ELECTRIC HOUSEWARES AND FANS

Newco Enterprise Inc
1735 S River Rd, Saint Charles
MO 63303-4122. 314/925-1202.
Employs: 100-249.

HOUSEHOLD APPLIANCES

Clean City Squares Inc
324 S Newstead Ave, St. Louis MO
63110-1113. 314/652-8622.
Employs: 50-99.

Universal Sewing Supply Inc
1011 E Park Indl Ct, St. Louis MO
63130. 314/862-0800. Employs: 50-99.

CURRENT-CARRYING WIRING DEVICES

American Electric
1525 Woodson Rd, St. Louis MO
63114-6126. 314/993-9430.
Employs: 100-249.

B-Line Systs Inc
816 Lions Dr, Troy IL 62294-2440.
618/667-6779. Employs: 50-99.

Lectronix/Assembly Systs Div
540 Little Hills Indl Blvd, Saint
Charles MO 63301-3710. 314/946-6430. Employs: 50-99.

RESIDENTIAL ELECTRIC LIGHTING FIXTURES

Dazor Mfg Corp
4483 Duncan Ave, St. Louis MO
63110-1111. 314/652-2400.
Employs: 50-99.

K S H Inc
10091 Manchester Rd, St. Louis
MO 63122-1825. 314/966-3111.
Employs: 100-249.

VEHICULAR LIGHTING EQUIPMENT

Public Safety Eqpt Inc
10986 N Warson Rd, St. Louis MO
63114-2029. 314/426-2700.
Employs: 100-249.

HOUSEHOLD AUDIO AND VIDEO EQUIPMENT

Atlas/Soundolier
600 Horine Rd, Festus MO 63028-1071. 314/937-9077. Employs: 100-249.

S L M Electronic
11880 Borman Dr, St. Louis MO 63146-4113. 314/569-0141. Employs: 100-249.

TELEPHONE AND TELEGRAPH APPARATUS

T A L X Corp
1850 Borman Ct, St. Louis MO 63146-4126. 314/434-0046. Employs: 100-249.

ELECTRONIC RESISTORS

B & K Cafe
113 N Main St, Brighton IL 62012-1033. 618/372-7071. Employs: 100-249.

ELECTRONIC COMPONENTS

American Electronic Labs Inc
140 E Circle Dr, East Alton IL 62024-2267. 618/259-7763. Employs: 100-249.

Central Microwave Co
12180 Prichard Farm Rd, Maryland Hts MO 63043-4201. 314/291-5270. Employs: 100-249.

Harvard Interiors Mfg Co
3000 Arnold Tenbrook Rd, Arnold MO 63010-4717. 314/296-5417. Employs: 100-249.

STORAGE BATTERIES

Acme Battery Mfg Co
3340 Morganford Rd, St. Louis MO 63116-1806. 314/776-2980. Employs: 100-249.

ELECTRICAL MACHINERY, EQUIPMENT AND SUPPLIES

ABB Power Distribution Inc
2388 Schuetz Rd, St. Louis MO 63146-3414. 314/567-7124. Employs: 50-99.

Allen-Bradley Co
3787 S Rider Trl, Earth City MO 63045-1114. 314/291-0083. Employs: 50-99.

Appleton Electric Products Co
12015 Manchester Rd, St. Louis MO 63131-4423. 314/966-8998. Employs: 50-99.

Arrow Hart
648 Oakwood Av, St. Louis MO 63119-2625. 314/962-2366. Employs: 50-99.

Arrow Hart
648 Oakwood Dr, Fenton MO 63026. 314/962-2366. Employs: 50-99.

Asea Brown Boveri Power T & D Co
11457 Olde Cabin Rd, St. Louis MO 63141-7139. 314/567-0963. Employs: 50-99.

B-Line Systems Inc
509 W Monroe Ave, St. Louis MO 63122-3839. 314/621-1594. Employs: 50-99.

Control Tech Sales Inc
S Outer Forty Rd, Chesterfield MO 63006. 314/469-6004. Employs: 50-99.

Cooper Distrb Equip Division
234 Old Meramec Station Rd # C, Ballwin MO 63021-5300. 314/256-4812. Employs: 50-99.

Crouse-Hinds Company
1750 S Brentwood Blvd, St. Louis MO 63144-1315. 314/961-1117. Employs: 50-99.

Crouse-Hinds Company-Ded
11 Hagers Mill Ct, Ballwin MO 63021-6807. 314/225-4770. Employs: 50-99.

Delta Electrical Sales
239 Schneider Dr, Fenton MO 63026-6019. 314/343-3582. Employs: 50-99.

Eaton Corporation
11775 Borman Dr, St. Louis MO 63146-4134. 314/569-0990. Employs: 50-99.

Emergi-Lite
2509 Westglen Farms Dr, Glencoe MO 63038. 314/458-2744. Employs: 50-99.

GE Company
2455 Cassens Dr, Fenton MO 63026-2540. 314/343-1777. Employs: 50-99.

GE Company
4333 Green Ash Dr, Earth City MO 63045-1207. 314/291-0410. Employs: 50-99.

Jones Electrical Enterprises
11520 Saint Charles Rock Rd, Bridgeton MO 63044-2732. 314/344-1930. Employs: 50-99.

Ken Way Co
8 The Pines Ct, St. Louis MO 63141. 314/469-9998. Employs: 50-99.

Ken Way Co
700 Office Pkwy, St. Louis MO 63141-7131. 314/567-0051. Employs: 50-99.

Lutron Electronics Company Inc
514 Earth City Expy, Earth City MO 63045-1303. 314/298-8077. Employs: 50-99.

P & A Equipment Co
7302 W Florissant Ave, St. Louis MO 63136-1302. 314/385-9446. Employs: 50-99.

Schlumberger Industries
110 Point West Blvd, Saint Charles MO 63301-4408. 314/724-0511. Employs: 100-249.

Square D Co
9735 Landmark Parkway Dr, St. Louis MO 63127-1646. 314/849-6330. Employs: 50-99.

Waterman & Waterman
745 Craig Rd, St. Louis MO 63141-7122. 314/432-6709. Employs: 50-99.

Amada Ltd
1580 Shannon Ln, Pacific MO 63069. 314/257-2162. Employs: 100-249.

Bowman & Associates Inc
7061 Forsyth Blvd, St. Louis MO 63105-2120. 314/863-8318. Employs: 50-99.

St Louis Laser Marking
10758 Trenton Ave, St. Louis MO 63132-1026. 314/423-1412. Employs: 50-99.

For more information on career opportunities in the electrical and electronic industry:

Associations

AMERICAN ELECTROPLATERS AND SURFACE FINISHERS SOCIETY
12644 Research Parkway, Orlando FL 32826. 407/281-6441.

AMERICAN CERAMIC SOCIETY
735 Ceramic Place, Westerville OH 43081. 614/890-4700.

ELECTROCHEMICAL SOCIETY
10 South Main Street, Pennington NJ 08534-2896. 609/737-1902.

ELECTRONIC INDUSTRIES ASSOCIATION
2001 Pennsylvania Avenue NW, Washington DC 20006. 202/457-4900.

ELECTRONICS TECHNICIANS ASSOCIATION
602 N. Jackson Street, Greencastle IN 46135. 317/653-8262.

INSTITUTE OF ELECTRICAL AND ELECTRONICS ENGINEERS
345 East 47th Street, New York NY 10017. 212/705-7900.

INTERNATIONAL BROTHERHOOD OF ELECTRICAL WORKERS
1125 15th Street NW, Washington DC 20005. 202/833-7000.

INTERNATIONAL SOCIETY OF CERTIFIED ELECTRONICS TECHNICIANS
2708 West Berry, Fort Worth TX 76109. 817/921-9101.

INTERNATIONAL SOCIETY FOR HYBRID MICROELECTRONICS
1861 Wiehle Avenue, Suite 340, Reston VA 22090. 703/471-0066.

NATIONAL ELECTRICAL MANUFACTURERS ASSOCIATION
2101 L Street NW, Suite 300, Washington DC 20037. 202/457-8400.

NATIONAL ELECTRONICS SALES AND SERVICES ASSOCIATION
2708 West Berry, Fort Worth TX 76109. 817/921-9061.

ROBOTICS INTERNATIONAL OF THE SOCIETY OF MANUFACTURING ENGINEERS
P.O. Box 930, One SME Drive, Dearborn MI 48121. 313/271-1500.

ENERGY, MINING AND PETROLEUM

The short-term future for the petroleum industry depends upon the world economy, OPEC production, and world oil prices. U.S. crude and natural gas production is expected to remain flat, while energy use is forecasted to rise 2-3 percent annually for oil and natural gas respectively. Environmental concerns will have a greater effect on the industry.
Jobseekers, especially those with engineering backgrounds, should keep an eye out for the growing emphasis on the development of alternative fuels like methanol, and for growth in hydroelectric, geothermal, and other environmentally sound energy sources.

AMOCO PETROLEUM ADDITIVES COMPANY
301 Evans, Wood River IL 62095. 618/251-2200. **Contact:** Mr. George A. Preston, Manager, Human Resources. **Description:** Manufacturers of petroleum additives products. **Employees:** 300. **Common positions:** Accountant; Buyer; Chemist; Computer Programmer; Chemical Engineering; Mechanical Engineer; Personnel and Labor Relations Specialist; Systems Analyst. **Educational backgrounds sought:** Accounting; Business Administration; Computer Science; Engineering. **Benefits:** medical insurance; dental insurance; pension plan; life insurance; tuition assistance; disability coverage; profit sharing; savings plan. **Corporate headquarters:** Chicago, IL.

ARCH MINERAL CORPORATION
City Place One, Suite 300, St. Louis MO 63141. 314/994-2700. **Contact:** Jane Fox, Office Manager. **Description:** Holding office for a company engaged in bituminous coal exploration and processing. **Employees:** 100.

CENTRAL MINE EQUIPMENT
6200 North Broadway Road, St. Louis MO 63147. 314/381-5900. **Contact:** Personnel Department. **Description:** A manufacturer of drilling rigs and related tools for mining and industry. **Employees:** 100.

CLARK OIL AND REFINING CORPORATION
201 East Hawthorne, Hartford IL 62048. 618/254-7301. **Contact:** Joyce Cunningham, Manager of Industrial Relations. **Description:** Manufacturers of petroleum products. **Employees:** 300.

COLUMBIA QUARRY COMPANY/ PLANTS #9, #3, AND #1
800 Quarry Road, Valmeyer IL 62295. 618/935-2201. **Contact:** Kevin Wilder, Superintendant. **Description:** Manufacturers of calcium carbonate and crushed stone. **Employees:** 100.

MISSISSIPPI LIME COMPANY
P.O. Box 2247, Alton IL 62002. 618/465-7741. **Contact:** Personnel Department. **Description:** A St. Louis company engaged in the manufacture of limestone, sand and rock.

MISSISSIPPI RIVER TRANSMISSION CORP.
A SUBSIDIARY OF ARKLA, INC.
9900 Clayton Road, St. Louis MO 63124. 314/991-7397. **Contact:** Wayne St. Claire, Manager, Human Resources. **Description:** A St. Louis company engaged in the wholesale of natural gas pipeline.

PEABODY HOLDING COMPANY, INC.
301 North Memorial Drive, St. Louis MO 63102. 314/342-3400. **Contact:** Peggy Nesbit, Supervisor/Employee Relations. **Description:** A holding company whose subsidiary operations include Peabody Coal Company which is engaged in coal mining, production and processing. **Common positions:** Accountant; Attorney; Computer Programmer; Geologist; Systems Analyst. **Educational backgrounds sought:** Accounting; Business Administration; Computer Science; Finance; Geology; Marketing; Mathematics. **Benefits:** medical insurance; dental insurance; pension plan; life insurance; tuition assistance; disability coverage; employee discounts; savings plan. **Corporate headquarters:** This location. **Operations at this facility:** administration; sales.

J.D. STREETT & COMPANY INC.
144 Weldon Parkway, Maryland Heights MO 63043. 314/432-6600. **Contact:** Jim Shuring, Personnel. **Description:** Retailers and wholesale marketers of petroleum products.

Additional large employers: 250+

BITUMINOUS COAL AND LIGNITE SURFACE MINING

Arch Of Il
R R 1, Percy IL 62272-9801.
618/497-2141. Employs: 250-499.

Peabody Coal Co
RR 2, Marissa IL 62257-9802.
618/295-2385. Employs: 250-499.

BITUMINOUS COAL UNDERGROUND MINING

Monterey Coal Co/Mine 2
P O Box 94, Albers IL 62215-0094.
618/248-5121. Employs: 250-499.

PETROLEUM REFINING

Godfrey Oil & Gas Co
Cannavan Dr, Godfrey IL 62035.
618/466-3666. Employs: 250-499.

Shell Oil Co
Wood River Mfg Complex, Wood River IL 62095. 618/254-7371.
Employs: 1,000+.

Additional small to medium sized employers: 50-249

BITUMINOUS COAL AND LIGNITE SURFACE MINING

Central Laboratory
8403 Peabody Rd, Freeburg IL 62243-2335. 618/539-5836. Employs: 50-99.

Consolidation Coal Co
RR 1, Pinckneyville IL 62274-9801. 618/3579381. Employs: 50-99.

Nerco Coal Corp
2043 Woodland Pkwy Ste 202, St. Louis MO 63146-4277. 314/993-2625. Employs: 50-99.

Peabody Coal Co
RR 3, Sparta IL 62286-9803. 618/443-4812. Employs: 50-99.

Peabody Coal Co
RR 2, Sparta IL 62286-9802. 618/443-3004. Employs: 50-99.

Peabody Coal Co
Baldwn Rd, New Athens IL 62264. 618/475-3311. Employs: 50-99.

Peabody Coal Co
RR 2, Mascoutah IL 62258 9802. 618/677-2788. Employs: 50-99.

Peabody Coal Co
RR 3, Marissa IL 62257. 618/443-2191. Employs: 50-99.

Peabody Coal Co
RR 1, Marissa IL 62257-9801. 618/295-2374. Employs: 50-99.

Peabody Flight Dept
Lambert St Louis Intl Airport, St. Louis MO 63145. 314/731-0988. Employs: 100-249.

Peabody R Parker
701 Market St Ste 700, St. Louis MO 63101-1826. 314/342-3400. Employs: 100-249.

Reserve Coal Properties Co
RR 1, Pinckneyville IL 62274-9801. 618/357-8341. Employs: 100-249.

Zeigler Coal Co
RR 2, Coulterville IL 62237-9802. 618/758-2311. Employs: 50-99.

BITUMINOUS COAL UNDERGROUND MINING

Consolidation Coal Co
12755 Olive Blvd, St. Louis MO 63141-6242. 314/275-2300. Employs: 50-99.

Zeigler Coal Co
50 Jerome Ln, E St. Louis IL 62208-2015. 618/394-2400. Employs: 50-99.

CRUSHED AND BROKEN LIMESTONE

Columbia Quarry Co
P O Box 128, Columbia IL 62236-0128. 618/281-7631. Employs: 50-99.

St Charles Quarry Co
2000 S River Rd, Saint Charles MO 63303-5713. 314/724-1344. Employs: 50-99.

CRUSHED AND BROKEN STONE

Bussen Quarries Inc
5000 Bussen Rd, St. Louis MO 63129-4405. 314/487-2300. Employs: 50-99.

CLAY, CERAMIC AND REFRACTORY MINERALS

Harbison Walker Refractories
Booker St, Vandalia MO 63382. 314/594-6425. Employs: 100-249.

PETROLEUM REFINING

Clark Oil & Refining Corp
2207 Camp Jackson Rd, E St. Louis IL 62206-2547. 618/332-0163. Employs: 100-249.

Clark Oil & Refining Corp
1001 Camp Jackson Rd, E St. Louis IL 62206-2277. 618/332-0138. Employs: 100-249.

Clark Oil & Refining Corp
913 Sherman St, Belleville IL 62221-4156. 618/277-6990. Employs: 100-249.

Clark Oil & Refining Corp
5404 Collinsville Rd, E St. Louis IL 62201-2336. 618/874-1482. Employs: 100-249.

Clark Oil & Refining Corp
800 E Broadway, E St. Louis IL 62201-2939. 618/874-3032. Employs: 100-249.

Clark Oil & Refining Corp
1701 State St, E St. Louis IL 62205-2503. 618/874-4632. Employs: 100-249.

Clark Oil & Refining Corp
3818 Saint Clair Ave, E St. Louis IL 62205-2632. 618/874-4630. Employs: 100-249.

Clark Oil & Refining Corp
1401 Kingshwy, E St. Louis IL 62204. 618/874-4629. Employs: 100-249.

Mobil Oil Corporation
2000 S 20th St, E St. Louis IL 62207-1917. 618/271-3155. Employs: 100-249.

ASPHALT PAVING MIXTURES AND BLOCKS

Elf Asphalt Inc
1000 Executive Pkwy, St. Louis MO 63141-6325. 314/878-0332. Employs: 100-249.

LUBRICATING OILS AND GREASES

Schaeffer Mfg
102 Barton St, St. Louis MO 63104-4728. 314/865-4100. Employs: 50-99.

CLAY REFRACTORIES

North American Refractories
300 W Locust St, Farber MO 63345. 314/249-2912. Employs: 100-249.

Wellsville Fire Brick Co
West Hwy 19, Wellsville MO 63384. 314/684-2222. Employs: 50-99.

CONCRETE BLOCK AND BRICK

F F Kirchner Inc
S Outer Rd I-70, Wentzville MO 63385. 314/291-3200. Employs: 50-99.

CUT STONE AND STONE PRODUCTS

Superior Home Prdtn
1743 Scherer Pkwy, Saint Charles MO 63303-3819. 314/947-0533. Employs: 50-99.

ABRASIVE PRODUCTS

V S M Abrasives Corp
1012 E Wabash St, O Fallon MO 63366-2774. 314/272-7432. Employs: 100-249.

MINERALS AND EARTHS, GROUND OR OTHERWISE TREATED

Intl Mill Svc
22nd & Edwardsville Rds, Granite City IL 62040. 618/451-7840. Employs: 50-99.

Tri State Mineral Consultants
9607 Dielman Rock Island Dr, St. Louis MO 63132-2149. 314/432-7755. Employs: 50-99.

International Mill Service Inc
4203 Earth City Expy, Earth City MO 63045-1304. 314/344-1096. Employs: 50-99.

NONCLAY REFRACTORIES

Christy Refractories Co
4641 McRee Ave, St. Louis MO 63110-2239. 314/773-7500. Employs: 50-99.

CRUDE PETROLEUM PIPELINES

Explorer Pipeline Co
4000 S 1st St, St. Louis MO 63118-3312. 314/752-2690. Employs: 50-99.

Explorer Pipeline Co
3300 Mississippi Ave, E St. Louis IL 62206-1048. 618/337-7190. Employs: 50-99.

Kock Pipelines Inc Wood Riv
Robbins Rd, Hartford IL 62048. 618/251-5850. Employs: 50-99.

Marathon Pipe Line Co
1700 S 20th St, E St. Louis IL 62207-1916. 618/875-3330. Employs: 50-99.

Missouri Pipe Line Co
91 Algana Ct, Saint Peters MO 63376-3968. 314/926-0387. Employs: 50-99.

PIPELINES

Platte Pipe Line Co
E 7th St, Hartford IL 62048. 618/254-1221. Employs: 50-99.

For more information on career opportunities in the energy, mining, and petroleum industries:

Associations

AMERICAN ASSOCIATION OF PETROLEUM GEOLOGISTS
P.O. Box 979, Tulsa OK 74101
918/584-2555.

AMERICAN GAS ASSOCIATION
1515 Wilson Boulevard, Arlington VA 22209. 703/841-8400.

AMERICAN GEOLOGICAL INSTITUTE
4220 King Street, Alexandria VA 22302. 703/379-2480.

AMERICAN INSTITUTE OF MINING, METALLURGICAL AND PETROLEUM
345 East 47th Street, New York NY 10017. 212/705-7695.

AMERICAN NUCLEAR SOCIETY
555 North Kensington Avenue, La Grange Park IL 60525. 708/352-6611.

AMERICAN PETROLEUM INSTITUTE
1220 L Street NW, Washington DC 20005. 202/682-8000.

AMERICAN SOCIETY OF TRIBOLOGISTS AND LUBRICATION ENGINEERS
840 Busse Highway, Park Ridge IL 60068. 708/825-5536.

CLEAN ENERGY RESEARCH INSTITUTE
P.O. Box 248294, Coral Gables FL 33124. 305/284-4666.

GEOLOGICAL SOCIETY OF AMERICA
3300 Penrose Place, P.O. Box 9140, Boulder CO 80301. 303/447-2020.

PETROLEUM EQUIPMENT INSTITUTE
P.O. Box 2380, Tulsa OK 74101. 918/494-9696.

PETROLEUM MARKETERS ASSOCIATION OF AMERICA
1120 Vermont Avenue NW, Washington DC 20005. 202/331-1198.

SOCIETY OF EXPLORATION GEOPHYSICISTS
P.O. Box 702740, Tulsa OK 74170-2740. 918/493-3516.

Directories

BROWN'S DIRECTORY OF NORTH AMERICAN AND INTERNATIONAL GAS COMPANIES
Advanstar Communications, 7500 Old Oak Boulevard, Cleveland OH 44130. 800/225-4569.

NATIONAL PETROLEUM NEWS FACT BOOK
Hunter Publishing Co., 950 Lee Street, Des Plaines IL 60016. 708/296-0770.

OIL AND GAS DIRECTORY
Geophysical Directory, Inc., P.O. Box 130508, Houston TX 77219. 713/529-8789.

Magazines

AMERICAN GAS MONTHLY
1515 Wilson Boulevard, Arlington VA 22209. 703/841-8686.

GAS INDUSTRIES AND APPLIANCE MAGAZINES
Gas Industries and Appliance News, Inc., P.O. Box 558, Park Ridge IL 60068. 312/693-3682.

NATIONAL PETROLEUM NEWS
Hunter Publishing Co., 950 Lee Street, Des Plaines IL 60016. 708/296-0770.

OIL AND GAS JOURNAL
PennWell Publishing Co., 1421 South Sheridan Road, Tulsa OK 74112. 918/835-3161.

ENGINEERING AND DESIGN

Job prospects for engineers have been good for a number of years, and will continue to improve into the next century. Employers will need more engineers as they increase investment in equipment in order to expand output. In addition, engineers will find work improving the nation's deteriorating infrastructure.

BOOKER ASSOCIATES, INC.
1139 Olive Street, St. Louis MO 63101. 314/421-1476. **Contact:** John E. Chew, Director of Personnel. **Description:** A St. Louis-area multi-discipline consulting firm specializing in engineering (civil, mechanical, electrical, structural), architecture/landscaping, and planning consultation. **Common positions:** Accountant; Administrator; Architect; Draftsperson; Architectural Engineer; Civil Engineer; Electrical Engineer; Industrial Engineer; Mechanical Engineer; Personnel and Labor Relations Specialist; Transportation and Traffic Specialist. **Educational backgrounds sought:** Accounting; Biology; Engineering; Architecture; Landscape Architecture. **Benefits:** medical, dental, and life insurance; pension plan; tuition assistance; disability coverage; stock options. **Corporate headquarters:** This location. **Other U.S. locations:** Fairview Heights, IL; Lexington, KY; Wichita, KS. **Operations at this facility:** administration; service; sales. **Revenues (1991):** $11 million. **Employees:** 200. **Projected hires for the next 12 months:** 10.

FRUCON ENGINEERING/SUBSIDIARY OF FRU-CON CORP.
15933 Clayton Road, Ballwin MO 63011. 314/391-6700. **Contact:** Personnel. **Description:** An engineering and architectural firm.

HELLMUTH OBATA & KASSABAUM INC.
1831 Chestnut Street, St. Louis MO 63103. 314/421-2000. **Contact:** John Mahon, Personnel Director. **Description:** A St. Louis architectural and engineering firm.

ZURHEIDE-HERRMANN INC.
4333w Clayton Avenue, St. Louis MO 63110. 314/652-6805. **Contact:** Harry Niederbremer, Administration. **Description:** A provider of engineering and architectural services. **Common positions:** Accountant; Architect; Architectural Engineer; Civil Engineer; Electrical Engineer; Industrial Engineer; Mechanical Engineer; Financial Analyst. **Educational backgrounds sought:** Engineering; Marketing. **Special programs:** Training programs and internships. **Benefits:** medical insurance; pension plan; life insurance; savings plan. **Corporate headquarters:** This location. **Other U.S. locations:** Champaign, IL. **Operations at this facility:** service. **Employees:** 45. **Projected hires for the next 12 months:** 1-3.

Additional large employers: 250+

ENGINEERING SERVICES

Monsanto Enviro-Chem Syst
800 N Lindbergh Bl, St. Louis MO 63166. 314/694-4131. Employs: 250-499.

Additional small to medium sized employers: 50-249

ENGINEERING SERVICES

Mc Michael Mc Cracken Et Al
915 Olive St, St. Louis MO 63101-1449. 314/241-1820. Employs: 50-99.

Burlington Environmental Inc
210 W Sand Bank Rd, Columbia IL 62236-1044. 618/281-7173. Employs: 50-99.

George H Knostman Junior & Ass
Farm Bus Bldg 102 N Main, Hillsboro IL 62049. 217/532-2140. Employs: 50-99.

Whitehead Roofing & Insltn Inc
800 N 3rd St, St. Louis MO 63102-2138. 314/421-4900. Employs: 50-99.

WVP Corporation
2810 S Grand Blvd, St. Louis MO 63118-1010. 314/664-8886. Employs: 50-99.

For more information on career opportunities in engineering and design:

<u>Associations</u>

AMERICAN ASSOCIATION OF COST ENGINEERS
209 Prairie Avenue, Suite 100, Morgantown WV 26507. 304/296-8444.

AMERICAN ASSOCIATION OF ENGINEERING SOCIETIES
1111 19th Street, Suite 608, Washington DC 20036. 202/296-2237.

AMERICAN CONSULTING ENGINEERS COUNCIL
1015 15th Street NW, Washington DC 20005. 202/347-7474.

AMERICAN INSTITUTE OF ARCHITECTS
1735 New York Ave NW, Washington DC 20006. 202/626-7300.

AMERICAN INSTITUTE OF PLANT ENGINEERS
3975 Erie Avenue, Cincinnati OH 45208. 513/561-6000.

AMERICAN SOCIETY FOR ENGINEERING EDUCATION
11 Dupont Circle NW, Suite 200, Washington DC 20036. 202/293-7080.

AMERICAN SOCIETY OF CIVIL ENGINEERS
345 East 47th Street, New York NY 10017. 212/705-7496.

Engineering and Design

AMERICAN SOCIETY OF HEATING, REFRIGERATING AND AIR CONDITIONING ENGINEERS
1791 Tullie Circle NE, Atlanta GA 30329. 404/636-8400.

AMERICAN SOCIETY OF LANDSCAPE ARCHITECTS
4401 Connecticut Avenue, Fifth Floor, Washington DC 20008. 202/686-2752.

AMERICAN SOCIETY OF MECHANICAL ENGINEERS
345 East 47th Street, New York NY 10017. 212/705-7722.

AMERICAN SOCIETY OF NAVAL ENGINEERS
1452 Duke Street, Alexandria VA 22314. 703/836-6727.

AMERICAN SOCIETY OF PLUMBING ENGINEERS
3617 Thousand Oaks Boulevard, Suite #210, Westlake CA 91362. 805/495-7120.

AMERICAN SOCIETY OF SAFETY ENGINEERS
1800 East Oakton Street, Des Plaines IL 60018-2187. 312/692-4121.

ILLUMINATING ENGINEERING SOCIETY OF NORTH AMERICA
345 East 47th Street, New York NY 10017. 212/705-7926.

INSTITUTE OF INDUSTRIAL ENGINEERS
25 Technology Park, Norcross GA 30092. 404/449-0460.

NATIONAL ACADEMY OF ENGINEERING
2101 Constitution Avenue NW, Washington DC 20418. 202/334-3200.

NATIONAL ACTION COUNCIL FOR MINORITIES IN ENGINEERING
3 West 35th Street, New York NY 10001. 212/279-2626.

NATIONAL ASSOCIATION OF MINORITY ENGINEERING
500 N. Michigan Avenue, Suite 1400, Chicago IL 60611. 312/661-1700.

NATIONAL ENGINEERING CONSORTIUM
303 E. Wacker Drive, Suite 740, Chicago IL 60601. 312/938-3500.

JUNIOR ENGINEERING TECHNICAL SOCIETY
1420 King Street, Suite 405, Alexandria VA 22314. 703/548-JETS.

NATIONAL INSTITUTE OF CERAMIC ENGINEERS
735 Ceramic Place, Westerville OH 43081. 614/890-4700.

NATIONAL SOCIETY OF BLACK ENGINEERS
1454 Duke Street, Alexandria VA 22314. 703/549-2207.

NATIONAL SOCIETY OF PROFESSIONAL ENGINEERS
1420 King Street, Alexandria VA 22314. 703/684-2800.

SOCIETY FOR THE ADVANCEMENT OF MATERIAL AND PROCESS ENGINEERS
1161 Parkview Drive, Covina CA 91724. 818/331-0616.

SOCIETY OF FIRE PROTECTION ENGINEERS
1 Liberty Square, Boston MA 02109. 617/482-0686.

SOCIETY OF MANUFACTURING ENGINEERS
P.O. Box 930, One SME Drive, Dearborn MI 48121. 313/271-1500.

UNITED ENGINEERING TRUSTEES
345 East 47th Street, New York NY 10017. 212/705-7000.

Directories

DIRECTORY OF ENGINEERING SOCIETIES
American Association of Engineering Societies, 1111 19th Street, Suite 608, Washington DC 20036. 202/296-2237.

DIRECTORY OF ENGINEERS IN PRIVATE PRACTICE
National Society of Professional Engineers, 1420 King Street, Alexandria VA 22314. 703/684-2800.

ENCYCLOPEDIA OF PHYSICAL SCIENCES & ENGINEERING INFORMATION SOURCES
Gale Research Inc., 835 Penobscot Building, Detroit MI 48226. 313/961-2242.

Magazines

CAREERS AND THE ENGINEER
Bob Adams, Inc., 260 Center Street, Holbrook MA 02343. 617/767-8100.

EDN CAREER NEWS
Cahners Publishing Co., 275 Washington Street, Newton MA 02158. 617/964-3030.

ENGINEERING TIMES
National Society of Professional Engineers, 1420 King Street, Alexandria VA 22314. 703/684-2800.

PROFESSIONAL ENGINEER
National Society of Professional Engineers, 1420 King Street, Alexandria VA 22314. 703/684-2800.

FABRICATED AND PRIMARY METALS

For steel manufacturers, the past few years have been a nightmare, with prices falling to ten-year lows. The industry should begin a modest recovery, however, if lower mortgage rates can spur the home construction industry. Foreign companies will become more and more important; look for more joint ventures between the U.S. and overseas firms. Big Steel's toughest competition is now the increasing number of minimills that have spun off from rivals.
Overall, employment prospects are weak, although metallurgical engineering is in demand.

ALUMAX FOILS INC.
6100 South Broadway, St. Louis MO 63111. 314/481-7000. **Contact:** Personnel Department. **Description:** A St. Louis-based manufacturer of metal foils. **Employees:** 300.

AMERICAN NATIONAL CAN COMPANY
3200 S. Kingshighway Boulevard, St. Louis MO 63139. 314/773-2200. **Contact:** Personnel Department. **Description:** St. Louis office of a manufacturer of metal cans. **Employees:** 800.

B-LINE SYSTEMS INC.
509 W. Monroe, Highland IL 62249. 618/654-2184. **Contact:** Personnel Department. **Description:** A St. Louis metal fabricating company, engaged primarily in the production of roll formers and welding of steel and aluminum products for the electrical and mechanical industry. **Employees:** 400.

BANJO IRON AND SUPPLY COMPANY
3209 Chouteau Avenue, St. Louis MO 63103. 314/772-6432. **Contact:** Personnel Department. **Description:** A metal service center specializing in the wholesale distribution of a variety of metal products. **Employees:** 100.

BIG RIVER ZINC CORPORATION
Route 3 and Monsanto Ave., Sauget IL 62201. 618/274-5000. **Contact:** Valerie Fulbright, Personnel Supervisor. **Description:** An area foundry, producing primary zinc. **Common positions:** Chemist; Computer Programmer; Metallurgical Engineer; Industrial Engineer; General Manager; Operations/Production Manager; Personnel and Labor Relations Specialist; Sales Representative; Sales Manager. **Educational backgrounds sought:** Accounting; Business Administration; Chemistry; Engineering. **Benefits:** medical insurance; dental insurance; life insurance; tuition assistance; disability coverage; profit sharing; savings plan; 401K. **Corporate headquarters:** Clayton, MO. **Parent company:** Big River Mineral. **Operations at this facility:** divisional headquarters; manufacturing; research and development; sales.

BODINE ALUMINUM INC.
2100 Walton Road, St. Louis MO 63114. 314/423-8200. **Contact:** Rick Gould, Human Resources Manager. **Description:** Manufacturers of aluminum castings. **Employees:** 300.

BULL MOOSE TUBE COMPANY
1819 Clarkson Road, Suite 100, Chesterfield MO 63017. 314/537-2600. **Contact:** Theresa Dwyer-Welch, Manager of Human Resources. **Description:** Manufacturers of electric welded steel tubing. **Employees:** 200.

CARONDELET CORPORATION
8600 Commercial Boulevard, Pevely MO 63070-0769. 314/479-4499. **Contact:** Dennis Simeone, Secretary/Treasurer. **Description:** Manufacturers of gray, alloy iron, and alloy steel castings. **Employees:** 100.

CONTINENTAL FABRICATORS
5601 W. Park Avenue, St. Louis MO 63110. 314/781-6300. **Contact:** Mark Rakers, Personnel Department. **Description:** Manufacturers of steel plate fabrication ducts, hoppers and pressure vessels. **Employees:** 100.

CUPPLES PRODUCTS DIVISION
ROBERTSON CECO CORPORATION
2650 South Hanley Road, St. Louis MO 63144. 314/781-4700. **Contact:** Ms. Judy Long, Manager/Human Resources. **Description:** Manufacturers of aluminum curtainwall. **Employees:** 135. **Common positions:** Accountant; Administrator; Blue-Collar Worker Supervisor; Chemist; Computer Programmer; Draftsperson; Architectural Engineer; Industrial Engineer; Mechanical Engineer; Personnel and Labor Relations Specialist; Purchasing Agent; Quality Controller; Sales Representative; Estimator. **Educational backgrounds sought:** Accounting; Business Administration; Chemistry; Computer Science; Engineering; Finance; Mathematics. **Benefits:** Medical, Dental, and Life Insurance; Pension Plan; Disability Coverage; Savings Plan. **Corporate headquarters:** Boston, MA. **Parent company:** Robertson Ceco. **Operations at this facility:** Manufacturing; Administration; Sales. **Listed on:** New York Stock Exchange.

DANVILLE METAL STAMPING COMPANY, INC.
20 Oakwood Avenue, Danville IL 61832. 217/446-0647. **Contact:** Greg Allard, Personnel Director. **Description:** Develops and produces fabricated metal components for the aerospace industry.

DIDION AND SONS FOUNDRY COMPANY
P.O. Box 520, St. Peters MO 63376. 314/928-1130. **Contact:** Ferdinand Potthast, Personnel Director. **Description:** Manufacturers of gray and ductile iron castings. **Employees:** 100. **Common positions:** Metallurgical Engineer. **Benefits:** medical insurance; pension plan; life insurance. **Corporate headquarters:** This location. **Operations at this facility:** manufacturing.

DIVERSIFIED INDUSTRIES INC.
101 South Hanley Road, Suite 1450, St. Louis MO 63105. 314/862-8200. **Contact:** Robert Garthe, Personnel Director. **Description:** Engaged in the manufacture of copper and aluminum granules; the reclamation of non-ferrous

metals and railroad freight car castings; the storage of brass strippings and structural steel. **Employees:** 300.

EG & G MISSOURI METAL SHAPING COMPANY
9970 Page Boulevard, St. Louis MO 63132. 314/428-3363. **Contact:** Bob Stone, Personnel Director. **Description:** A St. Louis company engaged in the manufacture of special metal fabricated parts for the aerospace industry. **Common positions:** Accountant; Blue-Collar Worker Supervisor; Buyer; Aerospace Engineer; General Manager; Operations/Production Manager; Personnel and Labor Relations Specialist; Purchasing Agent; Quality Control Supervisor; Sales Representative. **Educational backgrounds sought:** Accounting; Business Administration; Engineering; Marketing. **Special programs:** Training programs. **Benefits:** medical, dental, and life insurance; pension plan; tuition assistance; disability coverage; savings plan. **Corporate headquarters:** Wellesley, MA. **Parent company:** EG & G, Inc. **Operations at this facility:** manufacturing.

GENERAL METAL PRODUCTS COMPANY
3883 Delor Street, St. Louis MO 63116. 314/481-0300. **Contact:** Penny Ross, Personnel Director. **Description:** Manufacturers of metal stampings, fabrications, tools, dies and gauges. **Employees:** 400.

GRANITE CITY STEEL DIVISION/
NATIONAL STEEL COMPANY
1951 State Street, Granite City IL 62040. 618/451-3456. **Contact:** Troy Ward, Director/Human Resources. **Description:** A manufacturer of steel. **Employees:** 3,000.

GROSSMAN IRON & STEEL
5 North Market Street, St. Louis MO 63102. 314/231-9423. **Contact:** John Lorinc, Personnel Department. **Description:** A wholesaler of scrap and waste materials.

HARVARD INDUSTRIES/
ST. LOUIS DIECASTING DIVISION
201 Rock Industrial Park Drive, Bridgeton MO 63044. 314/291-3700. **Contact:** Mr. Gene Robinson, Personnel Director. **Description:** St. Louis manufacturers of zinc, aluminum, and magnesium diecasting.

HITCHINER MANUFACTURING COMPANY INC.
P.O. Box 280, O'Fallon MO 63366. 314/272-6176. **Contact:** Personnel Department. **Description:** Manufacture nonferrous investment castings.

LEONARD'S METAL, INC.
3030 Highway #94, North, P.O. Box 678, St. Charles MO 63302. 314/946-6525. **Contact:** Cindy Burleson, Personnel Director. **Description:** Manufacture stampings, fabricated metal products, tools and dies, aerospace parts and assemblies.

LYON SHEET METAL WORKS
4085 Bingham Avenue, St. Louis MO 63116. 314/352-8181. **Contact:** Payroll/Personnel. **Description:** A St. Louis metals company engaged in sheet metal fabrication and installation.

MARQUETTE TOOL & DIE COMPANY
3185 South Kingshighway, St. Louis MO 63139. 314/771-8509. **Contact:** Tom Hauska, Controller. **Description:** A St. Louis manufacturer of metal stampings, special machining and assemblies, tools and dies.

METAL GOODS
DIVISION OF ALCAN ALUMINUM CORPORATION
8800 Page Boulevard, St. Louis MO 63114. 314/427-1234. **Contact:** Personnel Department. **Description:** A wholesale service center for high-performance corrosion-resistant metals.

MISSOURI BOILER & TANK COMPANY
DIVISION OF NOOTER CORPORATION
P.O. Box 14704, St. Louis MO 63178. 314/231-5800. **Contact:** John Smegner, Personnel Director. **Description:** A St. Louis company engaged in the manufacture of steel alloy plate fabricators, heat exchangers, and pressure vessels.

NESCO STEEL BARREL COMPANY
P. O. Box N, Granite City IL 62040. 618/452-1190. **Contact:** Dale Cann, President. **Description:** A manufacturer of steel drums for food, chemicals and oil.

NOOTER CORPORATION
P.O. Box 451, St. Louis MO 63166. 314/621-6000. **Contact:** Robert Arb, Personnel. **Description:** A St. Louis company that fabricates and erects steel and alloy plate storage tanks and pressure vessels.

PAULO PRODUCTS COMPANY
5711 West Park Avenue, St. Louis MO 63110-1890. 314/647-7500. **Contact:** Lori Mueller, Personnel Director. **Description:** A St. Louis commercial heat treating and copper brazing services company.

PEA RIDGE IRON ORE CO.
HC65, P.O. Box 110, Sullivan MO 63080. 314/468-7251. **Contact:** Thomas D. Gallagher, Employee Relations Director. **Description:** Mining and processing of customized iron ore pellet and high grade iron oxide powders. **Common positions:** Accountant; Buyer; Chemist; Computer Programmer; Customer Service Representative; Electrical Engineer; Mechanical Engineer; Metallurgical Engineer; Mining Engineer; Personnel and Labor Relations Specialist; Purchasing Agent; Quality Control Supervisor. **Educational background sought:** Accounting. **Special programs:** Training programs. **Benefits:** medical insurance; dental insurance; pension plan; life insurance; tuition assistance; disability coverage. **Corporate headquarters:** St. Louis, MO. **Parent company:** Big River Minerals Corp. **Operations at this facility:** manufacturing; administration.

PROGRESSIVE SERVICE COMPANY
2720 Clark Avenue, St. Louis MO 63101. 314/531-4300. **Contact:** Tina Rauch, Personnel Director. **Description:** A St. Louis die-cutting company.

ROESCH INC.
100 North 24th Street, P.O. Box 328, Belleville IL 62222. 618/233-2760. **Contact:** Bonnie Voges, Personnel Director. **Description:** Southern Illinois manufacturers of steel stampings and porcelain enameling.

JOSEPH T. RYERSON & SON INC.
#5 Clinton Street, St. Louis MO 63102. 314/231-1020. **Contact:** Marilyn Eggerding, Personnel Department. **Description:** A St. Louis steel service center.

SOUTHWEST STEEL SUPPLY COMPANY
3401 Morganford Road, P.O. Drawer B, Gravois Station, St. Louis MO 63116. 314/664-6100. **Contact:** Alma Hansen, Controller. **Description:** A steel service center.

SPORLAN VALVE COMPANY
7525 Sussex Ave., St. Louis MO 63143. 314/647-2775. **Contact:** Steve Lange, Personnel Director. **Description:** A manufacturer of metallic valves.

ST. CLAIR DIE CASTING COMPANY
P.O. Drawer 280, St. Clair MO 63077-0280. 314/629-2550. **Contact:** Diana Sanders, Personnel Director. **Description:** Manufacturer of aluminum diecastings and zinc diecastings.

ST. LOUIS STEEL
133 McDonnell Boulevard, St. Louis MO 63042. 314/731-8000. **Contact:** Personnel. **Description:** A St. Louis company engaged in the manufacture of rolled steel sections, fence posts and hot dip galvanizing.

ST. LOUIS STEEL CASTING INC.
100 Mott Street, St. Louis MO 63111. 314/353-5800. **Contact:** Personnel. **Description:** Manufactures carbon, alloy and stainless steel castings.

STOUT INDUSTRIES INC.
6425 West Florissant Avenue, St. Louis MO 63136. 314/385-2280. **Contact:** Cheryl Goodman, Personnel Director. **Description:** St. Louis manufacturer of metal displays.

STUPP BROS. BRIDGE & IRON COMPANY
P.O. Box 6600, St. Louis MO 63125. 314/638-5000. **Contact:** John Stupp, Jr., Office Manager. **Description:** Manufacturers of fabricated structural steel.

TUBULAR STEEL INC.
1031 Executive Parkway, St. Louis MO 63141. 314/851-9200. **Contact:** Patricia Warchol, Personnel Specialist. **Description:** A St. Louis distributor of steel pipe and tubing. **Common positions:** Customer Service Representative; Sales Representative. **Educational backgrounds sought:** Accounting. **Corporate headquarters:** This location. **Operations at this facility:** Service.

U.S. RINGBINDER
6800 Arsenal Street, St. Louis MO 63139-2593. 314/645-7880. **Contact:** Ms. Pat Ahrens, Human Resources Manager. **Description:** Manufacture metal hardware parts for loose leaf binders.

VALENTEC KISCO
6300 St. Louis Avenue, St. Louis MO 63121. 314/381-9850. **Contact:** Cheryl Liebich, Personnel Manager. **Description:** Engaged in the manufacture of metal fabrication and stampings primarily for defense. **Common positions:** Blue-Collar Worker Supervisor; Mechanical Engineer; Operations/Production Manager; Quality Control Supervisor. **Educational backgrounds sought:** Business Administration; Engineering. **Benefits:** medical, dental, and life insurance; tuition assistance; disability coverage; profit sharing; savings plan. **Corporate headquarters:** Midland, TX. **Parent company:** Insilco. **Operations at this facility:** manufacturing.

Additional large employers: 250+

STEEL WORKS, BLAST FURNACES (INCLUDING COKE OVENS) AND ROLLING MILLS

Bethlehem Steel Corp
11701 Borman Dr, St. Louis MO 63146-4100. 314/993-6663. Employs: 250-499.

Grnt City Steel Division
7733 Forsyth Blvd, St. Louis MO 63105-1817. 314/726-4711. Employs: 250-499.

Inland Steel Co
12312 Olive Blvd, St. Louis MO 63141-6448. 314/542-0400. Employs: 250-499.

Laclede Steel Co
Cut St, Alton IL 62002. 618/474-2100. Employs: 1,000+.

Maverick Tube Corp
4 W Park Ave, Union MO 63084-1552. 314/583-5792. Employs: 250-499.

Missouri Rolling Mill Corp
6800 Manchester Ave, St. Louis MO 63143-2616. 314/645-3500. Employs: 250-499.

National Steel Corp
7733 Forsyth Blvd, St. Louis MO 63105-1817. 314/726-0707. Employs: 250-499.

COLD-ROLLED STEEL SHEET, STRIP AND BARS

Laclede Steel Co
211 N Broadway, St. Louis MO 63102-2733. 314/425-1400. Employs: 500-999.

STEEL PIPE AND TUBES

La Barge Pipe & Steel Co
901 N 10th St, St. Louis MO 63101-2900. 314/231-3400. Employs: 250-499.

STEEL FOUNDRIES

American Steel Foundries
1700 Walnut St, Granite City IL 62040-3100. 618/452-2111. Employs: 500-999.

PRIMARY PRODUCTION OF ALUMINUM

Consolidated Aluminum Corp
100960 Westline Industrial Dr, St. Louis MO 63146. 314/878-6950. Employs: 500-999.

SECONDARY SMELTING AND REFINING OF NONFERROUS METALS

Doe Run Co
881 Main St, Herculaneum MO 63048-1222. 314/479-5311. Employs: 500-999.

ROLLING, DRAWING AND EXTRUDING OF COPPER

Cerro Copper Products Co
Mississippi Ave, E St. Louis IL 62201. 618/337-6000. Employs: 1,000+.

ALUMINUM DIE-CASTINGS

Spartan Aluminum Products Inc
510 E McClurken St, Sparta IL 62286-1850. 618/443-4346. Employs: 250-499.

METAL CANS

Crown Cork & Seal Co Inc
7140 N Broadway, St. Louis MO 63147-2708. 314/679-7401. Employs: 250-499.

HEATING EQUIPMENT, EXCEPT ELECTRIC AND WARM AIR FURNACES

Arcoaire Comfortmaker
401 Randolph St, Red Bud IL 62278-1001. 618/282-6262. Employs: 500-999.

FABRICATED STRUCTURAL METAL

J S Alberici Cons Co Inc
2150 Kienlen Ave, St. Louis MO 63121-5505. 314/261-2611. Employs: 1,000+.

FABRICATED PLATE WORK (BOILER SHOPS)

Maverick Tube Corp
11 McBride Ctr Dr, Chesterfield MO 63005. 314/537-1314. Employs: 500-999.

AUTOMOTIVE STAMPINGS

Wagner
3700 Forest Pk Blvd, St. Louis MO 63108-3312. 314/658-5100. Employs: 250-499.

ELECTROPLATING, PLATING, POLISHING, ANODIZING AND COLORING

C & A Metal Finishing Co Inc
11048 Gravois Industrial Ct, St. Louis MO 63128-2013. 314/353-9434. Employs: 500-999.

Siegel Roberts Plating
8645 S Broadway St, St. Louis MO 63111-3810. 314/638-8300. Employs: 250-499.

ORDNANCE AND ACCESSORIES

Southwest Mobil Systems Corp
200 Sidney St, St. Louis MO 63104-4719. 314/771-3950. Employs: 250-499.

Valentec Kisco Inc
6300 St Louis Ave, St. Louis MO 63121-5721. 314/381-9850. Employs: 250-499.

FABRICATED METAL PRODUCTS

Contico Ark
105 Byassee Dr, Hazelwood MO 63042-3103. 314/731-0302. Employs: 250-499.

Additional small to medium sized employers: 50-249

METAL MINING SERVICES

Venice Convenient Mart
1101 4th St, Venice IL 62090-1110. 618/876-5749. Employs: 50-99.

STEEL WORKS, BLAST FURNACES (INCLUDING COKE OVENS), AND ROLLING MILLS

Bank Bldg Equip Co Amer
1130 Hampton Av, St. Louis MO 63139-3147. 314/647-3800. Employs: 50-99.

Carondelet Foundry Co
2101 S Kingshighway, St. Louis MO 63110-3217. 314/771-0906. Employs: 100-249.

Titan Tube Fabricators Inc
5739 Natural Bridge Ave, St. Louis MO 63120-1629. 314/381-2828. Employs: 100-249.

COLD-ROLLED STEEL SHEET, STRIP AND BARS

Midwest Metal Reducers Inc
315 W Pacific Ave, St. Louis MO 63119-2325. 314/961-1001. Employs: 100-249.

Missouri Heat Threat Inc
55 Mar Ln, Saint Charles MO 63303-9000. 314/441-0510. Employs: 50-99.

St Louis Cold Drawn Inc
1060 Pershall Rd, St. Louis MO 63137-3842. 314/867-4301. Employs: 50-99.

The Steel Works Corporation
1020 Niedringhaus Ave, Granite City IL 62040-3142. 618/452-2833. Employs: 100-249.

STEEL PIPE AND TUBES

Bull Moose Tube Co
Hwy 50, Gerald MO 63037. 314/764-3315. Employs: 100-249.

GRAY AND DUCTILE IRON FOUNDRIES

Duplex Metals Inc
1463 Pine Industrial, St. Louis MO 63132. 314/427-0905. Employs: 50-99.

Gene Bonds
5639 Chalet Manor Ct, St. Louis MO 63129-4106. 314/846-0630. Employs: 50-99.

Industrial Thermal Equipment
71 May Rd, Wentzville MO 63385-3312. 314/926-8501. Employs: 50-99.

Liberty Foundry Co
7600 S Vulcan St, St. Louis MO 63111-3449. 314/638-1800. Employs: 50-99.

Midwest Precision Castings Co
103 N Cool Springs Rd, O Fallon MO 63366-4403. 314/441-2602. Employs: 50-99.

Wirco Casting Inc
R R 1, New Athens IL 62264-9801. 618/475-2124. Employs: 50-99.

Neenah Foundry Co
55 Cherokee Dr, Saint Peters MO 63376-3927. 314/928-1023. Employs: 50-99.

STEEL INVESTMENT FOUNDRIES

STEEL FOUNDRIES

Excelsior Foundry Co Inc
1123 East B St, Belleville IL 62220-4149. 618/233-0232. Employs: 50-99.

Sterling Steel Foundry
2300 Falling Springs Rd, E St. Louis IL 62206-1102. 618/337-6123. Employs: 100-249.

PRIMARY SMELTING AND REFINING OF COPPER

Chemetco Inc
R R 3 & Oldenburg Rd, Hartford IL 62048. 618/254-4381. Employs: 100-249.

Cyprus Warrenton Refining Co
County Rd M, Warrenton MO 63383. 314/456-3488. Employs: 50-99.

PRIMARY SMELTING AND REFINING OF NONFERROUS METALS, EXCEPT COPPER AND ALUMINUM

Asarco Inc
S R 127, Hillsboro IL 62049. 217/532-3931. Employs: 50-99.

Grossman Iron & Steel Co
5 N Market St, St. Louis MO 63102-1415. 314/231-9423. Employs: 50-99.

St Louis Auto Shredding Inc
1200 N 1st St, Natl Stock Yd IL 62071. 618/271-7100. Employs: 50-99.

SECONDARY SMELTING AND REFINING OF NONFERROUS METALS

Becker Metals Corp
806 S 22nd St, St. Louis MO 63103-3039. 314/621-0566. Employs: 50-99.

Shapiro Sales Co
601 E Red Bud Ave, St. Louis MO 63147-3041. 314/381-9300. Employs: 50-99.

ROLLING, DRAWING AND EXTRUDING OF NONFERROUS METALS, EXCEPT COPPER AND ALUMINUM

Tradco Inc
1701 W Main St, Washington MO 63090-1003. 314/239-7816. Employs: 100-249.

DRAWING AND INSULATING OF NONFERROUS WIRE

Siemens Mfg Co Inc
410 W Washington St, Freeburg IL 62243-1333. 618/539-3000. Employs: 50-99.

ALUMINUM DIE-CASTINGS

H J Enterprises Inc
3010 High Ridge Blvd, High Ridge MO 63049-2214. 314/677-3421. Employs: 100-249.

Louisiana Mfg Co
1404 N Carolina St, Louisiana MO 63353-2209. 314/754-4191. Employs: 50-99.

NONFERROUS DIE-CASTINGS, EXCEPT ALUMINUM

Century Brass Works Inc
1100 N Illinois St, Belleville IL 62220-4378. 618/233-0182. Employs: 50-99.

ALUMINUM FOUNDRIES

Harvard Inds
201 Rock Indl Pk Dr, Bridgeton MO 63044. 314/291-3700. Employs: 100-249.

NONFERROUS FOUNDRIES, EXCEPT ALUMINUM AND COPPER

Midwest Precision Casting Co
102 N Cool Springs Rd, O Fallon MO 63366-4405. 314/272-6190. Employs: 50-99.

PRIMARY METAL PRODUCTS

Antonia Fabricators
3700 Highway M, Imperial MO 63052-2951. 314/942-2855. Employs: 50-99.

National Steel Granite City Div
1943 State St, Granite City IL 62040-4622. 618/451-3456. Employs: 50-99.

Spectrulite
College St, Venice IL 62090. 618/452-5190. Employs: 50-99.

Megamet Industries
743 Spirit Of St Louis Blvd, Chesterfield MO 63005. 314/537-5351. Employs: 50-99.

METAL CANS

American National Can Co
8750 Pevely Indl Dr, Pevely MO 63070. 314/479-4433. Employs: 100-249.

Metal Container Corp
42 Tenbrook Indl Pk, Arnold MO 63010. 314/296-2002. Employs: 100-249.

Mirax Chemical Products Corp
4999 Fyler Ave, St. Louis MO 63139-1111. 314/752-1500. Employs: 50-99.

Plaze Inc
9401 Watson Indl Pk, St. Louis MO 63126. 314/961-3564. Employs: 50-99.

METAL SHIPPING BARRELS, DRUMS, KEGS AND PAILS

Container Products
2391 Cassens Dr, Fenton MO 63026-2502. 314/343-7333. Employs: 50-99.

HAND AND EDGE TOOLS, EXCEPT MACHINE TOOLS AND HANDSAWS

Alexander Mfg Co
12978 Tesson Ferry Rd, St. Louis MO 63128-2961. 314/842-3344. Employs: 50-99.

Keller Tool Corp
1400 S Highway 141, Fenton MO 63026-5799. 314/343-8999. Employs: 50-99.

SAW BLADES AND HANDSAWS

Drake Corp
2723 Ivanhoe Ave, St. Louis MO 63139-2501. 314/645-3539. Employs: 100-249.

Kasco Corp
1569 Tower Grove Ave, St. Louis MO 63110-2215. 314/771-1550. Employs: 100-249.

HARDWARE

A I Manufacturing Corp
1611 Des Peres Rd, St. Louis MO 63131-1813. 314/821-7200. Employs: 100-249.

Hager Hinge Co
139 Victor St, St. Louis MO 63104-4724. 314/772-4400. Employs: 50-99.

Loose Leaf Metals Company Inc
6800 Arsenal St, St. Louis MO 63139-2526. 314/645-7880. Employs: 100-249.

ENAMELED IRON AND METAL SANITARY WARE

Ro Viso Supply Inc
217 Madison Av, Madison IL 62060-1107. 618/451-0172. Employs: 50-99.

HEATING EQUIPMENT, EXCEPT ELECTRIC AND WARM AIR FURNACES

Empire Comfort Systems Inc
918 Freeburg Ave, Belleville IL 62220-2623. 618/233-7420. Employs: 100-249.

Martin Inds
4200 St Clair Ave, E St. Louis IL 62203-1065. 618/271-1272. Employs: 100-249.

Watts Radiator Sales & Service
319 E Main St, Collinsville IL 62234-3008. 618/344-2534. Employs: 50-99.

FABRICATED STRUCTURAL METAL

E M E Inc
182 N W Indl Ct, Bridgeton MO 63044. 314/298-8300. Employs: 50-99.

Five Star Metal Fabricators
2701 Converse Ave, E St. Louis IL 62207-1728. 618/271-6250. Employs: 50-99.

Midwest Metal Fabricators Inc
201 E Indl Dr, New Haven MO 63068. 314/237-3003. Employs: 50-99.

Missouri Research Labs Inc
3800 W Clay St, Saint Charles MO 63301-4417. 314/946-6900. Employs: 100-249.

METAL DOORS, SASH, FRAMES, MOLDING AND TRIM

Clark Door Co Inc
2366 Centerline Ind Dr, St. Louis MO 63146-3302. 314/432-3112. Employs: 100-249.

Delsan Inds Inc
1644 Lotsie Blvd, St. Louis MO 63132-1427. 314/423-5900. Employs: 50-99.

Mc Alpine Co
18092 Chesterfield Airport Rd, Chesterfield MO 63005-1105. 314/532-3360. Employs: 50-99.

Moeller Reimer Co Inc
9245 Dielman Indl Dr, St. Louis MO 63132. 314/997-5310. Employs: 100-249.

Target Aluminum Inc
800 W State St, Vandalia MO 63382. 314/594-6433. Employs: 50-99.

Winco Mfg Co Inc
6200 Maple Ave, St. Louis MO
63130-3305. 314/725-8088.
Employs: 50-99.

FABRICATED PLATE WORK (BOILER SHOPS)

Airtherm Mfg Co
9339 Dielman Industrial Dr, St. Louis MO 63132-2212. 314/993-3400. Employs: 100-249.

Kickham Boiler & Eng Inc
625 E Carrie Ave, St. Louis MO 63147-3016. 314/261-4786. Employs: 50-99.

Lowell Mfg Co
3030 Laclede Sta Rd, St. Louis MO 63143-3806. 314/781-9058. Employs: 50-99.

Matco Machine & Tool Co
9550 Watson Indl Pk, St. Louis MO 63126. 314/962-9200. Employs: 100-249.

Missouri Boiler & Tank Co
2300 Papin St, St. Louis MO 63103-3026. 314/231-5800. Employs: 100-249.

Mitek Mfg
4203 Shoreline Dr E, Earth City MO 63045-1209. 314/298-8088. Employs: 50-99.

Permea Inc
11444 Lackland Rd, St. Louis MO 63146-3523. 314/694-8000. Employs: 100-249.

Systemaire Inc
4181 Shoreline Dr E, Earth City MO 63045-1217. 314/739-8310. Employs: 50-99.

SHEET METAL WORK

American Device Mfg Co
1003 W Broadway, Steeleville IL 62288-1311. 618/965-3491. Employs: 50-99.

C & R Heating & Svc Co Inc
12825 Pennridge Dr, Bridgeton MO 63044-1238. 314/739-1800. Employs: 100-249.

Charles E Jarrell Contracting
4208 Rider Trl N, Earth City MO 63045-1105. 314/291-0100. Employs: 100-249.

Fritz Inc
424 Lebanon Ave, Belleville IL 62220-4127. 618/277-1630. Employs: 100-249.

Gross Mechanical Contractors
7379 Pagedale Indl Ct, St. Louis MO 63133. 314/727-3688. Employs: 100-249.

Grossmann Contracting Co
2505 N Leffingwell St, St. Louis MO 63106-1919. 314/533-0690. Employs: 50-99.

Jackes Evans Mfg Co
4427 Geraldine Ave, St. Louis MO 63115-1217. 314/385-4132. Employs: 100-249.

Metalcraft Enterprise
202 Indl Dr, New Haven MO 63068. 314/237-3016. Employs: 50-99.

South Side Roofing/Sheet Metal
290 Hanley Indl Ct, St. Louis MO 63144. 314/968-4800. Employs: 50-99.

St Louis Blow Pipe
1948 N 9th St, St. Louis MO 63102-1343. 314/241-7316. Employs: 50-99.

ARCHITECTURAL AND ORNAMENTAL METAL WORK

G S Metals Corp
R R 4 Box 7, Pinckneyville IL 62274-9499. 618/357-5353. Employs: 100-249.

Tru-Weld Grating Inc
1501 Eilerman Ave, Litchfield IL 62056-3005. 217/324-6106. Employs: 50-99.

PREFABRICATED METAL BUILDINGS AND COMPONENTS

Arrow Group Inds
1101 N 4th St, Breese IL 62230-1755. 618/526-4546. Employs: 100-249.

Gismo
3445 Bent Ave, St. Louis MO 63116-2601. 314/772-5400. Employs: 100-249.

Henges Assoc Inc
12100 Prichard Farm Rd, Maryland Hts MO 63043-4201. 314/739-2600. Employs: 100-249.

Porta-King Building Systs
1020 Indl Pk Dr, Montgomery City MO 63361. 314/564-3766. Employs: 50-99.

SCREW MACHINE PRODUCTS

Apex Industries Inc
5931 Garfield Ave, St. Louis MO 63134-2303. 314/524-7400. Employs: 50-99.

Parts Fabricators Inc
7320 Hazelwood Ave, Hazelwood MO 63042-2910. 314/522-1000. Employs: 50-99.

Pohlman Inc
140 Long Rd, Chesterfield MO 63005-1206. 314/537-1909. Employs: 50-99.

Roton Products Inc
660 E Elliott Ave, St. Louis MO 63122-6408. 314/821-4400. Employs: 50-99.

Woodson Products Co Inc
1601 Woodson Rd, St. Louis MO 63114-6128. 314/997-4300. Employs: 50-99.

BOLTS, NUTS, SCREWS, RIVETS AND WASHERS

St Louis Screw & Bolt Co
6900 N Broadway, St. Louis MO 63147-2704. 314/389-7500. Employs: 50-99.

Western Wire Products Co
1415 S 18th St, St. Louis MO 63104-2501. 314/771-6100. Employs: 50-99.

NONFERROUS FORGINGS

Precision Forgings Inc
600 St Louis Ave, Valley Park MO 63088-1828. 314/225-5222. Employs: 50-99.

METAL STAMPINGS

Argo Products Co
3500 Goodfellow Blvd, St. Louis MO 63120-1109. 314/385-1803. Employs: 50-99.

Bachman Machine Co
4321 N Broadway, St. Louis MO 63147-3308. 314/231-4221. Employs: 50-99.

Highland Mach & Screw Prod Co
700 5th St, Highland IL 62249-1213. 618/654-2103. Employs: 50-99.

Metal Stamping Products
5101 Penrose St, St. Louis MO
63115-1222. 314/382-5300.
Employs: 50-99.

Wainwright Industries Inc
Arrowhead Industrial Pk, Saint
Peters MO 63376. 314/278-5850.
Employs: 100-249.

ELECTROPLATING, PLATING, POLISHING, ANODIZING AND COLORING

Fin Clair Corp
4001 Gratiot St, St. Louis MO
63110-1725. 314/535-7868.
Employs: 50-99.

COATING, ENGRAVING AND ALLIED SERVICES

Futura Coatings Inc
9200 Latty Ave, Hazelwood MO
63042-2805. 314/521-4100.
Employs: 50-99.

Precoat Metals
4301 S Spring Ave, St. Louis MO
63116-4436. 314/352-8000.
Employs: 100-249.

St Louis Metalizing Co
4123 Sarpy Ave, St. Louis MO
63110-1745. 314/531-5253.
Employs: 50-99.

Western Supplies Co
2920 Cass Ave, St. Louis MO
63106-1530. 314/531-0100.
Employs: 50-99.

U S Paint Corp
831 S 21st St, St. Louis MO 63103-3043. 314/621-0525. Employs: 100-249.

AMMUNITION, EXCEPT FOR SMALL ARMS

Propellex Corp
R R 159 N Springfield,
Edwardsville IL 62025. 618/656-3400. Employs: 100-249.

Propellex Corp
R R 1, Donnellson IL 62019-9801.
217/537-3312. Employs: 50-99.

Valentec Olivette
9315 Olive Blvd, St. Louis MO
63132-3211. 314/997-6656.
Employs: 100-249.

INDUSTRIAL VALVES

Sparklet Devices Inc
4400 Gustine Ave, St. Louis MO
63116-3418. 314/353-0400.
Employs: 50-99.

Sporlan Valve Co/Plt 2
1699 W Main St, Washington MO
63090-1001. 314/239-5266.
Employs: 100-249.

VALVES AND PIPE FITTINGS

Jefferson Products Co
711 Indl Ave, Washington MO
63090. 314/239-6524. Employs: 100-249.

Valley Steel Products Co
900 Walnut St, St. Louis MO
63102-1137. 314/231-2160.
Employs: 100-249.

MISCELLANEOUS FABRICATED WIRE PRODUCTS

Industrial Wire Products
2005 W N Service Rd, Sullivan
MO 63080. 314/468-5151.
Employs: 100-249.

Ludlow Saylor/Wire Cloth Div
1402 Old Hwy 40 E, Warrenton
MO 63383. 314/456-8200.
Employs: 100-249.

Nixdorff-Lloyd Chain Co
1009 Executive Parkway Dr, St. Louis MO 63141-6324. 314/576-4710. Employs: 100-249.

METAL FOIL AND LEAF

Highland Supply Corp
1111 6th St, Highland IL 62249-1408. 618/654-2161. Employs: 100-249.

Matteuzzi Decorators Inc
5347 Minerva Ave, St. Louis MO 63112-4116. 314/367-1352. Employs: 50-99.

FABRICATED PIPE AND PIPE FITTINGS

Bohn & Dawson Inc
3500 Tree Court Industr Bl, St. Louis MO 63122-6620. 314/225-5011. Employs: 50-99.

Maverick Tube Corp
1314 E Independence Dr, Union MO 63084-3101. 314/583-4950. Employs: 50-99.

Missouri Pipe Fittings Co
400 Withers Ave, St. Louis MO 63147-3128. 314/421-0790. Employs: 50-99.

FABRICATED METAL PRODUCTS

Beall Manufacturing Inc
112 N Shamrock Box 70, East Alton IL 62024-0070. 618/259-8154. Employs: 50-99.

For more information on career opportunities in the fabricated and primary metals industries:

Associations

AMERICAN FOUNDRYMEN'S SOCIETY
505 State Street, Des Plaines IL 60016. 708/824-0181.

AMERICAN IRON & STEEL INSTITUTE
1101 17th Street NW, 13th Floor, Washington DC 20036. 202/452-7100.

AMERICAN POWDER METALLURGY INSTITUTE
105 College Road East, Princeton NJ 08540. 609/452-7700.

AMERICAN SOCIETY FOR METALS
9639 Kinsman Road, Materials Park OH 44073-0002. 216/338-5151.

AMERICAN WELDING SOCIETY
P.O. Box 35140, 550 LeJeune Road NW, Miami FL 33135. 305/443-9353.

ASSOCIATION OF IRON AND STEEL ENGINEERS
Three Gateway Center, Suite 2350, Pittsburgh PA 15222. 412/281-6323.

ASSOCIATION OF STEEL DISTRIBUTORS
401 N. Michigan Avenue, Chicago IL 60611. 312/664-6610.

NATIONAL ASSOCIATION OF METAL FINISHERS
401 N. Michigan Avenue, Chicago IL 60611. 312/644-6610.

Directories

DIRECTORY OF STEEL FOUNDRIES IN THE UNITED STATES, CANADA, AND MEXICO
Steel Founder's Society of America, 455 State Street, Des Plaines IL 60016. 708/299-9160.

Magazines

AMERICAN METAL MARKET
Capital Cities ABC, 825 7th Avenue, New York NY 10019. 212/887-8580.

IRON AGE
191 S. Gary, Carol Stream IL 60188. 708/462-2285.

IRON & STEEL ENGINEER
Association of Iron and Steel Engineers, Three Gateway Center, Suite 2350, Pittsburgh PA 15222. 412/281-6323.

MODERN METALS
400 N. Michigan Avenue, Chicago IL 60611. 312/222-2000.

FINANCIAL SERVICES/MANAGEMENT CONSULTING

Since the 1987 crash, the financial services industry has been struggling to redefine itself. In response to the recession, companies have been cutting costs - and jobs - in order to become leaner and more efficient. Jobseekers should look to conservative firms for the most stable career tracks. Tip: Take a close look at mutual funds, one of the few current hot areas.

BOATMEN'S TRUST COMPANY
100 North Broadway, St. Louis MO 63102. 314/466-3377. **Contact:** Kristin Koppen, Vice President/Human Resources. **Description:** Among the largest trust institutions in the U.S., Boatmen's Trust Company is engaged exclusively in the trust and investment services. Founded in 1889. Operates with three divisions: Personal Trust Division, providing trust and investment services to families and individuals; Pension and Institutional Services Division, providing administration and investment services to employee benefits plans and other institutions; and Corporate Trust Division, providing stock and bond trust and agency services for corporations. Company is responsible for approximately $54 billion in total assets. **Employees:** 930+. **Common positions:** Accountant; Administrator for Trusts; Attorney; Financial Analyst; Department Manager; Operation Manager; Portfolio Manager; Security Analyst. **Educational backgrounds sought:** Accounting; Business Administration; Computer Science; Finance; Law. **Special programs:** Training programs. **Benefits:** medical, dental, and life insurance; pension plan; tuition assistance; disability coverage; daycare assistance; employee discounts; 401(K). **Parent company:** Boatmen's Bancshares, Inc. **Operations at this facility:** research and development; administration; service; sales.

CASHEX INC.
1600 South Brentwood Boulevard, Suite 220, St. Louis MO 63144. 800/627-4040. **Contact:** Human Resources. **Description:** Clearinghouse engaged in functions relating to banking. **Employees:** 100+.

CITICORP
CITICORP MORTGAGE, INC.
15851 Clayton Road, Ballwin MO 63011. 314/256-5000. **Contact:** Personnel Manager. **Description:** Citicorp Mortgage is the national mortgage division of Citibank, the country's largest financial institution. Headquartered in St. Louis, MO, the company develops mortgage products, policies, processes, systems and standards that have made the mortgage business a central part of Citibank's relationship with consumers across the country. Operates a nationwide network of mortgage lending offices which, together with other Citibank consumer mortgage operations, have provided more home loans than any other lender in the past five years. **Common positions:** Computer Programmer; Credit Manager; Customer Service Representative; Financial Analyst; Management Trainee; Operations/Production Manager; Marketing Specialist; Quality Control Supervisor; Sales Representative; Systems Analyst; Underwriter. **Educational backgrounds sought:** Accounting; Business Administration; Computer Science; Finance; Marketing; MBA. **Special programs:** Training programs and internships. **Benefits:** medical insurance; dental insurance; pension plan; life insurance; tuition assistance; disability coverage; daycare assistance; profit sharing; employee discounts; savings plan. **Corporate headquarters:** This location. **Parent company:** Citibank. **Operations at this facility:** research and development; administration; service; sales. **Listed on:** New York Stock Exchange.

MERRILL, LYNCH, PIERCE, FENNER & SMITH
1 Boatmens Plaza, 800 Market Street, Suite 2400, St. Louis MO 63101. 314/982-8000. **Contact:** Richard Paradise, Administrative Manager. **Description:** St. Louis office of the well-known world financial company. Nationally, company is organized to provide both traditional and innovative products and services to a broad range of individual and institutional customers. Merrill Lynch operates primarily through functional units which include: Individual Services; Capital Markets; Assets Management; Futures; International; Real Estate and Insurance. **Parent company:** Merrill Lynch & Co., Inc. **Corporate headquarters:** New York, NY. **Listed on:** New York Stock Exchange.

STIFEL NICOLAUS
500 North Broadway, St. Louis MO 63102. 314/342-2898. **Contact:** Robert Meyer, Director of Human Resources. **Description:** A regional investment firm. Services include: fixed income securities, corporate finance, syndicate participation, tax shelter, trading, broker dealer services, securities analysis, and options. **Corporate headquarters:** This location. **Common positions:** Sales Representative. **Educational backgrounds sought:** Accounting; Business Administration; Economics; Finance; Marketing. **Benefits:** medical insurance; dental insurance; life insurance.

WESTERN UNION FINANCIAL SERVICES INC
13022 Hollenberg Drive, Bridgeton MO 63044. 314/291-8000. **Contact:** Leslie Johnson, Manager of Personnel and Training. **Description:** One of three customer service centers which provide money transfer and message service to the public. Services include: Money transfer service via Western Union Agencies or by telephone with a credit card. Telegrams, mailgrams, cablegrams, and public opinion messages available by telephone. **Corporate headquarters:** Upper Saddle River, NJ. **Listed on:** New York Stock Exchange. International. **Common positions:** Customer Service Representative (part time and full time); Customer Service Specialist (part time and full time). **Special programs:** Paid training program. **Operations at this facility:** Service. **Benefits:** Employee Discounts. **Other U.S. locations:** Reno, NV. **Parent company:** New Valley Corp. **Employees:** 2,000. **Projected hires for the next 12 months:** 300 part-time employees.

Additional large employers: 250+

PERSONAL CREDIT INSTITUTIONS

Centerre Bank Na
One Centerre Plaza, St. Louis MO 63101. 314/554-6000. Employs: 1,000+.

SECURITY BROKERS, DEALERS AND FLOTATION COMPANIES

Edward D Jones & Co
201 Progress Pkwy, Maryland Hts MO 63043-3003. 314/851-2000. Employs: 1,000+.

OFFICES OF HOLDING COMPANIES

Townhouse Penthouse Ind Inc
1314 Hanley Industrial Ct, St. Louis MO 63144-1914. 314/968-1818. Employs: 500-999.

BUSINESS CONSULTING SERVICES

Harry H Kessler & Assoc Corp
9909 Clayton Rd, St. Louis MO 63124-1120. 314/994-3573. Employs: 500-999.

Additional small to medium sized employers: 50-249

PERSONAL CREDIT INSTITUTIONS

Boatmens National Bank St Louis
4249 Watson Rd, St. Louis MO 63109-1214. 314/781-7700. Employs: 100-249.

First Illinois Bank
327 Missouri Ave, E St. Louis IL 62201-3088. 618/271-8700. Employs: 50-99.

Jefferson Bank & Trust
2301 Market St, St. Louis MO 63103-2541. 314/621-0100. Employs: 50-99.

SHORT-TERM BUSINESS CREDIT INSTITUTIONS, EXCEPT AGRICULTURAL

Mercantile Bank
1005 Convention Plz, St. Louis MO 63101-1229. 314/444-4070. Employs: 50-99.

SECURITY BROKERS, DEALERS AND FLOTATION COMPANIES

Barney Smith Harris Upham & Co
34 N Meramec Ave, St. Louis MO 63105-3874. 314/863-2000. Employs: 50-99.

Brennan & Co
818 Olive St, St. Louis MO 63101-1554. 314/436-0006. Employs: 50-99.

Charles Schwab Co Inc
1 Metropolitan Sq, St. Louis MO 63102-2733. 314/436-4147. Employs: 50-99.

Cox Clark
314 N Broadway, St. Louis MO 63102-2035. 314/241-5057. Employs: 50-99.

Dain Bosworth Inc
1 City Centre, St. Louis MO 63101. 314/421-4560. Employs: 50-99.

Dapco Securities
906 Olive St, St. Louis MO 63101-1448. 314/621-8241. Employs: 50-99.

Dardas & Co
319 N 4th St, St. Louis MO 63102-1907. 314/241-4422. Employs: 50-99.

Edward D Jones & Co
4425 Hampton Ave, St. Louis MO 63109-2237. 314/352-8888. Employs: 50-99.

First Gateway Securities Inc
1000 Locust, St. Louis MO 63101. 314/231-6000. Employs: 50-99.

First St Louis Securities Inc
1010 Market St, St. Louis MO 63101-2000. 314/241-4949. Employs: 50-99.

George K Baum & Company
509 Olive St, St. Louis MO 63101-1844. 314/436-2811. Employs: 50-99.

Gershman Investment Corp
7 N Bemiston Ave, St. Louis MO 63105-3303. 314/889-0600. Employs: 50-99.

J A Glynn & Co
319 N 4th St, St. Louis MO 63102-1907. 314/241-2255. Employs: 50-99.

Mark Twain Brokerage Svc Inc
1630 S Lindbergh Blvd, St. Louis MO 63131-3513. 314/997-1322. Employs: 50-99.

Mercantile Investment Svc Inc
Mercantile Towers, St. Louis MO 63101. 314/425-3882. Employs: 50-99.

National Securities Corp
625 N Euclid Ave, St. Louis MO 63108-1660. 314/367-5477. Employs: 50-99.

Olde Discount
310 N 6th St, St. Louis MO 63101-1814. 314/241-6666. Employs: 50-99.

Olde Stock Report
310 N 6th St, St. Louis MO 63101-1814. 314/241-6533. Employs: 50-99.

Peacock Hislop Staley & Given
721 Olive St, St. Louis MO 63101-2235. 314/436-7722. Employs: 50-99.

R W Lee Investment Services
906 Olive St, St. Louis MO 63101-1448. 314/621-0087. Employs: 50-99.

Republic Securities Inc
5100 Oakland Ave, St. Louis MO
63110-1406. 314/534-3030.
Employs: 50-99.

Waterhouse Securities Inc
100 N Broadway, St. Louis MO
63102-2728. 314/421-2737.
Employs: 50-99.

A G Edwards & Sons Inc
10401 Clayton Rd, St. Louis MO
63131-2929. 314/991-7800.
Employs: 50-99.

Merrill Lynch Pierce Fenner
120 S Central Ave, St. Louis MO
63105-1705. 314/854-0400.
Employs: 50-99.

Planned Futures Inc
5523 Columbia Ave, St. Louis MO
63139-1621. 314/644-3565.
Employs: 50-99.

Shearson Lehman Brothers Inc
1 Gateway Mall, St. Louis MO
63101. 314/231-9580. Employs: 50-99.

INVESTMENT ADVICE

A G Edwards & Sons Inc
One City Centre, St. Louis MO
63101. 314/436-2060. Employs: 50-99.

Americorp Securities Svc Inc
501 N 7th St, St. Louis MO 63101-1605. 314/241-4002. Employs: 50-99.

UNIT INVESTMENT TRUSTS, FACE-AMOUNT CERTIFICATE OFFICES AND CLOSED-END MANAGEMENT INVESTMENT OFFICES

First Plan Investments
10800 Lincoln Trail Ste 16, E St. Louis IL 62208-2020. 618/277-1448. Employs: 50-99.

Trust Benefit Plans Inc
900 E 8th St Ste B, Washington MO 63090-3131. 314/239-7782.
Employs: 50-99.

U S P A & I R A
2620 West Blvd, Belleville IL
62221-5605. 618/234-3702.
Employs: 50-99.

PATENT OWNERS AND LESSORS

Medicine Shoppe Intl Inc
1100 N Lindbergh, St. Louis MO
63132-2914. 314/993-6000.
Employs: 100-249.

A & W Restaurants Inc
2240 Welsch Industrial Ct, St. Louis MO 63146-4222. 314/569-2044. Employs: 100-249.

Business Marketing Systems
12033 Gailcrest Ln, St. Louis MO
63131-3139. 314/997-5500.
Employs: 100-249.

Jani-King Of St Louis
11 Worthington Dr, Maryland Hts MO 63043. 314/576-4330.
Employs: 50-99.

Natl Restaurant Dev Corp
9 Junction Dr W, Edwardsville IL
62025-2931. 618/288-3178.
Employs: 100-249.

Subway Dev Corp Estrn Mo
320 Brookes Dr, Hazelwood MO
63042-2736. 314/895-4002.
Employs: 50-99.

MANAGEMENT CONSULTING SERVICES

Cobro Corp
4260 Shoreline Dr, Earth City MO
63045-1210. 314/291-8676.
Employs: 50-99.

MTS International Inc
1283 Research Blvd, St. Louis MO 63132-1713. 314/991-3721. Employs: 50-99.

Davis & James
555 N New Ballas Rd, St. Louis MO 63141-6825. 314/997-3331. Employs: 50-99.

Broeker & Associates Inc
655 Craig Rd, St. Louis MO 63141-7132. 314/991-2472. Employs: 50-99.

BUSINESS CONSULTING SERVICES

Dolgin & Associates
7800 Forsyth Blvd, St. Louis MO 63105-3311. 314/726-2900. Employs: 50-99.

Spectrum Emergency Care Inc
999 Executive Parkway Dr, St. Louis MO 63141-6336. 314/878-2280. Employs: 100-249.

Honeywell
11842 Borman Dr, St. Louis MO 63146-4113. 314/569-5400. Employs: 50-99.

For more information on career opportunities in financial services and management consulting:

<u>Associations</u>

AMERICAN FINANCIAL SERVICES ASSOCIATION
919 18th Street, 3rd Floor, Washington DC 20006. 202/296-5544.

AMERICAN MANAGEMENT ASSOCIATION
Management Information Service, 135 West 50th Street, New York NY 10020. 212/586-8100.

AMERICAN SOCIETY OF APPRAISERS
P.O. Box 17265, Washington DC 20041. 703/478-2228.

ASSOCIATION OF MANAGEMENT CONSULTING FIRMS
521 Fifth Avenue, 35th Floor, New York NY 10175. 212/697-9693.

COUNCIL OF CONSULTANT ORGANIZATIONS
521 Fifth Avenue, 35th Floor, New York NY 10175. 212/697-8262.

FEDERATION OF TAX ADMINISTRATORS
444 North Capital Street NW, Washington DC 20001. 202/624-5890.

ASSOCIATION FOR INVESTMENT MANAGEMENT AND RESEARCH
200 Park Avenue, 18th Floor, New York NY 10166. 212/957-2860.

FINANCIAL EXECUTIVES INSTITUTE
10 Madison Avenue, P.O. Box 1938, Morristown NJ 07962-1938. 201/898-4600.

INSTITUTE OF FINANCIAL EDUCATION
111 East Wacker Drive, Chicago IL 60601. 312/644-3100.

INSTITUTE OF INTERNATIONAL FINANCE
2000 Pennsylvania Ave NW, Washington DC 20006. 202/857-3600.

INSTITUTE OF MANAGEMENT CONSULTANTS
521 Fifth Avenue, 35th Floor, New York NY 10175. 212/697-8262.

NATIONAL ASSOCIATION OF BUSINESS ECONOMISTS
28790 Chagrin Boulevard, Suite 300, Cleveland OH 44122. 216/464-7986.

NATIONAL ASSOCIATION OF CREDIT MANAGEMENT
8815 Centre Park Drive, Suite 200, Columbia MD 21045-2117. 301/740-5560.

NATIONAL ASSOCIATION OF REAL ESTATE INVESTMENT TRUSTS
1129 20th Street NW, Suite 705, Washington DC 20036. 202/785-8717.

NATIONAL COMMERCIAL FINANCE ASSOCIATION
225 West 34th Street, New York NY 10122. 212/594-3490.

TREASURY MANAGEMENT ASSOCIATION
7315 Wisconsin Avenue, Suite 1250-W, Bethesda MD 20814. 301/907-2862.

SECURITIES INDUSTRY ASSOCIATION
120 Broadway, New York NY 10271. 212/608-1500.

PUBLIC SECURITIES ASSOCIATION
40 Broad Street, New York NY 10004. 212/809-7000.

Directories

DIRECTORY OF AMERICAN FINANCIAL INSTITUTIONS
McFadden Business Publications, 6195 Crooked Creek Road, Norcross GA 30092. 404/448-1011.

MOODY'S BANK AND FINANCE MANUAL
Moody's Investor Service, 99 Church Street, New York NY 10007. 212/553-0300.

Magazines

BARRON'S: NATIONAL BUSINESS AND FINANCIAL WEEKLY
Dow Jones & Co., 200 Liberty Street, New York NY 10281. 212/416-2700.

FINANCIAL PLANNING
40 W. 57th Street, 8th Floor, New York NY 10019. 212/765-5311.

INSURANCE TIMES
M & S Communications, 437 Newtonville Avenue, Newton MA 02160. 617/924-8161.

FINANCIAL WORLD
Financial World Partners, 1450 Broadway, New York NY 10001. 212/594-5030.

FUTURES: THE MAGAZINE OF COMMODITIES AND OPTIONS
250 South Wacker Drive, Suite 1150, Chicago IL 60606. 312/977-0999.

INSTITUTIONAL INVESTOR
488 Madison Avenue, New York NY 10022. 212/303-3300.

FOOD AND BEVERAGES: PROCESSING AND DISTRIBUTION

The best bets in the food industry are meats and poultry; processed fruits and vegetables; and soft drinks. One of the worst areas in the food industry is liquor and spirits.

ALLEN FOODS INC.
8543 Page, St. Louis MO 63114. 314/426-4100. **Contact:** Stanley Allen, President. **Description:** A distributor of international food products, food service supplies, and equipment.

ANHEUSER-BUSCH COMPANIES INC.
One Busch Place, St. Louis MO 63118. 314/577-0701. **Contact:** Curt Held, Employment Representative. **Description:** A diversified corporation whose products include beer, agricultural operations and products, and family entertainment complexes. **Corporate headquarters:** This location.

ARCHER DANIEL MIDLAND CO.
5020 Shreve Avenue, St. Louis MO 63115. 314/385-9100. **Contact:** Personnel Department. **Description:** St. Louis office of the well-known wholesaler and producer of a variety of baking products. **Corporate headquarters:** Minneapolis, MN.

RCHER DANIEL MIDLAND CO.
P.O. Box 1470, Decatur IL 62525. 217/424-5239. **Contact:** Sheila Witts-Mannweiler, Personnel Manager. **Description:** An agricultural products firm.

BEST BEERS INC.
5121 Manchester Avenue, St. Louis MO 63110. 314/647-7550. **Contact:** Bill Moss, Personnel Director. **Description:** A St. Louis beer distributing company.

BORDEN PASTA
611 E. Marceau, St. Louis MO 63111. 314/631-9000. **Contact:** Personnel Department. **Description:** Manufacturers of spaghetti and pasta products.

CONAGRA FLOUR MILLING COMPANY
145 West Broadway, Alton IL 62002. 618/463-4432. **Contact:** Oren Cummins, Manager. **Description:** Grain terminal operators engaged in the milling of flour and animal feed. **Employees:** 100.

CONTINENTAL BAKING COMPANY
6301 North Broadway, St. Louis MO 63147. 314/385-1600. **Contact:** Personnel Department. **Description:** Manufactures bread, cake, and other bakery products.

DIERBERG'S MARKETS
1422 Elbridge Payne Road, Suite 200, P.O. Box 1070, Chesterfield MO 63006. 314/532-8750. **Contact:** Fred Martels, Director of Personnel/Labor Relations. **Description:** A St. Louis-area chain of grocery stores. **Employees:** 700.

EAGLE BRAND SALES
4410 Gravois Avenue, St. Louis MO 63116. 314/481-0600. **Contact:** Personnel Department. **Description:** St. Louis food processor and distributor.

FLOUR MILLS DIVISION/ CON-AGRA
145 West Broadway, Alton IL 62002. 618/463-4411. **Contact:** Cindy Holt, Office Manager. **Description:** A division of the national agricultural products corporation. Specializes in the manufacture of grain terminal operators and the production of millers-flour and animal feed.

FRITO-LAY INC./ROLD GOLD
2445 South Wharf Street, St. Louis MO 63104. 314/773-1788. **Contact:** Winnie Paradise, Personnel Representative. **Description:** Pretzel products division of the well-known leader in the consumer food products market, nationally marketing a full-line of snack products, including Fritos Corn Chips, Lays Potato Chips, Doritos Tortilla Chips, and a wide range of other snack foods. **Common positions:** Administrator; Bank Officer/Manager; Blue-Collar Worker Supervisor; Computer Programmer; Department Manager; General Manager; Operations/Production Manager; Public Relations Worker; Quality Control Supervisor. **Corporate headquarters:** Dallas, TX. **Parent company:** Pepsico, Inc. **Listed on:** New York Stock Exchange; American Stock Exchange.

GREY EAGLE DISTRIBUTORS INC.
2340 Millpark Drive, Maryland Heights MO 63043. 314/429-9128. **Contact:** Personnel Department. **Description:** A wholesale distributor of beer.

HAAS BAKING COMPANY
9769 Reavis Park Drive, St. Louis MO 63123. 314/631-6100. **Contact:** Dolores Brunner, Office Manager. **Description:** A St. Louis bakery. **Benefits:** medical, dental, and life insurance; pension plan. **Corporate headquarters:** This location. **Operations at this facility:** manufacturing.

HUNTER/KREY FOODS
DIVISION OF JOHN MORRELL & COMPANY
6038 North Lindbergh, Hazelwood MO 63042. 314/731-5560. **Contact:** Personnel Department. **Description:** A distribution center for fresh pork, beef and processed meats.

LEAF INC./DIVISION OF SWITZER CLARK
1600 North Broadway, St. Louis MO 63102. 314/421-3474. **Contact:** Mark Chapman, Personnel Manager. **Description:** A St. Louis producer of candy and other confectionery products.

MFA INC.
615 Locust Street, Columbia MO 65201. 314/876-5206. **Contact:** Patty Miller, Manager of Personnel Services. **Description:** An agricultural cooperative supplying feed, seed, plant foods, farm supplies, agricultural chemicals and associated services. Purchase point for farmer-owned grain. Also provides complete agri-business sales and service. **Common positions:** Accountant; Administrator; Buyer; Commercial Artist; Computer Programmer; Credit Manager; Agricultural Engineer; Financial Analyst; Branch Manager; Department Manager; General Manager; Management Trainee; Operations/Production Manager; Marketing Specialist; Personnel and Labor Relations Specialist; Purchasing Agent; Quality Control Supervisor; Reporter/Editor; Sales Representative; Systems Analyst; Transportation and Traffic Specialist. **Educational backgrounds sought:** Accounting; Art/Design; Business Administration; Communications; Computer Science; Finance; Marketing; Agricultural Economics; Animal Nutrition; Animal Science; Agronomy. **Benefits:** medical insurance; pension plan; life insurance; disability coverage; savings plan. **Corporate headquarters:** This location. **Operations at this facility:** regional headquarters; divisional headquarters; administration; service; sales.

MERCK & COMPANY INC.
4545 Oleatha, St. Louis MO 63116. 314/353-7000. **Contact:** Kathy Aschenbrenner, Personnel Director. **Description:** A St. Louis company engaged in the manufacture of animal health and feed products, and medicinal chemicals.

MID-AMERICA DAIRYMEN INC.
3253 East Chestnut Expressway, Springfield MO 65802-2584. 417/865-7100. **Contact:** Mark Prevedel, Manager/Labor Relations. **Description:** A dairy cooperative which manufactures and markets numerous dairy food products. **Corporate headquarters:** This location. **Operations at this facility:** manufacturing; research and development; administration; service; sales. **Common positions:** Accountant; Administrator; Blue-Collar Worker Supervisor; Buyer; Chemist; Computer Programmer; Customer Service Representative; Mechanical Engineer; Food Technologist; Operations/Production Manager; Marketing Specialist; Quality Control Supervisor; Sales Representative; Systems Analyst. **Educational backgrounds sought:** Accounting; Chemistry; Computer Science; Engineering; Marketing; Dairy Food Science. **Special programs:** Internships offered. **Benefits:** medical insurance; dental insurance; pension plan; life insurance; disability coverage; savings plan. **Corporate headquarters:** Springfield, MO.

MRS. ALLISON'S COOKIE CO.
1780 Burns Avenue, St. Louis MO 63132. 314/429-2111. **Contact:** Donna Chadborn, Office Manager. **Description:** A St. Louis manufacturer of a variety of cookies.

MULTIPLEX COMPANY INC.
250 Old Ballwin Road, Ballwin MO 63021-4834. **Contact:** Personnel Department. Mailed inquiries only. **Description:** Engaged in the manufacture of beverage dispensing equipment.

NABISCO BRANDS INC.
2021 Congressional Drive, St. Louis MO 63177. 314/432-8116. **Contact:** John Dunleavy, Operations Manager. **Description:** The St. Louis warehouse, delivery, and sales office of the well-known manufacturer of crackers, packaged food products and wholesale bakery products. As one of the largest food companies in the United States, the firm has a strong market position in such areas as cookies, margarine, hot cereals and pet snacks. Production and distribution facilities are located throughout the United States, Canada, Europe, and the Asia/Pacific region. **Employees:** 69,000 people worldwide. **Listed on:** New York Stock Exchange

PARAMONT LIQUOR COMPANY
6501 Hall Street, St. Louis MO 63147. 314/382-9990. **Contact:** Personnel Department. **Description:** A St. Louis company engaged in the wholesale of wine and distilled beverages.

PEVELY DAIRY COMPANY
1001 South Grand Boulevard, St. Louis MO 63104. 314/771-4400. **Contact:** Vince Kubik, Personnel Director. **Description:** Manufactures wholesale and retail dairy products.

PRAIRIE FARMS DAIRY INC.
1800 Adams Street, Box W, Granite City IL 62040. 618/451-5600. **Contact:** Personnel Department. **Description:** St. Louis-area producer and wholesaler of dairy products.

RALSTON PURINA COMPANY
Checkerboard Square, St. Louis MO 63164. 314/982-1000. **Contact:** Ron Young, Personnel Director. **Description:** Producers of Ralston pet foods, cereals, snack foods, Eveready Batteries, Continental Baking Company's Wonder Bread, and Hostess Product lines.

SCHNUCK MARKETS INC.
11420 Lackland Road, P.O. Box 46928, St. Louis MO 63146-6928. 314/994-9900. **Contact:** Janice Rhodes, Employment Manager. Harry Moulton can be contacted at 4900 Manchester St., St. Louis, MO 63110. **Description:** Corporate headquarters location of a chain of retail supermarkets and restaurants. **Employees:** 2,530 nationwide.

SERVCO EQUIPMENT CO.
3189 Jamieson Avenue, St. Louis MO 63139. 314/781-3189. **Contact:** Sherry Mazur, CFO. **Description:** Manufacturer of food service equipment, supplying a variety of equipment to cafeterias, restaurants and hospitals.

THE SEVEN-UP COMPANY
8900 Page Street, Overlin MO 63114. 314/426-8200. **Contact:** Cheryl Deen, Administrator. **Description:** Headquarters location of the well-known producer of carbonated beverages. **Operations at this facility:** research and development, distribution and production.

ST. LOUIS NATIONAL STOCK YARDS COMPANY
P.O. Box 97, National Stock Yards IL 62071. 618/271-2405. **Contact:** Personnel Department. **Description:** A diversified livestock company engaged in a variety of activities, including livestock marketing; the operation of public stock yards and dry bulk warehousing; the operation of a switching railroad system; the operation of area restaurants; and the sale of real estate.

STAR MANUFACTURING INTERNATIONAL, INC.
9325 Olive Boulevard, St. Louis MO 63132. 314/994-0880. **Contact:** Vicky Hendrickson, Human Resources. **Description:** Manufacturers of commercial food service equipment and concession equipment. **Common positions:** Accountant; Buyer; Computer Programmer; Credit Manager; Customer Service Representative; Draftsperson; Mechanical Engineer; Purchasing Agent; Quality Controller; Sales Representative. **Educational backgrounds sought:** Accounting; Business Administration; Computer Science; Engineering; Finance; Marketing. **Benefits:** medical insurance; dental insurance; pension plan; life insurance; tuition assistance; disability coverage; profit sharing. **Corporate headquarters:** This location. **Other U.S. locations:** Tennessee (manufacturing, employing 134). **Operations at this facility:** research and development; administration; service; sales. **Employees:** 47.

SUNMARK, INC.
P.O. Box 14483, St. Louis MO 63178. 314/822-2800. **Contact:** Debra Stellhorn, Manager of Compensation and Benefits. **Description:** A regional manufacturer of consumer candies.

VALLEY FARM DAIRY COMPANY INC.
1114 East Road, Suite 110, Station Plaza, St. Louis MO 63110. 314/535-0800. **Contact:** Personnel Department. **Description:** Producers, processors, retailers, and wholesalers of fluid milk, cream, and related products.

VELVET FOODS INC./
VELVET FREEZE
7355 West Florissant, St. Louis MO 63136. 314/381-2384. **Contact:** Personnel Department. **Description:** Manufacturers and retailers of dairy and ice cream products.

WARNER-JENKINSON COMPANY
2526 Baldwin Street, St. Louis MO 63106. 314/889-7600. **Contact:** Mr. Mauri Smith, Personnel Department. **Description:** Manufacturers and distributors of vanilla, flavoring extracts and food colors.

WETTERAU INCORPORATED
8920 Pershall Road, Hazelwood MO 63042. 314/524-5000. **Contact:** Personnel Department. **Description:** Wholesaler of food and allied products. **Corporate headquarters:** This location.

182/The St. Louis JobBank

Additional large employers: 250+

POULTRY SLAUGHTERING AND PROCESSING

Banquet Foods Corp
13515 Bennet Pk, Ballwin MO 63011. 314/957-4000. Employs: 250-499.

CANNED SPECIALITIES

Pet Inc
400 S 4th St, St. Louis MO 63102-1807. 314/621-5400. Employs: 250-499.

FLOUR AND OTHER GRAIN MILL PRODUCTS

Gilster Mary Lee Co
1037 State St, Chester IL 62233-1657. 618/826-2361. Employs: 1,000+.

Golden Dipt Co
12813 Flushing Meadow Dr, St. Louis MO 63131-1823. 314/821-3113. Employs: 250-499.

CEREAL BREAKFAST FOODS

Kellogg Sales Co
111 Westport Plz, St. Louis MO 63146-3011. 314/434-6200. Employs: 250-499.

BREAD AND OTHER BAKERY PRODUCTS, EXCEPT COOKIES AND CRACKERS

Continental Baking Co
Checker Board Sq, St. Louis MO 63164. 314/982-4700. Employs: 1,000+.

Gateway Baking Co
1008 S Spring Ave, St. Louis MO 63110-2520. 314/865-1577. Employs: 250-499.

CANDY AND OTHER CONFECTIONERY PRODUCTS

Sunline Brands
8100 Water St, St. Louis MO 63111-3653. 314/638-5770. Employs: 250-499.

MALT BEVERAGES

Anheuser-Busch Companies Inc
10777 Sunset Office Dr, St. Louis MO 63127-1019. 314/957-4800. Employs: 1,000+.

Miller Brewing Co
930 Roosevelt Pkwy, Chesterfield MO 63017-2053. 314/532-4911. Employs: 1,000+.

BOTTLED AND CANNED SOFT DRINKS AND CARBONATED WATERS

Capri Sun Inc
2901 Hwy 3, Granite City IL 62040. 618/451-4820. Employs: 250-499.

Coca-Cola Bottling Co
19 Worthington Dr, Maryland Hts MO 63043. 314/878-0800. Employs: 250-499.

FOOD PREPARATIONS. NOT ELSEWHERE CLASSIFIED

Gilster-Mary Lee Corp
705 N Sparta St, Steeleville IL 62288-1547. 618/965-3426. Employs: 250-499.

GROCERY STORES

National Tea Co
6050 N Lindbergh Blvd, Hazelwood MO 63042-2804. 314/693-5100. Employs: 1,000+.

Additional small to medium sized employers: 50-249

MEAT PACKING PLANTS

Lanter Company
3 Caine Dr, Madison IL 62060.
618/452-7100. Employs: 100-249.

SAUSAGES AND OTHER PREPARED MEAT PRODUCTS

Frick's Meat Products Inc
805 Locust St, Washington MO
63090-4508. 314/239-3313.
Employs: 50-99.

Holten Meat Inc
8525 Page Ave, St. Louis MO
63114-6006. 314/423-8400.
Employs: 100-249.

NATURAL, PROCESSED AND IMITATION CHEESE

Pantera's Corporation
11933 Westline Industrial Dr, St.
Louis MO 63146. 314/275-8883.
Employs: 100-249.

Raskas Dairy Inc
1313 N Newstead Ave, St. Louis
MO 63113-2819. 314/531-1950.
Employs: 50-99.

DRY, CONDENSED AND EVAPORATED DAIRY PRODUCTS

Milnot Co
100 S Fourth St, St. Louis MO
63102-1800. 314/436-7667.
Employs: 50-99.

ICE CREAM AND FROZEN DESSERTS

Block S Ice Cream & Sandwich
2515 College Av, Alton IL 62002-4704. 618/465-9313. Employs: 50-99.

Prairie Farms Dairy Inc
1800 Adams St, Granite City IL
62040-3300. 618/451-5600.
Employs: 50-99.

FLUID MILK

Land-O-Sun Dairies Inc
610 E State St, Wood River IL
62095-1111. 618/632-6381.
Employs: 50-99.

Raskas Dairy Inc
165 N Meramec, St. Louis MO
63105-3772. 314/727-9992.
Employs: 50-99.

CANNED SPECIALTIES

Louisa Food Products
1918 Switzer Ave, St. Louis MO
63136-3756. 314/868-3000.
Employs: 50-99.

CANNED FRUITS, VEGETABLES, PRESERVES JAMS AND JELLIES

Shirley's Delicious Delights
RR 1, Fieldon IL 62031-9801.
618/376-6064. Employs: 100-249.

DRIED AND DEHYDRATED FRUITS, VEGETABLES AND SOUP MIXES

I P F Incorporated
703 W Main St, Collinsville IL
62234-3024. 618/345-3447.
Employs: 50-99.

PICKLED FRUITS AND VEGETABLES, VEGETABLE SAUCES AND SEASONINGS AND SALAD DRESSINGS

Heifetz Sales Div Grn Bay Food
75 Worthington Dr, Maryland Hts MO 63043. 314/434-0460. Employs: 50-99.

FROZEN SPECIALTIES

Nabisco Brands Inc
8501 Page Ave, St. Louis MO 63114-6001. 314/429-3636. Employs: 50-99.

FLOUR AND OTHER GRAIN MILL PRODUCTS

Conagra Inc
Water St, Chester IL 62233. 618/826-2371. Employs: 50-99.

Conagra Inc Grain Processing
145 W Broadway, St. Louis MO 63102. 314/741-6600. Employs: 50-99.

The Pillsbury Company
5020 Shreve Ave, St. Louis MO 63115-2226. 314/385-9100. Employs: 50-99.

DOG AND CAT FOOD

Purina Mills
1401 S Hanley Rd, St. Louis MO 63144-2902. 314/768-4100. Employs: 100-249.

PREPARED FEEDS AND FEED INGREDIENTS FOR ANIMALS AND FOWL, EXCEPT DOGS AND CATS

Continental Grain Co
901 N 59th St, E St. Louis IL 62203-1063. 618/274-3150. Employs: 50-99.

Nutribasics
1 Ultra Way Dr, Highland IL 62249-1241. 618/654-9856. Employs: 50-99.

BREAD AND OTHER BAKERY PRODUCTS, EXCEPT COOKIES AND CRACKERS

Dolly Madison Cake Co
1509 Madison Av, Granite City IL 62040-4427. 618/876-8602. Employs: 50-99.

National Bake Shops
8590 Page Ave, St. Louis MO 63114-6016. 314/731-5511. Employs: 100-249.

Theodoro Baking Co Inc
8559 Page Ave, St. Louis MO 63114-6008. 314/426-0080. Employs: 50-99.

COOKIES AND CRACKERS

Imperial Baking Co Of Mo
2141 Cass Ave, St. Louis MO 63106-2706. 314/621-3700. Employs: 50-99.

FROZEN BAKERY PRODUCTS, EXCEPT BREAD

Petrofsky's Enterprise Inc
701 Fee Fee Rd, Maryland Hts MO 63043-3209. 314/432-5101. Employs: 100-249.

CANE SUGAR, EXCEPT REFINING

Utah Packaging Inc
4240 Utah St, St. Louis MO 63116-1820. 314/773-8500. Employs: 100-249.

CANDY AND OTHER CONFECTIONERY PRODUCTS

Concorde Brands
8155 New Hampshire Ave, St. Louis MO 63123-2626. 314/832-7575. Employs: 100-249.

SALTED AND ROASTED NUTS AND SEEDS

David & Sons Co
8064 Chivvis Dr, St. Louis MO 63123-2333. 314/832-7575. Employs: 50-99.

SHORTENING, TABLE OILS, MARGARINE AND OTHER EDIBLE FATS AND OILS

P V O Foods Inc
2501 W 20th St, Granite City IL 62040-3101. 618/451-8868. Employs: 100-249.

WINES, BRANDY AND BRANDY SPIRITS

Beverage Concepts
4022 W Pine St, St. Louis MO 63108-3210. 314/531-7632. Employs: 50-99.

DISTILLED AND BLENDED LIQUORS

David Sherman Corp
5050 Kemper Ave, St. Louis MO 63139-1106. 314/772-2626. Employs: 50-99.

House Of Seagram
12400 Olive Blvd, St. Louis MO 63141-6431. 314/434-9177. Employs: 50-99.

BOTTLED AND CANNED SOFT DRINKS AND CARBONATED WATERS

Pepsi Cola Bottling Group
1875 Old State Hwy 94 S, Saint Charles MO 63303-3708. 314/724-6525. Employs: 50-99.

Pepsi Cola Btlg Co St Louis
4400 Clayton Ave, St. Louis MO 63110-1624. 314/658-0771. Employs: 100-249.

Pepsi Cola Btlg Co St Louis
Hwy Z, Pevely MO 63070. 314/296-5169. Employs: 50-99.

Pepsi-Cola Alton Bottling Inc
2521 E Broadway St, Alton IL 62002-1766. 618/465-3511. Employs: 50-99.

Pepsi-Cola Bottling Co
Highway Z, Pevely MO 63070. 314/789-3756. Employs: 50-99.

Pepsi-Cola Bottling Co
647 Tower Grove Ave, St. Louis MO 63110-1637. 314/533-2444. Employs: 100-249.

Seven-Up Bottling Co St Louis
555 Mc Donnell Blvd, Hazelwood MO 63042-2401. 314/895-7400. Employs: 100-249.

Vess Beverages Inc
2525 Schuetz Rd, Maryland Hts MO 63043-3316. 314/567-1300. Employs: 50-99.

Warrenton Products Inc
Old Hwy 40, Warrenton MO 63383. 314/456-3492. Employs: 50-99.

FLAVORING EXTRACTS AND FLAVORING SYRUPS

Beck Flavors
411 E Gano, St. Louis MO 63147-3210. 314/436-3133. Employs: 50-99.

Blanke Baer Bowey Krimko Inc
1572 Larkin Williams Rd, Fenton
MO 63026-3009. 314/343-1111.
Employs: 50-99.

Spicecraft Inc
Flottman Rd, Gerald MO 63037.
314/764-3396. Employs: 50-99.

ROASTED COFFEE

Old Judge Coffee Co
4410 Hunt Ave, St. Louis MO
63110-2112. 314/652-4200.
Employs: 50-99.

POTATO CHIPS, CORN CHIPS AND SIMILAR SNACKS

Eagle Snacks Inc
10777 Sunset Office Dr, St. Louis
MO 63127-1019. 314/966-7100.
Employs: 50-99.

Old Vienna Smack Inc
1945 Walton Rd, St. Louis MO
63114-5821. 314/426-2333.
Employs: 100-249.

MACARONI, SPAGHETTI, VERMICELLI AND NOODLES

Gilster-Mary Lee Corp
10 Industrial Pk, Steeleville IL
62288. 618/965-3449. Employs:
100-249.

Ravarino & Freschi Inc
611 E Marceau St, St. Louis MO
63111-3851. 314/773-2700.
Employs: 100-249.

FOOD PREPARATIONS

Nestle Beverage Co
2101 Adams St, Granite City IL
62040-3315. 618/225-4242.
Employs: 100-249.

Rold Gold Foods
2445 S Wharf St, St. Louis MO
63104-4727. 314/773-1788.
Employs: 50-99.

Schreiber Foods Inc
450 Cottonwood Rd Ste C, Glen
Carbon IL 62034. 618/656-5930.
Employs: 50-99.

Southern Products Co
2753 Magnolia Ave, St. Louis MO
63118-1426. 314/773-1456.
Employs: 50-99.

CHEWING AND SMOKING TOBACCO, AND SNUFF

R J Reynolds
11 Executive Park Dr Ste 10, E St.
Louis IL 62208-1357. 618/624-
4200. Employs: 100-249.

GROCERY STORES

Dierbergs Markets
Olive Street Rd & Hwy 141,
Chesterfield MO 63017. 314/469-
1400. Employs: 50-99.

Eastown Mini Mart
1410 West Blvd, Belleville IL
62221-5056. 618/234-2443.
Employs: 50-99.

Food For Less
14220 Old Halls Ferry Rd,
Florissant MO 63034-2402.
314/741-7011. Employs: 100-249.

Johnny's Super Market
11555 Gravois Rd, St. Louis MO
63126-3611. 314/8435760.
Employs: 50-99.

National Food Store
Bxf E Junction Dr, Edwardsville IL
62025. 618/692-0997. Employs:
50-99.

National Super Markets
20 Jefferson Sq, De Soto MO
63020-1031. 314/586-3900.
Employs: 100-249.

National Super Markets
655 Carlyle Rd, Belleville IL
62221-6224. 618/235-1626.
Employs: 100-249.

National Super Markets
1310 Big Bend Rd, Ballwin MO
63021. 314/225-3777. Employs:
100-249.

National Super Markets
6050 N Lindbergh Blvd,
Hazelwood MO 63042-2804.
314/731-5511. Employs: 100-249.

National Super Markets
810 Country Corners Shop Center,
Washington MO 63090-4603.
314/239-3577. Employs: 100-249.

National Super Markets
8319 Jennings Station Rd, St. Louis
MO 63136-3630. 314/383-3727.
Employs: 100-249.

National Super Markets
1589 Sierra Vista Plz, St. Louis
MO 63138-2040. 314/741-0282.
Employs: 100-249.

National Super Markets
8945 Riverview Dr, St. Louis MO
63137-2404. 314/867-1145.
Employs: 50-99.

National Super Markets
9445 Gravois Rd, St. Louis MO
63123-4529. 314/631-5200.
Employs: 100-249.

National Super Markets
421 N Kirkwood Rd, St. Louis MO
63122-3911. 314/821-2091.
Employs: 50-99.

National Super Markets
4617 Chippewa St, St. Louis MO
63116-1610. 314/773-5615.
Employs: 100-249.

National Super Markets
2700 S Grand Blvd, St. Louis MO
63118-1009. 314/664-7240.
Employs: 50-99.

National Super Markets
3830 S Grand Blvd, St. Louis MO
63118-3412. 314/664-6700.
Employs: 50-99.

National Super Markets
950 Loughborough Ave, St. Louis
MO 63111-2619. 314/752-5333.
Employs: 50-99.

National Super Markets
1030 Cass Ave, St. Louis MO
63106-4509. 314/621-4578.
Employs: 100-249.

National Super Markets
4171 Lindell Blvd, St. Louis MO
63108-2913. 314/533-8027.
Employs: 100-249.

Overland Thrift Markets
8711 Saint Charles Rock Rd, St.
Louis MO 63114-4337. 314/426-
2562. Employs: 50-99.

Schnuck Markets
4103 N Cloverleaf Dr, Saint
Charles MO 63303. 314/928-1078.
Employs: 50-99.

Schnuck's Supermarket
625 Lincoln Hwy, E St. Louis IL
62208-2121. 618/624-4310.
Employs: 100-249.

Schnuck's Supermarkets
2030 Doresett Village Center,
Maryland Hts MO 63043. 314/434-
3147. Employs: 100-249.

Shop 'N Save
Jerseyville Mall, Jerseyville IL 62052. 618/498-2136. Employs: 50-99.

Shop 'N Save
15446 Manchester Rd, Ballwin MO 63011-3029. 314/227-6332. Employs: 100-249.

Shop 'N Save
11355 Blake Dr, Bridgeton MO 63044-2912. 314/739-7398. Employs: 50-99.

Shop 'N Save
235 Hwy 175, O Fallon MO 63366. 314/272-2303. Employs: 100-249.

Shop 'N Save
5780 S Lindbergh Blvd, St. Louis MO 63123-6937. 314/842-0103. Employs: 50-99.

Shop 'N Save
2122 Troy Rd, Edwardsville IL 62025-2540. 618/692-9000. Employs: 100-249.

Shop 'N Save Warehouse Foods
1721 Homer M Adams Pkwy, Alton IL 62002-5604. 618/462-0056. Employs: 100-249.

Western Union
5433 Southwest Ave, St. Louis MO 63139-1465. 314/781-1277. Employs: 100-249.

7 Eleven Division Of Southland
40 New Sugar Creek Rd, Fenton MO 63026-4476. 314/343-5249. Employs: 50-99.

RETAIL BAKERIES

Knodels Wedding Cakes & Bakery
6621 W Florissant Ave, St. Louis MO 63136-3632. 314/385-2000. Employs: 50-99.

Petrofsky Enterprises
701 Fee Fee Rd, St. Louis MO 63146. 314/432-5101. Employs: 50-99.

MISCELLANEOUS FOOD STORES

Baily International Inc
2135 Schuetz Rd, St. Louis MO 63146-3537. 314/997-3389. Employs: 50-99.

Robata Of Japan
111 Westport Plz, St. Louis MO 63146-3011. 314/434-1007. Employs: 50-99.

For more information on career opportunities in food and beverage production and distribution:

Associations

ALLIED TRADES OF THE BAKING INDUSTRY
P.O. Box 398, Memphis TN 38101. 800/238-5765.

AMERICAN ASSOCIATION OF CEREAL CHEMISTS
3340 Pilot Knob Road, St. Paul MN 55121. 612/454-7250.

AMERICAN FROZEN FOOD INSTITUTE
1764 Old Meadow Lane, McLean VA 22102. 703/821-0770.

AMERICAN SOCIETY OF AGRICULTURAL ENGINEERS
2950 Niles Road, St. Joseph MI 49085. 616/429-0300.

AMERICAN SOCIETY OF BREWING CHEMISTS
3340 Pilot Knob Road, St. Paul MN 55121. 612/454-7250.

DAIRY AND FOOD INDUSTRIES SUPPLY ASSOCIATION
6245 Executive Boulevard, Rockville MD 20852. 301/984-1444.

DISTILLED SPIRITS COUNCIL OF THE UNITED STATES
1250 I Street NW, Suite 900, Washington DC 20005. 202/628-3544.

MASTER BREWERS ASSOCIATION OF THE AMERICAS
4513 Vernon Boulevard, Madison, WI 53705. 608/231-3446.

NATIONAL AGRICULTURAL CHEMICALS ASSOCIATION
1155 15th Street NW, Suite 900, Washington DC 20005. 202/296-1585.

NATIONAL BEER WHOLESALERS' ASSOCIATION
5205 Leesburg Pike, Suite 1600, Falls Church VA 22041. 703/578-4300.

NATIONAL DAIRY COUNCIL
10255 W. Higgins Road, Suite 900, Rosemont IL 60018. 708/803-2000.

NATIONAL FOOD PROCESSORS ASSOCIATION
1401 New York Avenue NW, Suite 400, Washington DC 20005. 202/639-5900.

NATIONAL SOFT DRINK ASSOCIATION
1101 16th Street NW, Washington DC 20036. 202/463 6732.

UNITED FOOD AND COMMERCIAL WORKERS INTERNATIONAL UNION
1775 K Street NW, Washington DC 20006. 202/223-3111.

Directories

FOOD ENGINEERING'S DIRECTORY OF U.S. FOOD PLANTS
Chilton Book Co., Chilton Way, Radnor PA 19089. 800/695-1214.

THOMAS FOOD INDUSTRY REGISTER
Thomas Publishing Co., One Penn Plaza, New York NY 10019. 212/695-0500.

Magazines

BEVERAGE INDUSTRY
Advanstar Communications, 7500 Old Oak Boulevard, Cleveland OH 44130. 216/243-8100.

BEVERAGE WORLD
150 Great Neck Road, Great Neck NY 11021. 516/829-9210.

FOOD MANAGEMENT
233 North Michigan, Chicago IL 60601. 312/938-2300.

FOOD PROCESSING
301 East Erie, Chicago IL 60611. 312/644-2020.

FROZEN FOOD AGE
Maclean Hunter Media, #4 Stamford Forum, Stamford CT 06901. 203/325-3500.

PREPARED FOODS
Gorman Publishing Co., 8750 West Bryn Mawr, Chicago IL 60631. 312/693-3200.

GENERAL MERCHANDISE: RETAIL

While much of the retail industry has been struggling against low consumer confidence, discount department stores have been booming. This trend holds true for both merchandise and apparel stores, as well as for other broad areas like health and beauty aides. Overall, retailing will continue to grow at a relatively slow pace. Unfortunately for professionals, most new jobs will be entry-level, where there is currently a major labor shortage.

ACKERMAN BUICK INC.
2900 Pershall, St. Louis MO 63136. 314/524-2900. **Contact:** Gerry Pavlovits, Office Manager. **Description:** Engaged in motor vehicle sales and automobile rental. **Employees:** 100.

CENTRAL HARDWARE COMPANY
111 Boulder Industrial Drive, Bridgeton MO 63044. 314/291-7000. **Contact:** Tom Tenhula, Vice-President/Human Resources. **Description:** A home center retailer. Parent company, Interco, is a broadly based manufacturer and retailer of consumer products and services with operations in apparel manufacturing, retailing, footwear manufacturing, and furniture and home furnishings. 40 locations in MO, IL, OH, IN, and TN. **Common positions:** Accountant; Department Manager; General Manager; Management Trainee. **Special programs:** Training programs; Internships. **Benefits:** Medical, Dental, and Life Insurance; Pension Plan; Tuition Assistance; Disability Coverage; Employee Discounts; Savings Plan. **Corporate headquarters:** This location. **Operations at this facility:** Administration; Service. **Employees:** 4,000. **Projected hires for the next 12 months:** 200.

DATAMAX OFFICE SYSTEMS
2121 Hampton Avenue, St. Louis MO 63139. 314/644-2800. **Contact:** Laurie Schreyer, Personnel Specialist. **Description:** A supplier of office equipment-an authorized Canon dealer, specializing in the sale of copying and duplicating equipment. **Common positions:** Credit Manager; Marketing Specialist; Sales Representative. **Special programs:** Training programs. **Parent company:** Sumner Group, Inc. **Operations at this facility:** administration; service; sales.

EDISON BROTHERS STORE, INC.
P.O. Box 14020, St. Louis MO 63178. 314/331-6125. **Contact:** Personnel Administration. **Description:** A nationwide retailer of shoes and apparel. Also operates entertainment chains. Stores include: Bakers/Leeds, Precis, The Wild Pair, Velocity, Sacha London Shoe Stores, JW/Jeans West, Oaktree, CODA, J. Riggings, Webster/Zeidler & Zeidler, Repp Ltd, Harry's, 5-7-9, Spirale, Dave and Buster's (restaurant/entertainment complexes); Time Out and Spaceport

family entertainment centers. **Corporate headquarters:** This location. **Listed on:** New York Stock Exchange. **Common positions:** Accounting; Administration; Marketing; Merchandising; Store Operations; Management Trainee. **Benefits:** medical and dental plans; life insurance; disability coverage; pension and 401K savings plans; employee merchandise discounts; and paid vacations.

FAMOUS-BARR COMPANY
601 Olive Street, St. Louis MO 63101. 314/444-3111. **Contact:** Human Resources. **Description:** A retail department store chain. Subsidiary of The May Department Stores Company. **Corporate headquarters:** This location. **Common positions:** Buyer; Department Manager. **Educational backgrounds sought:** Business Administration. **Benefits:** medical insurance; pension plan; life insurance; profit sharing; employee discounts.

FISHER SCIENTIFIC COMPANY
P.O. Box 14989, St. Louis MO 63178-4989. 314/991-2400. **Contact:** Employee Relations Supervisor. **Description:** Wholesalers of professional laboratory equipment and supplies. **Employees:** 100.

FOX MEYER DRUG COMPANY
P.O. Box 520, St. Louis MO 63166. 314/647-8000. **Contact:** Ron Bockstruck, Operations Manager. **Description:** A chain of drug stores. **Employees:** 100.

FRAME FACTORY LTD.
32 Worthington Drive, Maryland Heights MO 63043. 314/434-8882. **Contact:** Personnel Department. **Description:** The central office and warehouse for a chain of 10 area stores specializing in picture frames and framing for various business needs. **Employees:** 100. **Common positions:** Customer Service Representative; Management Trainee; Sales Representative. **Educational backgrounds sought:** Art/Design. **Special programs:** Training programs. **Benefits:** medical, dental, and life insurance; tuition assistance; employee discounts; savings plan. **Corporate headquarters:** This location. **Operations at this facility:** regional headquarters; administration; service; sales.

GRAMEX CORPORATION/
d.b.a. GRANDPA PIDGEON'S
11966 St. Charles Rock Road, Bridgeton MO 63044. 314/739-8300. **Contact:** Jane Gaitsch, Director of Human Resources. **Description:** A company which owns and operates a variety of discount department stores. **Common positions:** Accountant; Advertising Worker; Buyer; Branch Manager. **Educational backgrounds sought:** Business Administration; Liberal Arts. **Benefits:** medical, dental and life insurance; pension plan; tuition assistance; disability coverage; employee discounts. **Corporate headquarters:** This location. **Operations at this facility:** sales. **Employees:** 1,200.

HEWLETT-PACKARD COMPANY
530 Maryville Center Drive, St. Louis MO 63141. 800/752-0900. **Contact:** Audrey Bryant, Personnel Director. **Description:** Wholesaler of electrical apparatus and equipment. Parent company is engaged in the design and manufacture of measurement and computation products and systems used in business, industry, engineering, science, health care, and education; principal

products are integrated instrument and computer systems (including hardware and software), computer systems and peripheral products, and medical electronic equipment and systems. **Corporate headquarters:** Palo Alto, CA. **Listed on:** New York Stock Exchange.

HIT OR MISS, INC.
20 Hampton Village, St. Louis MO 63109. 314/481-2991. **Contact:** Judy Laing, Regional Manager. **Description:** A chain of women's fashion stores; over 550 stores in 35 states. A division of TJX, Inc. **Common positions:** Buyer; Assistant Buyer; Branch Manager; Store Manager; Assistant Store Manager; Assistant Store Manager-in-Training (for supervisors with no prior retail experience); Sales Associate; Loss Prevention Specialist; Store Detective. **Special programs:** Paid Training; Internships. **Benefits:** Medical, Dental, and Life Insurance; Tuition Assistance; Disability Coverage; Employee Discounts; 401K Retirement Plan; Referral Bonus Program; Scholarship Program; Savings/Profit Sharing Plan; Service Award Program; Stock Options. **Corporate headquarters:** Stoughton, MA. **Educational backgrounds sought:** College degree or experience in any customer service-based occupation; Art/Design; Business Administration; Liberal Arts. **Operations at this facility:** Sales. **Employees:** 5,000+. **Projected hires for the next 12 months:** Expect to hire several assistant managers-in-training. **Listed on:** New York Stock Exchange.

JCPENNEY COMPANY INC.
METRO DISTRICT OFFICE
2258 Schuetz Road, Suite 208, St. Louis MO 63146. 314/432-2038. **Contact:** Dennis Barbo, District Personnel Manager. **Description:** St. Louis offices of a domestic retailer, with store operations in all 50 states and Puerto Rico. The dominant portion of the company's business consists of providing merchandise and services to customers through stores, including catalog operations. Overall, the company operates and manages almost 600 full-line stores, and more than 1060 smaller soft-line stores. **Common positions:** Management Trainee. **Educational backgrounds sought:** Accounting; Business Administration; Communications; Economics; Finance; Liberal Arts; Marketing. **Benefits:** medical insurance; dental insurance; pension plan; life insurance; disability coverage; profit sharing; employee discounts; savings plan. **Corporate headquarters:** Dallas, TX. **Operations at this facility:** administration. **Listed on:** New York Stock Exchange.

K MART DISCOUNT STORES
DIVISION OF S.S. KRESGE COMPANY
11978 St. Charles Rock Road, Bridgeton MO 63044. 314/739-8800. **Contact:** Personnel Department. **Description:** A company which owns and operates a chain of discount department stores and food stores.

K'S MERCHANDISE
3103 North Charles Street, Decatur IL 62526. 217/875-1440. **Contact:** John Bell, Director of Personnel. **Description:** An expanding retail catalog showroom chain.

KLEIN'S DEPARTMENT STORES INC.
9957 Manchester Road, St. Louis MO 63122. 314/968-2900. **Contact:** Kevin Schmitt, Personnel Manager. **Description:** Engaged in general retail

merchandising. Parent company, Interco, is a broadly based manufacturer and retailer of consumer products and services with operations in apparel manufacturing, retailing, footwear manufacturing, and furniture and home furnishings group. **Employees:** 200.

LAMMERT FURNITURE COMPANY
8811 Ladue Road, St. Louis MO 63124. 314/725-0300. **Contact:** Martin Lammert V, Personnel Department. **Description:** A wholesaler and retailer of home and commercial furnishings. Also engaged in contract design.

LOWY ENTERPRISES INC.
4001 North Kingshighway Boulevard, St. Louis MO 63115. 314/383-2055. **Contact:** Ms. Ethel Maas, Personnel Director. **Description:** Wholesaler and retailer of home furnishings.

THE MAY DEPARTMENT STORES COMPANY
611 Olive Street, St. Louis MO 63101. 314/342-6300. **Contact:** Manager of Corporate Human Resources. **Description:** The corporate headquarters office of a retail organization with 13 department store companies and a shoe discount division. These department store companies are located in various areas scattered across the United States and operate under various names. **Common positions:** Accountant; Architect; Attorney; Claim Representative; Computer Programmer; Draftsperson; Civil Engineer; Electrical Engineer; Mechanical Engineer; Financial Analyst; Systems Analyst. **Educational backgrounds sought:** Accounting; Computer Science; Engineering; Finance; Mathematics. **Benefits:** medical and life insurance; pension plan; tuition assistance; disability coverage; profit sharing; employee discounts. **Corporate headquarters:** This location. **Listed on:** New York Stock Exchange.

MORGAN-WIGHTMAN SUPPLY COMPANY
10199 Woodfield Lane, Suite 300, Crevecoeur MO 63132-2922. 314/895-1111. **Contact:** Bonnie Hinds, Personnel Director. **Description:** A St. Louis distributor of wholesale building materials, including windows, doors, mouldings, and cabinets. **Common positions:** Buyer; Credit Manager; Operations/Production Manager; Sales Representative. **Benefits:** medical insurance; dental insurance; pension plan; life insurance; tuition assistance; disability coverage; employee discounts. **Corporate headquarters:** This location. **Operations at this facility:** administration.

MULTIPLEX DISPLAY FIXTURE COMPANY
1555 Larkin Williams Road, Fenton MO 63026. 314/343-5700. **Contact:** Al Hustead, Personnel Department. **Description:** A St. Louis company engaged in the display and selling of equipment, slide cabinets for the storing, viewing and retrieval of 35mm slides.

NEIMAN-MARCUS
100 Plaza Frontenac, St. Louis MO 63131. 314/567-9811. **Contact:** Roxane Holtzman, Human Resources Manager. **Description:** St. Louis branch of the national retail specialty store. Operating as a division of Neiman Marcus Group, Inc., which is a subsidiary of General Cinema Corp. **Corporate headquarters:** Dallas, TX. **Common positions:** Department Manager; General Manager; Management Trainee; Operations/Production Manager; Personnel; Public

Relations Specialist; Sales Representative. **Special programs:** Training programs; Internships. **Benefits:** Medical, Dental, and Life Insurance; Pension Plan; Tuition Assistance; Disability Coverage; Profit Sharing; Employee Discounts; Savings Plan. **Operations at this facility:** Service; Sales. **Listed on:** New York Stock Exchange.

NETTIE'S FLOWER GARDEN INC.
3801 South Grand Boulevard, St. Louis MO 63118. 314/771-9600. **Contact:** Personnel Office. **Description:** A retail florist specializing in fresh and artificial flowers, supplies, and custom decorating.

RADIO SHACK/
A TANDY CORPORATION
18 South County Center Way, St. Louis MO 63129. 314/892-1800. **Contact:** David McCoy, Store Manager. **Description:** Local office of the national consumer electronics retailer. Globally, company operates through more than 7000 stores worldwide. **Corporate headquarters:** Fort Worth, TX. **Listed on:** New York Stock Exchange.

SAKS FIFTH AVENUE
1 Plaza Frontenac, Frontenac MO 63131. 314/567-9200. **Contact:** Kathy Fornwalt, Personnel Director. **Description:** St. Louis office of the specialty retail stores. Company operates 32 fashion specialty stores located in Arizona, California, Florida, Georgia, Illinois, Maryland, Massachusetts, Michigan, Missouri, Nevada, New Jersey, New York, Ohio, Pennsylvania, and Texas. **Employees:** 10,000+ nationwide. Emphasis is on fashion-forward, high-quality soft goods, primarily apparel. Subsidiary of BATUS Inc. (Louisville, KY), a diversified corporation operating in three divisions: tobacco, retail, and paper. **Corporate headquarters:** New York, NY.

WILLIAM A. STRAUB INC.
8282 Forsyth Boulevard, St. Louis MO 63105. 314/725-2121. **Contact:** Personnel Department. **Description:** Owners and operators of a chain of retail grocery stores and restaurants.

SWANK AUDIO VISUALS INC.
211 S. Jefferson, St. Louis MO 63103. 314/534-1940. **Contact:** Sherry Senkfor, Vice President of Human Resources. **Description:** Film and tape distribution company.

VENTURE STORES INC.
2001 East Terra Lane, P.O. Box 110, O'Fallon MO 63366. 314/281-6601. **Contact:** Manager/Executive Recruitment. **Description:** Operates a chain of 91 discount department stores in seven Midwestern states. **Common positions:** Buyer; Computer Programmer; Financial Analyst; Management Trainee. **Educational backgrounds sought:** Business Administration; Computer Science; Finance; Marketing. **Benefits:** medical insurance; dental insurance; retirement plan; life insurance; tuition assistance; disability coverage; profit sharing; employee discounts; savings plan; fitness center; credit union. **Corporate headquarters:** This location. **Operations at this facility:** Administration. **Listed on:** New York Stock Exchange. **Revenues (1991):** $1.5 million.

General Merchandise: Retail/195

VI-JON LABORATORIES INC.
8515 Page Avenue, St. Louis MO 63114. 314/423-8000. **Contact:** Plant Manager. **Description:** Wholesalers of a variety of drugs and cosmetics.

WALGREEN DRUG STORES INC.
440 North Highway 67, Florissant MO 63031. 314/837-5500. **Contact:** Personnel Department. **Description:** Corporate office of a chain of retail drug stores.

WEHMUELLER JEWELERS
9671 Gielman Rock Island, Olivette MO 63132. 314/968-4211. **Contact:** Larry L. Beck, Operations Manager. **Description:** Owners and operators of a chain of retail jewelry stores. **Common positions:** Customer Service Representative; Management Trainee; Sales Representative. **Special programs:** Training programs. **Benefits:** medical insurance; dental insurance. **Corporate headquarters:** This location. **Operations at this facility:** sales. **Employees:** 120. **Projected hires for the next 12 months:** 6-8.

WEISS & NEUMAN SHOE COMPANY
1209 Washington Avenue, St. Louis MO 63103. 314/231-5125. **Contact:** Personnel Department. **Description:** An area chain of retail shoe stores.

WITTE HARDWARE CORPORATION
4600 Goodfellow Boulevard, St. Louis MO 63120. 314/381-1900. **Contact:** Personnel Department. **Description:** Wholesaler of hardware and kindred lines.

WOHL SHOE COMPANY
8350 Maryland Avenue, St. Louis MO 63105. 314/854-3133. **Contact:** Cheryl Schroer, Associate Human Resource Manager. **Description:** A large shoe retailer. Management and management trainee positions available in many locations throughout the United States. **Common positions:** General Manager; Management Trainee; Store Manager; Department Manager. **Special programs:** Training programs and internships. **Benefits:** medical insurance; pension plan; life insurance; daycare assistance; employee discounts; savings plan. **Corporate headquarters:** This location. **Parent company:** Brown Group, Inc. **Listed on:** New York Stock Exchange. **Operations at this facility:** administration.

F.W. WOOLWORTH COMPANY
3601 Olive Street, St. Louis MO 63108. 314/371-6522. **Contact:** Personnel Department. **Description:** St. Louis office of the well-known multinational retailer, distributing a wide variety of footwear, apparel, and department store merchandise through more than 6900 stores and leased departments throughout the world. The company operates retail units under the following names: Woolworth, Woolco, Kinney, Richman, Anderson-Little, J. Brannam, Shirt Closet, Susie's Casuals, Foot Locker, Lewis, Mankind, Fredelle, Williams the Shoeman, Frugal Frank's Shoe Outlet, Woolco Catalogue Stores, Shoppers World, B&Q (Retail) Ltd., Dodge City, Burgermaster, and Furnishing World. **Corporate headquarters:** New York, NY.

Additional large employers: 250+

FURNITURE

Weber Costello
200 Academic Way, Troy MO
63379-2708. 314/528-9500.
Employs: 250-499.

METALS SERVICE CENTERS
AND OFFICES

B-Line Systems Inc
509 W Monroe St, Highland IL
62249-1331. 618/654-2184.
Employs: 500-999.

ELECTRICAL APPARATUS
AND EQUIPMENT, WIRING
SUPPLIES AND
CONSTRUCTION
MATERIALS

Graybar Electric Co Inc
34 North Meramec Ave, St. Louis
MO 63105-3874. 314/727-3900.
Employs: 1,000+.

WARM AIR HEATING AND
AIR-CONDITIONING
EQUIPMENT AND SUPPLIES

Watlow Electric Mfg Co
12001 Lackland Rd, St. Louis MO
63146-4001. 314/878-4600.
Employs: 500-999.

INDUSTRIAL MACHINERY
AND EQUIPMENT

Sunnen Products Co
7910 Manchester Rd, St. Louis MO
63143-2712. 314/781-2100.
Employs: 500-999.

TRANSPORTATION
EQUIPMENT AND SUPPLIES,
EXCEPT MOTOR VEHICLES

ACF Industries Incorporated
3301 Rider Trail S, Earth City MO
63045-1309. 314/344-4900.
Employs: 500-999.

DURABLE GOODS

Uni Distribution Corp
Rte 154 E, Pinckneyville IL 62274.
618/357-2167. Employs: 250-499.

INDUSTRIAL AND PERSONAL
SERVICE PAPER

Distribix Inc
Drawer Ab Carr Station, Florissant
MO 63031-0148. 314/9217070.
Employs: 250-499.

GROCERIES, GENERAL LINE

Wetterau Inc
7100 Hazelwood Av, Hazelwood
MO 63042-2945. 314/524-4000.
Employs: 500-999.

GROCERIES AND RELATED
PRODUCTS

Bunge Corporation
11720 Borman Dr, St. Louis MO
63146-4129. 314/872-3030.
Employs: 1,000+.

Wetterau Incorporated
8920 Pershall Rd, Hazelwood MO
63042-2809. 314/524-5000.
Employs: 1,000+.

TOBACCO AND TOBACCO
PRODUCTS

Dolgin Candy & Tobacco Co
1024 S Vandeventer Av, St. Louis
MO 63110-3806. 314/531-5555.
Employs: 250-499.

General Merchandise: Retail/197

LUMBER AND OTHER BUILDING MATERIALS DEALERS

Hill-Behan Lumber Co
6515 Page Blvd, St. Louis MO 63133-1605. 314/725-1111. Employs: 500-999.

DEPARTMENT STORES

Famous-Barr Co
200 St Clair Sq, E St. Louis IL 62208-2134. 618/624-2000. Employs: 250-499.

Glik's Department Stores
3248 Nameoki Rd, Granite City IL 62040-5014. 618/876-6717. Employs: 250-499.

Sears Roebuck & Co
235 St Clair Sq, E St. Louis IL 62208-2134. 618/624-8980. Employs: 250-499.

Sears Roebuck & Co
8950 Pershall Rd, Hazelwood MO 63042-2825. 314/521-9710. Employs: 250-499.

Dillard Department Stores
100 Chesterfield Mall, Chesterfield MO 63017-4809. 314/532-4040. Employs: 250-499.

Famous-Barr Co
Northwest, Saint Ann MO 63074. 314/291-6404. Employs: 250-499.

MOTOR VEHICLE DEALERS (NEW AND USED)

Oldsmobile Div Gen Motors Corp
400 Chesterfield Ctr, Chesterfield MO 63017-4800. 314/532-7047. Employs: 500-999.

GASOLINE SERVICE STATIONS

Star Svc & Petroleum Co
800 N Skinker Bl, St. Louis MO 63130-4843. 314/863-7213. Employs: 500-999.

SHOE STORES

Edison Brothers Stores Inc
501 N Broadway, St. Louis MO 63102-2102. 314/331-6000. Employs: 1,000+.

MISCELLANEOUS APPAREL AND ACCESSORY STORES

Angelica Uniform Group
700 Rosedale Ave, St. Louis MO 63112-1408. 314/889-1111. Employs: 250-499.

FURNITURE STORES

A A Importing Co Inc
7734 Hall St, St. Louis MO 63147-2504. 314/383-4400. Employs: 250-499.

MISCELLANEOUS HOMEFURNISHINGS STORES

The Price L B Mercantile Co
4401 Ridgewood Ave, St. Louis MO 63116-1530. 314/481-8201. Employs: 250-499.

DRUG STORES AND PROPRIETARY STORES

Wal-Mart Discount Cities
2101 Barrett Station Rd, St. Louis MO 63131-1606. 314/822-3533. Employs: 250-499.

Wal-Mart Discount Cities
1150 Gannon Dr, Festus MO 63028. 314/937-3527. Employs: 250-499.

Venture Stores Inc
Christy Blvd & S Kingshighway, St. Louis MO 63116. 314/832-2600. Employs: 250-499.

OPTICAL GOODS STORES

J C Penney Co Inc
60 W County Ctr, St. Louis MO
63131-3701. 314/965-9100.
Employs: 250-499.

MISCELLANEOUS RETAIL STORES

Southwestern Bell Telecom
1000 Des Peres Rd, St. Louis MO
63131-2050. 314/822-6800.
Employs: 250-499.

Additional small to medium sized employers: 50-249

MOTOR VEHICLE SUPPLIES AND NEW PARTS

Chrysler St Louis Parts Dept
5790 Campus Pk, Hazelwood MO
63042-2337. 314/895-0740.
Employs: 50-99.

Boulevard Motors Inc
2222 Market St, St. Louis MO
63103-2516. 314/241-8768.
Employs: 50-99.

Hilltop Lincoln-Mercury
Page & Lindbergh, St. Louis MO
63114. 314/423-3555. Employs: 50-99.

Motor Parts Warehouse
2201 Washington Ave, St. Louis MO 63103-1521. 314/231-6677.
Employs: 50-99.

P & S Distributors
14243 New Halls Ferry Rd,
Florissant MO 63033-1607.
314/837-0080. Employs: 50-99.

Tractor-Trailer Supply Co
2525 Natural Bridge Ave, St. Louis MO 63107-3039. 314/241-3072.
Employs: 50-99.

FURNITURE

Bensinger's Inc
8543 Page Ave, St. Louis MO
63114-6008. 314/426-5100.
Employs: 50-99.

Office Depot Inc
12452 Saint Charles Rock Rd,
Bridgeton MO 63044-2506.
314/344-8989. Employs: 50-99.

IBT Inc-St Louis
4323 Woodson Rd, St. Louis MO
63134-3710. 314/428-4284.
Employs: 50-99.

HOMEFURNISHINGS

Interstate Supply Co
4445 Gustine Ave, St. Louis MO
63116-3417. 314/481-2222.
Employs: 50-99.

Clean-The Uniform Company
1316 S 7th St, St. Louis MO
63104-3634. 314/421-1220.
Employs: 50-99.

Brightman Distributing Co
10411 Baur Blvd, St. Louis MO
63132-1904. 314/993-6666.
Employs: 50-99.

LUMBER, PLYWOOD, MILLWORK AND WOOD PANELS

Misco-Shawnee Inc
2200 Forte Ct, Maryland Hts MO
63043-4204. 314/739-3337.
Employs: 50-99.

Millman Lumber Co
9264 Manchester Rd, St. Louis MO
63144-2636. 314/968-1700.
Employs: 100-249.

General Merchandise: Retail/199

Thomas & Proetz Lumber Co
3400 Hall St, St. Louis MO 63147-3430. 314/231-9343. Employs: 100-249.

BRICK, STONE AND RELATED CONSTRUCTION MATERIALS

Breckenridge Material Co
2829 Breckenridge Ind Ct, St. Louis MO 63144-2811. 314/962-1234. Employs: 50-99.

ROOFING, SIDING AND INSULATION MATERIALS

Brauer Supply Co
4260 Forest Park Ave, St. Louis MO 63108-2811. 314/534-7150. Employs: 50-99.

OFFICE EQUIPMENT

Mirex Corporation
5317 Mirex Dr, St. Louis MO 63119-5060. 314/968-5200. Employs: 100-249.

Beacon Paper Co
8537 Chapin Industrial Dr, St. Louis MO 63114-6005. 314/423-4100. Employs: 50-99.

COMMERCIAL EQUIPMENT

New Market Hardware Co
4064 Laclede Ave, St. Louis MO 63108-3218. 314/371-1720. Employs: 50-99.

Quip Industries Inc
1811 Jefferson St, Carlyle IL 62231-1334. 618/594-2437. Employs: 50-99.

MEDICAL, DENTAL AND HOSPITAL EQUIPMENT AND SUPPLIES

AAA Medical Equipment Co
1129 Macklind Av, St. Louis MO 63110-1440. 314/533-1611. Employs: 50-99.

Picker International
1278 N Warson Rd, St. Louis MO 63132-1806. 314/993-2590. Employs: 50-99.

Thompson-Cgr Medical
3324 Hollenberg Dr, Bridgeton MO 63044-2432. 314/432-3732. Employs: 100-249.

Midwest Medical Supply Co Inc
2349 Chaffee Dr, St. Louis MO 63146-3306. 314/872-8820. Employs: 50-99.

Profex Medical Products
8013 Maryland Ave, St. Louis MO 63105-3717. 314/727-2996. Employs: 50-99.

Smith & Davis Manufacturing
1100 Corporate Square Dr, St. Louis MO 63132-2908. 314/569-3515. Employs: 100-249.

PROFESSIONAL EQUIPMENT AND SUPPLIES

Mueller Optical Co
1625 Olive St, St. Louis MO 63103-2344. 314/621-9535. Employs: 50-99.

Don H Munger & Co Inc
1150 Hanley Industrial Ct, St. Louis MO 63144-1910. 314/961-8100. Employs: 50-99.

METALS SERVICE CENTERS AND OFFICES

Affiliated Metals Co Inc
1020 Niedringhaus Ave, Granite City IL 62040-3142. 618/451-4700. Employs: 50-99.

Feralloy Corp
2500 Nameoki Dr, Granite City IL 62040-2163. 618/452-2500. Employs: 50-99.

Heitman Steel Products Inc
10 Northgate Indus Dr, Granite City IL 62040-6805. 618/451-0052. Employs: 50-99.

Lapham Hickey Steel Corp
500 S Spring Ave, St. Louis MO 63110-1228. 314/535-8200. Employs: 50-99.

Tara Corporation
16th St, Granite City IL 62040. 618/451-4400. Employs: 100-249.

Tubular Steel Inc
1031 Executive Pkwy Dr Box, St. Louis MO 63141-6339. 314/851-9200. Employs: 100-249.

St Clair Die Casting Co
St Clair Industrial Park, Saint Clair MO 63077. 314/241-1066. Employs: 100-249.

Aladdin Steel Inc
Rt 16, Gillespie IL 62033. 217/839-2121. Employs: 50-99.

Joseph T Ryerson & Son Inc
5 Clinton St, St. Louis MO 63102-1424. 314/231-1020. Employs: 50-99.

McKinley Iron Inc
3620 Hall St, St. Louis MO 63147-3431. 314/231-6077. Employs: 50-99.

COAL AND OTHER MINERALS AND ORES

Arch Mineral-Sales Jv
200 N Broadway, St. Louis MO 63102-2730. 314/231-1010. Employs: 100-249.

ELECTRICAL APPARATUS AND EQUIPMENT, WIRING SUPPLIES AND CONSTRUCTION MATERIALS

Ahrens & McCarron Inc
4621 Beck Ave, St. Louis MO 63116-1605. 314/772-8400. Employs: 100-249.

ELECTRICAL APPLIANCES, TELEVISION AND RADIO SETS

W Schiller & Co
9240 Manchester Rd, St. Louis MO 63144-2636. 314/968-3650. Employs: 50-99.

Peerless Premier Appliance Co
119 S 14th St, Belleville IL 62220-1715. 618/233-0475. Employs: 100-249.

GPX Inc
108 Madison St, St. Louis MO 63102-1328. 314/621-3314. Employs: 100-249.

ELECTRONIC PARTS AND EQUIPMENT

AT&T Federal Systems
720 W Main St Ste 200, Belleville IL 62220-1551. 618/234-9310. Employs: 50-99.

Midwest Corp
11642 Lilburn Park Rd, St. Louis MO 63146-3535. 314/569-2240. Employs: 100-249.

Tech Electronics Inc
6437 Manchester Ave, St. Louis MO 63139-3457. 314/645-6200. Employs: 100-249.

General Merchandise: Retail/201

PLUMBING AND HEATING EQUIPMENT AND SUPPLIES (HYDRONICS)

Sidener Supply Company
11665 Lackland Rd, St. Louis MO 63146-3526. 314/432-4700. Employs: 50-99.

WARM AIR HEATING AND AIR-CONDITIONING EQUIPMENT AND SUPPLIES

Gillespie & Powers Inc
9550 True Dr, St. Louis MO 63132-1537. 314/423-9460. Employs: 50-99.

REFRIGERATION EQUIPMENT AND SUPPLIES

Dome Railway Service
435 N Old St Louis Rd, Wood River IL 62095-1129. 618/254-3040. Employs: 100-249.

Natl Auto Supply Co
1100 Martin Luther King Dr, E St. Louis IL 62201-1933. 618/271-1285. Employs: 50-99.

CONSTRUCTION AND MINING (EXCEPT PETROLEUM) MACHINERY AND EQUIPMENT

Vernon L Goedecke Co
4101 Clayton Ave, St. Louis MO 63110-1717. 314/652-1810. Employs: 50-99.

Allied Construction Equip Co
4015 Forest Park Ave, St. Louis MO 63108-3213. 314/371-1818. Employs: 50-99.

INDUSTRIAL MACHINERY AND EQUIPMENT

Continental Textile Corp
12046 Lackland Rd, St. Louis MO 63146-4002. 314/878-3800. Employs: 50-99.

Storage Systems Inc
6100 Lemay Ferry Rd, St. Louis MO 63129-2219. 314/993-3315. Employs: 50-99.

Ripley Industries Inc
4067 Folsom Ave, St. Louis MO 63110-2401. 314/664-5100. Employs: 100-249.

Cummins Gateway Inc
7210 Hall St, St. Louis MO 63147-2604. 314/389-5400. Employs: 50-99.

Shipping Utilities Inc
10539 Liberty Ave, St. Louis MO 63132-1218. 314/426-4800. Employs: 50-99.

Heat Transfer Systems Inc
8100 Polk St, St. Louis MO 63111-3642. 314/631-3311. Employs: 50-99.

United States Tape & Label
1561 Fairview, St. Louis MO 63132-1324. 314/423-4411. Employs: 50-99.

INDUSTRIAL SUPPLIES

Buffalo Tool Corp
1111 N Broadway, St. Louis MO 63102-2205. 314/231-6444. Employs: 100-249.

Berlin Packaging
8237 Brentwood Industrial Dr, St. Louis MO 63144-2814. 314/647-1551. Employs: 100-249.

Sporlan Valve Co
7525 Sussex Ave, St. Louis MO 63143-4124. 314/647-2775. Employs: 100-249.

Kaydon Spirolox Division
29 Cassens Ct, Fenton MO 63026-2542. 314/343-5885. Employs: 50-99.

Mineweld Inc
Rt 3 & Judith Ln, E St. Louis IL 62206. 618/332-0595. Employs: 50-99.

SERVICE ESTABLISHMENT EQUIPMENT AND SUPPLIES

Continental Research Corp
1540 Page Industrial, St. Louis MO 63132. 314/426-0410. Employs: 100-249.

Royal Papers Inc
1939 S Vandeventer Ave, St. Louis MO 63110-3219. 314/664-3900. Employs: 50-99.

SPORTING AND RECREATIONAL GOODS AND SUPPLIES

Markwort Sporting Goods Co
4300 Forest Park Ave, St. Louis MO 63108-2821. 314/652-3757. Employs: 100-249.

Roller Derby Skate Corp
311 W Edwards St, Litchfield IL 62056-1904. 217/324-3961. Employs: 50-99.

TOYS AND HOBBY GOODS AND SUPPLIES

Acme Premium Supply Corp
4100 Forest Park Av, St. Louis MO 63108-2809. 314/531-8880. Employs: 50-99.

DURABLE GOODS

C P Clare Corp
48 Progress Pkwy, Maryland Hts MO 63043-3706. 314/434-1450. Employs: 50-99.

St Louis Music Inc
1400 Ferguson Ave, St. Louis MO 63133-1720. 314/727-4512. Employs: 50-99.

STATIONERY AND OFFICE SUPPLIES

General Credit Forms
3595 S Rider Trl, Earth City MO 63045-1127. 314/291-8600. Employs: 50-99.

INDUSTRIAL AND PERSONAL SERVICE PAPER

Ford Hotel Supply Co
814 N Broadway, St. Louis MO 63102-2109. 314/231-8400. Employs: 50-99.

Lee Paper Co Inc
5010 Kemper, St. Louis MO 63139-1106. 314/771-7300. Employs: 50-99.

Shaughnessy Kniep Hawe Paper Co
4316 Duncan Ave, St. Louis MO 63110-1110. 314/533-2711. Employs: 50-99.

Zellerbach-A Mead Company
10805 Sunset Office Dr # L110, St. Louis MO 63127-1025. 314/652-3525. Employs: 50-99.

Smith-Scharff
722 S Vandeventer Ave, St. Louis MO 63110-1242. 314/533-0233. Employs: 50-99.

U-Haul Co
12060 Lusher Rd, St. Louis MO 63138-1302. 314/355-7900. Employs: 100-249.

General Merchandise: Retail/203

DRUGS, DRUG PROPRIETARIES AND DRUGGISTS' SUNDRIES

Invitron Corp
311 N Lindbergh Blvd # 100, St. Louis MO 63141-7842. 314/426-5000. Employs: 100-249.

Meyer Fox Co
5430 Wise Ave, St. Louis MO 63110-1857. 314/647-8000. Employs: 50-99.

WOMEN'S, CHILDREN'S AND INFANTS' CLOTHING AND ACCESSORIES

Fashions By Hugo
30 American Industrial Dr, Maryland Hts MO 63043-3006. 314/434-9300. Employs: 50-99.

FOOTWEAR

Missouri Industries
1017 Fernpark Dr, St. Louis MO 63141-6132. 314/878-8268. Employs: 50-99.

GROCERIES, GENERAL LINE

Assoc Grocers Co St Louis Mo
5030 Berthold Ave, St. Louis MO 63110-1409. 314/652-3715. Employs: 100-249.

Home Brands A Conagra
13523 Barrett Parkway Dr, Ballwin MO 63021-3802. 314/957-4400. Employs: 100-249.

Kraft Inc Food Service
10850 Ambassador Bl, St. Louis MO 63132-1708. 314/991-3122. Employs: 50-99.

P V O Foods Inc
3400 N Wharf St, St. Louis MO 63147-3443. 314/622-0200. Employs: 100-249.

The Fresh Fish Co
8501 Page Ave, St. Louis MO 63114-6001. 314/428-7777. Employs: 50-99.

DAIRY PRODUCTS, EXCEPT DRIED OR CANNED

Ice Cream Specialties
P O Box 19766, St. Louis MO 63144-0166. 314/962-2550. Employs: 100-249.

Midstates Dairy Co
2001 Chestnut St, St. Louis MO 63103-2201. 314/621-4312. Employs: 100-249.

Pevely Dairy Co
1001 S Grand Blvd, St. Louis MO 63104-1012. 314/771-4400. Employs: 100-249.

POULTRY AND POULTRY PRODUCTS

Crown Foods Inc
5243 Manchester Ave, St. Louis MO 63110-2015. 314/645-5300. Employs: 50-99.

FRESH FRUITS AND VEGETABLES

United Fruit & Produce Co
55 Produce Row, St. Louis MO 63102-1418. 314/621-9440. Employs: 100-249.

GROCERIES AND RELATED PRODUCTS

Foltz Distributing
Highway 54, Bowling Green MO 63334. 314/324-2442. Employs: 50-99.

Pepsi-Cola Bottling Company
8780 Metropolitan Blvd, Pevely MO 63070-1307. 314/479-5366. Employs: 50-99.

Joe Fazio's Bakery
1717 Sublette Ave, St. Louis MO 63110-1926. 314/645-6239. Employs: 50-99.

Hershey Choc USA Div Hershey
13545 Barrett Parkway Dr, Ballwin MO 63021-5896. 314/821-7778. Employs: 50-99.

GRAIN AND FIELD BEANS

Checkerboard Grain Co
835 S 8th St, St. Louis MO 63102-1002. 314/371-5090. Employs: 50-99.

Conagra Inc
PO Box 246, Alton IL 62002-0246. 618/463-4432. Employs: 100-249.

Italgrani U S A
7900 Van Buren, St. Louis MO 63111-3611. 314/638-1447. Employs: 50-99.

Archer Daniels Mdlnd Processing Co
3601 Cargill Rd, Granite City IL 62040-4255. 618/797-2449. Employs: 50-99.

CHEMICALS AND ALLIED PRODUCTS

Chevron Chemical Co
2497 Adie Rd, Maryland Hts MO 63043-3503. 314/432-8234. Employs: 100-249.

Northwestern Bottle Co
1033 Corporate Square Dr, St. Louis MO 63132-2928. 314/569-3633. Employs: 100-249.

Servicemaster
249 Old Meramec Station Rd, Ballwin MO 63021-5310. 314/256-3569. Employs: 50-99.

PETROLEUM AND PETROLEUM PRODUCTS

WHOLESALERS, EXCEPT BULK STATIONS AND TERMINALS

Chart Automotive Group Inc
8801 Frost Ave, St. Louis MO 63134-1001. 314/522-1112. Employs: 50-99.

Fkg Oil Co
721 W Main St, Belleville IL 62220-1514. 618/233-6754. Employs: 100-249.

BEER AND ALE

William D Pizzini Inc
110 E College St, Edwardsville IL 62025-1607. 618/656-5390. Employs: 50-99.

Lohr Distributing Co Inc
1100 S 9th St, St. Louis MO 63104-3511. 314/231-6400. Employs: 50-99.

WINE AND DISTILLED ALCOHOLIC BEVERAGES

St Louis Liquor Co
6501 Hall St, St. Louis MO 63147-2910. 314/382-9400. Employs: 100-249.

FARM SUPPLIES

Quincy Soybean Company
PO Box 158, Laddonia MO 63352-0158. 314/373-5311. Employs: 50-99.

Chem Lawn Services Corporation
655 Axminister Dr, Fenton MO 63026-2905. 314/343-1973. Employs: 50-99.

Greene County Svc Co
Rt 67 N, Greenfield IL 62044. 217/368-2916. Employs: 50-99.

BOOKS, PERIODICALS AND NEWSPAPERS

Capitol City Distribution Inc
801 Bradbury, Sparta IL 62286.
618/443-5323. Employs: 100-249.

PAINTS, VARNISHES AND SUPPLIES

Brod-Dugan Company
2145 Schuetz Rd, St. Louis MO
63146-3547. 314/567-1111.
Employs: 100-249.

NONDURABLE GOODS

Hermann Marketing
1400 N Price Rd, St. Louis MO
63132-2308. 314/432-1595.
Employs: 100-249.

LUMBER AND OTHER BUILDING MATERIALS DEALERS

Central Hardware Stores
Big Bend & Lindbergh Blvd, St. Louis MO 63143. 314/822-3600.
Employs: 50-99.

Illinois Lumber Company
3 Club Sentre Ste C, Edwardsville IL 62025-3519. 618/656-1905.
Employs: 50-99.

Kienstar Inc
2801 Circle Dr, Granite City IL
62040-2121. 618/876-4150.
Employs: 50-99.

La Crosse Lumber Co
200 N Main St, Louisiana MO
63353-1747. 314/754-4533.
Employs: 50-99.

O'Neil Lumber Co Inc
104 Saint Clair Ave, E St. Louis IL
62201-1432. 618/271-1400.
Employs: 50-99.

Cox Brothers Door Co
3924 Shrewsbury Ave, St. Louis
MO 63119-2112. 314/781-0651.
Employs: 50-99.

Glasco Electric Company
24 Worthington Dr, Maryland Hts
MO 63043. 314/469-2233.
Employs: 100-249.

PAINT, GLASS AND WALLPAPER STORES

Flanagan Paint & Wallpaper Co
3500 Hampton Ave, St. Louis MO
63139-1918. 314/351-0691.
Employs: 50-99.

Grandpa Pidgeon's
7077 Chippewa St, St. Louis MO
63119-5601. 314/781-9130.
Employs: 100-249.

Kenstan Distributors
10401 Trenton Ave, St. Louis MO
63132-1222. 314/427-0770.
Employs: 50-99.

RETAIL NURSERIES, LAWN AND GARDEN SUPPLY STORES

Forrest Keeling Nursery
Highway 79, Elsberry MO 63343.
314/898-5571. Employs: 50-99.

DEPARTMENT STORES

Dillards
Hwy 366/145 Crestw Pl, St. Louis
MO 63126. 314/532-4040.
Employs: 100-249.

Dollar General Store
700 Carlyle Rd, Belleville IL
62221. 618/235-1338. Employs: 50-99.

Dollar General Store
13 Northtown Shopping Center,
Highland IL 62249. 618/654-9013.
Employs: 50-99.

Dollar General Store
18 East Gate Plaza, East Alton IL 62024-1057. 618/254-8335. Employs: 50-99.

Dollar General Store
56 Airport Plaza, Bethalto IL 62010-1774. 618/377-5524. Employs: 50-99.

F W Woolworth Co
1327 19th St, Granite City IL 62040-4604. 618/451-9935. Employs: 50-99.

Famous-Barr Co
100 Alton Sq, Alton IL 62002-5917. 618/463-4100. Employs: 50-99.

Famous-Barr Co
47 Crestwood Pl, St. Louis MO 63126-1700. 314/961-8686. Employs: 100-249.

Famous-Barr Co
7601 W Florissant/Northln, St. Louis MO 63121. 314/389-9099. Employs: 100-249.

Glik's Department Store
1506 Troy Rd, Edwardsville IL 62025-2550. 618/656-3875. Employs: 50-99.

Grandpa Pidgeons
2801 N Illinois St, Belleville IL 62221-2300. 618/234-1798. Employs: 50-99.

J C Penney Co Inc
1355 Mark Twain Shop Center, Saint Charles MO 63301-2457. 314/724-3100. Employs: 100-249.

J C Penney Co Inc
245 St Clair Sq, E St. Louis IL 62208-2134. 618/632-2300. Employs: 100-249.

J C Penney Co Inc
150 Alton Sq, Alton IL 62002-5917. 618/463-9595. Employs: 100-249.

K-Mart
2120 Troy Rd, Edwardsville IL 62025-2540. 618/692-0050. Employs: 50-99.

Sears Roebuck & Co
1050 Washington Sq, Washington MO 63090-5302. 314/239-2751. Employs: 50-99.

Sears Roebuck & Co
8650 Big Bend Bl, St. Louis MO 63119-3839. 314/968-7623. Employs: 100-249.

Sears Roebuck & Co Inc
6802 Gravois Ave, St. Louis MO 63116-1128. 314/577-0679. Employs: 100-249.

The Dollar Store
1974 Vandalia St, Collinsville IL 62234-4846. 618/345-7844. Employs: 50-99.

Venture Stores Inc
6525 N Illinois St, E St. Louis IL 62208-2001. 618/397-8300. Employs: 100-249.

Venture Stores Inc
2600 Homer M Adams Pkwy, Alton IL 62002-5430. 618/462-1281. Employs: 100-249.

Wal-Mart
Bx1 E Junction Dr, Edwardsville IL 62025. 618/692-0550. Employs: 50-99.

Wal-Mart
700 Carlyle Rd, Belleville IL 62221. 618/277-5210. Employs: 50-99.

Wal-Mart
1530 Highway 50 W, O Fallon IL 62269. 618/632-9066. Employs: 50-99.

Wal-Mart Super Center
1200 E Highway 100, Washington MO 63090. 314/239-1993. Employs: 50-99.

J C Penney Co Inc
56 Grandview Plaza Shopping Ctr, Florissant MO 63033-6105. 314/8383384. Employs: 100-249.

J C Penney Co Inc
1169 Gannon Dr, Festus MO 63028. 314/937-4888. Employs: 50-99.

J C Penney Co Inc
50 Hampton Village Plaza, St. Louis MO 63109-2127. 314/351-5050. Employs: 100-249.

K-Mart Stores
3861 Gravois Ave, St. Louis MO 63116-4657. 314/771-2396. Employs: 50-99.

K-Mart Stores
4560 Gravois Village Ctr, High Ridge MO 63049-1838. 314/677-7258. Employs: 50-99.

K-Mart Stores High Ridge
7335 Manchester Rd, St. Louis MO 63143-3107. 314/781-7900. Employs: 50-99.

Sears Roebuck and Co
9059 Watson Rd, St. Louis MO 63126-2220. 314/961-5448. Employs: 100-249.

Wal-Mart Discount Cities
N Market, Sparta IL 62286. 618/443-3021. Employs: 100-249.

Wal-Mart Discount Cities
2511 Franklin St, Carlyle IL 62231-2403. 618/594-2465. Employs: 50-99.

Wal-Mart Discount Cities
1511 Camp Jackson Rd, E St. Louis IL 62206-2537. 618/332-1771. Employs: 50-99.

Wal-Mart Discount Cities
4550 Gravois Village Ctr, High Ridge MO 63049-1838. 314/671-0505. Employs: 50-99.

Wal-Mart Discount Cities
Hwy 50 E, Union MO 63084. 314/583-2531. Employs: 50-99.

Wal-Mart Discount Cities
655 Gravois Rd, Fenton MO 63026-4136. 314/349-3007. Employs: 50-99.

Wal-Mart Discount Cities
I-44 & Viola Lane, Eureka MO 63025. 314/587-2201. Employs: 50-99.

Wal-Mart Discount Cities
Hwy 21 Route N, De Soto MO 63020. 314/586-6878. Employs: 50-99.

Wal-Mart Discount Cities
15 Shopping Plaza, Litchfield IL 62056-1042. 217/324-6195. Employs: 100-249.

Wal-Mart Discount Cities
Mall, Jerseyville IL 62052. 618/498-6861. Employs: 100-249.

Wal-Mart Discount Cities
10741 W Florissant Ave, St. Louis MO 63136-2403. 314/521-2565. Employs: 100-249.

Wal-Mart Discount Cities
Twin Pike Shopping Center, Louisiana MO 63353. 314/754-4573. Employs: 50-99.

Dollar General Stores
931 Fairfax St, Carlyle IL 62231-1811. 618/594-4403. Employs: 50-99.

Dollar General Stores
160 N Main St, Breese IL 62230-1630. 618/526-2911. Employs: 50-99.

Ten Dollars & Less
300 Junction Dr, Edwardsville IL 62025-4320. 618/692-6550. Employs: 50-99.

Big Lots
3801 Nameoki Rd, Granite City IL 62040-3722. 618/452-8001. Employs: 50-99.

Big Lots
1721 Homer M Adams Pkwy, Alton IL 62002-5604. 618/462-0174. Employs: 50-99.

Big Lots
1070 Lemay Ferry Rd, St. Louis MO 63125-1744. 314/544-0480. Employs: 100-249.

Bill's Dollar Store
10738 Highway 21, Hillsboro MO 63050. 314/789-5139. Employs: 50-99.

Burlington Coat Factory
11977 Saint Charles Rock Rd, Bridgeton MO 63044-2613. 314/739-4545. Employs: 50-99.

Burlington Coat Factory
12750 Manchester Rd, St. Louis MO 63131-1818. 314/821-7890. Employs: 100-249.

Dillard Department Stores
220 S County Center Way, St. Louis MO 63129-1088. 314/487-1600. Employs: 50-99.

Dillard Department Stores
1105 St. Louis Galleria, St. Louis MO 63117-1159. 314/725-8363. Employs: 100-249.

Dillard Department Stores
400 Jamestown Mall, Florissant MO 63034-2932. 314/355-8600. Employs: 100-249.

Dillard Department Stores
496 Northwest Plaza, Saint Ann MO 63074-2203. 314/291-5191. Employs: 100-249.

Dillard Department Stores
601 Washington Ave, St. Louis MO 63101-1207. 314/231-5080. Employs: 100-249.

Dillard Department Stores
Mid Rivers Mall, Saint Peters MO 63376. 314/279-2555. Employs: 50-99.

Dollar General Corp
117 Main, White Hall IL 62092. 217/374-2002. Employs: 50-99.

Dollar General Corp
114 S Elm St, Staunton IL 62088-1467. 618/6353011. Employs: 50-99.

Dollar General Corp
108 W State St, Nokomis IL 62075-1657. 217/563-2211. Employs: 50-99.

Dollar General Store
116 N Main St, Marissa IL 62257-1342. 618/295-3222. Employs: 50-99.

Dollar General Store
203 N Sturgeon St, Montgomery City MO 63361-1822. 314/564-3368. Employs: 50-99.

Dollar General Store
4242 Telegraph Rd, St. Louis MO 63129-2658. 314/845-2414. Employs: 100-249.

Dollar General Stores
2717 Cherokee St, St. Louis MO
63118-3035. 314/776-7072.
Employs: 100-249.

Dollar General Stores
63 Grasso Plaza, St. Louis MO
63123-3107. 314/631-5406.
Employs: 100-249.

Dollar General Stores
12115 Bellefontaine Rd, St. Louis
MO 63138-1906. 314/355-1141.
Employs: 100-249.

Dollar General Stores
Highway Z, Pevely MO 63070.
314/479-3581. Employs: 50-99.

Dollar General Stores
518 E Osage St, Pacific MO
63069-1706. 314/257-3493.
Employs: 50-99.

Dollar General Stores
Twin City Mall, Crystal City MO
63019. 314/937-8501. Employs:
50-99.

Design Exclusively Levis Straus
213 Northwest Plaza, Saint Ann
MO 63074-2201. 314/739-6662.
Employs: 50-99.

Family Dollar Stores Inc
RR 2, Chester IL 62233-9802.
618/826-3221. Employs: 50-99.

Family Dollar Stores Inc
2 Bellevue Park Plaza, Belleville
IL 62223-5201. 618/277-1915.
Employs: 50-99.

Family Dollar Stores Inc
1835 Kingshwy, E St. Louis IL
62204. 618/875-3900. Employs:
50-99.

Family Dollar Stores Inc
2318 State St, E St. Louis IL
62205-2319. 618/875-9806.
Employs: 50-99.

Family Dollar Stores Inc
531 S State St, Jerseyville IL
62052-2241. 618/498-3611.
Employs: 50-99.

Family Dollar Stores Inc
6321 W Florissant Ave, St. Louis
MO 63136-4935. 314/389-0281.
Employs: 100-249.

Famous-Barr Co
601 Olive, Collinsville IL 62234.
618/345-7667. Employs: 50-99.

Famous-Barr Co
2505 Mentor Pl, St. Louis MO
63144-2129. 314/569-0771.
Employs: 100-249.

Famous-Barr Co
South County, St. Louis MO
63129. 314/892-0110. Employs:
100-249.

Famous-Barr Co
West County, St. Louis MO 63131.
314/966-0017. Employs: 50-99.

Fridge's Top Fashion
305 Collinsville Ave, E St. Louis
IL 62201-2912. 618/271-8001.
Employs: 50-99.

Grandpa Pidgeon's Stores
14650 Manchester Rd, Ballwin MO
63011-3751. 314/227-8600.
Employs: 50-99.

J C Penney Co Inc
2404 Northline Industrial Dr,
Maryland Hts MO 63043-3309.
314/872-8120. Employs: 50-99.

J C Penney Co Inc
4337 Butler Hill Rd # A, St. Louis
MO 63128-3717. 314/845-0668.
Employs: 100-249.

J C Penney Co Inc
12521 Olive Blvd, St. Louis MO
63141-6311. 314/542-0490.
Employs: 100-249.

Joseph's Apparel
111 S State St, Jerseyville IL
62052-1850. 618/498-2312.
Employs: 50-99.

K-Mart Stores
15909 Manchester Rd, Ballwin MO
63011-2101. 314/391-3226.
Employs: 50-99.

Little Tot Shop
1453 St. Louis Galleria, St. Louis
MO 63117-1112. 314/727-8880.
Employs: 100-249.

Marshall's
248 Mid Rivers Mall Dr, Saint
Peters MO 63376. 314/279-2070.
Employs: 50-99.

Marshall's
10780 Sunset Hills Plaza, St. Louis
MO 63127. 314/821-7630.
Employs: 100-249.

Marshall's
15029 Manchester Rd, Ballwin MO
63011-4626. 314/227-3520.
Employs: 50-99.

McCrory Store
95 Northland Shopping Ctr, St.
Louis MO 63136-1413. 314/385-3991. Employs: 100-249.

Paesano Pizza & Pasta
3025 High Ridge Blvd, High Ridge
MO 63049-2216. 314/677-6611.
Employs: 50-99.

Pennys Worth
601 N Highway 47, Union MO
63084. 314/583-6181. Employs:
50-99.

Places

808 N Sturgeon St, Montgomery
City MO 63361-1426. 314/564-3555. Employs: 50-99.

Poslosky Department Stores
117 Lemay Ferry Rd, St. Louis MO
63125-1245. 314/631-1929.
Employs: 100-249.

Sears Hardware Store
3833 Lemay Ferry Rd, St. Louis
MO 63125-4535. 314/894-7324.
Employs: 100-249.

Stuarts
158 Jamestown Mall, Florissant
MO 63034-2926. 314/741-7437.
Employs: 100-249.

Target Stores
15025 Manchester Rd, Ballwin MO
63011-4626. 314/391-7500.
Employs: 50-99.

Target Stores
12275 Saint Charles Rock Rd,
Bridgeton MO 63044-2502.
314/291-0600. Employs: 100-249.

Target Stores
5252 S Lindbergh Blvd, St. Louis
MO 63126-3519. 314/842-2000.
Employs: 100-249.

Target Stores
2677 Dunn Rd, St. Louis MO
63136-4627. 314/741-7500.
Employs: 100-249.

Target Stores
4255 Hampton Ave, St. Louis MO
63109-2120. 314/481-9100.
Employs: 100-249.

Target Stores
3940 W Clay St, Saint Charles MO
63301-4419. 314/723-7223.
Employs: 100-249.

General Merchandise: Retail/211

Ten Dollars & Less
1415 Vaughn Rd, Wood River IL 62095-1853. 618/259-3318. Employs: 50-99.

Tucker's Department Store
2810 N Grand Blvd, St. Louis MO 63107-2605. 314/533-7103. Employs: 100-249.

Venture Return Center
2600 Homer M Adams Pkwy, Alton IL 62002-5430. 618/462-5077. Employs: 50-99.

Venture Stores Inc
3979 I-70 & Cave Springs Rd, Saint Charles MO 63303. 314/278-6595. Employs: 50-99.

Venture Stores Inc
5401 Collinsville Rd, E St. Louis IL 62201-2335. 618/874-8555. Employs: 50-99.

Venture Stores Inc
200 Andersohn, Ballwin MO 63011. 314/527-5774. Employs: 50-99.

Venture Stores Inc
3200 Laclede Station Rd, St. Louis MO 63143-3709. 314/644-1100. Employs: 100-249.

Venture Stores Inc
3901 Lemay Ferry Rd, St. Louis MO 63125-4521. 314/892-9900. Employs: 100-249.

Venture Stores Inc
8901 Page Ave, St. Louis MO 63114-6119. 314/429-7800. Employs: 100-249.

Venture Stores Inc
1225 S Kirkwood Rd, St. Louis MO 63122-7224. 314/821-8200. Employs: 100-249.

Wal-Mart Discount Cities
635 Gravois Rd, Fenton MO 63026-4136. 314/349-3116. Employs: 50-99.

Wal-Mart Discount Cities
100 Hilltop Village Center Dr, Eureka MO 63025-1107. 314/938-6618. Employs: 50-99.

Wal-Mart Discount Cities
740 N Market St, Waterloo IL 62298-1014. 618/939-3416. Employs: 50-99.

Wal-Mart Discount Cities
4000 Centre Pt S, Saint Charles MO 63304-2817. 314/447-5853. Employs: 50-99.

Wal-Mart Store Discount Cities
Wentzville Center, Wentzville MO 63385. 314/327-5155. Employs: 100-249.

Wal-Mart Store Discount Cities
The Plaza, Troy MO 63379. 314/528-6111. Employs: 50-99.

50-50 Stores
680 N Highway 67, Florissant MO 63031. 314/831-3767. Employs: 100-249.

VARIETY STORES

Abel Oil Co Inc
Hwy 79 S Box 532, Louisiana MO 63353-0532. 314/754-5595. Employs: 50-99.

K-Mart Stores
237 Arnold Crossroads Ctr, Arnold MO 63010-1434. 314/296-4600. Employs: 50-99.

K-Mart Stores
10041 Lewis & Clark Blvd, St. Louis MO 63136. 314/868-8815. Employs: 50-99.

MISCELLANEOUS GENERAL MERCHANDISE STORES

Dollar General Store
620 Berkshire Blvd, East Alton IL 62024-1325. 618/259-7111. Employs: 50-99.

K-Mart Discount Stores
2851 Homer M Adams Pkwy, Alton IL 62002-4856. 618/462-8720. Employs: 50-99.

Wal-Mart Discount City
348 State Hwy 143 N, Highland IL 62249. 618/654-4596. Employs: 100-249.

Svc Merchandise
5881 Suemandy Rd, Saint Peters MO 63376-4327. 314/278-3312. Employs: 50-99.

Sears Roebuck and Co
455 North Hwy 67, Florissant MO 63031. 314/838-4000. Employs: 100-249.

MOTOR VEHICLE DEALERS (NEW AND USED)

Cassens & Sons Inc
121 Hillsboro Av, Edwardsville IL 62025-1621. 618/656-6070. Employs: 100-249.

Rauscher Chevrolet Co Inc
Page & Lindbergh, St. Louis MO 63122. 314/423-5700. Employs: 50-99.

Roberts Ford Chrysler Plymouth
4350 N Alby Street Rd, Alton IL 62002-5913. 618/466-7220. Employs: 50-99.

Schmitt Chev Inc
512 Main, St. Louis MO 63136. 314/436-0288. Employs: 50-99.

Carlson Oldsmobile
885 S Lindbergh Blvd, St. Louis MO 63131-2824. 314/994-1400. Employs: 50-99.

Charles Brock Oldsmobile Inc
8917 Dunn Rd, Hazelwood MO 63042-2004. 314/921-6111. Employs: 50-99.

West County BMW-SAAB
14417 Manchester Rd, Ballwin MO 63011-4044. 314/227-5454. Employs: 50-99.

Plaza Motor Company
11830 Olive Blvd, St. Louis MO 63141-6718. 314/432-1003. Employs: 100-249.

Southland Volks Nissan Suzuki
6000 S Lindbergh Blvd, St. Louis MO 63123-7019. 314/892-8200. Employs: 50-99.

Lou Fusz
1025 N Lindbergh Blvd, St. Louis MO 63132-2911. 314/994-1500. Employs: 100-249.

Seeger Toyota
12833 Olive Blvd, St. Louis MO 63141-6205. 314/434-5000. Employs: 50-99.

Dave Sinclair Ford Inc
7466 S Lindbergh Blvd, St. Louis MO 63125-4845. 314/892-2600. Employs: 100-249.

Pundmann Ford
2727 W Clay St, Saint Charles MO 63301-2539. 314/946-6611. Employs: 50-99.

St Louis Freightliner Co
747 E Taylor Ave, St. Louis MO 63147-2807. 314/381-3800. Employs: 50-99.

MOTOR VEHICLE DEALERS (USED ONLY)

Hertz Rent A Car
Lambert Field, St. Louis MO 63145. 314/426-2724. Employs: 50-99.

Meyer Pontiac Honda & Subaru
301 West A St, Belleville IL 62220-1177. 618/233-8280. Employs: 50-99.

AUTO AND HOME SUPPLY STORES

Napa Auto Parts
525 S Jefferson Ave, St. Louis MO 63103-3021. 314/533-0243. Employs: 100-249.

Reuther Jeep Eagle
11654 Olive Blvd, St. Louis MO 63141-7002. 314/432-8408. Employs: 50-99.

Precision Rebuilders Inc
350 N Commercial, St. Louis MO 63102. 314/652-8296. Employs: 100-249.

H & H Goodyear Tire Centers
14268 Manchester Rd, Ballwin MO 63011-4510. 314/394-2400. Employs: 50-99.

K-Mart Stores
7220 N Lindbergh Blvd, Hazelwood MO 63042-2019. 314/731-4610. Employs: 100-249.

Sears Roebuck & Co
490 Northwest Plaza, Saint Ann MO 63074-2203. 314/344-5628. Employs: 100-249.

GASOLINE SERVICE STATIONS

Bauer Oil Co
9812 Sappington Rd, St. Louis MO 63128-1242. 314/842-4800. Employs: 50-99.

J D Street & Co
144 Weldon Pkwy, Maryland Hts MO 63043-3102. 314/432-6600. Employs: 50-99.

Jefferson Sixty-Six Station
505 Jefferson St, Saint Charles MO 63301-2702. 314/724-0317. Employs: 50-99.

BOAT DEALERS

Western Diesel Services Inc
1424 Ashby Rd, St. Louis MO 63132-1211. 314/429-2131. Employs: 100-249.

MEN'S, BOYS' CLOTHING AND ACCESSORY STORES

Knickerbocker Clothing Co
1308 Washington Ave, St. Louis MO 63103-1919. 314/421-3908. Employs: 100-249.

WOMEN'S CLOTHING STORES

Coats and Things
8049 Litzsinger Rd, St. Louis MO 63144-2505. 314/647-6621. Employs: 50-99.

CHILDREN'S AND INFANTS' WEAR STORES

Fashion Lane Inc
2745 Locust St, St. Louis MO 63103-1413. 314/533-6600. Employs: 50-99.

FAMILY CLOTHING STORES

Venture
7230 Old St Louis Rd, Belleville IL 62223-3502. 618/236-1800. Employs: 100-249.

SHOE STORES

Senack Shoes
101 S Hanley Rd, St. Louis MO 63105-3406. 314/997-0330. Employs: 100-249.

Wild Pair Shoe Store
St Louis Centre, St. Louis MO 63101. 314/421-1795. Employs: 50-99.

FURNITURE STORES

Aristokraft Cabinets
4999 Tyler, St. Louis MO 63119. 314/351-5294. Employs: 50-99.

Buford Rhodes Furnishing Co
8000 Bonhomme Av, St. Louis MO 63105-3515. 314/727-9440. Employs: 50-99.

HOUSEHOLD APPLIANCE STORES

Magic Chef Factory Service
4888 Baumgartner Rd, St. Louis MO 63129-2800. 314/487-2433. Employs: 50-99.

RADIO, TELEVISION AND CONSUMER ELECTRONICS STORES

Silo
969 Anglum Rd, Hazelwood MO 63042-2328. 314/731-5616. Employs: 100-249.

COMPUTER AND COMPUTER SOFTWARE STORES

Computer Sales International Inc
10845 Olive Blvd, St. Louis MO 63141-7760. 314/997-7010. Employs: 50-99.

NCR Corporation
9811 S Forty Dr, St. Louis MO 63124. 314/991-5511. Employs: 100-249.

Unisys Corporation
55 Westport Plaza, St. Louis MO 63146-3109. 314/434-6000. Employs: 100-249.

RECORD AND PRERECORDED TAPE STORES

Sight & Sound Distributors
2055 Walton Rd, St. Louis MO 63114-5805. 314/426-2388. Employs: 50-99.

MUSICAL INSTRUMENT STORES

Ludwig Music House Inc
3600 Rider Trail S, Earth City MO 63045-1115. 314/739-7007. Employs: 100-249.

St Anns School Music Svc Inc
10005 Saint Charles Rock Rd, Saint Ann MO 63074-2021. 314/428-7100. Employs: 50-99.

DRUG STORES AND PROPRIETARY STORES

Reese Drug Stores Inc
2044 Madison Ave # 4, Granite City IL 62040-4641. 618/877-0828. Employs: 100-249.

Wal-Mart Discount Cities
2897 I 70, Saint Charles MO 63303-3526. 314/723-4233. Employs: 50-99.

Wal-Mart Discount Cities
10835 Saint Charles Rock Rd, Saint Ann MO 63074-1507. 314/291-8110. Employs: 50-99.

Wal-Mart Discount Cities
Hwy 66 S & Cumberland, Sullivan MO 63080. 314/468-5121. Employs: 100-249.

Colman's
12950 New Halls Ferry Rd,
Florissant MO 63033-4035.
314/838-9101. Employs: 100-249.

Jim Neels Boatmens Bldg Pharm
9705 Watson Rd, St. Louis MO
63126-1853. 314/966-4010.
Employs: 50-99.

Kare Drugs
8319 Jennings Station Rd, St. Louis
MO 63136-3630. 314/389-3600.
Employs: 50-99.

Kare Pharmacies
2511 State St, E St. Louis IL
62205-2322. 618/274-2000.
Employs: 100-249.

Rinderer's Drug Stores
3855 Lucas and Hunt Rd # 224, St.
Louis MO 63121-2935. 314/534-1311. Employs: 50-99.

Venture Pharmacy
5401 Collinsville Rd, E St. Louis
IL 62201-2335. 618/874-2525.
Employs: 100-249.

SPORTING GOODS STORES AND BICYCLE SHOPS

Johnny Macs Sporting Goods
5051 Gravois Av, St. Louis MO
63116-2342. 314/352-3339.
Employs: 50-99.

Rawlings Sporting Goods Co
PO Box 22000, St. Louis MO
63126-0090. 314/349-3500.
Employs: 100-249.

STATIONERY STORES

Buschart Office Products Inc
1834 Walton Rd, St. Louis MO
63114-5820. 314/426-7171.
Employs: 100-249.

JEWELRY STORES

Grndpa Pidgeons Jewelry & Musk
8020 Olive Blvd, St. Louis MO
63130-2021. 314/991-3783.
Employs: 100-249.

Zales Jewelers
244 Saint Clair Sq, E St. Louis IL
62208-2134. 618/632-6333.
Employs: 50-99.

GIFT, NOVELTY AND SOUVENIR SHOPS

Pettymark
112 Crestwood Plaza, St. Louis
MO 63126-1701. 314/962-0465.
Employs: 100-249.

Zootique
St Louis Zoo, St. Louis MO 63110.
314/781-2070. Employs: 100-249.

SEWING, NEEDLEWORK AND PIECE GOODS STORES

Cloth World
8500 Maryland Ave, St. Louis MO
63124-2017. 314/854-4000.
Employs: 50-99.

OPTICAL GOODS STORES

Sears Roebuck and Co
Jamestown Mall, Florissant MO
63034. 314/6534654. Employs:
100-249.

J C Penney Co Inc
100 S County Center Way, St.
Louis MO 63129-1009. 314/892-9630. Employs: 100-249.

J C Penney Co Inc
Jennings River Roads Mall, St.
Louis MO 63136. 314/868-9700.
Employs: 100-249.

Sears Optical
Crestwood Plaza, St. Louis MO
63126. 314/968-7654. Employs:
50-99.

MISCELLANEOUS RETAIL STORES

Busch Creative Services Corp
5240 Oakland Ave, St. Louis MO 63110-1436. 314/289-7700. Employs: 50-99.

Contel Of Missouri Inc
1000 Contel Dr, Wentzville MO 63385. 314/6393812. Employs: 50-99.

Rolm Company
1807 Park 270 Dr, St. Louis MO 63146-4021. 314/878-6500. Employs: 50-99.

Motor Coils Manufacturing Co
4084 Bingham Ave, St. Louis MO 63116-3534. 314/481-1400. Employs: 100-249.

Frame Factory Ltd
11467 Olive Blvd, St. Louis MO 63141-7108. 314/367-8333. Employs: 50-99.

Able Safe Co
5th St & Boonslick, Saint Charles MO 63301. 314/946-5300. Employs: 50-99.

James River Corporation
310 McDonnell Blvd, Hazelwood MO 63042-2514. 314/731-6700. Employs: 100-249.

For more information on career opportunities in general merchandise - retail:

Associations

AMERICAN INTERNATIONAL AUTOMOTIVE DEALERS ASSOCIATION
99 Canal Center Plaza, Suite 500, Alexandria VA 22314-1538. 703/519-7800.

INTERNATIONAL ASSOCIATION OF CHAIN STORES
38100 Moor Place, Alexandria VA 22305. 703/549-4525.

INTERNATIONAL COUNCIL OF SHOPPING CENTERS
665 Fifth Avenue, New York NY 10022. 212/421-8181.

MENSWEAR RETAILERS OF AMERICA
2011 I Street NW, Suite 300, Washington DC 20006. 202/347-1932.

NATIONAL AUTOMOTIVE DEALERS ASSOCIATION
8400 Westpark Drive, McLean VA 22102. 703/821-7000.

NATIONAL INDEPENDENT AUTOMOTIVE DEALERS ASSOCIATION
2521 Brown Boulevard, Suite 100, Arlington TX 76006. 817/640-3838.

NATIONAL RETAIL MERCHANTS ASSOCIATION
100 West 31st Street, New York NY 10001. 212/244-8780.

Directories

AUTOMOTIVE NEWS MARKET DATA BOOK
Automotive News, 1400 Woodbridge Avenue, Detroit MI 48207. 313/446-6000.

GOVERNMENT

Large employers: 250+

EXECUTIVE, LEGISLATIVE AND GENERAL GOVERNMENT

Bulk Mail Center
5800 Phantom Dr, Hazelwood MO 63042-2436. 314/895-9241. Employs: 500-999.

Regional Office
1520 Market St, St. Louis MO 63103-2620. 314/342-1171. Employs: 250-499.

U S Farmers Home Admin
1520 Market St, St. Louis MO 63103-2620. 314/539-2403. Employs: 1,000+.

Veterans Affairs
915 N Grand Blvd, St. Louis MO 63106-1621. 314/652-4100. Employs: 500-999.

Lambert St Louis International Airport
Lambert St Louis Airport, St. Louis MO 63145. 314/426-8000. Employs: 250-499.

Human Resources Dept Vocational Educ
555 S Brentwood Blvd, St. Louis MO 63105-2522. 314/889-3453. Employs: 250-499.

Small to medium sized employers: 50-249

EXECUTIVE, LEGISLATIVE AND GENERAL GOVERNMENT

Belleville Twp High School W
2600 W Main St, Belleville IL 62223-5032. 618/233-5070. Employs: 100-249.

County Probation
2125 Troy Rd, Edwardsville IL 62025-2572. 618/692-6255. Employs: 50-99.

County Sheriff
405 Randle St, Edwardsville IL 62025-1933. 618/692-6087. Employs: 100-249.

Madison City Supt Of Schools
1707 4th St, Madison IL 62060-1505. 618/877-1712. Employs: 50-99.

O F City Cmty School Dist 90
707 N Smiley St, O Fallon IL 62269-1353. 618/632-3666. Employs: 50-99.

ARBORETA AND BOTANICAL OR ZOOLOGICAL GARDENS

Zoo
Forest Park, St. Louis MO 63110-1300. 314/781-0900. Employs: 100-249.

Attorney-Us
1114 Market St, St. Louis MO 63101-2043. 314/539-2200. Employs: 50-99.

Equal Employment Opportunity Comm
625 N Euclid Ave, St. Louis MO 63108-1660. 314/425-6585. Employs: 50-99.

Missouri Dept Of Housing
210 N Tucker Blvd, St. Louis MO
63101-1947. 314/425-4783.
Employs: 100-249.

U S Food & Drug Administration
1114 Market St, St. Louis MO
63101-2043. 314/539-2135.
Employs: 50-99.

Ballwin City Of City Hall
300 City Hall Dr, Ballwin MO
63011-3717. 314/227-8580.
Employs: 50-99.

Berkeley-City Of Civic Center
6120 Madison Ave, St. Louis MO
63134-2104. 314/522-9872.
Employs: 100-249.

Bridgeton City Of Admn
11925 Natural Bridge Rd,
Bridgeton MO 63044-2040.
314/739-7500. Employs: 100-249.

Clayton City For All Other Dept
10 N Bemiston Ave, St. Louis MO
63105-3304. 314/727-8100.
Employs: 50-99.

Jail
124 S 14th St, St. Louis MO
63103-2702. 314/622-4741.
Employs: 100-249.

Municipal Courts Bldg
1320 Market St, St. Louis MO
63103-2717. 314/622-4000.
Employs: 100-249.

Overland-City Of City Hall
9119 Lackland Rd, St. Louis MO
63114-5410. 314/428-4321.
Employs: 100-249.

Recreation Division Office Comsnr
Forest Park, St. Louis MO 63110-1300. 314/535-5050. Employs: 50-99.

Refuse Collection Div
4100 S 1st St, St. Louis MO 63118-3313. 314/353-8877. Employs: 100-249.

St Louis Housing Auth
4100 Lindell Blvd, St. Louis MO
63108-2914. 314/531-4770.
Employs: 100-249.

Treasurer
City Hall, St. Louis MO 63103.
314/622-3305. Employs: 100-249.

Workhouse
7600 Hall St, St. Louis MO 63147-2618. 314/381-1872. Employs: 100-249.

St Louis County Offices
1500 S Big Bend Blvd, St. Louis
MO 63117-2206. 314/647-3657.
Employs: 50-99.

GOVERNMENT TRANSPORTATION ORGANIZATIONS

Tri City Regional Port Authority
2801 Rock Rd, Granite City IL
62040-6839. 618/877-8444.
Employs: 50-99.

HEALTH CARE AND PHARMACEUTICALS

Employment in the health care industry has gone up steadily from 7 million in 1989, to over 9 million just three years later, with an average annual growth rate of 8 percent - and that doesn't include medical equipment manufacturers or pharmaceutical companies, which are also booming. Health care expenditures are now rising to over $800 billion a year. Various approaches to controlling the cost of health care have been proposed, although Washington has yet to take any specific action. Reforms to the health care system should lead to more efficient and effective services. The hottest areas in this hot industry are HMOs and home health care.

A.G.I.-DELHAVEN MANOR, INC.
5460 Delmar Boulevard, St. Louis MO 63112. 314/361-2902. **Contact:** Geraldine Potter, Administrator. **Description:** Skilled nursing care facilities. **Employees:** 100. **Corporate headquarters:** Sikeston, MO.

ALTON MEMORIAL HOSPITAL
1 Memorial Drive, Alton IL 62002. 618/463-7320. **Contact:** N. Dawn Wakeford, Manager of Human Resources. **Description:** A St. Louis-area general acute care hospital. **Common positions:** Health Care RN; OT; PT; MT. **Educational backgrounds sought:** Appropriate health care major. **Special programs:** Internships offered. **Benefits:** medical insurance; dental insurance; pension plan; life insurance; tuition assistance; disability coverage; savings plan; TSA. **Corporate headquarters:** St. Louis, MO. **Parent company:** Christian Health Services.

ALTON MENTAL HEALTH CENTER
4500 College Avenue, Alton IL 62002. 618/465-5593. **Contact:** Joe Foehrkolv, Head of Personnel. **Description:** A St. Louis medical facility, specializing in treatment of psychiatric developmental disabilities. **Employees:** 300.

BARNES HOSPITAL
One Barnes Hospital Plaza, St. Louis MO 63110. 314/362-0700. **Contact:** Carol Esrock, Director of Employment/Recruitment. **Description:** A St. Louis-area teaching hospital consistently listed as one of the top 10 in the nation. **Employees:** 6,200. **Common positions:** Accountant; Administrator; Advertising Worker; Attorney; Claim Representative; Computer Programmer; Credit Manager; Dietician; Draftsperson; Biomedical Engineer; Financial Analyst; Department Manager; Marketing Specialist; Personnel and Labor Relations Specialist; Public Relations Worker; Purchasing Agent; Reporter/Editor; Registered Nurse; Laboratory Technologist; Respiratory Therapist; Pharmacist; Social Worker. **Educational backgrounds sought:** Accounting; Business Administration; Chemistry; Communications; Computer Science; Liberal Arts; Marketing; Nursing; Medical Technology; Respiratory Therapy; Pharmacy. **Special programs:** Training programs and internships in

nursing. **Benefits:** medical, dental, and life insurance; pension plan; tuition assistance; disability coverage; daycare assistance; profit sharing; employee discounts. **Corporate headquarters:** This location.

BARNES ST. PETER'S HOSPITAL
10 Hospital Drive, St. Peters MO 63376. 314/447-6600. **Contact:** Andrea Bull, Personnel Director. **Description:** A general hospital.

BARNES WEST COUNTY HOSPITAL
12634 Olive Boulevard, St. Louis MO 63141. 314/434-0600. **Contact:** Cindy Baker, Human Resources Administrator. **Description:** A St. Louis general hospital. **Employees:** 200.

BETHESDA GENERAL HOSPITAL AND HOMES
3655 Vista Avenue, St. Louis MO 63110. 314/772-9200. **Contact:** Ellis Hough, Personnel Manager. **Description:** A St. Louis health-care company that owns and operates a general hospital, as well as homes for the aged and professional nursing homes. **Employees:** 800. **Benefits:** medical insurance; dental insurance; pension plan; life insurance; tuition assistance; disability coverage; daycare assistance; employee discounts; savings plan. **Corporate headquarters:** This location.

BEVERLY FARM FOUNDATION INC.
6301 Humbert Road, Godfrey IL 62035. 618/466-0367. **Contact:** Steven Tatsaros, Personnel Director. **Description:** A residential care facility for mentally handicapped children and adults from ages 5 to 85. **Employees:** 200.

CALGON VESTAL LABORATORIES
P.O. Box 147, St. Louis MO 63166-0147. 314/535-1810. **Contact:** Heather Cammarata, Human Resources Specialist. **Description:** Produces healthcare products primarily in the wound management and skin care fields. In addition, company produces biodecontamination products. **Common positions:** Biologist; Chemist; Customer Service Representative; Sales Representative. **Educational backgrounds sought:** Biology; Business Administration; Chemistry; Marketing. **Special programs:** training programs; internships. **Benefits:** medical, dental and life insurance; pension plan; tuition assistance; disability coverage; savings plan. **Corporate headquarters:** This location. **Parent company:** Merck & Co., Inc. **Operations at this facility:** manufacturing; research and development; administration; service; sales. **Listed on:** New York Stock Exchange. **Employees:** 650.

CARDINAL GLENNON CHILDREN'S HOSPITAL
1465 South Grand Boulevard, Human Resource Department, St. Louis MO 63104. 314/577-5389. **Contact:** John Tighe Jr., Employment Manager. **Description:** A St. Louis pediatric hospital. **Employees:** 1,600. **Common positions:** Accountant; Nurse; Dietician; Biomedical Engineer; Rehab Nurse. **Benefits:** medical, dental, and life insurance; tuition assistance; disability coverage; employee discounts; savings plan; pension plan. **Corporate headquarters:** This location. **Operations at this facility:** Service.

CARDINAL RITTER INSTITUTE
4483 Lindell Boulevard, St. Louis MO 63108. 314/652-3600. **Contact:** Joan Martin, Assistant Personnel Director. **Description:** Specializes in services to the aged: home health service, housing service, social service, employment programs, and volunteer programs. **Employees:** 350. **Common positions:** Social Worker; Home Health Nurse. **Educational backgrounds sought:** Nursing; Social Services. **Benefits:** Medical, Dental, and Life Insurance; Disability Coverage; Savings Plan. **Corporate headquarters:** This location. **Operations at this facility:** Administration.

CARLE FOUNDATION HOSPITAL
611 West Park Street, Urbana IL 61801. 217/383-3048. **Contact:** Kathy McCasky, Manager of Employment. **Description:** 300-bed tertiary care and regional trauma center. Also includes a 240-bed long-term care facility, home care agency, durable medical equipment, retail pharmacy, day care center, psychiatric and chemical dependency services. **Employees:** 1,994.

THE CATHOLIC HEALTH ASSOCIATION OF THE UNITED STATES
4455 Woodson Road, St. Louis MO 63134. 314/427-2500. **Contact:** Joe Smoltz, Personnel Director. **Description:** A company engaged in a wide variety of services for member hospitals and organizations across the United States.

CEDARCREST MANOR INC.
324 West 5th Street, Washington MO 63090. 314/239-7848. **Contact:** Ed Maschmann, Administrator/Supervisor. **Description:** Skilled nursing care facility. **Employees:** 100.

CEDARCROFT NURSING CENTER INC.
110 Highland Avenue, Valley Park MO 63088. 314/225-5144. **Contact:** Harold Pascal, Administrator. **Description:** Nursing and personal care facility. **Employees:** 100.

CENTOCOR, INC.
4649 Le Bourget Drive, St. Louis MO 63134. 314/426-5000. **Contact:** Betty Wendland, Manager, Human Resources. **Description:** Company is engaged in biopharmaceutical manufacturing. **Common positions:** Biochemist; Biologist; Buyer; Chemist; Computer Programmer; Draftsperson; Biomedical Engineer; Electrical Engineer; Department Manager; Operations/Production Manager; Quality Control Supervisor. **Educational backgrounds sought:** Biology; Chemistry; Computer Science; Engineering. **Special programs:** Training programs. **Benefits:** medical insurance; dental insurance; life insurance; tuition assistance; disability coverage; savings plan. **Corporate headquarters:** Malvern, PA. **Parent company:** Centocor, Inc. **Operations at this facility:** manufacturing; administration.

CENTRAL MEDICAL CENTER
4411 N. Newstead Avenue, St. Louis MO 63115. 314/382-7979, ext. 504. **Contact:** Donna M. Webb, Employment Specialist. **Description:** A St. Louis general medical facility. **Employees:** 300. **Common positions:** Accountant; Administrator; Counselor. **Educational backgrounds sought:** Finance; Marketing; Business Administration; Communications. **Benefits:** medical,

dental, and life insurance; tuition assistance. **Corporate headquarters:** This location. **Operations at this facility:** Service. **Special programs:** Internships. **Employees:** 430.

CENTREVILLE TOWNSHIP HOSPITAL
5900 Bond Avenue, Centreville IL 62207. 618/332-3060. **Contact:** Administrative Assistant. **Description:** A medical facility. **Employees:** 300.

CHILDREN'S HOSPITAL
1 Children's Place, St. Louis MO 63110. 314/454-6000. **Contact:** Carol Sullivan, Employment Coordinator. **Description:** St. Louis hospital that specializes in health care for children.

DEACONESS HEALTH SYSTEM/CENTRAL CAMPUS
6150 Oakland Avenue, St. Louis MO 63139. 314/768-3059. **Contact:** Employment Specialist/Nurse Recruiter. **Description:** Deaconess Health System operates three full-service medical centers: Deaconess Central, a 527 bed facility, Deaconess West (530 Des Peres Road, St Louis MO 63131, 168 beds) and Deaconess North (7840 Natural Bridge Road, St. Louis, MO 63131, 198 beds). Deaconess Central is a St. Louis hospital which employs over 2600. **Common positions:** Health Care Professionals. **Benefits:** medical, dental, and life insurance; pension plan; tuition assistance; disability coverage; daycare assistance (on-site daycare); employee discounts.

DEPARTMENT OF VETERANS AFFAIRS
MEDICAL CENTER
Personnel Office (05JB), St. Louis MO 63125. 314/894-6624. **Contact:** Carol Blair, Personnel Management Specialist. **Description:** A tertiary care, teaching, affiliated, medical center. **Common positions:** Biologist; Computer Programmer; Biomedical Engineer; Civil Engineer; Systems Analyst; Occupational Therapist; Physical Therapist; Registered Nurse. **Educational backgrounds sought:** Computer Science; Engineering; Health Care Professions. **Special programs:** training programs and internships offered. **Benefits:** medical, dental, and life insurance; pension plan; tuition assistance; disability coverage; liberal vacation time. **Corporate headquarters:** Washington DC. **Parent company:** US Department of Veterans Affairs. **Operations at this facility:** research and development; administration; service.

DEPAUL HEALTH CENTER
12303 DePaul Drive, Bridgeton MO 63044. 314/344-6267. **Contact:** Karen Wales, Director, Employee Services. **Description:** A general and psychiatric hospital. **Employees:** 2,000. **Common positions:** Health Care Professionals; Dietician; Biomedical Engineer. **Educational backgrounds sought include:** Health Care Disciplines. **Benefits:** medical, dental, and life insurance; pension plan; tuition assistance; disability coverage; employee discounts; savings plan. **Corporate headquarters:** St. Louis, MO. **Parent company:** Daughters of Charity National Health System.

FOREST PHARMACEUTICALS
2510 Metro Boulevard, St. Louis MO 63043. 314/569-3610. **Contact:** Personnel Department. **Description:** A St. Louis company engaged in the manufacture of pharmaceuticals.

INCARNATE WORD HOSPITAL
3545 Lafayette Avenue, St. Louis MO 63104. 314/865-6500. **Contact:** Sharon Bateman, Personnel Director. **Description:** Metropolitan St. Louis general hospital.

JEFFERSON MEMORIAL HOSPITAL
P.O. Box 350, Crystal City MO 63019. 314/933-1000. **Contact:** Lory Halbrook, Human Resources Director. **Description:** A general medical facility.

JEWISH CENTER FOR AGED
13190 South Outer 40 Road, Chesterfield MO 63017. 314/434-3330. **Contact:** Athea Webster, Employment Coordinator. **Description:** A skilled nursing facility for the aged and Adult Care Program. **Common positions:** RN; LPN; Physical Therapists, Occupational Therapist; Certified Occupational Therapy Assistant; Physical Therapist Assistant. Must have applicable licenses, degrees, and/or certification. **Benefits:** medical and life insurance; pension plan; tuition reimbursement; liberal vacation. **Operations at this facility:** service.

THE JEWISH HOSPITAL OF ST. LOUIS
216 South Kingshighway, St. Louis MO 63110. 314/454-8208. **Contact:** Marty Lenihan, Manager of Staffing. **Description:** A St. Louis general hospital. **Common positions:** Dietician; Biomedical Engineer; RN's; Medical Technologists; Pharmacists. **Educational backgrounds sought:** Accounting; Art/Design; Biology; Business Administration; Chemistry; Communications; Computer Science; Economics; Finance; Liberal Arts; Marketing; Nursing. **Benefits:** medical, dental, and life insurance; pension plan; tuition assistance; disability coverage; profit sharing; employee discounts; savings plan. **Corporate headquarters:** This location. **Operations at this facility:** research.

K-V PHARMACEUTICAL CO.
2503 South Hanley Road, St. Louis MO 63144. 314/645-6600. **Contact:** Staffing. **Description:** A pharmaceutical research and development firm.

LUTHERAN MEDICAL CENTER
2639 Miami Street, St. Louis MO 63118. 314/577-5762. **Contact:** Personnel Director. **Description:** A St. Louis general acute medical facility. **Common positions:** Dietician; Registered Nurses; Occupational Therapist; Physical Therapist; Medical Technologist. **Educational backgrounds sought:** Nursing; Physical Therapy. **Benefits:** medical, dental, and life insurance; pension plan; tuition assistance; disability coverage; profit sharing; employee discounts. **Corporate headquarters:** Los Angeles, CA. **Parent company:** National Medical Enterprises, Inc. **Operations at this facility:** service. **Listed on:** New York Stock Exchange.

MEMORIAL HOSPITAL
4500 Memorial Drive, Belleville IL 62223. 618/233-7750. **Contact:** Barbara L. Schneider, Director of Personnel. **Description:** A St. Louis metropolitan area acute care hospital, operating 346 adult and pediatric beds and 32 bassinets, and a 108 bed skilled nursing facility. **Common positions:** RN's; Pharmacist; Radiologic Technician; MTASCP; MLT ASPC.

MISSOURI BAPTIST HOSPITAL OF SULLIVAN
751 Sappington Bridge, P.O. Box 190, Sullivan MO 63080. 314/468-4186. **Contact:** Personnel Department. **Description:** A general hospital.

MISSOURI BAPTIST MEDICAL CENTER
11710 Ballas Road, St. Louis MO 63141. 314/569-0390. **Contact:** Joan Ketterer, Employment Manager. **Description:** Multifaceted 400-bed acute-care hospital located in West St. Louis county. **Common positions:** Accountant; Computer Programmer; Customer Service Representative; Dietician; Financial Analyst; Marketing Specialist; Public Relations Specialist; Purchasing Agent; Statistician; Physical Therapist; Radiologic Technician. **Special programs:** Training programs; Internships sometimes offered. **Benefits:** Medical, Dental, and Life Insurance; Pension Plan; Tuition Assistance; Disability Coverage; Daycare Assistance; Employee Discounts; Savings Plan; Tax Shelter Annuity. **Operations at this facility:** Administration; Service. **Employees:** 2,000. **Projected hires for the next 12 months:** 500.

NATIONAL HEALTH CARE
2920 Fee Fee Road, Maryland Heights MO 63043. 314/291-0121. **Contact:** Bernice Taylor, Personnel Department. **Description:** A skilled nursing care facility. **Employees:** 150.

OVERLAND MEDICAL CENTER
2428 Woodson Road, Overland MO 63114. 314/427-2424. **Contact:** Gerry Westrich, Administrator. **Description:** A St. Louis medical clinic.

SSM REHABILITION INSTITUTE
555 North New Ballas, P.O. Box 150, St. Louis MO 63141. 314/994-2120. **Contact:** Human Resources. **Description:** A specialty hospital providing rehabilitation for persons with head injuries, spinal cord injuries, and general rehabilitation needs. **Common positions:** RN's, PT's and OTR's. **Special programs:** Internships. **Benefits:** medical insurance; dental insurance; pension plan; life insurance; tuition assistance; disability coverage; employee discounts; savings plan. **Corporate headquarters:** St. Louis, MO. **Employees:** 200. **Projected hires for the next 12 months:** 40.

STI
2550 Hermelin Drive, St. Louis MO 63144. 314/781-4975. **Contact:** Donna Hurley, Human Resources Administrator. **Description:** A technology-based health care company that designs, develops, and produces automatic injectors, prefilled syringes, and medical electronics, with a focus on safe and convenient participation by the patient in injection therapy. Also supplies delivery system design; pharmaceutical research and development; and sterile product manufacturing to pharmaceutical companies worldwide. **Common positions:** Accountant; Biologist; Blue-Collar Worker Supervisor; Buyer; Chemist; Electrical Engineer; Industrial Engineer; Mechanical Engineer; Financial Analyst; Industrial Manager; Instructor/Trainer/Teacher; General Manager; Management Trainee; Personnel and Labor Relations Specialist; Purchasing Agent; Quality Controller; Statistician. **Educational backgrounds sought:** Biology; Chemistry; Engineering. **Benefits:** Medical, Dental, and Life Insurance; Disability Coverage; Profit Sharing; Savings Plan. **Corporate headquarters:** Rockville, MD. **Operations at this facility:** Manufacturing;

Research and Development; Administration. **Listed on:** American Stock Exchange. **Employees:** 270. **Projected hires for the next 12 months:** 5.

SHERWOOD MEDICAL COMPANY
1915 Olive Street, St. Louis MO 63103. 314/241-5700. **Contact:** Lola M. Contestabile, Employment Manager. **Description:** A St. Louis manufacturer of medical equipment and supplies for use in hospitals, physicians' offices and laboratories. **Common positions:** Accountant; Administrator; Biochemist; Commercial Artist; Customer Service Representative; Draftsperson; Electrical Engineer; Mechanical Engineer; Business Administration; Engineering. **Special programs:** Training programs. **Benefits:** medical insurance; dental insurance; pension plan; life insurance; tuition assistance; disability coverage; employee discounts; savings plan. **Corporate headquarters:** This location.

SHRINERS HOSPITAL FOR CRIPPLED CHILDREN
2001 South Lindbergh Boulevard, St. Louis MO 63131. 314/432-3600. **Contact:** Lynn Flekal, Personnel Director. **Description:** Charitable hospital for orthopedically handicapped children.

ST. ANTHONY'S HOSPITAL
P.O. Box 340, Alton IL 62002-0340. 618/463-5151. **Contact:** Personnel Director. **Description:** A Southern Illinois general hospital.

ST. ANTHONY'S MEDICAL CENTER
10010 Kennerly Road, St. Louis MO 63128. 314/525-1000. **Contact:** Mr. Dale Kreienkamp, Personnel Director. **Description:** A medical center and general hospital.

ST. CLEMENT HOSPITAL
325 Spring Street, Red Bud IL 62278. 618/282-3831. **Contact:** Human Resource Director. **Description:** A St. Louis-area general hospital. **Common positions:** Accountant; Credit Manager; Personnel and Labor Relations; Purchasing Agent; RNs; Radiology Technicians; Lab Technicians. **Educational backgrounds sought:** Business Administration; Finance; Nursing; Health Care. **Benefits:** medical insurance; pension plan; life insurance; tuition assistance; disability coverage; employee discounts; savings plan. **Corporate headquarters:** O'Fallon, IL. **Parent company:** ASC Health System. **Operations at this facility:** administration; service.

ST. ELIZABETH'S HOSPITAL
211 South 3rd Street, Belleville IL 62222. 618/234-2120. **Contact:** Susan Silver, Personnel Director. **Description:** A Southern Illinois general hospital.

ST. JOHN'S MERCY HOSPITAL
200 Madison Avenue, Washington MO 63090. 314/239-8000. **Contact:** John Swope, Administration. **Description:** A St. Louis-area general hospital.

ST. JOHN'S MERCY MEDICAL CENTER
615 South New Ballas Road, St. Louis MO 63141. 314/569-6000. **Contact:** Pat Tubbesing, Personnel Director. **Description:** A St. Louis general hospital.

ST. JOSEPH HOSPITAL
525 Couch Avenue, Kirkwood MO 63122. 314/966-1551. **Contact:** Ms. Chris Rossino, Director of Personnel. **Description:** A St. Louis-area general hospital. **Common positions:** Accountant; Administrator; Blue-Collar Worker Supervisor; Buyer; Claim Representative; Commercial Artist; Computer Programmer; Credit Manager; Dietician; Biomedical Engineer; Financial Analyst; Department Manager; Marketing Specialist; Personnel and Labor Relations Specialist; Reporter/Editor; RNs; X-Ray Technologists. **Educational backgrounds sought:** Accounting; Business Administration; Chemistry; Communications; Computer Science; Engineering; Finance; Liberal Arts; Marketing; Mathematics; Nursing; Medical Technologist. **Special programs:** Training programs and internships. **Benefits:** medical insurance; dental insurance; pension plan; life insurance; tuition assistance; disability coverage; daycare assistance; employee discounts; savings plan. **Corporate headquarters:** St. Louis, MO. **Operations at this facility:** administration; service; sales.

ST. JOSEPH HOSPITAL
1515 Main Street, Highland IL 62249. 618/654-7421. **Contact:** Kim Kampwerth, Personnel Assistant. **Description:** A Southern Illinois general hospital. **Benefits:** medical, dental, and life insurance; pension plan; tuition assistance; disability coverage.

ST. LOUIS CHILDREN'S HOSPITAL
1 Children's Place, St. Louis MO 63110. 314/454-6000. **Contact:** Personnel Department. **Description:** A hospital for children from birth through 21 years.

ST. LOUIS REGIONAL MEDICAL CENTER
63112 Delmar Boulevard, St. Louis MO 63112. 314/361-1212. **Contact:** Personnel Department. **Description:** A St. Louis-area medical center.

ST. LOUIS STATE HOSPITAL
5400 Arsenal Street, St. Louis MO 63139. 314/644-8036. **Contact:** Yale Wolff, Director of Human Resources. **Description:** A St. Louis hospital dedicated to treatment of mental illness. Fully accredited by JCAH, Medicare and Medicaid. Treatment programs for Geriatrics, Acute Care, Continuing Care, Substance Abuse, Forensic and Community Placement. Intern and research affiliations. **Common positions:** Accountant; Administrator; Blue-Collar Worker Supervisor; Claim Representative; Dietician; Psychiatrist; Occupational Therapist; Registered Nurses; Master Social Worker. **Educational backgrounds sought:** Accounting; Psychiatry; Nursing; Social Work; Psychology; Adjunct Therapies. **Benefits:** medical insurance; pension plan; life insurance; disability coverage; savings plan; vacation and sick leave. **Corporate headquarters:** Jefferson City MO. **Parent company:** Missouri Department of Mental Health.

ST. LUKE'S HOSPITAL
425 South Woods Mill Road, Suite 250, Chesterfield MO 63017. 314/576-2320. **Contact:** Personnel Department. **Description:** A St. Louis general hospital. **Common positions:** Accountant; Dietician; Dietary Staff; Entry Level Housekeeping. **Educational backgrounds sought:** Accounting; Business Administration; Finance. **Benefits:** medical insurance; dental insurance; tuition

assistance; disability coverage (long-term); employee discounts; use of sports medicine equipment; free meals and parking.

ST. MARY'S HEALTH CENTER
6420 Clayton Road, St. Louis MO 63117. 314/768-8000. **Contact:** Terry Fellon, Director of Human Resources. **Description:** A general hospital.

ST. PAUL'S HOMES FOR THE AGED
1021 West E Street, Belleville IL 62220. 618/233-2095. **Contact:** Arthur H. Peters, Administrator. **Description:** Residential and nursing care for the aged.

ST. PETER'S HOSPITAL
10 Hospital Drive, St. Peters MO 63376. 314/447-6600. **Contact:** Human Resources. **Description:** A general hospital.

STORZ INSTRUMENT COMPANY
3365 Tree Court Industrial Boulevard, St. Louis MO 63122. 314/225-7600, ext. 5546. **Contact:** Theresa Czolgosz, Employment Supervisor. **Description:** Manufacturers and distributors of micro-surgical instruments and diagnostic medical equipment. **Common positions:** Accountant; Buyer; Chemist; Computer Programmer; Customer Service Representative; Draftsperson; Biomedical Engineer; Electrical Engineer; Industrial Engineer; Mechanical Engineer; Industrial Manager; Operations/Production Manager; Marketing Specialist; Purchasing Agent; Sales Representative; Technical Writer/Editor; Quality Control Inspector. **Educational backgrounds sought:** Accounting; Business Administration; Chemistry; Computer Science; Engineering; Marketing; Technical Education; Biomedical Science; Material Sciences. **Special programs:** Training programs and internships. **Benefits:** medical, dental, and life insurance; pension plan; tuition assistance; disability coverage; employee discounts; supplemental life; savings plan; vision care. **Corporate headquarters:** This location. **Parent company:** American Cyanamid. **Operations at this facility:** manufacturing; research and development; administration; service; sales.

UNIVERSITY HOSPITAL/ST. LOUIS
3635 Vista Grand Boulevard, University Medical Center, St. Louis MO 63110-0250. 314/577-8000. **Contact:** Personnel Department. **Description:** A St. Louis hospital.

VISITING NURSE ASSOCIATION OF GREATER ST. LOUIS
1129 Macklind Avenue, St. Louis MO 63110. 314/533-9680. **Contact:** Human Resources Department. **Description:** Health services provided to patients in their home or place of residence including nursing, physical therapy, occupational therapy, speech pathology, nutritional therapy, mental health and enterostomal therapy, aide, medical social services and hospice care.

WOOD RIVER TOWNSHIP HOSPITAL
Edwardsville Road, Wood River IL 62095. 618/254-3821. **Contact:** Personnel Department. **Description:** A general hospital.

Additional large employers: 250+

PHARMACEUTICAL PREPARATIONS

Bristol Myers Products
8877 Ladue Rd, St. Louis MO 63124-2045. 314/862-1100. Employs: 250-499.

Mallinckrodt Medical Inc
2703 Wagner Pl, Maryland Hts MO 63043-3421. 314/344-3800. Employs: 250-499.

Smithkline Beecham
300 S Broadway St, St. Louis MO 63102-2800. 314/621-2304. Employs: 250-499.

SURGICAL AND MEDICAL INSTRUMENTS AND APPARATUS

Allied Health Care Products Inc
1720 Sublette Ave, St. Louis MO 63110-1927. 314/771-2400. Employs: 500-999.

Survival Technology Inc
2550 Hermelin Dr, St. Louis MO 63144-2520. 314/781-4975. Employs: 500-999.

Vitek Systs Inc
595 Anglum Dr, Hazelwood MO 63042-2320. 314/731-8500. Employs: 250-499.

OFFICES AND CLINICS OF DOCTORS OF MEDICINE

St Louis County Health Centers
111 S Meramec Ave, St. Louis MO 63105-1711. 314/854-6000. Employs: 1,000+.

OFFICES AND CLINICS OF OPTOMETRISTS

Sears Roebuck & Co Bernita
Chesterfield Mall, Chesterfield MO 63017. 314/532-8654. Employs: 250-499.

SKILLED NURSING CARE FACILITIES

Memorial Convalescent Center
4315 Memorial Dr, Belleville IL 62223-5342. 618/233-7750. Employs: 500-999.

NURSING AND PERSONAL CARE FACILITIES

Hillsboro Hospital
1200 E Tremont St, Hillsboro IL 62049-1912. 217/532-6111. Employs: 250-499.

GENERAL MEDICAL AND SURGICAL HOSPITALS

Care Unit
1755 S Grand Bl, St. Louis MO 63104-1540. 314/771-0500. Employs: 500-999.

Comprehensive Care Corp
1795 Clarkson Rd, Chesterfield MO 63017-4975. 314/537-1288. Employs: 1,000+.

Malcolm Bliss Mntl Health Ctr
5400 Arsenal St, St. Louis MO 63139-1403. 314/241-7600. Employs: 500-999.

Lincoln County Mem Hospital
1000 E Cherry, Troy MO 63379-1513. 314/528-8551. Employs: 250-499.

Metropolitan Med Ctr
7840 Natural Bridge Rd, St. Louis MO 63121-4626. 314/389-0015. Employs: 500-999.

MEDICAL LABORATORIES

Smithkline Beecham Clinic Labs
11636 Administration Dr, St. Louis MO 63146-3534. 314/567-3905. Employs: 250-499.

Additional small to medium sized employers: 50-249

MEDICINAL CHEMICALS AND BOTANICAL PRODUCTS

Merck & Co Inc
4545 Oleatha Ave, St. Louis MO 63116-1719. 314/353-7000. Employs: 50-99.

Midco Products Company
11697 Fairgrove Ind Blvd, Maryland Hts MO 63043-3437. 314/567-1710. Employs: 50-99.

PHARMACEUTICAL PREPARATIONS

Dios Chemical Co
4200 Laclede Ave, St. Louis MO 63108-2815. 314/533-9600. Employs: 50-99.

Jones Medical Inds Inc
11604 Lilburn Pk Rd, St. Louis MO 63146-3535. 314/432-7557. Employs: 50-99.

Ni-Med Inc
3127 Cliff Dr, Arnold MO 63010-5502. 314/287-3333. Employs: 100-249.

Purina Mills Inc
13001 St Charles Rock Rd, Bridgeton MO 63044-2421. 314/291-6720. Employs: 100-249.

Smithkline Beecham Labs
E Lincoln Rd, White Hall IL 62092. 217/374-2102. Employs: 50-99.

SURGICAL AND MEDICAL INSTRUMENTS AND APPARATUS

Smith & Nephew Equipment Group
1920 S Jefferson, St. Louis MO 63104-2621. 314/772-7000. Employs: 100-249.

ORTHOPEDIC, PROSTHETIC AND SURGICAL APPLIANCES AND SUPPLIES

Oxycon
401 S Outer Svc Rd, Wright City MO 63390. 314/745-3713. Employs: 100-249.

Puritan-Bennett Corp
4073 Wedgeway Ct, Earth City MO 63045-1213. 314/739-7070. Employs: 100-249.

Sherwood Medical Co
11311 Hammack Dr, Bridgeton MO 63044-2305. 314/731-1500. Employs: 100-249.

Sterile Products Corp
Fourth & Marshall, Valley Park MO 63088. 314/225-5151. Employs: 100-249.

W K Mfg Corp
3127 Cliff Dr, Arnold MO 63010-5502. 314/296-5554. Employs: 50-99.

Yungck Medical & Surgical Sup
2600 State St, Alton IL 62002-5150. 618/466-5632. Employs: 50-99.

DENTAL EQUIPMENT AND SUPPLIES

Keller Lab Inc
10966 Gravois Indl Ct, St. Louis MO 63128. 314/842-4320. Employs: 100-249.

Young Dental Mfg Co
13705 Shoreline Ct E, Earth City MO 63045-1202. 314/344-0010. Employs: 50-99.

X-RAY APPARATUS AND TUBES AND RELATED IRRADIATION APPARATUS

Computerized Medical Systs Inc
56 Worthington Dr, Maryland Hts MO 63043. 314/434-4394. Employs: 50-99.

ELECTROMEDICAL AND ELECTROTHERAPEUTIC APPARATUS

Jones Medical Electronics Inc
1418 Floraville Rd, Waterloo IL 62298-3116. 618/939-7802. Employs: 100-249.

Mb Industries Inc
1707 Madison Ave, Granite City IL 62040-4429. 618/451-2992. Employs: 50-99.

OFFICES AND CLINICS OF DOCTORS OF MEDICINE

Specialists In Ob-Gyn Inc
675 Old Ballas Rd, St. Louis MO 63141-7011. 314/872-9206. Employs: 50-99.

OFFICES AND CLINICS OF DENTISTS

Overland Medical Center
2428 Woodson Rd, St. Louis MO 63114-5423. 314/427-2424. Employs: 100-249.

OFFICES AND CLINICS OF HEALTH PRACTITIONERS

Head Injury Resource Center
755 S New Ballas Rd, St. Louis MO 63141-8703. 314/652-8857. Employs: 50-99.

Hillhaven Rehabilitation Center
11692 Manchester Rd, St. Louis MO 63131-4612. 314/966-3350. Employs: 100-249.

SKILLED NURSING CARE FACILITIES

Anna-Henry Nursing Home
637 Hillsboro Av, Edwardsville IL 62025-1818. 618/656-1136. Employs: 50-99.

Calvin Johnson Care Center
727 N 17th St, Belleville IL 62223-6552. 618/234-3323. Employs: 50-99.

Caseyville Health Care Center
601 W Lincoln St, Caseyville IL 62232-1306. 618/345-3072. Employs: 50-99.

Castle Haven Nursing Center
225 Castellano Dr, Belleville IL 62221-3027. 618/235-1300. Employs: 100-249.

Charlevoix Nursing Center
1221 Boonslick Rd, Saint Charles MO 63301-2328. 314/946-6140. Employs: 50-99.

Colonial Haven Nursing Homes
3900 Stearns Av, Granite City IL 62040-4154. 618/9313900. Employs: 50-99.

Community Life Care Ent Inc
2349 Virden St, Alton IL 62002-5160. 618/466-5331. Employs: 50-99.

D'Adrian Convalescent Center
1318 W Delmar Av, Godfrey IL 62035-1705. 618/466-0153. Employs: 50-99.

Edwardsville Care Center East
6 Saddlebrook Dr, Edwardsville IL 62025. 618/692-1330. Employs: 50-99.

Eldercare Of Alton Inc
3523 Wickenhauser Av, Alton IL 62002-2118. 618/465-8887. Employs: 100-249.

Eunice C Smith Nursing Home
1251 College Av, Alton IL 62002-6735. 618/463-7337. Employs: 50-99.

Faith Couuntryside Homes
1216 27th St, Highland IL 62249-2735. 618/654-2393. Employs: 50-99.

Grandview Healthcare Center
201 Grand Av, Washington MO 63090-1209. 314/239-9190. Employs: 50-99.

Hillhaven Of Highland
2510 Lemon Street Rd, Highland IL 62249-2627. 618/654-2368. Employs: 50-99.

Meadow View Care Nursing Home
Rt 70 Route 70, Maryville IL 62062. 618/344-7750. Employs: 50-99.

Mill Haven Care Center Inc
415 Veteran Dr, Millstadt IL 62260-1335. 618/4763575. Employs: 50-99.

O'Fallon Healthcare Center
700 Weber Dr, O Fallon IL 62269-2248. 618/632-3511. Employs: 100-249.

Pleasant Rest Nursing Home
614 Summit Av, Collinsville IL 62234-3728. 618/344-8476. Employs: 50-99.

Rosewood Care Center
100 Rosewood Dr, Belleville IL 62221-2301. 618/236-1391. Employs: 50-99.

Rosewood Care Center
3490 Humbert Rd, Alton IL 62002-7101. 618/465-2626. Employs: 50-99.

Saint Ann S Healthcare Center Inc
770 State St, Chester IL 62233-1642. 618/826-2314. Employs: 50-99.

Saint Paul's Home For The Aged
1021 West E St, Belleville IL 62220. 618/233-2095. Employs: 100-249.

Sisters St Francis
2120 Central Av, Alton IL 62002-4546. 618/463-2750. Employs: 50-99.

Weier Retirement Home
5 Gundlach Pl, Belleville IL 62220-4227. 618/233-6625. Employs: 50-99.

Alexian Brothers Lansdowne Mnr
4624 Lansdowne Ave, St. Louis MO 63116-1523. 314/351-6888. Employs: 50-99.

Americana Healthcare Center
1200 Graham Rd, Florissant MO 63031-8015. 314/838-6555. Employs: 100-249.

Barnes Extended Care
401 Corporate Park Dr, St. Louis MO 63105-4201. 314/725-7447. Employs: 50-99.

Barr Smith Manor
2407 Georgia St, Louisiana MO 63353-2557. 314/754-6279. Employs: 50-99.

Bent-Wood Nursing Center
1501 Charbonier Rd, Florissant MO 63031-5308. 314/921-2700. Employs: 50-99.

Bernard West Pine Nursing Home
4335 W Pine Blvd, St. Louis MO 63108-2205. 314/371-0200. Employs: 50-99.

Beverly Enterprises Regl Office
50 Crestwood Executive Ctr, St. Louis MO 63126-1945. 314/849-0037. Employs: 50-99.

Blind Girls Home
221 W Washington Ave, St. Louis MO 63122-3916. 314/966-6034. Employs: 50-99.

Christian Care Home
800 Chambers Rd, St. Louis MO 63137-2901. 314/522-8100. Employs: 50-99.

Country View Nurse & Retirement Center
6 S 20th St, Bowling Green MO 63334-1702. 314/324-2216. Employs: 50-99.

Community Care Center Festus Inc
RR 1, Festus MO 63028-9801. 314/937-3150. Employs: 50-99.

Delmar Gardens Nursing Centers
4401 Parker Rd, Florissant MO 63033-4262. 314/355-1516. Employs: 50-99.

Delmar Gardens Nursing Centers
13550 S Outer 40 Rd, Chesterfield MO 63017. 314/878-1330. Employs: 100-249.

Delmar Gardens Nursing Centers
15197 Clayton Rd, Ballwin MO 63011. 314/394-7515. Employs: 50-99.

Delmar Gardens Nursing Centers
14855 N Outer 40 Rd, Chesterfield MO 63017. 314/532-0150. Employs: 50-99.

Festus Manor Nursing Center
627 Westwood Dr S, Festus MO 63028-2062. 314/937-9066. Employs: 50-99.

Florissant Nursing Center
615 Rancho Ln, Florissant MO 63031-1717. 314/839-2150. Employs: 50-99.

Forest Haven Care Center
3201 Parkwood Ln, Maryland Hts MO 63043-1334. 314/291-5911. Employs: 50-99.

Gamma Road Nursing Center
250 Gamma Rd, Wellsville MO 63384-1422. 314/684-2002. Employs: 50-99.

Garden View Care Center
700 Garden Path, O Fallon MO 63366-3052. 314/272-2840. Employs: 50-99.

Integrated Health Services
110 Highland Ave, Valley Park MO 63088-1422. 314/225-5144. Employs: 100-249.

Jonesburg Caring Center
Cedar Av & William Tell, Jonesburg MO 63351. 314/488-5400. Employs: 50-99.

Jonesburg Nursing Home Inc
Hwy Y, Jonesburg MO 63351.
314/488-5516. Employs: 50-99.

Lincoln County Caring Center
1145 E Cherry St, Troy MO 63379-1520. 314/528-5712. Employs: 50-99.

Mari De Villa Retirement Center Inc
13900 Clayton Rd, Ballwin MO 63011-2913. 314/227-5347. Employs: 100-249.

Mary Queen & Mother Center
7601 Watson Rd, St. Louis MO 63119-5001. 314/961-8485. Employs: 50-99.

Marymount Manor Nursing Center
313 Augustine Rd, Eureka MO 63025-1935. 314/938-6770. Employs: 50-99.

Medicalodge Of Troy
200 Thompson Dr, Troy MO 63379-2308. 314/528-8446. Employs: 50-99.

Meeks Rest Haven
9732 Natural Bridge Rd, St. Louis MO 63134-3306. 314/427-7907. Employs: 50-99.

Mother Of Good Counsel Home
6825 Natural Bridge Rd, St. Louis MO 63121-5314. 314/383-4765. Employs: 100-249.

Northshore Health Care Center
610 Prigge Rd, St. Louis MO 63138-3543. 314/741-9393. Employs: 50-99.

Parkside Towers
4960 Laclede Ave, St. Louis MO 63108-1404. 314/361-6240. Employs: 100-249.

Peace Haven Association
12630 Rott Rd, St. Louis MO 63127-1214. 314/965-3833. Employs: 50-99.

South County Manor
Highway 21, Arnold MO 63010. 314/296-5141. Employs: 50-99.

St Clair Nursing Center
1035 Plaza Ct, Saint Clair MO 63077. 314/629-2100. Employs: 50-99.

Sunset Nursing & Retirement Homes
113 W Clinton Pl, St. Louis MO 63122-5809. 314/821-7007. Employs: 50-99.

The Edgewater
5500 S Broadway, St. Louis MO 63111-2025. 314/832-5800. Employs: 100-249.

Tower Village Inc
4518 Blair Ave, St. Louis MO 63107-1404. 314/534-4000. Employs: 50-99.

Truman Restorative Center
5700 Arsenal St, St. Louis MO 63139-1610. 314/768-6600. Employs: 50-99.

Village North Manor
6768 N Highway 67, Florissant MO 63034. 314/741-9101. Employs: 50-99.

West County Care Center Inc
312 Solley Ave, Ballwin MO 63021-5248. 314/391-0666. Employs: 50-99.

Woodland Manor Nursing Center
100 Woodland Mnr, Arnold MO 63010-2030. 314/296-1400. Employs: 50-99.

INTERMEDIATE CARE FACILITIES

Alan Barry Nursing Home
3338 Eminence Ave, St. Louis MO 63114-4220. 314/427-0988. Employs: 50-99.

Bethesda Lutheran Home
2310 Elm St, Saint Charles MO 63301-1441. 314/949-0308. Employs: 50-99.

Bridgeton Nursing Center
12145 Bridgeton Sq, Bridgeton MO 63044-2616. 314/298-7444. Employs: 50-99.

Brook View Nursing Home
2963 Doddridge Ave, Maryland Hts MO 63043-1736. 314/291-4557. Employs: 50-99.

Castle Acres Nursing Home Inc
PO Box 308, Hillsboro MO 63050-0308. 314/789-2882. Employs: 50-99.

Chesterfield Manor
14001 Olive Blvd, Chesterfield MO 63017-2607. 314/469-3500. Employs: 50-99.

Elsberry Health Care Center Inc
Highway B, Elsberry MO 63343. 314/898-2880. Employs: 50-99.

Good Samaritan Home
5200 S Broadway, St. Louis MO 63111-2019. 314/352-2400. Employs: 100-249.

Harris Ferrier Residential Care
3636 Page Blvd, St. Louis MO 63113-3808. 314/533-0300. Employs: 50-99.

Heritage Of St Louis Inc
4401 N Hanley Rd, St. Louis MO 63134-2710. 314/521-7471. Employs: 50-99.

Integrated Health Services
10954 Kennerly Rd, St. Louis MO 63128-2018. 314/843-4242. Employs: 50-99.

Jonora Rest Home
RR 4, De Soto MO 63020-9804. 314/586-4078. Employs: 50-99.

Little Flower Nursing Home
2500 S 18th St, St. Louis MO 63104-4304. 314/664-2267. Employs: 50-99.

Maple Grove Lodge Nursing Home
2407 Kentucky St, Louisiana MO 63353-2503. 314/754-5456. Employs: 50-99.

Mark Twain Manor
11988 Mark Twain Ln, Bridgeton MO 63044-2825. 314/291-8240. Employs: 50-99.

Mercy Convalescent Center
3450 Russell Blvd, St. Louis MO 63104-1548. 314/664-1020. Employs: 50-99.

Normandy Nursing Center Inc
7301 Saint Charles Rock Rd, St. Louis MO 63133-1737. 314/726-5514. Employs: 50-99.

Northwoods Garden Nursing Center
11400 Mehl Ave, Florissant MO 63033-7204. 314/741-3138. Employs: 50-99.

Oak Knoll Health Care Facility
37 N Clark Ave, St. Louis MO 63135-2323. 314/521-7419. Employs: 50-99.

Pacific Care Center Inc
105 S 6th St, Pacific MO 63069-1328. 314/257-4222. Employs: 50-99.

Rosewood Care Center St Louis
11278 Schuetz Rd, St. Louis MO 63146-4957. 314/991-4066. Employs: 50-99.

South Gate Care Center
5943 Telegraph Rd, St. Louis MO 63129-4715. 314/846-2000. Employs: 50-99.

St Josephs Hill Infirmary
Rural Route 1, Eureka MO 63025-9801. 314/938-5095. Employs: 50-99.

Troy House
350 Cap Au Gris St, Troy MO 63379-1744. 314/528-4915. Employs: 50-99.

Villa Gesu
11755 Riverview Dr, St. Louis MO 63138-3610. 314/741-6830. Employs: 100-249.

Wentzville Park Care Center
401 Mar Le Dr, Wentzville MO 63385-1647. 314/327-5274. Employs: 50-99.

Westwinds Park
16062 Manchester Rd, Ballwin MO 63011-2104. 314/394-7213. Employs: 50-99.

NURSING AND PERSONAL CARE FACILITIES

Alcoholic Rehabilitation Community
1313 21st St, Granite City IL 62040-4756. 618/876-9601. Employs: 50-99.

Alton Ursuline Infirmary
845 Danforth St, Alton IL 62002-2204. 618/465-0791. Employs: 50-99.

Aviston Terrace
349 W First, Aviston IL 62216. 618/228-7040. Employs: 50-99.

Breese Nursing Home
N 1st, Breese IL 62230. 618/526-4521. Employs: 50-99.

Cahokia Health Care Center
2 Annable Ct, E St. Louis IL 62206-2204. 618/332-0114. Employs: 50-99.

Carlyle Healthcare Center Inc
501 Clinton St, Carlyle IL 62231-1503. 618/594-3112. Employs: 100-249.

Children S Home & Aid Society Il
2133 Johnson Rd, Granite City IL 62040-3986. 618/452-8900. Employs: 50-99.

Clinton Manor Living Center
111 E Illinois St, New Baden IL 62265-1817. 618/588-4924. Employs: 50-99.

Columbia Convalescent
253 Bradington Dr, Columbia IL 62236-2519. 618/281-6800. Employs: 50-99.

Country Care Center Gillespie
RR 2, Gillespie IL 62033-9802. 217/839-2171. Employs: 50-99.

Countryside Manor
450 W 1st, Aviston IL 62216. 618/228-7615. Employs: 50-99.

Edwardsville Care Center
1095 University Dr, Edwardsville IL 62025-3961. 618/656-1081. Employs: 50-99.

Florence New Nurse & Care Center
Hwy 19 & Picnic Road, New Florence MO 63363-9709. 314/835-2025. Employs: 50-99.

Four Fountains Conval Center
101 South Belt-West, Belleville IL 62220. 618/277-7700. Employs: 50-99.

Freeburg-Care Center
RR 2, Freeburg IL 62243-9649. 618/539-5856. Employs: 50-99.

Friendship Manor Inc
305 Friendship Dr, Nashville IL 62263-1316. 618/327-3041. Employs: 100-249.

Garnet's Chateau
608 W Pearl St, Jerseyville IL 62052-1525. 618/498-4312. Employs: 50-99.

Geri-Wear Co
416 W St. Louis St, Lebanon IL 62254-1518. 618/537-4563. Employs: 50-99.

Group Home Residential Care
1824 Main St, Alton IL 62002-4724. 618/465-4431. Employs: 50-99.

Highland Home
1600 Walnut St, Highland IL 62249-2013. 618/654-2395. Employs: 50-99.

Hillsboro Health Care Center
1300 E Tremont St, Hillsboro IL 62049-1913. 217/532-6191. Employs: 50-99.

Hospice Of Southern Il Inc
305 S Illinois St, Belleville IL 62220-2133. 618/235-1703. Employs: 50-99.

King Management Co
625 S Mill St, Nashville IL 62263-1800. 618/327-3064. Employs: 100-249.

Mar-Ka Nursing Home
201 S 10th St, Mascoutah IL 62258-1736. 618/566-8000. Employs: 50-99.

Mariacare Nursing Home
350 W South 1st St, Red Bud IL 62278-1116. 618/282-3891. Employs: 50-99.

Maryville Manor
700 Vadalabene Dr, Maryville IL 62062. 618/288-5999. Employs: 50-99.

Missouri Baptist Hospice
763 S New Ballas Rd, St. Louis MO 63141-8704. 314/569-5595. Employs: 50-99.

Monroe County Nursing Home
500 Illinois Ave, Waterloo IL 62298-1111. 618/939-3488. Employs: 100-249.

Mt Gilead Shelter Care Home
RR 3, Carrollton IL 62016-9803. 217/942-5362. Employs: 50-99.

New Haven Care Center
201 Hwy 100 W, New Haven MO 63068. 314/237-2103. Employs: 50-99.

Park Haven Care Center
107 S Lincoln, Belleville IL 62220. 618/235-4600. Employs: 50-99.

River Bluffs Of Cahokia
3354 Jerome Ln, E St. Louis IL 62206-2604. 618/337-9823. Employs: 50-99.

Robings Manor
502 N Main St, Brighton IL 62012-1042. 618/372-3232. Employs: 50-99.

Saint Joseph's Home
723 1st Capitol Dr, Saint Charles MO 63301-2729. 314/724-6380. Employs: 50-99.

Sparta Terrace
1501 Melmar Dr, Sparta IL 62286-1088. 618/443-2122. Employs: 50-99.

Sullivan Nursing Center
875 Dunsford Dr, Sullivan MO 63080-1238. 314/468-3128. Employs: 50-99.

Virgil Calvert Care Center
5050 Summit Ave, E St. Louis IL 62203-1026. 618/874-3597. Employs: 50-99.

West Main Nursing Home
1244 W Main St, Mascoutah IL 62258-1060. 618/566-7327. Employs: 50-99.

Hospice Care
Collins & West Main, Festus MO 63028. 314/933-2760. Employs: 50-99.

Hospice Care
3545 Lafayette Ave, St. Louis MO 63104-1314. 314/865-6842. Employs: 50-99.

Hospice Of Southern Illinois
251 N Market St, Sparta IL 62286-2068. 618/443-4559. Employs: 50-99.

St Elizabeth Medical Center
2100 Madison St, St. Louis MO 63106-2607. 314/621-3378. Employs: 50-99.

VNA Community Hospice Care
1129 Macklind Ave, St. Louis MO 63110-1440. 314/533-1113. Employs: 50-99.

GENERAL MEDICAL AND SURGICAL HOSPITALS

Edward Utlaut Mem Hospital
Health Cafe Dr, Greenville IL 62246. 618/664-1230. Employs: 50-99.

Thomas Boyd Mem Hospital
800 School St, Carrollton IL 62016-1436. 217/942-6946. Employs: 50-99.

SPECIALTY HOSPITALS, EXCEPT PSYCHIATRIC

CPC Weldon Spring Hospital
5931 Hwy 94 S, Saint Charles MO 63304. 314/441-7300. Employs: 100-249.

SPECIALTY OUTPATIENT FACILITIES

The Edgewood Program
615 S New Ballas Rd, St. Louis MO 63141-8221. 314/569-6500. Employs: 50-99.

HEALTH AND ALLIED SERVICES

St Josephs Hospital
Jamestown Rd, Breese IL 62230. 618/526-4511. Employs: 100-249.

For more information on career opportunities in health care and pharmaceuticals:

Associations

ACCREDITING BUREAU OF HEALTH EDUCATION SCHOOLS
Oak Manor Office, 29089 US 20 West, Elkhart IN 46514. 219/293-0124.

AMERICAN ACADEMY OF FAMILY PHYSICIANS
8880 Ward Parkway, Kansas City MO 64114. 816/333-9700.

AMERICAN ACADEMY OF PHYSICIAN ASSISTANTS
950 North Washington Street, Alexandria VA 22314. 703/836-2272.

AMERICAN ASSOCIATION FOR CLINICAL CHEMISTRY
2029 K Street NW, 7th Floor, Washington DC 20006. 202/857-0717.

AMERICAN ASSOCIATION OF BLOOD BANKS
8101 Glenbrook Road, Bethesda MD 20814. 301/907-6977.

AMERICAN ASSOCIATION OF COLLEGES OF OSTEOPATHIC MEDICINE
6110 Executive Boulevard, Suite 405, Rockville MD 20852. 301/468-2037.

AMERICAN ASSOCIATION OF COLLEGES OF PHARMACY
1426 Prince Street, Alexandria VA 22314. 703/739-2330.

AMERICAN ASSOCIATION OF COLLEGES OF PODIATRIC MEDICINE
1350 Piccard Drive, Suite 322, Rockville MD 20850. 301/990-7400.

AMERICAN ASSOCIATION OF DENTAL SCHOOLS
1625 Massachusetts Avenue NW, Washington DC 20036. 202/667-9433.

AMERICAN ASSOCIATION OF HOMES FOR THE AGED
901 E Street NW, Suite 500, Washington DC 20004. 202/783-2242.

AMERICAN ASSOCIATION OF MEDICAL ASSISTANTS
20 North Wacker Drive, Suite 1575, Chicago IL 60606. 312/899-1500.

AMERICAN ASSOCIATION OF NURSE ANESTHETISTS
216 Higgins Road, Park Ridge IL 60068. 708/692-7050.

AMERICAN ASSOCIATION OF RESPIRATORY CARE
11030 Ables Lane, Dallas TX 75229-4593. 214/243-2272.

AMERICAN CHIROPRACTIC ASSOCIATION
1701 Clarendon Boulevard, Arlington VA 22209. 703/276-8800.

AMERICAN COLLEGE OF HEALTHCARE ADMINISTRATORS
325 South Patrick Street, Alexandria VA 22314. 703/549-5822.

AMERICAN COLLEGE OF HEALTHCARE EXECUTIVES
840 North Lake Shore Drive, Chicago IL 60611. 312/943-0544.

AMERICAN COUNCIL ON PHARMACEUTICAL EDUCATION
311 West Superior Street, Chicago IL 60610. 312/664-3575.

AMERICAN DENTAL ASSOCIATION
211 East Chicago Avenue, Chicago IL 60611. 312/440-2500.

AMERICAN DENTAL HYGIENISTS ASSOCIATION
Division of Professional Development, 444 North Michigan Avenue, Suite 3400, Chicago IL 60611. 312/440-8900.

AMERICAN DIETETIC ASSOCIATION
216 West Jackson Street, Chicago IL 60606. 312/899-0040.

AMERICAN HEALTH CARE ASSOCIATION
1201 L Street NW, Washington DC 20005. 202/842-4444.

AMERICAN HOSPITAL ASSOCIATION
840 North Lake Shore Drive, Chicago IL 60611. 312/280-6000.

AMERICAN MEDICAL ASSOCIATION
515 North State Street, Chicago IL 60605. 312/464-5000.

AMERICAN HEALTH INFORMATION MANAGEMENT ASSOCIATION
919 North Michigan Avenue, Suite 1400, Chicago IL 60611. 312/787-2672.

AMERICAN MEDICAL TECHNOLOGISTS
Registered Medical Assistants, 710 Higgins Road, Park Ridge IL 60068. 708/823-5169.

AMERICAN NURSES ASSOCIATION
600 Maryland Avenue SW, Suite 100W, Washington DC 20024. 202/554-4444.

AMERICAN OCCUPATIONAL THERAPY ASSOCIATION
1383 Piccard Drive, P.O. Box 1725, Rockville MD 20849-1725. 301/948-9626.

AMERICAN OPTOMETRIC ASSOCIATION
243 North Lindbergh Boulevard, St. Louis MO 63141. 314/991-4100.

AMERICAN PHARMACEUTICAL ASSOCIATION
2215 Constitution Avenue NW, Washington DC 20037. 202/628-4410.

AMERICAN PHYSICAL THERAPY ASSOCIATION
1111 North Fairfax Street, Alexandria VA 22314. 703/684-2782.

AMERICAN SOCIETY FOR BIOCHEMISTRY AND MOLECULAR BIOLOGY
9650 Rockville Pike, Bethesda MD 20814. 301/530-7145.

AMERICAN SOCIETY OF HOSPITAL PHARMACISTS
4630 Montgomery Avenue, Bethesda MD 20814. 301/657-3000.

AMERICAN VETERINARY MEDICAL ASSOCIATION
1931 North Meacham Road, Suite 100, Schaumburg IL 60173-4360. 708/925-8070.

CARDIOVASCULAR CREDENTIALING INTERNATIONAL
P.O. Box 611, Dayton OH 45419. 513/294-5225.

MEDICAL GROUP MANAGEMENT ASSOCIATION
104 Invernes Terrace E, Englewood CO 80112. 303/799-1111.

NATIONAL ASSOCIATION OF PHARMACEUTICAL MANUFACTURERS
747 Third Avenue, New York NY 10017. 212/838-3720.

NATIONAL ASSOCIATION OF PRIVATE PSYCHIATRIC HOSPITALS
1319 F Street NW, Washington DC 20004. 202/393-6700.

NATIONAL HEALTH COUNCIL
1730 M Street NW, Suite 500, Washington DC 20036. 202/785-3910.

NATIONAL MEDICAL ASSOCIATION
1012 Tenth Street NW, Washington DC 20001. 202/347-1895.

NATIONAL PHARMACEUTICAL COUNCIL
1894 Preston White Drive, Reston VA 22091. 703/620-6390.

Directories

BLUE BOOK DIGEST OF HMOs
National Association of Employers on Health Care Alternatives, P.O. Box 220, Key Biscayne FL 33149. 305/361-2810.

DRUG TOPICS RED BOOK
Medical Economics Co., P.O. Box 1935, Marion OH 43306-4035. 201/358-7200.

ENCYCLOPEDIA OF MEDICAL ORGANIZATIONS AND AGENCIES
Gale Research Inc., 835 Penobscot Building, Detroit MI 48226. 313/961-2242.

HEALTH ORGANIZATIONS OF THE UNITED STATES, CANADA, AND THE WORLD
Gale Research Inc., 835 Penobscot Building, Detroit MI 48226. 313/961-2242.

MEDICAL AND HEALTH INFORMATION DIRECTORY
Gale Research Inc., 835 Penobscot Building, Detroit MI 48226. 313/961-2242.

NATIONAL DIRECTORY OF HEALTH MAINTENANCE ORGANIZATIONS
Group Health Association of America, 1129 20th Street NW, Washington DC 20036. 202/778-3200.

Magazines

AMERICAN MEDICAL NEWS
American Medical Association, 515 North State Street, Chicago IL 60605. 312/464-5000.

CHANGING MEDICAL MARKETS
Theta Corporation, Theta Building, Middlefield CT 06455. 203/349-1054.

DRUG TOPICS
Medical Economics Co., 5 Paragon Drive, Montvale NJ 07645. 201/358-7200.

HEALTH CARE EXECUTIVE
American College of Health Care Executives, 840 North Lake Shore Drive, Chicago IL 60611. 312/943-0544.

MODERN HEALTHCARE
Crain Communications, 740 North Rush Street, Chicago IL 60611. 312/649-5374.

PHARMACEUTICAL ENGINEERING
International Society of
Pharmaceutical Engineers, 3816 W.
Linebaugh Avenue, Suite 412,
Tampa FL 33624. 813/960-2105.

HOSPITALITY: HOTELS AND RESTAURANTS

In the restaurant segment, the fastest-growing sector of the market continues to be fast-food-style establishments, although increased public concern has led industry leaders to develop new products and marketing strategies. McDonald's has released its lower-fat "McLean Deluxe", and Kentucky Fried Chicken has changed its name to "KFC" to de-emphasize the word "Fried". The take-out trend, spurred by changing demographics and eating habits, is changing the industry as a whole, not just at the fast-food end.

Managerial prospects are better than average, but the industry is hampered by a shortage of entry-level workers. The hotel industry is tied closely to other segments of the travel industry, which in turn relies on the U.S. economy as a whole. International arrivals are the fastest-growing segment of the travel industry, so hotels in major American international destinations are better positioned. Look for greater specialization within the industry, with specific companies advertising as "budget", "luxury", or "corporate/meeting", for example. Hotels will also need to respond to the growing number of working couples who take shorter vacations together.

ARBY'S ROAST BEEF RESTAURANTS
SAGE SYSTEMS INC.
8860 Ladue Road, 2nd Floor, Ladue MO 63124. 314/727-9701. **Contact:** Mrs. Charleen Breese, Office Manager. **Description:** Regional office of the well-known national chain of fast food restaurants. **Employees:** 400.

CLARION HOTEL/ST. LOUIS
200 South Fourth Street, St. Louis MO 63102. 314/241-9500. **Contact:** Mr. Carey Sharpe, Director of Human Resources. **Description:** A downtown hotel with 850 rooms, extensive banquet facilities, two restaurants, and a bar. Full-service hotel. **Employees:** 600, with a management staff of over 50. **Common positions:** Accountant; Hotel Manager/Assistant Manager; Food and Beverage Director; Rooms Division Manager; Executive Housekeeper. **Educational backgrounds sought:** Hospitality/Service. **Benefits:** medical and life insurance; disability coverage; employee discounts. **Corporate headquarters:** Denver, CO. **Parent company:** AIRCOA. **Operations at this facility:** service; sales.

242/The St. Louis JobBank

COLLINSVILLE HOLIDAY INN N/I
1000 Eastport Plaza Drive, Collinsville IL 62234. 618/345-2800. **Contact:** Eva Kisow, Personnel Department. **Description:** Operates a full-service hotel as part of the Holiday Inn chain, whose operations include the management of more than 1,750 company-owned and franchised hotels, gaming operations, restaurants, and a sea transportation subsidiary. **Corporate headquarters:** Memphis, TN. **Employees:** 100. MARY SHANKS

COLLINSVILLE MAC INC./
McDONALD'S RESTAURANT OFFICE
3673 Highway 111, Granite City IL 62040. 618/931-2100. **Contact:** Dave Embry, Head of Operations. **Description:** A regional home office which owns and operates 15 area fast food restaurants. Parent company is a worldwide developer, operator, franchisor, and servicer of a system of restaurants which process, package, and sell a limited menu of fast foods. Internationally, company is one of the largest restaurant chains, and the largest food service organization, operating more than 6,000 McDonald's restaurants in all 50 states and in more than 25 foreign countries. **Corporate headquarters:** Oak Brook, IL. **Listed on:** New York Stock Exchange. **Employees:** 100.

ERKER CATERING COMPANY INC.
8066 Clayton Road, St. Louis MO 63117. 314/727-3366. **Contact:** John Vlatkovich, Personnel Director. **Description:** A St. Louis caterer and industrial food service company. **Employees:** 100.

EXECUTIVE INTERNATIONAL INN
4530 N. Lindbergh, Bridgeton MO 63044. 314/731-3800. **Contact:** David Green, General Manager. **Description:** An area motel, restaurant, and bar. **Employees:** 200+.

FINNINGER'S CATERING SERVICE INC.
8370 N. Broadway, St. Louis MO 63147. 314/389-7680. **Contact:** Pat Meyer, Personnel Director. **Description:** A St. Louis food service catering company. **Employees:** 100.

FISCHER'S RESTAURANT
2100 W. Main Street, Belleville IL 62223. 618/233-1131. **Contact:** Vel Crabtree, Manager. **Description:** A restaurant which also provides catering services. **Employees:** 100.

HARDEE'S INC.
3451 Rider Trail South, Earth City MO 63045. 314/291-0068. **Contact:** Bill Nichols, Director of Human Resources. **Description:** The nation's third largest chain of fast food hamburger restaurants. **Common positions:** Food Technologist; Hotel Manager/Assistant Manager; Management Trainee. **Educational backgrounds sought:** Business Administration; Liberal Arts. **Benefits:** medical insurance; dental insurance; pension plan; life insurance; tuition assistance; disability coverage; employee discounts; savings plan. **Corporate headquarters:** Rocky Mountain, NC. **Parent company:** Imaso Ltd. **Operations at this facility:** regional headquarters.

HENRY VIII INN & LODGE BEST WESTERN
4690 North Lindbergh Boulevard, St. Louis MO 63044. 314/731-3040. **Contact:** Jeff Rockers, Personnel Director. **Description:** A motel.

HOLIDAY INN DOWNTOWN/CONVENTION CENTER
811 North 9th Street, St. Louis MO 63101. 314/421-4000. **Contact:** Ms. Seema Moorman, Personnel Manager. **Description:** A St. Louis hotel. **Common positions:** Accountant; Credit Manager; Customer Service Representative; Mechanical Engineer; Hotel Manager/Assistant Manager; Department Manager; General Manager; Personnel and Labor Relations Specialist; Food and Beverage Director; Executive Housekeeper. **Educational backgrounds sought:** Business Administration. **Special programs:** Training programs. **Benefits:** medical, dental, and life insurance; employee discounts; savings plan; credit union. **Corporate headquarters:** Minneapolis, MN. **Parent company:** Seymour Logan and Assoc. **Employees:** 130.

HOLIDAY INNS INC./ST. LOUIS AREA
4545 North Lindbergh Boulevard, Bridgeton MO 63044. 314/731-2100. **Contact:** Georganna Condor, Personnel. **Description:** Operates a full-service hotel as part of the Holiday Inn chain, whose operations include the management of more than 1,750 company-owned and franchised hotels, gaming operations, restaurants. International facilities. **Common positions:** Accountant; Hotel Manager/Assistant Manager; Personnel; All Service Type Personnel; Sales Representative. **Educational backgrounds sought:** Accounting; Business Administration; Marketing. **Benefits:** medical, dental, and life insurance; tuition assistance; disability coverage; profit sharing; employee discounts; savings plan. **Corporate headquarters:** Atlanta GA. **Operations at this facility:** service. **Listed on:** New York Stock Exchange.

HOST INTERNATIONAL, INC.
Lambert-St. Louis International Airport, P.O. Box 10187, St. Louis MO 63145. 314/429-3400. **Contact:** Regina Rayburn, Human Resource Manager. **Description:** A company which provides catering services to restaurants, bars, and airlines. **Common positions:** Department Manager; Management Trainee; Operations/Production Manager, Food and Beverage Assistant Manager. **Educational background sought:** Business Administration; Hotel/Restaurant Management. **Benefits:** medical, dental and life insurance; pension plan; tuition assistance; disability coverage; profit sharing; employee discounts; savings plan. **Corporate headquarters:** Washington, DC. **Parent company:** Marriott.

LION'S CHOICE
12015 Manchester, Suite 180, St. Louis MO 63131. 314/821-8665. **Contact:** Jim Tobias, Personnel Director. **Description:** Corporate office for a company which owns and operates a chain of fast food restaurants.

MARRIOTT AIRPORT HOTEL/ST. LOUIS
I-70 at Lambert International Airport, St. Louis MO 63134. 314/423-9700. **Contact:** Mr. Wynn Watkis, Director of Human Resources. **Description:** Lambert International Airport branch of the well-known national chain of hotels. Parent corporation's operations include hotels, contract and in-flight food

services, fast food restaurants and Great America theme parks. **Corporate headquarters:** Washington, D.C. **Listed on:** New York Stock Exchange.

MARRIOTT PAVILION HOTEL
One South Broadway, St. Louis MO 63102. 314/421-1776. **Contact:** Janet Brobeck, Personnel Director. **Description:** A branch location of the well-known Marriott chain of hotels.

McDONALD'S CORPORATION
ST. LOUIS REGIONAL OFFICE
922 Roosevelt Parkway, Suite 300, Chesterfield MO 63017. 314/537-0809. **Contact:** Regional Personnel Manager. **Description:** Regional office of the world famous quick service restaurant chain. Primary opportunities are in the Restaurant Management area. **Common positions:** Management Trainee; Operations/Production Manager; Restaurant Manager. **Educational backgrounds sought:** Business Administration. **Benefits:** medical, dental, and life insurance; pension plan; tuition assistance; disability coverage; profit sharing; savings plan. **Corporate headquarters:** Oak Brook, IL. **Operations at this facility:** regional headquarters. **Listed on:** New York Stock Exchange.

MISS HULLING'S CAFETERIAS
MISSOURI CAFETERIA INC.
1103 Locust Street, St. Louis MO 63101. 314/436-0840. **Contact:** Personnel Department. **Description:** A St. Louis eating complex with several cafeterias and restaurants.

PIZZA HUT OF ST. LOUIS INC.
13801 Riverport Drive, Suite 101, Maryland Heights MO 63043. 314/770-2727. **Contact:** Sharon Lawrence, Director of Human Resources. **Description:** St. Louis office of the well-known national chain of family pizza restaurants. **Common positions:** Accountant; Administrator; Management Trainee; Operations/Production Manager. **Educational backgrounds sought:** Business Administration. **Special programs:** Training programs. **Benefits:** medical, dental, and life insurance; pension plan; tuition assistance; disability coverage; daycare assistance; profit sharing; savings plan. Parent Company, Pepsico, Inc., operates nationally in four business segments: beverages, food products, food service, and sporting goods. Products include a wide range of consumer items. **Corporate headquarters:** Wichita, KS. **Operations at this facility:** divisional headquarters; administration. **Listed on:** New York Stock Exchange.

H.A. POPE & SONS INC.
25 South County Center Way, St. Louis MO 63129. 314/487-3606. **Contact:** Dianna Clooney, Personnel Director. **Description:** A food service company specializing in the operation of a variety of cafeterias, restaurants and contract food services.

RAX RESTAURANTS, INC.
1147 S. Kirkwood Rd., Kirkwood MO 63122. 314/821-6305. **Contact:** Personnel. **Description:** Operators of a fast food restaurant chain. **Corporate headquarters:** This location.

LT. ROBERT E. LEE RESTAURANT
100 Lenore K. Sullivan Boulevard, St. Louis MO 63102. 314/241-1282. **Contact:** Personnel Department. **Description:** Owners of Lt. Robert E. Lee Restaurants. **Employees:** 1,000.

SCHNEITHORST'S
1600 South Lindbergh Boulevard, St. Louis MO 63131. 314/993-5600. **Contact:** Tom Lyons, Personnel Director. **Description:** A St. Louis company that owns and operates restaurants and catering services.

SHERATON WEST PORT INN
191 West Port Plaza Drive, Maryland Heights MO 63146. 314/878-1500. **Contact:** Personnel Department. **Description:** One of several area locations of the international hotel chain, specializing in accommodations for business travelers. **Corporate headquarters:** Boston, MA. In turn, Sheraton Corporation is a subsidiary of ITT Corporation, a diversified company engaged principally in the businesses of Telecommunications and Electronics; Engineered Products; Consumer Products and Services; Natural Resources; and Insurance and Finance. Company maintains manufacturing or sales operations in approximately 100 countries. Telecommunications and Electronics Group operations include managing the largest international record carrier through land, undersea, and satellite networks, and the design and manufacture of navigation and marine electronics systems for commercial and military customers worldwide, as well as operating and maintaining support services at NASA facilities through defense and avionics unit. Engineered Products Group produces automotive products (through subsidiaries Teves, Koni, and SWF); pumps, valves, and fluid-handling products; and electronic memories, and distribution of electrical and electronic connectors, controls and other instrumentation. Consumer Products and Services includes operations through 'Sheraton' hotels and inns subsidiary, lawn care and gardening products through Scotts and Burpee subsidiaries, and publishing through the 'Marquis Who's Who' directories. Natural Resources Group produces forest products (including the production of wood pulps and other wood products through subsidiary ITT Rayonier and others); and energy and mineral products through subsidiary Eason Oil Company, involved in oil and gas exploration, and in the mining, preparation, and sale of metallurgical and steam coal, silica, and attapulgite. Insurance and Finance Group writes a broad range of life, property, and casualty insurance through subsidiary The Hartford Insurance Group (New York, NY); and makes consumer and commercial loans, and provides financing to ITT customers through ITT Financial Corporation. Subsidiaries operate independently. International. **Listed on:** New York Stock Exchange.

SHONEY'S INC.
320 Brookes Drive, Suite 115, Hazelwood MO 63042. 314/895-1201. **Contact:** Personnel Department. **Description:** An area chain of family restaurants.

TONY'S INC.
410 Market Street, St. Louis MO 63102. 314/231-7007. **Contact:** Arthur J. Schomaker, Controller. **Description:** Owners and operators of a Mobil 5 Star and AAA Diamond rated restaurant, specializing in fine Italian Continental cuisine. **Common positions:** Cooks/Chefs; Waiters. **Educational backgrounds**

sought: experience. **Special programs:** Training programs. **Benefits:** medical insurance; union plans. **Employees:** 90.

WHITE CASTLE SYSTEM INC.
1111 Macklind Avenue, St. Louis MO 63110. 314/535-7430. **Contact:** Martha Fischer, Personnel Department. **Description:** Corporate office of the chain of family hamburger restaurants.

Additional large employers: 250+

EATING PLACES

Sheraton Plaza Hotel
900 Westport Plaza, St. Louis MO 63146-3104. 314/434-5010. Employs: 250-499.

Central Missouri Pizza Inc
1350 Elbridge Payne Rd, Chesterfield MO 63017-8531. 314/537-1120. Employs: 250-499.

HOTELS AND MOTELS

Sheraton St Louis Hotel
910 N 7th St, St. Louis MO 63101-1023. 314/231-5100. Employs: 250-499.

Additional small to medium sized employers: 50-249

EATING PLACES

Athens Cafe
954 Crestwood Plaza, St. Louis MO 63126-1709. 314/962-0107. Employs: 50-99.

Burger King
5025 Delmar Blvd, St. Louis MO 63108-1043. 314/361-1336. Employs: 50-99.

Denny's Restaurant
10820 Lincoln Trail, E St. Louis IL 62208-2010. 618/397-9344. Employs: 50-99.

Gianni's Italian Restaurant
7435 Watson Rd, St. Louis MO 63119-4403. 314/961-3700. Employs: 100-249.

Grone Cafeteria
4409 Woodson Rd, St. Louis MO 63134-3701. 314/423-7880. Employs: 50-99.

Hardee's Business Office
2304 E Main St, Belleville IL 62221-5026. 618/234-4007. Employs: 100-249.

Kennedy's 2nd Street Company
612 N 2nd St, St. Louis MO 63102-2553. 314/421-3655. Employs: 50-99.

Marciano's
333 Westport Plaza, St. Louis MO 63146-3003. 314/878-8180. Employs: 50-99.

McDonald's Restaurants
4015 Lemay Ferry Rd, St. Louis MO 63129-1857. 314/892-0550. Employs: 50-99.

Nantucket Cove
40 N Kingshighway Blvd, St. Louis MO 63108-1355. 314/361-0625. Employs: 50-99.

Paula's Family Restaurant
15484 Manchester Rd, Ballwin MO
63011-3053. 314/394-3310.
Employs: 50-99.

Perkins Restaurant
1881 Sherman Dr, Saint Charles
MO 63303-3966. 314/946-9662.
Employs: 50-99.

Pietro's
3801 Watson Rd, St. Louis MO
63109-1238. 314/645-9263.
Employs: 50-99.

Pizza Hut
760 Saint Francois St, Florissant
MO 63031-4922. 314/838-8732.
Employs: 100-249.

Ponderosa Steakhouse
2895 N Highway 67, Florissant
MO 63033. 314/838-2366.
Employs: 50-99.

Red Lobster
170 Homer M Adams Pkwy, Alton
IL 62002-5924. 618/465-6554.
Employs: 50-99.

The Edge
2300 Lasalle St, St. Louis MO
63104-2421. 314/776-0445.
Employs: 50-99.

The Pasta House Company
295 Plaza, St. Louis MO 63131.
314/569-3040. Employs: 50-99.

Trotter's Bar-B-Que
9960 Watson Rd, St. Louis MO
63126-1827. 314/965-7795.
Employs: 50-99.

Aunt Heidi's Deli & Ice Crm
720 Westport Plaza, St. Louis MO
63146-3010. 314/576-6717.
Employs: 50-99.

I G A Capri
Old Rt 66 & 16, Litchfield IL
62056. 217/324-5367. Employs:
50-99.

Cecil Whittaker's Pizzeria
4412 Lemay Ferry Rd, St. Louis
MO 63129-1758. 314/894-3100.
Employs: 50-99.

Domino's Pizza
10805 Sunset Office Dr Ste 208, St.
Louis MO 63127-1026. 314/843-
8622. Employs: 50-99.

Red Lobster Restaurants
12235 Saint Charles Rock Rd,
Bridgeton MO 63044-2502.
314/291-8680. Employs: 50-99.

McDonald's Restaurants
Rt 16 & Hwy 66, Litchfield IL
62056. 217/324-2635. Employs:
50-99.

McDonald's Restaurants
809 St. Louis Ave, E St. Louis IL
62201-2930. 618/274-3343.
Employs: 50-99.

McDonald's Restaurants
4011 Bayless Ave, St. Louis MO
63125-1315. 314/544-5151.
Employs: 50-99.

Ponderosa Steakhouse
3225 Hampton Ave, St. Louis MO
63139-2325. 314/647-4919.
Employs: 50-99.

Shoney's Restaurants
7468 Manchester Rd, St. Louis MO
63143-3032. 314/645-9244.
Employs: 50-99.

Denny's Restaurant
2925 N Highway 67, Florissant
MO 63033. 314/831-0471.
Employs: 50-99.

Little Nashville Catering
RR 1, Nashville IL 62263-9801.
618/478-5588. Employs: 50-99.

DRINKING PLACES (ALCOHOLIC BEVERAGES)

Saintcso
300 Monsanto Av, E St. Louis IL 62201-1064. 618/274-4500. Employs: 50-99.

Terrance Blackmons
127 Collinsville Av, E St. Louis IL 62201-3008. 618/271-9678. Employs: 50-99.

Club Soda
2002 N Truman Blvd, Crystal City MO 63019-1021. 314/937-3115. Employs: 50-99.

HOTELS AND MOTELS

Holiday Inn
1000 Eastport Plaza Dr, Collinsville IL 62234-6103. 618/345-2800. Employs: 50-99.

Holiday Inn Alton Parkway
3800 Homer M Adams Pkwy, Alton IL 62002-5063. 618/462-1220. Employs: 100-249.

Ramada Westport
12031 Lackland Rd, St. Louis MO 63146-4001. 314/878-1400. Employs: 50-99.

Days Inn At The Arch
4th & Washington, St. Louis MO 63102. 314/621-7900. Employs: 50-99.

Drury Inns
20th & Market, St. Louis MO 63103. 314/231-3900. Employs: 50-99.

Embassy Suites Hotel
901 N 1st St, St. Louis MO 63102-2548. 314/241-4200. Employs: 50-99.

Gardens Motel
S Route 66, Litchfield IL 62056. 217/324-2181. Employs: 50-99.

Gil Hess Motel
3106 N Newstead Ave, St. Louis MO 63115-2631. 314/534-9790. Employs: 50-99.

Harley Hotel Of St Louis
I-270 & I-70, Earth City MO 63045. 314/291-6800. Employs: 50-99.

Royalty Motel
3951 W Florissant Ave, St. Louis MO 63107-1620. 314/383-8223. Employs: 50-99.

Alcorn Hotel
4165 Washington Blvd, St. Louis MO 63108-3134. 314/534-9329. Employs: 50-99.

Atlantis Management Inc
1133 Washington Ave, St. Louis MO 63101-1121. 314/421-0052. Employs: 50-99.

Cheshire Inn & Lodge
6306 Clayton Rd, St. Louis MO 63117-2500. 314/647-7300. Employs: 50-99.

Drury Inns
7th & Broadway, St. Louis MO 63101. 314/231-8100. Employs: 50-99.

Grandel Square Hotel
3716 Grandel Sq, St. Louis MO 63108-3628. 314/534-9312. Employs: 50-99.

Holiday Inn
9 St At Convention Plaza, St. Louis MO 63101. 314/421-4000. Employs: 50-99.

Lincoln Retirement Home
2228 Olive St, St. Louis MO 63103-1529. 314/241-5511. Employs: 50-99.

Mayfair Suites
806 St Charles, St. Louis MO
63101. 314/421-2500. Employs:
50-99.

North Western Inn
5720 Natural Bridge Ave, St. Louis
MO 63120-1630. 314/383-9631.
Employs: 50-99.

St Louis Marriott Pavillion
One Broadway, St. Louis MO
63102. 314/421-1776. Employs:
100-249.

St Louisian Hotel
1133 Washington Ave, St. Louis
MO 63101-1121. 314/421-4727.
Employs: 50-99.

Stadium Motor Hotel
201 S 20th St, St. Louis MO
63103-2222. 314/621-4718.
Employs: 50-99.

Old Convent Guesthouse
2049 Sidney St, St. Louis MO
63104-2828. 314/772-3531.
Employs: 50-99.

Midway Hotel Best Western
2434 Old Dorsett Rd, Maryland Hts
MO 63043-2415. 314/291-8700.
Employs: 50-99.

Days Inn South
3660 S Lindbergh Blvd, St. Louis
MO 63127-1204. 314/821-3000.
Employs: 100-249.

Holiday Inn
7730 Bonhomme Ave, St. Louis
MO 63105-1909. 314/863-0400.
Employs: 50-99.

Holiday Inn
4th & Pine, St. Louis MO 63102.
314/621-8200. Employs: 100-249.

Hyatt Hotels & Resorts
1820 Market St, St. Louis MO
63103-2208. 314/436-7524.
Employs: 50-99.

Red Roof Inn
I-44 & Hampton Av, St. Louis MO
63139. 314/645-0101. Employs:
50-99.

Courtyard By Marriott
2340 Market St, St. Louis MO
63103-2517. 314/241-9111.
Employs: 50-99.

Residence Inn By Marriott
1881 Craigshire Rd, St. Louis MO
63146-4015. 314/469-0060.
Employs: 50-99.

Huckleberry Finn Youth Hostel
1906 S 12th St, St. Louis MO
63104-3951. 314/241-0076.
Employs: 50-99.

ROOMING AND BOARDING HOUSES

Goodfellow Manor
1119 Goodfellow Blvd, St. Louis
MO 63112-2816. 314/361-9118.
Employs: 50-99.

For more information on career opportunities in hospitality - hotels and restaurants:

Associations

COUNCIL ON HOTEL, RESTAURANT AND INSTITUTIONAL EDUCATION
1200 17th Street NW, Washington DC 20036. 202/331-5990.

THE EDUCATIONAL FOUNDATION OF THE NATIONAL RESTAURANT ASSOCIATION
250 South Wacker Drive, 14th Floor, Chicago IL 60606. 312/715-1010.

HOSPITALITY SALES AND MARKETING ASSOCIATION INTERNATIONAL
1300 L Street NW, Suite 800, Washington DC 20005. 202/789-0089.

NATIONAL RESTAURANT ASSOCIATION
1200 17th Street NW, Washington DC 20036. 202/331-5900.

Directories

DIRECTORY OF CHAIN RESTAURANT OPERATORS
Business Guides, Inc., Lebhar-Friedman, Inc., 3922 Coconut Palm Drive, Tampa FL 33619-8321. 813/664-6700.

DIRECTORY OF HIGH-VOLUME INDEPENDENT RESTAURANTS
Lebhar-Friedman, Inc., 3922 Coconut Palm Drive, Tampa FL 33619-8321. 813/664-6700.

Magazines

CORNELL HOTEL AND RESTAURANT ADMINISTRATION QUARTERLY
Cornell University School of Hotel Administration, 327 Statler Hall, Ithaca NY 14853. 607/255-2093.

HOTEL AND MOTEL MANAGEMENT
120 West 2nd Street, Duluth MN 55802. 218/723-9440.

INNKEEPING WORLD
Box 84108, Seattle WA 98124. 206/362-7125.

NATION'S RESTAURANT NEWS
425 Park Avenue, New York NY 10022. 212/756-5200.

INSURANCE

The fastest-growing segment of the insurance industry will be in annuities. Premiums of property-casualty insurers should increase by about 5 percent, according to the Bureau of Labor Statistics. Competition and mergers will increase, while life insurance companies are expected to experience further problems. The industry as a whole has been trimming back through layoffs, although the worst may be over.

ALEXANDER & ALEXANDER OF MISSOURI
120 South Central Avenue, St. Louis MO 63105. 314/889-9200. **Contact:** Alicia K. Koch, Human Resources Manager. **Description:** A St. Louis provider of insurance services. **Employees:** 200. **Common positions:** Actuary; Claim Representative; Insurance Agent/Broker; Sales Representative; Underwriter. **Educational backgrounds sought:** CPCU. **Benefits:** medical insurance; dental insurance; pension plan; life insurance; tuition assistance; disability coverage; savings plan. **Corporate headquarters:** New York, NY. **Operations at this facility:** divisional headquarters; service; sales. **Listed on:** New York Stock Exchange.

ALLSTATE INSURANCE COMPANY
P.O. Box 7110, St. Louis MO 63177. 314/434-4477. **Contact:** Marva B. Gaylor, Staff Claim Analyst. **Description:** Regional office of the national insurance company.

BLUE CROSS AND BLUE SHIELD OF MISSOURI
1831 Chestnut Street, St. Louis MO 63103. 314/923-4444. **Contact:** Cheryl Slaughter, Personnel Manager. **Description:** A prepaid health care benefits company. Nationally, Blue Cross and Blue Shield provides hospitalization and medical coverage to individuals and groups. **Employees:** 1,000. **Common positions:** Actuary; Attorney; Claim Representative; Computer Programmer; Customer Service Representative; Electrical Engineer; Mechanical Engineer; Financial Analyst; Marketing Specialist; Technical Writer/Editor; Underwriter. **Educational backgrounds sought:** Accounting; Business Administration; Computer Science; Engineering; Finance; Marketing; Mathematics. **Benefits:** medical, dental, and life insurance; pension plan; tuition assistance; disability coverage; savings plan. **Corporate headquarters:** This location. **Operations at this facility:** service.

CHARLES L. CRANE AGENCY COMPANY
100 South Fourth Street, Suite 800, St. Louis MO 63102. 314/241-8700. **Contact:** Jerry Burnett, General Manager. **Description:** A St. Louis insurance agency. **Employees:** 100. **Common positions:** Accountant; Claim Representative; Computer Programmer; Customer Service Representative; Industrial Engineer; Financial Analyst; Insurance Agent/Broker; Department Manager; General Manager; Marketing Specialist; Systems Analyst; Underwriter. **Benefits:** medical insurance; dental insurance; life insurance;

tuition assistance; profit sharing; savings plan. **Corporate headquarters:** This location. **Operations at this facility:** administration; service; sales.

THE DANIEL AND HENRY COMPANY
2350 Market Street, Suite 400, St. Louis MO 63103. 314/421-1525. **Contact:** Nancy Keiser, Personnel Manager. **Description:** A St. Louis insurance agency and brokerage firm. **Employees:** 150. **Common positions:** Accountant; Insurance Agent/Broker; Quality Controller; Underwriter. **Benefits:** medical, dental, and life insurance; pension plan; tuition assistance; disability coverage. **Corporate headquarters:** This location. **Operations at this facility:** administration; service; sales. **Employees:** 150.

FIREMAN'S FUND INSURANCE COMPANY
727 Craig Road, St. Louis MO 63141. 314/569-7311. **Contact:** Sheila Hutchinson, Human Resources Representative. **Description:** Underwriters of all insurance. The umbrella company for the group of property/liability insurance companies, operating primarily in the United States. **Common positions:** Attorney; Claim Representative; Customer Service Representative; Operations/Production Manager; Electrical Engineer; Industrial Engineer; Mechanical Engineer; Financial Analyst; Engineer, HPR. **Educational backgrounds sought:** Business Administration; Finance; Liberal Arts; Marketing; Accounting; Engineering. **Special programs:** Training programs. **Benefits:** medical insurance; dental insurance; pension plan; life insurance; tuition assistance; disability coverage; savings plan; profit sharing; employee discounts. **Corporate headquarters:** Novato, CA. **Parent company:** Allianz AG. **Operations at this facility:** Administration; Service; Sales. **Revenues (1991):** $89.5 million. **Employees:** 175. **Projected hires for the next 12 months:** 6-12.

ISO COMMERCIAL RISK SERVICES
3660 South Geyer Road, Suite 100, St. Louis MO 63127. 314/965-2700. **Contact:** Mr. R.E. Harnisch, Regional Director. **Description:** Insurance rating, statistical and advisory service.

MARSHALL-McLENNON INSURANCE AGENCY
10 South Broadway, St. Louis MO 63102. 314/621-5540. **Contact:** Claire Britt, Personnel Director. **Description:** A St. Louis insurance agency.

MISSOURI MEDICAL SERVICE INC.
BLUE SHIELD
1831 Chestnut, St. Louis MO 63103. 314/923-4444. **Contact:** Robert Bolesta, Personnel Director. **Description:** St. Louis affiliate of the well-known non-profit corporation providing prepaid medical health insurance to subscribers through a variety of health care providers. Member of the Blue Shield Association, an organization that provides national coordination on behalf of 69 local, autonomous Blue Shield Plans which together serve about 70 million people. **Corporate headquarters:** San Francisco, CA.

NATIONAL CASUALTY COMPANY
515 N. 6th Street, St. Louis MO 63101. 314/421-4626. **Contact:** George Karris, Human Resource Associate. **Description:** An individual health insurer. **Common positions:** Accountant; Actuary; Claim Representative; Computer

Programmer; Customer Service Representative; Management Trainee; General Manager. **Educational backgrounds sought:** Accounting; Business Administration; Computer Science; Finance; Marketing. **Special programs:** Training programs; Internships. **Benefits:** medical, dental, and life insurance; tuition assistance; pension plan; disability coverage; savings plan. **Corporate headquarters:** This location. **Parent company:** Nationwide Insurance. **Employees:** 200. **Operations at this facility:** Administration; Service; Sales.

NATIONAL GENERAL INSURANCE COMPANY
(A GENERAL MOTORS INSURANCE COMPANY)
P.O. Box 66937, St. Louis MO 63166-6937. 314/298-0500. **Contact:** Barbara J. Trabert, Vice President/Human Resources. **Description:** Engaged in the direct-response marketing of personal lines insurance (homeowners, automobile, and motorcycle); data management services to sponsoring associations in 48 states. **Common positions:** Accountant; Actuary; Administrator; Claim Representative; Computer Programmer; Customer Service Representative; Department Manager; Management Trainee; Underwriter; Customer Sales Agent; Administrative Assistant; Word Processor; Computer Operator; CRT Operator; Secretarial. **Educational backgrounds sought:** Business Administration; Computer Science; Liberal Arts. **Benefits:** medical, dental and life insurance; pension plan; tuition assistance; disability coverage; savings plan; credit union; 401K. **Corporate headquarters:** This location. **Revenues (1991):** $196 million. **Employees:** 600+. **Projected hires for the next 12 months:** 50+.

THE RELIABLE LIFE INSURANCE CO.
231 West Lockwood Avenue, Webster Groves MO 63119. 314/968-4900. **Contact:** Personnel Department. **Description:** A St. Louis insurance carrier.

SAFECO INSURANCE GROUP
P.O. Box 461, St. Louis MO 63166. 314/965-0400. **Contact:** Parker Nelson, Personnel Director. **Description:** St. Louis division office of a insurance carrier.

STATE FARM INSURANCE COMPANIES
8945 Dunn Road, Hazelwood MO 63042. 314/839-6200. **Contact:** Jeanette LaPlante, Personnel Representative. For employment information, Art Ruiz can be contacted at 11885 Lackland, Suite 315, St. Louis MO 63146, #14/993-3076. **Description:** Regional office of the well-known insurance companies. Company offers a complete range of life, accident and health, automobile and fire insurance. **Common positions:** Claim Representative; Underwriter. **Educational backgrounds sought:** Business Administration; Liberal Arts. **Benefits:** medical, dental, and life insurance; pension plan; tuition assistance; disability coverage; profit sharing; savings plan. **Corporate headquarters:** Bloomington, IL. **Operations at this facility:** divisional headquarters.

THE TRAVELERS INSURANCE COMPANY
701 Market Street, St. Louis MO 63101. 314/425-8500. **Contact:** Human Resource Representative. **Description:** Branch office of one of the world's largest investor-owned insurance and financial service institutions in the world. Writes every principal form of life, accident, health and casualty/property insurance. Offers a broad range of pension and other investment management services. Operates in more than 375 field offices throughout the country, and has assets of over $20 billion and more than $100 billion of life insurance in force

Common positions: Attorney; Claim Representative; Customer Service Representative; Industrial Engineer; Mechanical Engineer; Financial Analyst; Insurance Agent/Broker; Marketing Specialist; Sales Representative; Underwriter. **Educational backgrounds sought:** Accounting; Business Administration; Computer Science; Engineering; Finance; Liberal Arts; Marketing; Mathematics. **Benefits:** medical, dental, and life insurance; pension plan; tuition assistance; employee discounts; savings plan. **Corporate headquarters:** Hartford, CT. **Operations at this facility:** regional headquarters; divisional headquarters; research and development; administration; service; sales. **Listed on:** New York Stock Exchange.

WORLD WIDE INSURANCE GROUP
WORLD WIDE UNDERWRITERS INC.
11975 Westline Drive, St. Louis MO 63146. 314/878-1800. **Contact:** Paul Yakulis, Vice President of Human Resources. **Description:** A national insurance company. **Corporate headquarters:** Wausau, WI.

Additional large employers: 250+

ACCIDENT AND HEALTH INSURANCE

General American Life Ins Co
700 Market St Box 396-63166, St. Louis MO 63101-1829. 314/231-1700. Employs: 1,000+.

HOSPITAL AND MEDICAL SERVICE PLANS

Admar Corp
509 Olive St, St. Louis MO 63101-1844. 314/421-1005. Employs: 500-999.

Benefit Plan Administrators
10 S Broadway, St. Louis MO 63102-1712. 314/241-6888. Employs: 500-999.

Blue Cross & Blue Shield Of Mo
4444 Forest Park Ave, St. Louis MO 63108-2212. 314/658-4444. Employs: 500-999.

FIRE, MARINE AND CASUALTY INSURANCE

Nat Bonding Account Ins Co
4242 Lindell Bl, St. Louis MO 63108-2916. 314/652-1414. Employs: 250-499.

SURETY INSURANCE

ITT Financial Corp
12555 Manchester Rd, St. Louis MO 63131-3716. 314/821-6060. Employs: 1,000+.

INSURANCE CARRIERS

Frick Company
1260 Andes Bl, St. Louis MO 63132-1702. 314/997-2100. Employs: 250-499.

INSURANCE AGENTS, BROKERS AND SERVICE

Millers Mutual Ins Assn Il
111 E 4th St, Alton IL 62002-6241. 618/463-3636. Employs: 250-499.

General American Life Ins Co
13045 Tesson Ferry Rd, St. Louis MO 63128-3407. 314/843-8700. Employs: 500-999.

Insurance/255

Transprotection Service Co
1 United Dr, Fenton MO 63026-2535. 314/343-9889. Employs: 250-499.

Additional small to medium sized employers: 50-249

ACCIDENT AND HEALTH INSURANCE

Florists' Mutual Insurance Co
500 St Louis St, Edwardsville IL 62025-1502. 618/656-4240. Employs: 50-99.

HOSPITAL AND MEDICAL SERVICE PLANS

Accident & Health Plans Agency
6631 Delmar Blvd, St. Louis MO 63130-4544. 314/725-7776. Employs: 50-99.

Assocd Drs Health & Life Ins Co
301 Sovereign Ct, Ballwin MO 63011-4435. 314/227-3388. Employs: 50-99.

Gulf Agency Inc
1515 N Warson Rd, St. Louis MO 63132-1111. 314/423-9666. Employs: 50-99.

Insured Research Service
15444 Clayton Rd, Ballwin MO 63011 3166. 314/394 4620. Employs: 50-99.

Missouri Brokerage Svcs Inc
235 Cedar Grove Dr, Saint Charles MO 63304-7379. 314/947-1840. Employs: 100-249.

Secure Marketing Co Amer Inc
1600 Heritage Lndg, Saint Charles MO 63303-8489. 314/441-1813. Employs: 100-249.

PENSION, HEALTH AND WELFARE FUNDS

Kirke-Van Orsdel Inc

1 Metropolitan Sq, St. Louis MO 63102-2733. 314/621-0040. Employs: 50-99.

Massachusetts Mutual Life Ins Co
1 Boatmens Plaza, St. Louis MO 63101-2602. 314/241-6585. Employs: 50-99.

INSURANCE CARRIERS

McMurray Quality Car Wash
8 N 22nd St, E St. Louis IL 62205-1102. 618/874-7210. Employs: 50-99.

INSURANCE AGENTS, BROKERS AND SERVICE

Genelco
1600 S Brentwood Blvd, St. Louis MO 63144-1320. 314/962-2040. Employs: 100-249.

Charter National Life Ins Co
8301 Maryland Ave, St. Louis MO 63105-3644. 314/725-7575. Employs: 50-99.

General American Life Ins Co
1611 Des Peres Rd, St. Louis MO 63131 1813. 314/957 9900. Employs: 50-99.

Rollins Burdick Hunter Mo Inc
500 Washington Ave, St. Louis MO 63101-1261. 314/241-8010. Employs: 50-99.

State Farm Insurance
339 Mid Rivers Mall Dr, Saint Peters MO 63376-1516. 314/279-4100. Employs: 50-99.

Wausau Insurance Companies
12101 Woodcrest Executive Dr, St. Louis MO 63141-5047. 314/878-1030. Employs: 50-99.

Metropolitan Life Insurance Co
650 Community Federal Center, St. Louis MO 63131. 314/822-1618. Employs: 100-249.

Prudential Insurance Co Amer
12312 Olive Blvd, St. Louis MO 63141-6448. 314/542-4500. Employs: 50-99.

Home Agency Inc
12680 Olive Blvd, St. Louis MO 63141-6322. 314/576-6161. Employs: 100-249.

For more information on career opportunities in insurance:

Associations

ALLIANCE OF AMERICAN INSURERS
1501 Woodfield Road, Suite 400 West, Schaumburg IL 60173-4980. 708/330-8500.

AMERICAN COUNCIL OF LIFE INSURANCE
1001 Pennsylvania Avenue NW, 5th Floor South, Washington DC 20004-2599. 202/624-2000.

AMERICAN INSURANCE ASSOCIATION
1130 Connecticut Avenue NW, Suite 1000, Washington DC 20036. 202/828-7100.

HEALTH INSURANCE ASSOCIATION OF AMERICA
1025 Connecticut Avenue NW, Suite 1200, Washington DC 20036-3998. 202/223-7780.

INSURANCE INFORMATION INSTITUTE
110 William Street, New York NY 10038. 212/669-9200.

LIFE INSURANCE RESEARCH AND MARKETING ASSOCIATION
8 Farm Springs Road, Farmington CT 06032. 203/677-0033.

NATIONAL ASSOCIATION OF LIFE UNDERWRITERS
1922 F Street NW, Washington DC 20006-4387. 202/331-6000.

SOCIETY OF ACTUARIES
475 North Martingale Road, Suite 800, Schaumburg IL 60173-2227. 708/706-3500.

Directories

INSURANCE ALMANAC
Underwriter Printing and Publishing Co., 50 East Palisade Avenue, Englewood NJ 07631. 201/569-8808.

INSURANCE MARKET PLACE
Rough Notes Company, Inc., P.O. Box 564, Indianapolis IN 46206. 317/634-1541.

INSURANCE PHONE BOOK AND DIRECTORY
121 Chanlon Road, New Providence NJ 07974. 800/521-8110.

Magazines

BEST'S REVIEW
A. M. Best Co., A. M. Best Road, Oldwick NJ 08858. 908/439-2200.

INSURANCE JOURNAL
80 Southlake Avenue, Suite 550, Pasadena CA 91101. 818/793-7717.

INSURANCE REVIEW
Journal of Commerce, 2 World Trade Center, 27th Floor, New York NY 10048. 212/837-7000.

LEGAL SERVICES

The legal profession is undergoing a major adjustment, largely due to the rapid rise in the number of lawyers over the past two decades. In the '70s the number of lawyers doubled, and in the '80s the number rose by another 48 percent. Meanwhile, a decline in civil litigation, coupled with the recent economic downturn, has led to a "produce or perish" climate. Law schools are reporting a 10-20 percent decline in placements, and firms are laying off associates, freezing rates, and firing unproductive partners.
Graduates of prestigious law schools and those who rank high in their classes will have the best opportunities.

ARMSTRONG, TEASDALE, SCHAFLEY, DAVIS, DICUS
One Metropolitan Square, Suite 2600, St. Louis MO 63102. 314/621-5070. **Contact:** Debra Bollinger, Recruitment Coordinator. **Description:** A St. Louis general practice law firm. **Employees:** 200. **Common positions:** Attorney. **Benefits:** medical and life insurance; pension plan; disability coverage.

BRYAN AND CAVE
211 North Broadway, Suite 3600, One Metropolitan Square, St. Louis MO 63102-2750. 314/259-2000. **Contact:** Jean Belford, Personnel Manager. **Description:** A St. Louis legal services firm. **Employees:** 200.

GREENSFELDER, HEMKER, AND GALE
10 South Broadway, Suite 1800, St. Louis MO 63102. 314/241-9090. **Contact:** Sarah Allen, Personnel Director. **Description:** A St. Louis legal services firm. **Employees:** 100+.

Small to medium sized employers: 50-249

LEGAL SERVICES

Coburn Croft & Putzell
1 Mercantile Ctr, St. Louis MO 63101-1643. 314/621-8575. Employs: 100-249.

Husch & Eppenberger
100 N Broadway, St. Louis MO 63102-2728. 314/421-4800. Employs: 100-249.

Lashly & Baer
714 Locust, St. Louis MO 63101. 314/621-2939. Employs: 100-249.

Lewis Rice & Fingersh
611 Olive St, St. Louis MO 63101-1721. 314/444-7600. Employs: 100-249.

Martin Peper Jensen Maichel
720 Olive St, St. Louis MO 63101-2338. 314/421-3850. Employs: 50-99.

Moser & Marsalek
200 N Broadway, St. Louis MO 63102-2730. 314/421-5364. Employs: 50-99.

Stolar Partnership
911 Washington Ave, St. Louis MO 63101-1243. 314/231-2800. Employs: 100-249.

Ziercher & Hocker Pc
130 S Bemiston Ave, St. Louis MO 63105-1913. 314/727-5822. Employs: 50-99.

For more information on career opportunities in legal services:

Associations

AMERICAN BAR ASSOCIATION
North Lake Shore Drive, Chicago IL 60611. 312/988-5000.

FEDERAL BAR ASSOCIATION
1815 H. Street NW, Suite 408, Washington DC 20006. 202/638-0252.

NATIONAL ASSOCIATION FOR LAW PLACEMENT
1666 Connecticut Avenue, Suite 450, Washington DC 20009. 202/667-1666.

NATIONAL ASSOCIATION OF LEGAL ASSISTANTS
1601 South Main Street, Suite 300, Tulsa OK 74119. 918/587-6828.

NATIONAL FEDERATION OF PARALEGAL ASSOCIATIONS
P.O. Box 33108, Kansas City MO 64114-0108. 816/941-4000.

NATIONAL PARALEGAL ASSOCIATION
P.O. Box 629, 6186 Honey Hollow Road, Doylestown PA 18901. 215/297-8333.

MANUFACTURING: MISCELLANEOUS CONSUMER

Because the consumer products industry is so diversified, industry outlooks depend more on specific product categories. Here's a sampling: <u>Soaps and Detergents</u>: One of the biggest trends in this category has been to move away from the environmentally damaging phosphates used in detergents. In fact, about 40 percent of the nation has banned phosphates altogether, instead using natural soaps made of tallow and tropical oils. Overall, employment in this area will be increasing. <u>Household Products</u>: The short-term prognosis depends on consumer confidence. Although disposable incomes have risen slightly, many consumers are replenishing savings and paying off debts instead of buying expensive new items. A recovery in housing and the aging baby-boom generation should contribute to the long-term health of this segment.

THE ABSORBENT COTTON COMPANY
DIVISION OF STERILE PRODUCTS CORPORATION
401 Marshall Road, Valley Park MO 63088. 314/225-5151. **Contact:** Jan Kelly, Personnel Assistant. **Description:** Engaged in the manufacture of consumer cotton products. **Employees:** 190. **Corporate headquarters:** This location.

AMERICAN TRADING & PRODUCTION CORP.
HAZEL DIVISION
1200 South Stafford Street, Washington MO 63090. 314/239-2781. **Contact:** Judy Reed, Personnel Director. **Description:** Manufactures vinyl and leather specialty-advertising items and county record binders.

THE BENJAMIN ANSEHL COMPANY
1555 Page Industrial Boulevard, St. Louis MO 63132. 314/429-4300. **Contact:** Kim McPherson, Personnel Assistant. **Description:** Manufacturers of toiletries and cosmetics. **Employees:** 100.

AUTOMATION INTERNATIONAL, INC.
1020 Balils Street, Danville IL 61832. 217/446-9500. **Contact:** Verna M. Quick, Human Resources Manager. **Description:** Newly founded in July, 1991, Automation International is engaged in the production of custom designed resistance and arc welding equipment. **Common positions:** Customer Service Representative; Electrical Engineer; Mechanical Engineer; Sales Representative. **Educational backgrounds sought:** Business Administration; Engineering. **Special programs:** Training programs. **Benefits:** medical insurance; dental insurance; life insurance; tuition assistance. **Corporate headquarters:** Walcott, IA. **Parent company:** Titan Wheel, Inc. **Operations at this facility:**

manufacturing; research and development; administration; service; sales. **Employees:** 42. **Projected hires for the next 12 months:** 25.

BARNHART INDUSTRIES INC.
P.O. Box 278, Barnhart MO 63012. 314/942-3133. **Contact:** Kerry Clack, Vice President. **Description:** Manufacturers of a wide variety of items, including feminine hygiene products, garters, elastic notions, sewing accessories, surgical garments, hospital accessories, advertising novelties, and orthodontic appliances. **Employees:** 100.

BARRY-WEHMILLER COMPANY
8020 Forsyth Boulevard, Clayton MO 63105. 314/862-8000. **Contact:** Terry McBride, Administrative Assistant. **Description:** Manufacturers of food processing equipment. **Employees:** 400.

BEALL MANUFACTURING DIVISION/ VARLEN CORP.
P.O. Box 70, East Alton IL 62024. 618/259-8154. **Contact:** Scott Patsaros, Personnel. **Description:** Manufacturers of spring lock washers, agriculture implement parts, leaf spring steel items, flat washers. **Employees:** 100.

BECKITT & COLEMAN
30 Arrowhead Industrial Boulevard, St. Peters MO 63376. 314/278-5211. **Contact:** Cindy Lapinski, Human Resources Director. **Description:** Engaged in the manufacture of a variety of nationally-marketed detergents and air fresheners. **Employees:** 100.

BELL SPORTS
East Highway 136, Rantoul IL 61866. 217/893-9300. **Contact:** Director of Human Resources. **Description:** Manufactures safety helmets and other safety equipment. **Common positions:** Accountant; Buyer; Computer Programmer; Mechanical Engineer; Financial Analyst; Operations/Production Manager; Purchasing Agent; Systems Analyst. **Educational backgrounds sought:** Accounting; Business Administration; Computer Science Engineering. **Special programs:** Training programs; internships. **Benefits:** medical, dental, and life insurance; tuition assistance; disability coverage; employee discounts; savings plan; 401K. **Corporate headquarters:** This location. **Other U.S. locations:** Norwalk, CA, Providence, RI. **Operations at this facility:** Manufacturing. **Revenues (1991):** $65 million. **Employees:** 625. **Projected hires for the next 12 months:** 20.

CPI CORP.
1706 Washington Avenue, St. Louis MO 63103. 314/231-1575. **Contact:** Employment Manager. **Description:** A company engaged in a variety of consumer products and services including portrait photography, one-hour photofinishing and electronic publishing. **Common positions:** Accountant; Advertising Worker; Computer Programmer; Marketing Specialist. **Educational backgrounds sought:** Accounting; Business Administration; Computer Science; Marketing. **Benefits:** medical, dental and life insurance; pension plan; tuition assistance; disability coverage; profit sharing; employee discounts; savings plan. **Corporate headquarters:** This location. **Operations at this facility:** manufacturing; administration. **Listed on:** New York Stock Exchange.

Revenues (1991): $414 million. **Employees:** 1,000. **Projected hires for the next 12 months:** 30.

CENTRAL COUNTER COMPANY
6260 North Broadway Street, St. Louis MO 63147. 314/385-6322. **Contact:** Charles Van Nest, Personnel Director. **Description:** Manufacturers of shoe counters and shanks. **Employees:** 100.

CENTRAL MICROFILM SERVICE
DIVISION OF BUSINESS PRODUCTS CENTER
1601 Washington Avenue, St. Louis MO 63103. 314/436-2800. **Contact:** Personnel Department. **Description:** A manufacturer of microfilm equipment and supplies. Also engaged in reproducing and developing microfilm. **Employees:** 200.

COIN ACCEPTORS INC.
300 Hunter Avenue, St. Louis MO 63124. 314/725-0100. **Contact:** Personnel Department. **Description:** Manufacturers of coin mechanisms for vending machines. **Employees:** 200.

CONTICO INTERNATIONAL, INC.
1129 Warson Road, St. Louis MO 63132. 314/997-2160. **Contact:** Sharon Duey, V.P. Human Resources. **Description:** A manufacturer of plastic, metal and chemical products for the industrial, consumer, and automotive markets. Headquartered in St. Louis, MO with offices and plants in El Paso, TX, Juarez, Mexico, Houston, TX, Los Angeles, CA, and the United Kingdom. **Common positions:** Accountant; Administrator; Advertising Worker; Blue Collar Worker Supervisor; Buyer; Chemist; Claim Representative; Computer Programmer; Credit Manager; Customer Service Representative; Draftsperson; Chemical Engineer; Electrical Engineer; Industrial Engineer; Mechanical Engineer; Metallurgical Engineer; Financial Analyst; Industrial Designer; Branch Manager; Department Manager; General Manager; Management Trainee; Operations/Production Manager; Personnel and Labor Relations Specialist; Purchasing Agent; Quality Control Supervisor; Sales Representative; Statistician; Transportation and Traffic Specialist. **Educational backgrounds sought:** Accounting; Business Administration; Chemistry; Communications; Engineering; Finance; Marketing; Mathematics. **Benefits:** medical, dental and life insurance; pension plan; disability coverage; profit sharing; employee discounts; savings plan. **Corporate headquarters:** This location. **Operations at this facility:** manufacturing; research and development; administration; service; sales.

THE DIAL CORPORATION
6901 McKissock Avenue, St. Louis MO 63147. 314/382-8535. **Contact:** Carol Croft, Employment and Training Manager. **Description:** Well-known manufacturers of soap, bleach and detergent washing compounds, household ammonia, and plastic containers. **Common positions:** Accountant; Blue-Collar Worker Supervisor; Buyer; Draftsperson; Electrical Engineer; Industrial Engineer; Mechanical Engineer; Industrial Manager; Department Manager; General Manager; Operations/Production Manager; Personnel and Labor Relations Specialist; Purchasing Agent; Quality Control Supervisor; Sales Representative; Systems Analyst; Transportation and Traffic Specialist.

Educational backgrounds sought: Accounting; Business Administration; Chemistry; Computer Science; Engineering. **Special programs:** Training programs and internships. **Benefits:** medical, dental, and life insurance; pension plan; tuition assistance; disability coverage; profit sharing; employee discounts; savings plan. **Corporate headquarters:** Phoenix AZ. **Parent company:** The Greyhound/Dial Corporation. **Operations at this facility:** manufacturing; administration; sales. **Listed on:** New York Stock Exchange.

DUKE MANUFACTURING COMPANY
2305 North Broadway, St. Louis MO 63102. 314/231-1130. **Contact:** Ms. Frances Milliere, Personnel Director. **Description:** Manufacturers of commercial food service equipment. **Employees:** 100.

EMPIRE STOVE COMPANY
918 Freeburg Avenue, P.O. Box 529, Belleville IL 62222. 618/233-7420. **Contact:** Betty Senulis, Personnel Director. **Description:** Manufacturers of gas heating appliances. **Employees:** 100.

FALCON PRODUCTS INC.
9387 Dielman Industrial Drive, St. Louis MO 63132. 314/991-9200. **Contact:** John Becker, Personnel Director. **Description:** Manufacturers of table bases, table tops (laminated, folding, fiberglass) metal and wood chairs, plastic shell chairs and restaurant booths. **Employees:** 100.

HAGER HINGE COMPANY
139 Victor Street, St. Louis MO 63104. 314/772-4400. **Contact:** Blake Earnest, Human Resources Director. **Description:** A manufacturer and wholesaler of building hardware.

HARVARD INTERIORS MANUFACTURING CO.
HARVARD INDUSTRIES INC.
4321 Semple Avenue, St. Louis MO 63120. 314/382-5590. **Contact:** Tom Barry, Personnel Director. **Description:** Manufacture office furniture, dormitory furniture, electric bed controls, and electronic assemblies.

HIGHLAND SUPPLY CORPORATION
1111 6th Street, Highland IL 62249. 618/654-2161. **Contact:** Personnel. **Description:** Manufacture foils, polypropolene film, cellophane and film bags (printed and plain). **Common positions:** Accountant; Chemist; Computer Programmer; Mechanical Engineer; General Manager; Operations/Production Manager; Quality Control Supervisor; Sales Representative. **Educational backgrounds sought:** Accounting; Business Administration; Chemistry; Computer Science; Engineering; Marketing. **Benefits:** medical insurance; life insurance; tuition assistance. **Corporate headquarters:** This location. **Operations at this facility:** manufacturing; administration; sales.

HOME NURSERY GREENHOUSES INC.
P.O. Box 307, Edwardsville IL 62025. 618/656-1790. **Contact:** Carol Balke, Personnel Director. **Description:** A nursery engaged in the wholesale and retail sales of lawn and garden supplies.

JACKES-EVAN MANUFACTURING COMPANY
4427 Geraldine Avenue, St. Louis MO 63115. 314/385-4132. **Contact:** Tom Tracy, Personnel Manager. **Description:** Manufacturers of stove pipe, barbecue accessories, fireplace accessories, and galvanized wire.

JAKEL INCORPORATED
400 Broadway, Highland IL 62249. 618/654-2371. **Contact:** Human Resources. **Description:** Manufacture sub-fractional horse power electric motors.

LEE-ROWAN COMPANY
6333 Etzel Avenue, St. Louis MO 63133. 314/721-3363. **Contact:** Jill Bogner, Personnel Department. **Description:** Manufacture wood, plastic and metal closet accessories; bath accessories.

LEGGETT & PLATT, INC.
1 Leggett Road, Carthage MO 64836. 417/358-8131. **Contact:** Valerie Glaze, Employment/Compensation Coordinator. **Description:** Leggett & Platt specializes in manufacturing and marketing a broad line of components used by companies making furniture and bedding for homes, offices and institutions. Other home furnishings products include a select line of finished furniture and carpet cushioning materials. **Corporate headquarters:** This location. **Listed on:** Pacific Stock Exchange. **Listed on:** New York Stock Exchange. **Common positions:** Accountant; Administrator; Advertising Worker; Attorney; Commercial Artist; Computer Programmer; Credit Manager; Department Manager; Operations/Production Manager; Marketing Specialist; Personnel and Labor Relations Specialist; Public Relations Specialist; Purchasing Agent; Sales Representative; Systems Analyst; Transportation and Traffic Specialist. **Educational backgrounds sought:** Accounting; Business Administration; Computer Science; Finance; Marketing. **Benefits:** Medical Insurance; Pension Plan; Tuition Assistance; Disability Coverage; Stock Plans. **Corporate headquarters:** This location. **Other U.S. locations:** 100+ facilities in the United States and Canada. **Listed on:** New York Stock Exchange. **Employees:** 11,000.

JOSEPH LIPIC PEN COMPANY
2200 Gravois Avenue, St. Louis MO 63104. 314/664-2111. **Contact:** Wayne Hoover, Personnel Director. **Description:** Manufacture advertising specials, pens and pencils and desk sets.

LOWELL MANUFACTURING COMPANY
100 Integram Drive, Pacific MO 63069. 314/257-3400. **Contact:** Dorothy H. Lowell, President. **Description:** Manufacture loud speaker baffles and accessories. **Common positions:** Blue-Collar Worker Supervisor; Electrical Engineer; Operations/Production Manager; Purchasing Agent. **Educational backgrounds sought:** Engineering; Marketing. **Benefits:** medical insurance; pension plan. **Corporate headquarters:** This location. **Operations at this facility:** manufacturing; research and development; administration; service; sales. **Employees:** 77. **Projected hires for the next 12 months:** 12.

MARSH COMPANY
707 East B Street, Belleville IL 62222. 618/234-1122. **Contact:** Fred Drayer, Director, Human Resources. **Description:** A St. Louis-area company engaged in

the manufacture of microprocessor controlled and mechanical marking, coding, and packing equipment for industrial use. **Common positions:** Buyer; Chemist; Computer Programmer; Customer Service Representative; Draftsperson; Electrical Engineer; Mechanical Engineer; Sales Representative. **Educational backgrounds sought:** Chemistry; Computer Science; Engineering; Marketing. **Special programs:** Training programs and internships. **Benefits:** medical insurance; dental insurance; life insurance; tuition assistance; disability coverage; savings plan. **Corporate headquarters:** This location. **Operations at this facility:** manufacturing; research and development; administration; sales.

MARTIN INDUSTRIES
4200 St. Clair Avenue, Washington Park IL 62204. 618/271-1272. **Contact:** Rita Enskat, Personnel Director. **Description:** Manufacture heat stoves (wood and gas), gas fired incinerators.

NATIONAL LOCK CORPORATION
104 Keystone Drive, Sikeston MO 63801. 314/472-0220. **Contact:** Tammy Byrd, Personnel Director. **Description:** A manufacturer of residential door locks. **Operations at this facility:** manufacturing. **Corporate headquarters:** Lancaster, OH. **Common positions:** Accountant; Blue-Collar Worker Supervisor; Buyer; Credit Manager; Customer Service Representative; Draftsperson; Industrial Engineer; Mechanical Engineer; General Manager; Marketing Specialist; Personnel and Labor Relations Specialist; Purchasing Agent; Quality Control Supervisor. **Educational backgrounds sought:** Accounting; Business Administration; Computer Science; Engineering; Marketing. **Benefits:** medical insurance; pension plan; life insurance; tuition assistance; disability coverage; employee discounts; savings plan.

NIXDORFF KREIN INDUSTRIES INC.
P.O. Box 419050, St. Louis MO 63141. 314/872-8500. **Contact:** Personnel Department. **Description:** A St. Louis company engaged in the manufacture of athletic equipment.

OLIN CORPORATION/
BRASS AND WINCHESTER GROUPS
427 North Shamrock Street, East Alton IL 62024. 618/258-2909. **Contact:** Mr. Lee Schnieder, Personnel. **Description:** A St. Louis company engaged in the manufacture of commercial and military ammunition; ramset powder activated fastening systems; copper and alloy sheet and strip, stamped and drawn parts and clad metals.

RITEPOINT CORPORATION/
DIVISION OF PENN CORPORATION
1733 Gilsinn Lane, Fenton MO 63026. 314/343-4400. **Contact:** Karen Shore, Personnel Director. **Description:** A division of the well-known manufacturer of a variety of mechanical pencils, marking pens, ball point pens, and plastic specialties.

ROADMASTER CORPORATION
P.O. Box 344, Olney IL 62450. 618/393-2991. **Contact:** Carol Rennier, Personnel Supervisor. **Description:** Manufactures bicycles, tricycles, and junior riding products for children; and fitness equipment. Other facility sites in Tyler,

Texas and Delavan, Wisconsin. **Common positions:** Accountant; Blue-Collar Worker Supervisor; Buyer; Chemist; Computer Programmer; Credit Manager; Customer Service Representative; Draftsperson; Industrial Engineer; Mechanical Engineer; Financial Analyst; Department Manager; Operations/Production Manager; Purchasing Agent; Quality Control Supervisor; Sales Representative; Systems Analyst; Technical Writer/Editor; Transporation and Traffic Specialist; Industrial Designer. **Educational backgrounds sought:** Accounting; Art/Design; Business Administration; Engineering; Finance; Marketing; Industrial Technology. **Benefits:** medical insurance; life insurance; tuition assistance; disability coverage; employee discounts. **Corporate headquarters:** This location. **Operations at this facility:** manufacturing; quality administration; service; sales; accounting; marketing. **Listed on:** NASDAQ.

SWING-A-WAY MANUFACTURING COMPANY
4100 Beck Avenue, St. Louis MO 63116. 314/773-1487. **Contact:** Joyce Crook, Personnel. **Description:** Manufacturers of a variety of consumer items, including can openers, ice crushers, and jar openers.

TARACORP INDUSTRIES
1200 16th Street, Granite City IL 62040. 618/451-4400. **Contact:** Carla R. Jones, Personnel Administrator. **Description:** Manufactures and sells lead products. **Common positions:** Accountant; Administrator; Blue-Collar Worker Supervisor; Buyer; Chemist; Claim Representative; Customer Service Representative; Engineer; Industrial Engineer; Purchasing Agent; Quality Control Supervisor; Transportation and Traffic Specialist. Currently in a hiring freeze. **Educational backgrounds sought:** Accounting; Chemistry; Engineering. **Benefits:** medical insurance; pension plan; life insurance; disability coverage; profit sharing. Divisional headquarters location. **Corporate headquarters:** Atlanta, GA. **Operations at this facility:** manufacturing; sales.

THOMPSON & MITCHELL
One Mercantile Center, Suite 3400, St. Louis MO 63101. 314/231-7676, ex. 1363. **Contact:** Tracey Allen, Personnel Assistant. **Description:** A corporate legal services company. **Common positions:** Accountant; Attorney; Computer Programmer; Instructor/Trainer; Department Manager; Personnel and Labor Relations Specialist; Public Relations Specialist; Paralegal; Legal Secretary; Mailroom. **Educational backgrounds sought:** Computer Science; Economics; Finance; Liberal Arts. **Special programs:** Training programs and internships. **Benefits:** medical insurance; pension plan; life insurance; disability coverage; profit sharing; employee discounts; pre-tax options. **Corporate headquarters:** This location. **Operations at this facility:** administration; legal services. **Employees:** 431. **Projected hires for the next 12 months:** 35.

WELSH COMPANY
1535 South 8th Street, St. Louis MO 63104. 314/231-8822. **Contact:** Mark Thompson, Accounting. **Description:** A manufacturer of a variety of consumer items, including baby carriages, beds, strollers, seats, and baby swings.

WICKS ORGAN COMPANY
1100 Fifth Street, Highland IL 62249. 618/654-2191. **Contact:** Martin Wick, President. **Description:** A manufacturer of church pipe organs.

WILLERT HOME PRODUCTS INC.
4044 Park Avenue, St. Louis MO 63110. 314/772-2822. **Contact:** Phil Wells, Personnel Director. **Description:** A consumer products manufacturer specializing in the production of such items as household deodorants, moth preventatives, plastic ash trays, and potpourri products. **Common positions:** Accountant; Chemist; Customer Service Representative; Marketing Specialist; Personnel and Labor Relations Specialist. **Educational backgrounds sought:** Accounting; Marketing. **Benefits:** medical insurance; life insurance; disability coverage; profit sharing; employee discounts. **Corporate headquarters:** This location. **Employees:** 300+.

Additional large employers: 250+

WOOD HOUSEHOLD FURNITURE, EXCEPT UPHOLSTERED

Charleswood Corp
305-E S 1st St, Wright City MO 63390. 314/745-3351. Employs: 250-499.

Gusdorf Corp
11440 Lackland Rd, St. Louis MO 63146-3523. 314/567-5249. Employs: 500-999.

Interco Inc
101 S Hanley Rd, St. Louis MO 63105-3406. 314/863-1100. Employs: 1,000+.

OFFICE FURNITURE, EXCEPT WOOD

Esselte Pendaflex Corp
W Park Rd, Union MO 63084. 314/583-4400. Employs: 250-499.

SOAP AND OTHER DETERGENTS, EXCEPT SPECIALTY CLEANERS

Procter & Gamble Mfg Co
169 E Grand Ave, St. Louis MO 63147-3213. 314/622-8200. Employs: 250-499.

SPECIALTY CLEANING, POLISHING AND SANITATION PREPARATIONS

Calgon Vestal Laboratories
7501 Page Ave, St. Louis MO 63133-1031. 314/535-1810. Employs: 500-999.

SPORTING AND ATHLETIC GOODS

American Recreation Prdts Inc
1224 Fern Ridge Pkwy, St. Louis MO 63141-4451. 314/576-8000. Employs: 250-499.

Rawlings Sporting Goods Co
1859 Intertech Dr, Fenton MO 63026-1926. 314/349-3500. Employs: 1,000+.

MARKING DEVICES

Marsh Company
707 E "B" St, Belleville IL 62220-4065. 618/234-1122. Employs: 250-499.

LINOLEUM, ASPHALTED-FELT-BASE AND OTHER HARD SURFACE FLOOR COVERINGS

Lowy Enterprises
4001 N King Hwy, St. Louis MO 63115. 314/383-2055. Employs: 250-499.

Additional small to medium sized employers: 50-249

WOOD HOUSEHOLD FURNITURE, EXCEPT UPHOLSTERED

Berco Inds Inc
1120 Montrose Ave, St. Louis MO 63104-1828. 314/772-4700. Employs: 50-99.

Gerber Inds Inc
1 Gerber Indl Dr, Saint Peters MO 63376. 314/278-5710. Employs: 50-99.

WOOD HOUSEHOLD FURNITURE, UPHOLSTERED

Contour Chair Lounge Co/Plt 1
5200 Virginia Ave, St. Louis MO 63111-1946. 314/352-8300. Employs: 100-249.

METAL HOUSEHOLD FURNITURE

Fredman Bros
6000 Goodfellow Ave, St. Louis MO 63147-1207. 314/382-6007. Employs: 50-99.

MATTRESSES, FOUNDATIONS AND CONVERTIBLE BEDS

Serta Midwest
1819 S Hanley Rd, St. Louis MO 63144-2911. 314/647-5200. Employs: 50-99.

WOOD OFFICE FURNITURE

EAC Corporation
347 N Lindbergh Blvd, St. Louis MO 63141-7811. 314/993-8100. Employs: 100-249.

OFFICE FURNITURE, EXCEPT WOOD

Orna-Metal Inc
12th & Stafford Sts, Washington MO 63090. 314/239-7867. Employs: 50-99.

PUBLIC BUILDING AND RELATED FURNITURE

B & M Of Illinois Inc
R R 1 Box 711, Carlyle IL 62231-9511. 618/594-4091. Employs: 100-249.

Huntco Healthcare Inc
1180 Central Indl Ave, St. Louis MO 63110. 314/771-7145. Employs: 50-99.

Integram St Louis Seating
1000 Integram Dr, Pacific MO 63069. 314/257-5511. Employs: 100-249.

WOOD OFFICE AND STORE FIXTURES, PARTITIONS, SHELVING AND LOCKERS

Loughman Cabinet Co
5151 Mattis Rd, St. Louis MO 63128-2775. 314/428-0321. Employs: 50-99.

Midwest Woodworking/Fixture Co
11634 Gravois Rd, St. Louis MO 63126-3014. 314/843-3001. Employs: 50-99.

OFFICE AND STORE FIXTURES, PARTITIONS, SHELVING AND LOCKERS, EXCEPT WOOD

Allied Fixtures
2344 Grissom Dr, St. Louis MO 63146-3311. 314/997-7800. Employs: 50-99.

Multiplex Display Fixture Co
1555 Larkin Williams Road, Fenton MO 63026-3008. 314/343-5700. Employs: 50-99.

Porta-Fab Corp
18080 Chesterfield Airport Rd, Chesterfield MO 63005-1105. 314/537-5555. Employs: 50-99.

Shure Mfg Corp
1601 S Hanley Rd, St. Louis MO 63144-2907. 314/781-2505. Employs: 100-249.

Tiffany Industries Inc
1015 Corporate Sq Dr, St. Louis MO 63132-2926. 314/991-1700. Employs: 100-249.

DRAPERY HARDWARE AND WINDOW BLINDS AND SHADES

Sunshine Drapery Co Inc
11660 Page Svc Rd, St. Louis MO 63146. 314/569-2980. Employs: 50-99.

FURNITURE AND FIXTURES

Spartan Showcase Inc
W Park Rd, Union MO 63084. 314/583-4050. Employs: 100-249.

Vitro Prdts Inc
201 Madison St, St. Louis MO 63102-1329. 314/241-2265. Employs: 50-99.

SOAP AND OTHER DETERGENTS, EXCEPT SPECIALTY CLEANERS

Chemsico Inc
8494 Chapin Indl Dr, St. Louis MO 63114. 314/427-4886. Employs: 100-249.

Navy Brand Mfg Inc
5111 Southwest Ave, St. Louis MO 63110-3429. 314/865-5500. Employs: 50-99.

SPECIALTY CLEANING, POLISHING AND SANITATION PREPARATIONS

Monsanto/Wesport Plt
2381 Centerline Indl Dr, St. Louis MO 63146. 314/997-8600. Employs: 50-99.

Peck's Products Co
610 E Clarence Ave, St. Louis MO 63147-3020. 314/385-5454. Employs: 50-99.

Reckitt & Colman Inc
30 Arrowhead Indl Blvd, Saint Peters MO 63376. 314/278-5211. Employs: 100-249.

PERFUMES, COSMETICS AND OTHER TOILET PREPARATIONS

Benjamin Ansehl Co
1555 Page Ind Blvd, St. Louis MO 63132-1309. 314/429-4300. Employs: 100-249.

Vi Jon Labs Inc
6300 Etzel Ave, St. Louis MO 63133-1904. 314/721-2990. Employs: 100-249.

MUSICAL INSTRUMENTS

Wicks Organ Co
1100 5th St, Highland IL 62249-1270. 618/654-2191. Employs: 100-249.

GAMES, TOYS AND CHILDREN'S VEHICLES, EXCEPT DOLLS AND BICYCLES

Shreddi-Mix
501 N Market, Brighton IL 62012. 618/372-3432. Employs: 50-99.

SPORTING AND ATHLETIC GOODS

American Recreation Prdts Inc
502 Orchard St, New Haven MO 63068-9781. 314/237-4200. Employs: 100-249.

Gared Sports
1107 Mullanphy St, St. Louis MO 63106-4334. 314/421-0044. Employs: 50-99.

Nixdorff Krein Industries Inc
P O Box 27479, St. Louis MO 63141. 314/872-8500. Employs: 50-99.

P C A Industries Inc
5642 Natural Bridge Ave, St. Louis MO 63120-1628. 314/389-4140. Employs: 50-99.

Schutt Mfg Co Inc
610 S Indl Dr, Litchfield IL 62056. 217/324-3978. Employs: 50-99.

PENS, MECHANICAL PENCILS AND PARTS

Ritepoint
1733 Gilsinn Ln, Fenton MO 63026-2000. 314/343-4400. Employs: 100-249.

MARKING DEVICES

Cosco Graphics
11548 Adie Rd, Maryland Hts MO 63043-3508. 314/872-9181. Employs: 50-99.

BROOMS AND BRUSHES

S M Arnold Inc
7901 Michigan, St. Louis MO 63111-3504. 314/544-4103. Employs: 50-99.

SIGNS AND ADVERTISING SPECIALTIES

Gannett Outdoor Group
6767 N Hanley Rd, St. Louis MO 63134-1013. 314/524-0800. Employs: 50-99.

Jos Lipic Pen Co
2200 Gravols Ave, St. Louis MO 63104-2848. 314/664-2111. Employs: 100-249.

Magnet Inc
4 Wayne Ave, Washington MO 63090. 314/239-5661. Employs: 100-249.

Nevco Scoreboard Co
301 E Harris Ave, Greenville IL 62246-2151. 618/664-0360. Employs: 50-99.

Quick Point Inc
1717 Fenpark Dr, Fenton MO 63026-2919. 314/343-9400. Employs: 50-99.

Signet Graphic Prdts Inc
10751 Midwest Indl Blvd, St. Louis MO 63132. 314/426-0200. Employs: 50-99.

U S Display Co
Main St, Hawk Point MO 63349. 314/338-9211. Employs: 50-99.

Universal Display Corp
4540 Swan Ave, St. Louis MO 63110-2132. 314/652-9050. Employs: 50-99.

MANUFACTURING INDUSTRIES

Janco Design
555 N New Ballis, St. Louis MO 63141-6825. 314/993-1332. Employs: 50-99.

Koken Manufacturing Co Inc
1631 Dr Martin Luther King Dr, St. Louis MO 63106-3720. 314/231-7383. Employs: 100-249.

For more information on career opportunities in consumer manufacturing:

Associations

ASSOCIATION OF HOME APPLIANCE MANUFACTURERS
20 North Wacker Drive, Chicago IL 60606. 312/984-5800.

NATIONAL ASSOCIATION OF MANUFACTURERS
1331 Pennsylvania Avenue, NW, Suite 1500, Washington DC 20004. 202/637-3000.

NATIONAL HOUSEWARES MANUFACTURERS ASSOCIATION
6400 Schafer Court, Suite 650, Rosemont IL 60018. 708/292-4200.

ASSOCIATION FOR MANUFACTURING TECHNOLOGY
7901 Westpark Drive, McLean VA 22102. 703/893-2900.

SOAP AND DETERGENT ASSOCIATION
475 Park Avenue South, New York NY 10016. 212/725-1262.

Directories

APPLIANCE MANUFACTURER ANNUAL DIRECTORY
Corcoran Communications, Inc., 29100 Aurora Road, Suite 200, Solon OH 44139. 216/349-3060.

HOUSEHOLD AND PERSONAL PRODUCTS INDUSTRY BUYERS GUIDE
Rodman Publishing Group, 17 South Franklin Turnpike, Ramsey NJ 07446. 201/825-2552.

Magazines

APPLIANCE
1110 Jorie Boulevard, Oak Brook IL 60522-9019. 708/990-3484.

COSMETICS INSIDERS REPORT
Advanstar Communications, 7500 Old Oak Boulevard, Cleveland OH 44130. 216/243-8100.

HOUSEWARES
Harcourt Brace Jovanovich, 1 East First Street, Duluth MN 55802. 714/231-6616.

MANUFACTURING: MISCELLANEOUS INDUSTRIAL

Trend to watch for: In the machinery manufacturing segment, many of the biggest company names will continue to disappear due to mergers and buy outs. While hundreds of U.S. companies still make machine tools, materials handling equipment, and compressors for American factories, the fastest-growing machinery markets are now overseas. This means that U.S. firms will have to build overseas presences just to survive. In fact, foreign orders for a number of American-made tools remain strong.

Although mergers are often followed by layoffs, workers who survive these cuts should be better positioned for the long-term. Many manufacturers are giving workers a much greater degree of across-the-board involvement, with team-based product management allowing individual workers to gain training in a number of different job functions.

ALLIED AFTERMARKET
1200 East Highland, Nevada MO 64772. 417/667-3051. **Contact:** Personnel Director. **Description:** Manufactures heavy-duty air and fuel filters. Parent company, Allied Signal Corporation, serves a broad spectrum of industries through its more than 40 strategic businesses, which are grouped into five sectors: Aerospace; Automotive; Chemical; Industrial and Technology; and Oil and Gas. Allied Signal is one of the nation's largest industrial organizations, and has 115,000 employees in over 30 countries. **Corporate headquarters:** Morristown, NJ.

ALVEY INC.
9301 Olive Boulevard, St. Louis MO 63132. 314/993-4700. **Contact:** Bob Schafer, Personnel Director. **Description:** Manufacturers of conveyors of various types including gravity conveyors belt and live roller conveyors, apron conveyors, chain conveyors, complete automated conveyor systems, pallet loaders, depalletizers, pallet-dispensing units, and related equipment. **Employees:** 400.

CENTRIFUGAL AND MECHANICAL INDUSTRIES INC.
146 President Street, St. Louis MO 63118. 314/776-2848. **Contact:** Ken Geldmacher, Personnel Director. **Description:** Manufacturers of continuous centrifugal dryers, clarifiers and chip wringers; custom machine shop work. **Employees:** 100.

COURION INDUSTRIES INC.
SECURITY FIRE DOOR DIVISION
3044 Lambdin Avenue, St. Louis MO 63115. 314/533-5700. **Contact:** Kevin O'Meara, General Manager. **Description:** Manufacturers of freight elevator doors, material dumbwaiter systems, detention windows, fire doors and electrical operators. **Employees:** 100.

CRANE NATIONAL VENDORS
12955 Enterprise Way, Bridgeton MO 63044. 314/298-3500. **Contact:** Edwin J. Barutio, Vice President/Human Resources. **Description:** A St. Louis company engaged in the manufacture of vending machines, currency products and contract manufacturing. **Common positions:** Accountant; Buyer; Credit Manager; Draftsperson; Electrical Engineer; Industrial Engineer; Mechanical Engineer; Operations/Production Manager; Personnel and Labor Relations Specialist; Purchasing Agent; Quality Assurance Manager; Systems Analyst; Technical Writer/Editor. **Educational backgrounds sought:** Accounting; Business Administration; Computer Science; Engineering; Liberal Arts. **Benefits:** medical insurance; dental insurance; life insurance; pension plan; tuition assistance; disability coverage; savings plan. **Corporate headquarters:** Stamford, CT. **Parent company:** Crane Co. **Operations at this facility:** manufacturing; research and development; administration; service; sales. **Listed on:** New York Stock Exchange. **Revenues (1991):** $125 million. **Employees:** 700. **Projected hires for the next 12 months:** 30.

CUMMINS GATEWAY
7210 Hall Street, St. Louis MO 63147. 314/389-5400. **Contact:** John Wagner, President. **Description:** A Missouri company specializing in the sale and service of diesel engines. **Employees:** 100+.

CURTIS-TOLEDO-A WYLE COMPANY
1905 Kienlen Avenue, St. Louis MO 63133. 314/383-1300. **Contact:** Personnel Department. **Description:** A manufacturer of machinery, specializing in the production of air compressors, clutch discs, pipe threading machines and hand tools. **Employees:** 100.

DIEMAKERS, INC.
P.O. Box 278, Monroe City MO 63456. **Contact:** Personnel Manager. **Description:** A supplier of zinc, aluminum, and magnesium diecastings to world-wide markets. Primary customers include the automotive industry, and hand-tool and computer manufacturers. Other services include complete in-house diemaking; advanced product development; engineering support; and die design. **Corporate headquarters:** This location. **Common positions:** Accountant; Blue-Collar Worker Supervisor; Buyer; Computer Programmer; Draftsperson; Electrical Engineer; Industrial Engineer; Mechanical Engineer; Metallurgical Engineer; Operations/ Production Manager; Purchasing Agent; Quality Control Supervisor; Sales Representative; Tool and Diemaker; CAD Operator. **Benefits:** medical insurance; dental insurance; life insurance; tuition assistance; profit sharing; savings plan. **Corporate headquarters:** This location. **Other U.S. locations:** Palmyra, MO. **Parent company:** Kanematsu, U.S.A. **Operations at this facility:** Manufacturing; Administration; Sales. **Employees:** 760. **Projected hires for the next 12 months:** 20-30. **Educational**

backgrounds sought: Business Administration; Computer Science; Engineering; Finance. **Special programs:** Training programs.

JOHN FABICK TRACTOR COMPANY
#1 Fabick Drive, Fenton MO 63026. 314/343-5900. **Contact:** Cindy Kleekamp, Personnel Director. **Description:** Sales and service of caterpillar products-diesel engines, electric generator sets, road construction and earth moving equipment, mining equipment, materials handling equipment, and oil and gas pipelining equipment. **Employees:** 200.

FERGUSON MACHINE COMPANY/
DIVISION OF UMC INDUSTRIES INC.
11820 Lackland Road, St. Louis MO 63146. 314/567-3200. **Contact:** Tom Schreiber, Personnel Director. **Description:** A St. Louis manufacturer of special machinery. **Employees:** 100.

T.J. GUNDLACH MACHINE COMPANY
1 Freedom Drive, P.O. Box 385, Belleville IL 62222. 618/233-7208. **Contact:** T.E. Dinges, Vice President, Administration. **Description:** Engaged in the manufacture and sales of mining machinery and equipment.

HUSSMANN CORPORATION
DIVISION OF WHITMAN
12999 St. Charles Rock Road, Bridgeton MO 63044. 314/291-2000. **Contact:** Roger O'Neill, Manager of Industrial Relations. **Description:** Manufacturers of refrigerated display fixtures and cases, walk-in coolers, condensing units, shelving, checkouts, and refrigeration systems.

JEFFERSON PRODUCTS
P.O. Box 230, Washington MO 63090. 314/239-6524. **Contact:** Art Shelich, President/General Manager. **Description:** Manufactures air conditioning and refrigeration components, and valve parts.

KASCO CORPORATION
1569 Tower Grove Avenue, St. Louis MO 63110. 314/771-1550. **Contact:** Philip Zampogna, Human Resources Manager. **Description:** Manufacture and service meat cutting equipment. **Common positions:** Accountant; Administrator; Buyer; Computer Programmer; Credit Manager; Customer Service Representative; Draftsperson; Mechanical Engineer; Financial Analyst; Industrial Manager; Operations/Production Manager; Sales Representative. **Educational backgrounds sought:** Accounting; Business Administration; Communications; Computer Science; Engineering. **Special programs:** Training programs. **Benefits:** medical insurance; pension plan; life insurance; tuition assistance; disability coverage. **Corporate headquarters:** Maitland, FL. **Parent company:** Bairnco Corporation. **Operations at this facility:** divisional headquarters; manufacturing; research and development; administration; service; sales. **Listed on:** New York Stock Exchange.

KICKHAM BOILER & ENGINEERING COMPANY
625 East Carrie Avenue, St. Louis MO 63147. 314/261-4786. **Contact:** Personnel. **Description:** Manufacture and repair boiler shop worktanks, pressure vessels and welding plate fabrication.

LINCOLN
A PENTAIR COMPANY
One Lincoln Way, St. Louis MO 63120. 314/679-4200. **Contact:** Personnel. **Description:** Manufacture automotive, industrial, and agricultural lubricating equipment.

MARLO COIL NUCLEAR COOLING INC.
P.O. Box 171, High Ridge MO 63049. 314/677-6600. **Contact:** David Ault, President. **Description:** St. Louis-area manufacturers of component parts (cooling for ships and submarines), air handling equipment, cooling coils and steam coils for hospitals, schools and industry.

ORCHARD CORPORATION OF AMERICA
1154 Reco Avenue, St. Louis MO 63126. 314/822-3880. **Contact:** Mary Anna Schnieder, Personnel. **Description:** A St. Louis company engaged in the manufacture of gravure printing and coatings for laminite industries.

L.E. SAUER MACHINE COMPANY
3535 Tree Court Industrial, St. Louis MO 63122. 314/225-5358. **Contact:** Personnel Department. **Description:** Manufactures rotary die cutting equipment, scorers and associated parts for paper cutting.

SOUTHERN EQUIPMENT COMPANY
P.O. Box 7115, St. Louis MO 63116. 314/481-0660. **Contact:** Donna Cheevers, Personnel Director. Southern Equipment Company is located at 4550 Gustine Avenue, St. Louis MO 63116. **Description:** Manufactures of commercial and institutional food serving and handling equipment.

ST. LOUIS REFRIGERATOR CAR CO.
103 Cherokee Street, St. Louis MO 63118. 314/577-1700. **Contact:** Personnel Department. **Description:** A repair company specializing in work on all types of railroad cars.

STANDARD MACHINE & MANUFACTURING COMPANY
10014 Big Bend Boulevard, St. Louis MO 63122. 314/966-4500. **Contact:** Personnel Director. **Description:** An industrial manufacturer, specializing in the production of water, oil and air filters, refrigerant filters and valves, and industrial controls.

SUNNEN PRODUCTS COMPANY
7910 Manchester Avenue, St. Louis MO 63143. 314/781-2100. **Contact:** Jean Miller, Manager of Personnel Services. **Description:** Manufacturers of precision honing equipment and internal gauges, as well as a variety of automotive tools.

TEMPMASTER CORPORATION
2001 West Business 136 Highway, P.O. Box 267, Albany MO 64402. 816/726-3956. **Contact:** LaNell Beil, Director of Employee Relations. **Description:** A manufacturer of air conditioning and air handling products (commercial and industrial). **Corporate headquarters:** This location. **Operations at this facility:** manufacturing; research and development; administration; service; sales. **Common positions:** Accountant; Administrator; Blue-Collar Worker

Supervisor; Buyer; Computer Programmer; Customer Service Representative; Draftsperson; Engineer; Electrical Engineer; Industrial Engineer; Mechanical Engineer; Manager; Department Manager; Operations/Production Manager; Personnel and Labor Relations Specialist; Purchasing Agent; Quality Control Supervisor; Reporter/Editor; Systems Analyst; Technical Writer/Editor; Transportation and Traffic Specialist. **Educational backgrounds sought:** Accounting; Business Administration; Computer Science; Engineering. **Benefits:** medical, dental, and life insurance; pension plan; tuition assistance; disability coverage; profit sharing; savings plan.

TITANIUM RESEARCH & DEVELOPMENT COMPANY/ TRADCO
1701 West Main Street, Washington MO 63090. 314/239-7816. **Contact:** George Schrecengost, Vice President and General Manager. **Description:** Manufacturers and processors of titanium sheets; titanium hot forming, blanking, economy blanking dies; aircraft component parts and assemblies.

WESTERN SUPPLIES COMPANY
2920 Cass Avenue, St. Louis MO 63106. 314/531-0100. **Contact:** Jeffrey Altuater, Vice President. **Description:** Manufacturer of cutting dies and shoe machinery. Engaged in machine shop work specializing in dies and machinery for heat sealing thermoplastics.

WIESE PLANNING & ENGINEERING INC.
1445 Woodson Road, St. Louis MO 63132. 314/427-5200. **Contact:** Pat Luhman, Personnel Department. **Description:** A wholesaler of industrial machinery and equipment.

WILLIAMS PATENT CRUSHER & PULVERIZER COMPANY
813 Montgomery Street, St. Louis MO 63102. 314/621-3348. **Contact:** Randy Williams, Personnel Department. **Description:** Manufacturers of crushing and pulverizing equipment, air moving equipment, and material conveyors.

ZERO MANUFACTURING COMPANY
1 Cablecar Drive, Washington MO 63090. 314/239-0300. **Contact:** Personnel Department. **Description:** Manufacturers of blasting, peening, and finishing equipment; beverage and food tanks in stainless steel; refrigerated dairy farm bulk milk tanks in stainless steel; computerized feed management systems for dairy farms; and dairy farm milking machines.

Additional large employers: 250+

INTERNAL COMBUSTION ENGINES

Sierra
725 McKinley Ave, Litchfield IL 62056-2701. 217/324-9400.
Employs: 500-999.

INDUSTRIAL TRUCKS, TRACTORS, TRAILERS AND STACKERS

MACHINE TOOLS, METAL CUTTING TYPES

Hunter Engineering Co
11250 Hunter Dr, Bridgeton MO 63044-2306. 314/731-3020. Employs: 250-499.

INDUSTRIAL PATTERNS

Owens-Illinois Machine Mfg Inc
315 Tolle Ln, Godfrey IL 62035-2455. 618/466-8811. Employs: 500-999.

SPECIAL DIES AND TOOLS, DIE SETS, JIGS AND FIXTURES AND INDUSTRIAL MOLDS

Leonard's Metal Inc
3030 N Hwy 94, Saint Charles MO 63301. 314/946-6525. Employs: 250-499.

Owens-Brockway Glass Container
1625 E Broadway St, Alton IL 62002-6662. 618/463-3100. Employs: 250-499.

CUTTING TOOLS, MACHINE TOOL ACCESSORIES AND MACHINISTS' PRECISION MEASURING DEVICES

General Metal Products Co
3883 Delor St, St. Louis MO 63116-3327. 314/481-0300. Employs: 250-499.

ELECTRIC AND GAS WELDING AND SOLDERING EQUIPMENT

Thermadyne Industries
101 S Hanley, St. Louis MO 63105-3406. 314/721-5573. Employs: 1,000+.

FOOD PRODUCTS MACHINERY

Golden Dipt Co
100 E Washington St, Millstadt IL 62260-1224. 618/476-9912. Employs: 250-499.

GENERAL INDUSTRIAL MACHINERY AND EQUIPMENT

Mark Andy Inc
18081 Chesterfield Airport Rd, Chesterfield MO 63005-1116. 314/532-4433. Employs: 250-499.

CALCULATING AND ACCOUNTING MACHINES, EXCEPT ELECTRONIC COMPUTERS

H R Electronics
6217 Hwy Pp, High Ridge MO 63049-2922. 314/677-3377. Employs: 250-499.

AUTOMATIC VENDING MACHINES

Coin Acceptors Inc
300 Hunter Ave, St. Louis MO 63124-2081. 314/725-0100. Employs: 250-499.

AIR-CONDITIONING AND WARM AIR HEATING EQUIPMENT AND COMMERCIAL AND INDUSTRIAL REFRIGERATION EQUIPMENT

Moog Automotive Inc
6565 Wells Ave, St. Louis MO 63133-2122. 314/385-3400. Employs: 1,000+.

Nordyne Inc
7100 S Grand Blvd, St. Louis MO 63111-2607. 314/352-2700. Employs: 250-499.

SEARCH, DETECTION, NAVIGATION, GUIDANCE, AERONAUTICAL AND NAUTICAL SYSTEMS AND INSTRUMENTS

Engineered Air Systs Inc
1270 N Price Rd, St. Louis MO 63132-2316. 314/993-5880. Employs: 250-499.

AUTOMATIC CONTROLS FOR REGULATING RESIDENTIAL AND COMMERCIAL ENVIRONMENTS AND APPLIANCES

White-Rodgers
9797 Reavis Rd, St. Louis MO 63123-5329. 314/577-1300. Employs: 250-499.

INSTRUMENTS FOR MEASURING AND TESTING OF ELECTRICITY AND ELECTRICAL SIGNALS

Fisher Controls Intl Inc
8000 Maryland Ave, St. Louis MO 63105-3752. 515/754-2452. Employs: 1,000+.

Additional small to medium sized employers: 50-249

FARM MACHINERY AND EQUIPMENT

Williams Pat Crshr & Pulv Co
813 Montgomery St, St. Louis MO 63102-1513. 314/621-3348. Employs: 100-249.

Worksaver Inc
S State Rd, Litchfield IL 62056. 217/324-5973. Employs: 50-99.

MINING MACHINERY AND EQUIPMENT, EXCEPT OIL AND GAS FIELD MACHINERY AND EQUIPMENT

Central Mine Equipment Co
6200 N Broadway, St. Louis MO 63147-2801. 314/381-5900. Employs: 100-249.

ELEVATORS AND MOVING STAIRWAYS

Guilbert Inc
3044 Lambdin, St. Louis MO 63115-2814. 314/533-5700. Employs: 50-99.

CONVEYORS AND CONVEYING EQUIPMENT

Beltservice Corporation
2025 Concourse Dr, St. Louis MO 63146-4118. 314/567-6255. Employs: 50-99.

MACHINE TOOLS, METAL CUTTING TYPES

John Ramming Machine Co
4591 McRee Ave, St. Louis MO 63110-2237. 314/771-3211. Employs: 50-99.

Modern Engineering Co
P O Box 31725, St. Louis MO 63131-0725. 314/965-6901. Employs: 50-99.

MACHINE TOOLS, METAL FORMING TYPES

Fulton Iron Works Co
3844 Walsh, St. Louis MO 63116-3354. 314/752-2400. Employs: 50-99.

INDUSTRIAL PATTERNS

Star Manufacturing Intl Co
9325 Olive Blvd, St. Louis MO
63132-3211. 314/994-0880.
Employs: 100-249.

SPECIAL DIES AND TOOLS, DIE SETS, JIGS AND FIXTURES AND INDUSTRIAL MOLDS

Carr Lane Mfg Co
4200 Carr Lane Ct, St. Louis MO
63119-2129. 314/647-6200.
Employs: 50-99.

Mueller Machine & Tool Co
5932 Jackson Ave, St. Louis MO
63134-2310. 314/522-8080.
Employs: 50-99.

Progressive Service Die Co
2720 Clark Ave, St. Louis MO
63103-2504. 314/531-4300.
Employs: 50-99.

Roto-Die Co Inc
800 Howerton Ln, Eureka MO
63025-1027. 314/587-3600.
Employs: 100-249.

Westhoff Tool & Die Co
9462 Watson Indl Pk, St. Louis
MO 63126. 314/968-5091.
Employs: 50-99.

CUTTING TOOLS, MACHINE TOOL ACCESSORIES AND MACHINISTS' PRECISION MEASURING DEVICES

Eclipse Industrial Product
10801 Pear Tree Lane, St. Louis
MO 63134. 314/429-0022.
Employs: 50-99.

METALWORKING MACHINERY

Engel Inds Inc
8122 Reilly Ave, St. Louis MO
63111-3645. 314/638-0100.
Employs: 50-99.

TEXTILE MACHINERY

Cardinal Technologies Inc
10820 Sunset Office Dr, St. Louis
MO 63127-1016. 314/821-7322.
Employs: 50-99.

PRINTING TRADES MACHINERY AND EQUIPMENT

Allied Gear & Machine Co Inc
1101 Research Blvd, St. Louis MO
63132-1711. 314/991-5900.
Employs: 50-99.

Southern Gravure Svc Inc
1022 N 6th St, St. Louis MO
63101-3100. 314/231-6240.
Employs: 50-99.

FOOD PRODUCTS MACHINERY

Multiplex Co Inc
250 Old Ballwin Rd, Ballwin MO
63021-4834. 314/256-7777.
Employs: 100-249.

Seco Products
Old Hwy 100 E, Washington MO
63090. 314/239-4788. Employs:
100-249.

SPECIAL INDUSTRY MACHINERY

Barry-Wehmiller Co
8020 Forsyth Blvd, St. Louis MO
63105-1707. 314/381-1504.
Employs: 100-249.

Clemco Industries Corp
One Cable Car Dr, Washington
MO 63090-1119. 314/239-0300.
Employs: 100-249.

Marquette Tool & Die Co
3185 S Kingshighway, St. Louis MO 63139-1121. 314/771-8509. Employs: 100-249.

Mitek Inds Inc
11710 Old Ballas Rd, St. Louis MO 63141-7023. 314/567-7127. Employs: 50-99.

PUMPS AND PUMPING EQUIPMENT

Charles S Lewis & Co Inc
8625 Grant Rd, St. Louis MO 63123-1009. 314/843-4437. Employs: 50-99.

BALL AND ROLLER BEARINGS

Rates Bearing & Trnsmsn Co
10 Central Industrial Dr, Granite City IL 62040-6801. 618/452-1115. Employs: 50-99.

SPEED CHANGERS, INDUSTRIAL HIGH-SPEED DRIVES AND GEARS

C & M Services
6 Executive Park Dr Ste 2, E St. Louis IL 62208-1331. 618/632-9595. Employs: 50-99.

Delta Gear Co
9825 Meeks Blvd, St. Louis MO 63132-1408. 314/993-2800. Employs: 50-99.

Dorris Co
8610 Page Blvd, St. Louis MO 63114-6102. 314/423-7300. Employs: 50-99.

INDUSTRIAL PROCESS FURNACES AND OVENS

Godfrey Utility Office
4725 Brecht La, Godfrey IL 62035-1303. 618/466-3334. Employs: 50-99.

GENERAL INDUSTRIAL MACHINERY AND EQUIPMENT

Diagraph Corporation
3401 Rider Trail South, Earth City MO 63045-1110. 314/739-1221. Employs: 100-249.

Indeeco
425 Hanley Indl Ct, St. Louis MO 63144. 314/644-4300. Employs: 100-249.

Swing-A-Way Mfg Co
4100 Beck Ave, St. Louis MO 63116-2634. 314/773-1487. Employs: 50-99.

Thermo Science
2200 Cassens Dr, Fenton MO 63026-2521. 314/349-1233. Employs: 50-99.

OFFICE MACHINES

V C R Clinic
309 S Lincoln St, O Fallon IL 62269-2141. 618/624-2058. Employs: 50-99.

AUTOMATIC VENDING MACHINES

Stout Industries Inc
6425 W Florissant Ave, St. Louis MO 63136-3622. 314/385-2280. Employs: 100-249.

COMMERCIAL LAUNDRY, DRYCLEANING AND PRESSING MACHINES

Rug Doctor L P
997 Horan Dr, Fenton MO 63026-2401. 314/343-5106. Employs: 50-99.

AIR-CONDITIONING AND WARM AIR HEATING EQUIPMENT AND COMMERCIAL AND INDUSTRIAL REFRIGERATION EQUIPMENT

Nordyne Inc
10820 Sunset Office Dr, St. Louis MO 63127-1016. 314/822-9600. Employs: 50-99.

Servco Equipment Co
3189 Jamieson Ave, St. Louis MO 63139-2519. 314/781-3189. Employs: 50-99.

INDUSTRIAL AND COMMERCIAL MACHINERY AND EQUIPMENT

Construction & Mining Svcs Inc
3126-3200 Missouri Ave, E St. Louis IL 62205-1127. 618/271-7210. Employs: 50-99.

Davlan Engrg Inc
3644 Scarlet Oak Blvd, St. Louis MO 63122-6606. 314/225-5310. Employs: 50-99.

United Engrg Co
8800 Pevely Indl Dr, Pevely MO 63070. 314/479-7132. Employs: 50-99.

United Engrg Co
Hwy 61-67, Imperial MO 63052. 314/464-5171. Employs: 50-99.

Carden Machine Shop Inc
975 N Outer Rd W, Sullivan MO 63080. 314/468-4194. Employs: 50-99.

SEARCH, DETECTION, NAVIGATION, GUIDANCE, AERONAUTICAL AND NAUTICAL SYSTEMS AND INSTRUMENTS

Surface Systs Inc
10420 Baur Blvd, St. Louis MO 63132-1905. 314/569-1002. Employs: 50-99.

AUTOMATIC CONTROLS FOR REGULATING RESIDENTIAL AND COMMERCIAL ENVIRONMENTS AND APPLIANCES

Mallinckrodt Anesthesia Products
107 Eastgate Indl Ct, New Haven MO 63068. 314/237-2193. Employs: 50-99.

Specialty Waste Services Inc
2398 Belle St, Alton IL 62002-6847. 618/465-0269. Employs: 100-249.

Tempset Inc
4204 Miami, St. Louis MO 63116-2618. 314/772-8855. Employs: 100-249.

INDUSTRIAL INSTRUMENTS FOR MEASUREMENT, DISPLAY AND CONTROL OF PROCESS VARIABLES; AND RELATED PRODUCTS

Tri-Onics Inc
Highland Indl Ct, Highland IL 62249. 618/654-9831. Employs: 50-99.

TOTALIZING FLUID METERS AND COUNTING DEVICES

All Chemical Process Eqpt Corp
250 Quindaro Dr, Florissant MO 63034-1210. 314/837-8811. Employs: 50-99.

For more information on career opportunities in industrial manufacturing:

Associations

APPLIANCE PARTS DISTRIBUTORS ASSOCIATION
228 East Baltimore Street, Detroit MI 48202. 313/875-8455.

NATIONAL ASSOCIATION OF MANUFACTURERS
1331 Pennsylvania Avenue, NW, Suite 1500, Washington DC 20004. 202/637-3000.

ASSOCIATION FOR MANUFACTURING TECHNOLOGY
7901/ Westpark Drive, McLean VA 22102. 703/893-2900.

NATIONAL SCREW MACHINE PRODUCTS ASSOCIATION
6700 West Snowville Road, Breckville OH 44141. 216/526-0300.

NATIONAL TOOLING AND MACHINING ASSOCIATION
9300 Livingston Road, Fort Washington MD 20744. 301/248-1250.

MISCELLANEOUS SERVICES

BURNS INTERNATIONAL SECURITY SERVICES INC.
320 Brooks Drive, Suite 207, Hazelwood MO 63042. 314/895-4440. **Contact:** Personnel Assistant. **Description:** An area detective agency providing security and protection services. **Employees:** 300.

CLEAN INDUSTRIAL SERVICE
1316 South 7th Street, St. Louis MO 63104. 314/421-1220. **Contact:** Joan Reheis, Office Manager. **Description:** A St. Louis company engaged in the rental and laundry service of uniforms, dust mops, and dust mats. **Employees:** 100.

CLEAN-TECH COMPANY AND SUBSIDIARIES
2815 Olive Street, St. Louis MO 63103. 314/652-2388. **Contact:** Mr. John Hanson, Vice President of Operations. **Description:** A St. Louis company engaged in a variety of services including janitorial and security guard services. **Employees:** 1,000.

DIRECTORY DISTRIBUTING ASSOCIATION INC.
P.O. Box 10066, St. Louis MO 63145. 314/427-2800. **Contact:** John Richardson, Personnel Director. **Description:** Distribution of telephone books. **Employees:** 100.

FACTORY MUTUAL ENGINEERING AND RESEARCH
3300 Rider Trail South, Suite 600, Earth City MO 63045. 314/298-9966. **Contact:** Personnel Department. **Description:** A loss-prevention service organization maintained by the Factory Mutual System, with district offices strategically located throughout the United States and Canada. The Loss Prevention Consultants inspect insured properties on a periodic basis to help pinpoint hazards or conditions that could cause fires or explosions and result in damage to property and lost production. During inspections, the company also determines if fire protection systems and equipment are adequate and in good condition. **Corporate headquarters:** Norwood, MA.

P.J. HOLLORAN COMPANY
222 South 21st Street, St. Louis MO 63103. 314/231-4932. **Contact:** Personnel Department. **Description:** A greater-St. Louis industrial and commercial laundry service.

HUDSON CHEMICAL COMPANY
110-1/2 North Kirkwood Road, St. Louis MO 63122. 314/965-1929. **Contact:** Personnel Department. **Description:** A St. Louis company engaged in a variety of janitorial, maintenance, and total building services.

MAINTENANCE UNLIMITED JANITORIAL
UNLIMITED WATER PROCESSING INC.
5200 Helen, St. Louis MO 63136. 314/381-8585. **Contact:** Mary Walters, Office Manager. **Description:** A St. Louis cleaning and maintenance service, also engaged in delivery of drinking water to area construction sites.

MORGAN SYSTEMS INC.
3124 Olive Street, P.O. Box 14110-A, St. Louis MO 63178. 314/531-7800. **Contact:** Personnel Department. **Description:** A St. Louis linen supply service company.

NATIONAL CLEANING
915 Olive, Suite 142, St. Louis MO 63101. 314/436-4050. **Contact:** Personnel Department. **Description:** A St. Louis company engaged in janitorial and contract custodial window cleaning. **Common positions:** Management Trainee; Operations/Production Manager; Sales Representative. **Educational backgrounds sought:** Accounting; Business Administration; Finance; Marketing. **Benefits:** medical, dental, and life insurance; disability coverage. **Corporate headquarters:** New York NY. **Operations at this facility:** divisional headquarters; service; sales. **Listed on:** New York Stock Exchange.

NATIONAL INDUSTRIAL SECURITY CORPORATION
2025 South Brentwood Boulevard, St. Louis MO 63144. 314/962-1414. **Contact:** Bill Gucciardo, Personnel Director. **Description:** A St. Louis security guard and private investigations company. **Corporate headquarters:** This location.

NATIONAL LINEN SERVICE
P.O. Box 14467, St. Louis MO 63118. 314/865-4500. **Contact:** Lisa Haley, Human Resource Manager. **Description:** A St. Louis linen supply service. **Common positions:** Administrator; Blue-Collar Worker Supervisor; Credit

Manager; Customer Service Representative; Industrial Manager; Branch Manager; Management Trainee; Operations/Production Manager; Personnel and Labor Relations Specialist; Sales Representative; General Office Worker; Route Sales Representative (Driver). **Educational backgrounds sought:** Business Administration. **Special programs:** Training programs. **Benefits:** Medical and Life Insurance; Pension Plan; Tuition Assistance; Stock Options. **Corporate headquarters:** Atlanta, GA. **Parent company:** National Services Industries. **Operations at this facility:** Service. **Listed on:** Dunn and Bradstreet. **Employees:** 115.

PINKERTON SECURITY SERVICES
10121 Paget Drive, Suite 175, St. Louis MO 63132. 314/997-7801. **Contact:** Wanda Landi, Personnel Manager. **Description:** St. Louis office of the oldest and largest non-governmental security service organization in the world today, operating for over 130 years. Principal business is providing high-quality security, investigative, and consulting services to a multitude of commercial, industrial, institutional, governmental, and residential clients. Operates from 129 offices in the United States, Canada, and Great Britain. Services include: industrial plant security, retail security, nuclear plant security, institutional security, commercial and residential building security, construction security, patrol and inspection service, courier service, inventory service, community security, sports and special events service, K-9 patrol service, investigation services, security consultation, and equipment evaluation. **Employees:** 35,000+ worldwide. **Corporate headquarters:** Van Nuys, CA.

SHADE TREE SERVICE COMPANY
520 South Highway Drive, Fenton MO 63026. 314/343-1212. **Contact:** Personnel Department. **Description:** An eastern Missouri tree trimming service.

SPANN BUILDING MAINTENANCE COMPANY
2025 Olive Street, St. Louis MO 63103. 314/241-1975. **Contact:** Sheila Cernicek, Personnel Director. **Description:** A St. Louis janitorial service. **Common positions:** Accountant; Blue-Collar Worker Supervisor; Branch Manager; Management Trainee; Sales Representative. **Educational backgrounds sought:** Accounting; Business Administration; Finance; Marketing. **Benefits:** medical insurance; pension plan; life insurance; disability coverage. **Corporate headquarters:** This location. **Operations at this facility:** administration; service; sales.

WHELAN SECURITY COMPANY INC.
1750 South Hanley Road, St. Louis MO 63144. 314/644-1974. **Contact:** Daniel Twardowski, Administration. **Description:** A detective agency and contract security guard service. **Common positions:** Security Supervisor; Security Officer. **Educational backgrounds sought:** Criminal Justice. **Special programs:** Training programs and internships. **Benefits:** medical and life insurance; pension plan. **Corporate headquarters:** This location. **Operations at this facility:** administration.

284/The St. Louis JobBank

Additional large employers: 250+

GARMENT PRESSING AND AGENTS FOR LAUNDRIES AND DRYCLEANERS

American Cleaners
8562 Watson Rd, St. Louis MO 63119-5219. 314/842-3271.
Employs: 250-499.

SUPPLY SERVICES

TLI Inc
15400 S Outer 40 Rd, Chesterfield MO 63017. 314/532-9007.
Employs: 500-999.

DETECTIVE, GUARD AND ARMORED CAR SERVICES

National Industrial Secur Corporation
2025 S Brentwood, St. Louis MO 63144-1833. 314/962-1414.
Employs: 250-499.

Additional small to medium sized employers: 50-249

LAWN AND GARDEN SERVICES

Evergreen Lawns Regional Office
1390 Charlestown Industrial D, Saint Charles MO 63303-5157. 314/946-9700. Employs: 100-249.

LAUNDRY AND GARMENT SERVICES

Jims Formal Wear Co
11 E Wisconsin St, Trenton IL 62293-1403. 618/2249211.
Employs: 50-99.

BEAUTY SHOPS

J C Penney Co Inc
Northwest Plaza, Saint Ann MO 63074. 314/739-6026. Employs: 100-249.

FUNERAL SERVICE AND CREMATORIES

Baue Funeral Home
620 Jefferson St, Saint Charles MO 63301-2704. 314/724-0073.
Employs: 50-99.

Fieser Funeral Home
401 Gravois Rd, Fenton MO 63026-4132. 314/343-4344.
Employs: 50-99.

SECRETARIAL AND COURT REPORTING SERVICES

A-1 Resume Company
111 S Bemiston Ave, St. Louis MO 63105-1912. 314/721-1288.
Employs: 50-99.

First Impression Best Impress
2910 Devondale Pl, St. Louis MO 63131-2518. 314/997-7011.
Employs: 50-99.

BUILDING CLEANING AND MAINTENANCE SERVICES

New System Carpet & Bldg Car
18 Worthington Dr, St. Louis MO 63128. 314/878-5050. Employs: 50-99.

Abbco Service Corporation
2125 Gravois Ave, St. Louis MO 63104-2845. 314/771-3221.
Employs: 100-249.

Brite Maintenance Corp
1099 Headquarters Park, Fenton MO 63026-1910. 314/343-7766.
Employs: 100-249.

HEAVY CONSTRUCTION EQUIPMENT RENTAL AND LEASING

Big Boy Steel Erection Inc
11843 Missouri Bottom Rd, Hazelwood MO 63042-2400. 314/731-4157. Employs: 50-99.

EQUIPMENT RENTAL AND LEASING

Admiral Chair Co
10665 Baur Blvd, St. Louis MO 63132-1612. 314/993-3600. Employs: 50-99.

EMPLOYMENT AGENCIES

C and P Marketing Ltd
555 N New Ballas Rd, St. Louis MO 63141-6825. 314/997-6553. Employs: 50-99.

HELP SUPPLY SERVICES

Temps Inc
2368 Meadow Park Ct, Maryland Hts MO 63043-1518. 314/878-7878. Employs: 50-99.

Olsten Temporary Services
2025 Craigshire Rd, St. Louis MO 63146-4014. 314/434-2800. Employs: 50-99.

Bee Line Leasing Company
3300 Chouteau Ave, St. Louis MO 63103-2912. 314/772-7202. Employs: 50-99.

DETECTIVE, GUARD AND ARMORED CAR SERVICES

Security Armored Car Svc Inc
1022 S 9th St, St. Louis MO 63104-3509. 314/231-4030. Employs: 50-99.

SSI Global Security Service
8 Seclusion Woods, Festus MO 63028-4110. 314/296-6200. Employs: 50-99.

Investigative Research Svcs
132 W Main St, Belleville IL 62220-1502. 618/234-5500. Employs: 50-99.

NEWS SYNDICATES

St Louis Post Dispatch
112A N Main St, Edwardsville IL 62025-1902. 618/692-1666. Employs: 50-99.

BUSINESS SERVICES

Aerofil Technology Inc
225 Indl Pk Dr, Sullivan MO 63080. 314/468-5551. Employs: 50-99.

Cliff Kelley Inc
2850 S Jefferson Ave, St. Louis MO 63118-1509. 314/664-0023. Employs: 100-249.

Ralston Purina Ars
711 W Fuesser Rd, Mascoutah IL 62224-0001. 618/566-4645. Employs: 50-99.

Street Inds Inc
1 River Rd, St. Louis MO 63125-4113. 314/892-2958. Employs: 50-99.

Cervantes Convention Center
801 Convention Plz, St. Louis MO 63101-1215. 314/342-5000. Employs: 100-249.

Peckham Guyton Albers & Viets
200 N Broadway, St. Louis MO 63102-2730. 314/231-7318. Employs: 50-99.

Hastings & Chivetta Archts Inc
101 S Hanley Rd, St. Louis MO 63105-3406. 314/863-5717. Employs: 50-99.

Bell & Howell Co
149 Weldon Pkwy, Maryland Hts MO 63043-3103. 314/567-0893. Employs: 50-99.

Eastman Kodak Co
11525 Olde Cabin Rd, St. Louis MO 63141-7118. 314/993-2700. Employs: 100-249.

REFRIGERATION AND AIR-CONDITIONING SERVICE AND REPAIR SHOPS

J & L Refrigeration
295 San Juan, Saint Charles MO 63303-4128. 314/946-6402. Employs: 50-99.

Climate Control
152 E Kirkham Ave, St. Louis MO 63119-1753. 314/968-8400. Employs: 50-99.

Johnson Controls Inc
2188 Welsch Industrial Ct, St. Louis MO 63146-4221. 314/569-1570. Employs: 50-99.

ELECTRICAL AND ELECTRONIC REPAIR SHOPS

Sears Roebuck & Co
4600 Bellevue Park Dr No 27, Belleville IL 62223. 618/234-5098. Employs: 100-249.

REPAIR SHOPS AND RELATED SERVICES

Broad Bros Service Center
11038 Olive Blvd, St. Louis MO 63141-7615. 314/567-6565. Employs: 100-249.

SERVICES

Corroon & Black Consulting Group
231 S Bemiston Ave, St. Louis MO 63105-1914. 314/725-0114. Employs: 100-249.

NEWSPAPER PUBLISHING

Throughout the recession, the newspaper industry has been suffering from a severely shrinking share of advertising dollars. Classified advertising was especially hard hit, and recovery will depend on improvement in the retail, automotive, and real estate industries, as well as on a growing employment market. For the long-term, look for newspaper companies to target specific readers in order to attract advertisers. Lifestyle, health care, and business sections will grow in importance.

ALTON TELEGRAPH PRINTING COMPANY
111 East Broadway, Alton IL 62002. 618/463-2500. **Contact:** Personnel Department. **Description:** A regional newspaper publisher. **Employees:** 100.

JOURNAL NEWSPAPERS OF SOUTH COUNTY
SOUTH SUBURBAN PUBLICATIONS, INC.
4210 Chippewa, St. Louis MO 63116. 314/664-2700. **Contact:** Leonard Woolsey, Advertising Manager. **Description:** Holding company for a group of area newspapers.

THE NEWS DEMOCRAT
120 South Illinois, P.O. Box 427, Belleville IL 62222. 618/234-1000. **Contact:** Personnel Director. **Description:** A Southern Illinois newspaper publisher.

THE SPORTING NEWS
A TIMES MIRROR COMPANY
1212 North Lindbergh Boulevard, St. Louis MO 63132. 314/997-7111. **Contact:** George Moskowitz, Director, Human Resources. **Description:** Corporate offices of a well-known national newspaper, covering a complete range of sports-related news.

ST. LOUIS POST-DISPATCH/
PULITZER PUBLISHING CO.
900 North Tucker Boulevard, St. Louis MO 63101. 314/340-8000. **Contact:** Preston Vanderford, Personnel Director. **Description:** Offices of St. Louis' daily newspaper.

Small to medium sized employers: 50-249

NEWSPAPERS: PUBLISHING
OR PUBLISHING AND
PRINTING

219 N Illinois St, Belleville IL 62220-1316. 618/277-7000.
Employs: 50-99.

Belleville Journal

Bethalto News
1307 Sir Galahad La, Godfrey IL 62035-2658. 618/466-8240. Employs: 50-99.

Cahokia Herald
713 Range Ln, E St. Louis IL 62206-2020. 618/337-7309. Employs: 50-99.

Cahokia-Dupo Journal
1010 Camp Jackson Rd, E St. Louis IL 62206-2228. 618/332-6000. Employs: 50-99.

East St Louis News
1010 Camp Jackson Rd, E St. Louis IL 62206-2228. 618/337-6502. Employs: 50-99.

Edwardsville Intelligencer
117 N 2nd St, Edwardsville IL 62025-1938. 618/656-4700. Employs: 50-99.

Gospel Gazette Christian Msn
715 N Vandeventer Ave, St. Louis MO 63108-3527. 314/534-6420. Employs: 50-99.

Metro Citizen
242 Collinsville Ave, E St. Louis IL 62201-3009. 618/271-9500. Employs: 50-99.

Mid America Printing Co
4356 Duncan Av, St. Louis MO 63110-1110. 314/961-9997. Employs: 100-249.

Missourian Publishing Co Inc
14 W Main St, Washington MO 63090-2518. 314/239-7701. Employs: 100-249.

New Athens Journal Press
904 Old Baldwin Rd # A, New Athens IL 62264-1574. 618/475-2166. Employs: 50-99.

News Democrat
998 E Gannon Dr, Festus MO 63028-2600. 314/937-9811. Employs: 100-249.

North County Publications
9320 Lewis & Clark Blvd, St. Louis MO 63136. 314/868-8000. Employs: 50-99.

Press Journal Publishing Co
3406 Georgia St, Louisiana MO 63353-2734. 314/754-5566. Employs: 50-99.

Saint Charles Journal
340 N Main St, Saint Charles MO 63301-2033. 314/724-1111. Employs: 50-99.

South County Publications Inc
4210 Chippewa St, St. Louis MO 63116-2636. 314/481-1111. Employs: 50-99.

Spotlight Publications
PO Box 63423, St. Louis MO 63163-3523. 314/725-7734. Employs: 50-99.

St Louis Business Journal
612 N 2nd St, St. Louis MO 63102-2553. 314/421-6200. Employs: 50-99.

St Louis Post-Dispatch
123 N Main St, St. Louis MO 63101. 314/621-6666. Employs: 50-99.

St Louis Veterans Home Cmmte
4092 Robert Ave, St. Louis MO 63116-2754. 314/353-1355. Employs: 50-99.

St Louis Whirl Examiner
8544 Riverview Blvd, St. Louis MO 63147-1322. 314/383-3875. Employs: 50-99.

Suburban Journals Corporate Office
1714 Deer Tracks Trl, St. Louis MO 63131-1838. 314/821-1110. Employs: 100-249.

Suburban Journals E Side Publ
1815 N 19th St, St. Louis MO 63106-3015. 314/621-5801. Employs: 50-99.

Times-Tribune
201 E Market St, Troy IL 62294-1511. 618/667-3111. Employs: 50-99.

Wall St Journal Classified
10 S Broadway, St. Louis MO 63102-1712. 314/621-3389. Employs: 50-99.

West County Publications
1215 Fern Ridge Pkwy #100, St. Louis MO 63141-4405. 314/434-9400. Employs: 50-99.

For more information on career opportunities in newspaper publishing:

Associations

AMERICAN NEWSPAPER PUBLISHERS ASSOCIATION
Newspaper Center, 11600 Sunrise Valley Drive, Reston VA 22091. 703/648-1000.

AMERICAN SOCIETY OF NEWSPAPER EDITORS
P.O. Box 17004, Washington DC 20041. 703/648-1144.

THE DOW JONES NEWSPAPER FUND
P.O. Box 300, Princeton NJ 08543-0300. 609/520-4000.

INTERNATIONAL CIRCULATION MANAGERS ASSOCIATION
P.O. Box 17420, Washington DC 20041. 703/620-9555.

NATIONAL NEWSPAPER ASSOCIATION
1627 K Street NW, Suite 400, Washington DC 20006. 202/466-7200.

NATIONAL PRESS CLUB
529 14th St. NW, 13th Floor, Washington DC 20045. 202/662-7500.

THE NEWSPAPER GUILD
Research and Information Department, 1125 15th Street NW, Washington DC 20005. 301/585-2990.

Directories

EDITOR & PUBLISHER INTERNATIONAL YEARBOOK
Editor & Publisher Co. Inc., 11 West 19th Street, New York NY 10011. 212/675-4380.

JOURNALISM CAREER AND SCHOLARSHIP GUIDE
The Dow Jones Newspaper Fund, P.O. Box 300, Princeton NJ 08543-0300. 609/520-4000.

Magazines

EDITOR AND PUBLISHER
Editor & Publisher Co. Inc., 11 West 19th Street, New York NY 10011. 212/675-4380.

NEWS, INC.
49 East 21st Street, New York NY 10010. 212/979-4600.

PAPER AND PACKAGING/GLASS AND FOREST PRODUCTS

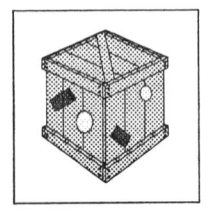

The next few years hold both promise and problems for the paper industry. If the economy strengthens and export markets regain the momentum lost during the last few years, the industry should see revenues grow about 10 percent by the end of 1996. Technological advances should strengthen the industry both at home and abroad. In addition, environmental concerns should give the paper packaging segment the upper hand over plastics.

DRUG PACKAGE INC.
901 Drug Package Lane, O'Fallon MO 63366. 314/272-6261. **Contact:** Tracy Sherman, Personnel Department. **Description:** Manufacturers of prescription boxes and labels for drug trade. **Employees:** 100.

GAYLORD CONTAINER DIVISION
5300 Bircher Boulevard, St. Louis MO 63120. 314/679-6000. **Contact:** Tom Rellergert, Comptroller. **Description:** A St. Louis manufacturer of corrugated shipping containers. **Employees:** 300.

GEORGIA PACIFIC
P.O. Box 100, Mt. Olive IL 62069. 217/999-2511. **Contact:** Personnel Department. **Description:** One of several area divisions of the well-known diversified manufacturer of packaging products.

GEORGIA PACIFIC
HOPPER PAPER DIVISION
P.O. Box 380, Taylorville IL 62568. 217/824-9611. **Contact:** Bob Morrison, Personnel Director. **Description:** Manufactures printing papers.

INLAND CONTAINER CORPORATION
1201 North Highway Drive, P.O. Box 780, Fenton MO 63026. 314/225-4900. **Contact:** Harry Moppins, Employee Relations Supervisor. **Description:** Manufacturers of shipping containers.

JAMES RIVER CORPORATION
310 McDonnell Road, Hazelwood MO 63042. 314/731-6700. **Contact:** Martin Gabbert, Personnel Director. **Description:** An area manufacturer of flexible packaging. **Employees:** 300.

JEFFERSON SMURFIT
CONTAINER DIVISION
6th and Zscholkke Sts., Highland IL 62249. 618/654-2141. **Contact:** Loma Thomas, Personnel Controller. **Description:** A metropolitan manufacturer of corrugated containers.

JEFFERSON SMURFIT
CORRUGATED BOX DIVISION
577 Goddard Avenue, Chesterfield MO 63005. 314/532-3492. **Contact:** Sharon Williams, Personnel Manager. **Description:** Manufacturers of corrugated fibreboard boxes. **Employees:** 100.

JEFFERSON SMURFIT
ALTON PACKAGING CORPORATION
8182 Maryland Avenue, Clayton MO 63105. 314/746-1100. **Contact:** Mike Harrington, Personnel Director. **Description:** Manufacture paperboard packaging, boxes, paper cores.

OWENS-ILLINOIS INC.
MACHINE DIVISION
315 Tolle Lane, Godfrey IL 62035. 618/466-8811. **Contact:** Verlene Schwalb, Assistant Industrial Relations Director. **Description:** One of several area divisions of the well-known diversified manufacturer of packaging products. Company's principal products are glass containers, blown plastic containers, plastic beverage bottles, plastic drums, metal and plastic closures, tamper-resistant closures, plastic and glass prescription containers, pharmaceutical items, labels, and multipack plastic carriers for containers. Specialized glass products made and sold by the company include Libbey Tumblers, stemware, and decorative glassware, television blubs for picture tubes, and Kimble scientific and laboratory ware. Some overseas affiliates also manufacture flat glass and related products. **Common positions:** Machinist. **Special programs:** Training programs. **Benefits:** medical, dental, and life insurance; pension plan; tuition assistance; disability coverage; savings plan. **Corporate headquarters:** Toledo, OH. **Parent company:** Owens-Illinois Inc. **Operations at this facility:** manufacturing.

OWENS-ILLINOIS INC./
MOLD SHOP
1625 East Broadway, Alton IL 62002. 618/463-3130. **Contact:** David Bailey, Personnel Coordinator. **Description:** One of several area divisions of the well-known diversified manufacturer of packaging products. Company's principal products are glass containers, although the company also produces and sells blown plastic containers, plastic beverage bottles, plastic drums, metal and plastic closures, tamper-resistant closures, plastic and glass prescription containers, pharmaceutical items, labels, and multipack plastic carriers for containers. Specialized glass products made and sold by the company include Libbey Tumblers, stemware, and decorative glassware, television blubs for picture tubes, and Kimble scientific and laboratory ware. Some overseas affiliates also manufacture flat glass and related products. **Common positions:** Moldmaker. **Educational backgrounds sought:** Moldmaker Apprenticeship. **Special programs:** Training programs. **Benefits:** medical, dental, and life insurance; pension plan; tuition assistance; disability coverage; savings plan. **Corporate headquarters:** Toledo, OH. **Parent company:** Owens-Illinois Inc.

OWENS-ILLINOIS INC./ PLASTICS PRODUCTS DIVISION
2122 Hereford Avenue, St. Louis MO 63110. 314/664-8390. **Contact:** Personnel Department. **Description:** One of several area divisions of the well-known diversified manufacturer of packaging products. Company's principal products are glass containers, although the company also produces and sells containerboard, corrugated containers, printing plates and ink, plywood and demension lumber, blown plastic containers, plastic beverage bottles, plastic drums, metal and plastic closures, tamper-resistant closures, plastic and glass prescription containers, pharmaceutical items, labels, and multipack plastic carriers for containers. Specialized glass products made and sold by the company include Libbey Tumblers, stemware, and decorative glassware, television blubs for picture tubes, and Kimble scientific and laboratory ware. Some overseas affiliates also manufacture flat glass and related products.

PACKAGING CORPORATION OF AMERICA
10750 Baur Boulevard, St. Louis MO 63132. 314/994-7600. **Contact:** Becca Dotson, Personnel. **Description:** St. Louis office of the national manufacturer of a variety of packaging products. Principal products include shipping containers and containerboard products, folding cartons, molded pulp products, and solid wood products. Products are used in the packaging of food, paper, and paper products, metal products, rubber and plastics, automotive products and point of purchase displays; packaging soap, detergent, and food products; and residential construction. Operates more than 60 plants throughout the Midwest, South and East.

SMURFIT RECYCLING
600 Biddle Street, St. Louis MO 63101. 314/231-1567. **Contact:** Steve Brooks, Personnel Director. **Description:** Packers and sorters of reclaimed waste paper and folding paperboard boxes.

UNION CAMP CORPORATION
8300 Valcour Avenue, St. Louis MO 63123. 314/832-1201. **Contact:** Terri Helvy, Personnel Director. **Description:** Manufacturer of multiwall papers bags.

WEYERHAEUSER PAPER COMPANY
3001 Otto Street, Belleville IL 62223. 618/233-5460. **Contact:** Human Resource Manager. **Description:** Manufacturer of corrugated cardboard shipping containers. **Corporate headquarters:** Tacoma, WA. **Listed on:** American Stock Exchange.

Additional large employers: 250+

TIMBER TRACTS

Stark Brothers Nursery & Orch Co
Rfd 2, Louisiana MO 63353-9802. 314/754-5511. Employs: 250-499.

Huttig Sash & Door Co
14500 S Forty Outer Dr, Chesterfield MO 63017. 314/878-2222. Employs: 1,000+.

MILLWORK

PAPER MILLS

Federal International Inc
3948 Lindell Blvd, St. Louis MO 63108-3204. 314/531-0335. Employs: 250-499.

FOLDING PAPERBOARD BOXES, INCLUDING SANITARY

Jefferson Smurfit Corp
1101 S Denton Rd, Pacific MO 63069-2201. 314/257-1400. Employs: 250-499.

PACKAGING PAPER AND PLASTICS FILM, COATED AND LAMINATED

Flexible Packaging Technology
310 Mc Donnell Blvd, Hazelwood MO 63042-2514. 314/731-6700. Employs: 250-499.

SANITARY PAPER PRODUCTS

Central States Diversified
9322 Manchester Rd, St. Louis MO 63119-1450. 314/961-4300. Employs: 250-499.

STATIONERY, TABLETS AND RELATED PRODUCTS

Atapco Office Products Group
12312 Olive Blvd Ste 400, St. Louis MO 63141-6448. 314/542-5400. Employs: 1,000+.

GLASS CONTAINERS

Foster-Forbes Glass Div
1500 Foster Forbes Dr, Pevely MO 63070-1503. 314/479-4421. Employs: 250-499.

Hillsboro Glass Co
Schram Ave, Hillsboro IL 62049. 217/532-3976. Employs: 250-499.

Additional small to medium sized employers: 50-249

SAWMILLS AND PLANING MILLS, GENERAL

Kerr-Mc Gee Chemical Corp
Washington St, Madison IL 62060. 618/452-4116. Employs: 50-99.

STRUCTURAL WOOD MEMBERS

Truss Components Inc
102 S Elam Ave, Valley Park MO 63088-2025. 314/861-1120. Employs: 50-99.

WOOD PALLETS AND SKIDS

Kauling Wood Products Co
Old Hwy 50 E, Beckemeyer IL 62219. 618/594-2901. Employs: 50-99.

Madison County Wood Products Inc
5101 Farlin Ave, St. Louis MO 63115-1206. 314/383-5700. Employs: 100-249.

MOBILE HOMES

Mobile Structures Inc
R R 1, Pinckneyville IL 62274-9801. 618/357-2138. Employs: 50-99.

WOOD PRESERVING

Jennison Wright Corp
22nd & RR Tracks, Granite City IL 62040. 618/452-3114. Employs: 50-99.

RECONSTITUTED WOOD PRODUCTS

Rite Paper Products Inc
1100 S Outer Rd, Wright City MO 63390. 314/928-5121. Employs: 50-99.

WOOD PRODUCTS

Wilson Trophy Co
9495 Aero Space Dr, St. Louis MO 63134-3825. 314/427-2700. Employs: 50-99.

PAPER MILLS

Baxter Distributing Co
912 E Broadway St, Alton IL 62002-6405. 618/465-9347. Employs: 50-99.

Central States Diversified Inc
5221 Natural Bridge Rd, St. Louis MO 63115-1102. 314/261-8000. Employs: 100-249.

Flesh Co
2118 S 59th St, St. Louis MO 63110-2808. 314/781-4400. Employs: 50-99.

Georgia Pacific Corp
420 Hadley Ave, Edwardsville IL 62025-2505. 618/656-1365. Employs: 50-99.

Hexagon Honeycomb Corp
7980 Clayton Rd #201, St. Louis MO 63117-1354. 314/647-0701. Employs: 50-99.

St Regis Envelope
601 Cannonball Ln, O Fallon MO 63366. 314/272-7500. Employs: 100-249.

White House Mfg Corp
Rt 267, White Hall IL 62092-9614. 217/374-2141. Employs: 50-99.

PAPERBOARD MILLS

Alton Box Board Co
6344 Lake Dr, Godfrey IL 62035-2208. 618/463-6266. Employs: 100-249.

Quality Partitions Mfg
1401 W Eilerman Ave, Litchfield IL 62056. 217/324-6591. Employs: 50-99.

CORRUGATED AND SOLID FIBER BOXES

Consolidated Packaging Corp
3601 Rider Trl S, Earth City MO 63045-1116. 314/739-1212. Employs: 100-249.

Container Corp Of America
577 Goddard Ave, Chesterfield MO 63005-1110. 314/532-3492. Employs: 100-249.

Loy-Lange Box Co
222 Russell Ave, St. Louis MO 63104-4608. 314/776-4712. Employs: 50-99.

Midland Container Corp
827 Koeln Ave, St. Louis MO 63111-3226. 314/638-0028. Employs: 50-99.

Shillington Box Co
3501 Tree Ct Indl Blvd, St. Louis MO 63122-6619. 314/225-5353. Employs: 50-99.

Stone Container Corp
9150 Latty Ave, St. Louis MO 63134-1029. 314/522-6600. Employs: 100-249.

FIBER CANS, TUBES, DRUMS AND SIMILAR PRODUCTS

Sonoco Fibre Drum
8401 St Charles Rock Rd, St. Louis MO 63114-4501. 314/427-5525. Employs: 100-249.

FOLDING PAPERBOARD BOXES, INCLUDING SANITARY

Packaging Corp Of America
10750 Baur Blvd, St. Louis MO 63132-1625. 314/994-7600. Employs: 100-249.

Service Paper Box Co
4248 Forest Park Blvd, St. Louis MO 63108-2811. 314/535-2200. Employs: 100-249.

Superior Box Co
4170 Geraldine Ave, St. Louis MO 63115-1211. 314/383-3800. Employs: 50-99.

PACKAGING PAPER AND PLASTICS FILM, COATED AND LAMINATED

Creative Data Svcs
13748 Shoreline Ct E, Earth City MO 63045-1202. 314/291-0699. Employs: 50-99.

R X Systems Inc
20 Point West Blvd, Saint Charles MO 63301-4430. 314/925-0001. Employs: 50-99.

COATED AND LAMINATED PAPER

National Graphics Inc
2711 Miami St, St. Louis MO 63118-3831. 314/773-1744. Employs: 50-99.

Superior Insulating Tape Co
800 N Oak St, Union MO 63084-1548. 314/583-4500. Employs: 50-99.

PLASTICS, FOIL AND COATED PAPER BAGS

Chase Packaging
5051 Southwest Ave, St. Louis MO 63110-3427. 314/771-3535. Employs: 100-249.

UNCOATED PAPER AND MULTIWALL BAGS

Packaging Concepts Inc
4971 Fyler Ave, St. Louis MO 63139-1111. 314/481-1155. Employs: 100-249.

Sisco Corp
Rt 127 S, Nashville IL 62263. 618/327-3066. Employs: 50-99.

DIE-CUT PAPER AND PAPERBOARD AND CARDBOARD

Serv U Mfg Co Inc
4161 Beck Ave, St. Louis MO 63116-2632. 314/776-7038. Employs: 50-99.

ENVELOPES

Ambassador Envelope Co
10655 Gateway Blvd, St. Louis MO 63132-1889. 314/534-5252. Employs: 50-99.

American Envelope Co
601 Cannonball Ln, O Fallon MO 63366. 314/272-2500. Employs: 100-249.

Hampton Envelope Co
200 Hanley Indl Ct, St. Louis MO 63144. 314/644-1222. Employs: 50-99.

National Envelope Central
13871 Parks Steed Dr, Earth City MO 63045-1406. 314/291-2722. Employs: 100-249.

Orchard Corporation Of America
1154 Reco Ave, St. Louis MO 63126-1027. 314/822-3880. Employs: 100-249.

Roodhouse Envelope Co
414 S State St, Roodhouse IL
62082-1544. 217/589-4321.
Employs: 50-99.

Tension Envelope Corp Of Mo
5001 Southwest Ave, St. Louis MO
63110-3427. 314/773-7700.
Employs: 100-249.

STATIONERY, TABLETS AND RELATED PRODUCTS

Sunshine Art Studios Inc
1123 Washington Ave, St. Louis
MO 63101-1121. 314/241-1404.
Employs: 50-99.

CONVERTED PAPER AND PAPERBOARD PRODUCTS

Hexagon Honeycomb Corp
Hwy 50 W, Lebanon IL 62254-9508. 618/934-4311. Employs: 50-99.

Denny-Reyburn Co
7806 Cross Mont Dr, St. Louis MO
63123-3543. 314/822-3102.
Employs: 50-99.

FLAT GLASS

Arco Glass & Mirror
1117 Laurel St, Highland IL
62249-1812. 618/654-4541.
Employs: 50-99.

H G P Industries Inc
E Hwy M, Truesdale MO 63380.
314/456-3452. Employs: 100-249.

GLASS CONTAINERS

Air Products & Chemicals Inc
PO Box 3768, St. Louis MO
63122-0768. 314/821-2950.
Employs: 100-249.

Continental Glass & Plas Inc
8511 Mid County Industrial Dr, St.
Louis MO 63114-6011. 314/423-5557. Employs: 100-249.

Northwestern Bottle Co
12927 Gravois Rd, St. Louis MO
63127-1714. 314/842-8800.
Employs: 100-249.

Owens-Illinois Inc
1655 Des Peres Rd, St. Louis MO
63131-1832. 314/965-1701.
Employs: 100-249.

Pentagon Software Systems Inc
1750 S Brentwood Blvd, St. Louis
MO 63144-1315. 314/961-4500.
Employs: 100-249.

Silgan Plastics Corp
16216 Baxter Rd, Chesterfield MO
63017-4778. 314/537-3223.
Employs: 50-99.

Silgan Plastics Corp
2337 Centerline Industrial Dr,
Maryland Hts MO 63043. 314/997-3288. Employs: 100-249.

PRESSED AND BLOWN GLASS AND GLASSWARE

Baker Glass
703 S Library St, Waterloo IL
62298-1440. 618/939-7105.
Employs: 50-99.

Becton Dickinson Accu-Glass
10765 Trenton Ave, St. Louis MO
63132-1025. 314/423-0300.
Employs: 50-99.

Intaglio Designs Ltd
450 N Wood River, Wood River IL
62095-1557. 618/254-1230.
Employs: 50-99.

G W Fiberglass Inc
1700 W Terra Ln, O Fallon MO
63366-2348. 314/441-6910.
Employs: 100-249.

Fibertek
3601 Goodfellow Blvd, St. Louis MO 63120-1103. 314/383-5575. Employs: 50-99.

Resurfacing Plus
500 Marie Dr, Saint Charles MO 63301-0500. 314/949-0825. Employs: 50-99.

GLASS PRODUCTS, MADE OF PURCHASED GLASS

David Marshall
2319 Grissom Dr, St. Louis MO 63146-3310. 314/997-3003. Employs: 50-99.

Krane Mfg Co
2222 N 2nd St, St. Louis MO 63102-1431. 314/231-7005. Employs: 50-99.

For more information on career opportunities in the paper, packaging, glass, and forest products industries:

Associations

AMERICAN FOREST COUNCIL
1250 Connecticut Avenue NW, Washington DC 20036. 202/463-2455.

AMERICAN PAPER INSTITUTE
260 Madison Avenue, New York NY 10016. 212/340-0600.

FOREST PRODUCTS RESEARCH SOCIETY
2801 Marshall Court, Madison WI 53705. 608/231-1361.

NATIONAL FOREST PRODUCTS ASSOCIATION
1250 Connecticut Avenue NW, Washington DC 20036. 202/463-2700.

NATIONAL PAPER TRADE ASSOCIATION
111 Great Neck Road, Great Neck NY 11021. 516/829-3070.

PAPERBOARD PACKAGING COUNCIL
1101 Vermont Avenue NW, Suite 411, Washington DC 20005. 202/289-4100.

TECHNICAL ASSOCIATION OF THE PULP AND PAPER INDUSTRY
P.O. Box 105113, Atlanta GA 30348. 404/446-1400.

Directories

DIRECTORY OF THE FOREST PRODUCTS INDUSTRY
Miller Freeman Publications, Inc., 600 Harrison Street, San Francisco CA 94107. 415/905-2200.

LOCKWOOD-POST'S DIRECTORY OF THE PAPER AND ALLIED TRADES
Miller Freeman Publications, Inc., 600 Harrison Street, San Francisco CA 94107. 415/905-2200.

POST'S PULP AND PAPER DIRECTORY
Miller Freeman Publications, Inc., 600 Harrison Street, San Francisco CA 94107. 415/905-2200.

Magazines

FOREST INDUSTRIES
Miller Freeman Publications, Inc., 600 Harrison Street, San Francisco CA 94107. 415/905-2200.

PAPERBOARD PACKAGING
Advanstar Communications, 1 E. First Street, Duluth MN 55802. 218/723-9200.

PULP AND PAPER WEEK
Miller Freeman Publications, Inc., 600 Harrison Street, San Francisco CA 94107. 415/905-2200.

PRINTING/GRAPHIC ARTS

As the U.S. economy improves, accompanied by growth in print advertising, the printing industry should begin to rebound. The price of paper is expected to remain soft, with paper mill capacity outstripping demand. The printing industry's employment levels will rise.

S.G. ADAMS PRINTING AND STATIONERY
1611 Locust Street, St. Louis MO 63103. **Contact:** Personnel Director. **Description:** Engaged in the manufacture of printing products; rubber stamps, seals, stencils; the retail sales of office supplies; and the wholesale sales of office furniture. **Employees:** 200+.

AMERICAN LOOSE-LEAF BUSINESS PRODUCTS
4015 Papin Street, St. Louis MO 63110. 314/535-1414. **Contact:** Personnel Department. **Description:** A St. Louis-based manufacturer of custom and stock loose leaf and data binders. Distributor of office supplies. **Common positions:** Blue-Collar Worker Supervisor; Buyer; Credit Manager; Customer Service Representative; Industrial Manager; Operations/Production Manager; Purchasing Agent; Sales Representative. **Educational backgrounds sought:** Accounting; Business Administration. **Benefits:** medical, dental, and life insurance; disability coverage; 401K. **Corporate headquarters:** This location. **Operations at this facility:** manufacturing; administration; service; sales.

BERNADETTE BUSINESS FORMS INC.
9800 Halls Ferry Road, St. Louis MO 63136. 314/868-7200. **Contact:** Jeff Davis, Personnel Director. **Description:** St. Louis business form manufacturers, specializing in one-time carbon business forms and continuous forms. **Employees:** 100.

CENTRAL STATES DIVERSIFIED INC.
5221 Natural Bridge Road, St. Louis MO 63115. 314/261-8000. **Contact:** Marc Groppe, Personnel Director. **Description:** Manufacturers of extrusions, printing and converting of polyethylene, dielectric sealing and converting of vinyl, and health care disposals. Wholesalers of fabricated plastics. **Employees:** 400+.

COLOR ART INC.
10300 Watson Road, St. Louis MO 63127. 314/966-2000. **Contact:** Lea Alexander, Executive Secretary. **Description:** A St. Louis commercial printing company engaged in offset and letter press printing. Other operations include the retail sales of office furniture and office interior design. **Employees:** 100.

COMFORT PRINTING AND STATIONERY COMPANY
1611 Locust Street, St. Louis MO 63103. 314/241-6991. **Contact:** Lisa Warfel, Personnel Director. **Description:** A St. Louis commercial printing/lithography company. Also engaged in the wholesale and retail sales of office supplies and furniture. **Employees:** 100.

DELUXE CHECK PRINTERS, INC.
2331 Schuetz Road, St. Louis MO 63146. 314/432-5503. **Contact:** Martin Kingsbury, Human Resources. **Description:** A leader in the financial document printing industry with an expanded line of products and services offered in the payment systems market, the business systems market, and the consumer specialty products market. Fortune 500 rating is 339. **Employees:** 250 in St. Louis and over 15,000 nationwide. **Common positions:** Customer Service Representative; Production Management Trainee; Production Worker; Sales Representative Trainee. **Educational backgrounds sought:** Business Administration; Communications; Liberal Arts; Marketing. **Benefits:** medical, dental, vision and life insurance; tuition assistance; disability coverage; profit sharing; employee discounts. **Corporate headquarters:** St. Paul, MN. **Operations at this facility:** manufacturing; service; sales. **Listed on:** New York Stock Exchange.

FORESTER ENTERPRISES, INC.
d/b/a BUXTON & SKINNER PRINTING CO.
2419 Glasgow Avenue, St. Louis MO 63106. 314/535-9700. **Contact:** Rockford R. Abbott, Vice President and Administrator. **Description:** An offset, flexo, and letter press printer engaged in book manufacturing, labels, coasters, and general commercial printing. **Employees:** 95. **Common positions:** Accountant; Blue-Collar Worker Supervisor; Customer Service Representative; Department Manager; General Manager; Management Trainee; Purchasing Agent; Sales Representative; Printing Pressman; Bindery and Prep Workers. **Educational backgrounds sought:** Accounting; Business Administration; Finance; Printing. **Special programs:** Training programs and internships. **Benefits:** medical insurance; disability coverage; savings plan. **Corporate headquarters:** This location.

FOX PHOTO
2838 Market Street, St. Louis MO 63103. 314/652-1300. **Contact:** Theresa Kirkpatrick, Personnel Clerk. **Description:** Wholesalers of photographic supplies, and retailers of photo finishing services. **Employees:** 100.

NIES-KAISER PRINTING COMPANY
5900 Berthold Avenue, St. Louis MO 63110. 314/647-3400. **Contact:** Chuck Stout, Personnel. **Description:** A St. Louis company engaged in commercial printing.

SAYERS PRINTING COMPANY
9600 Manchester Road, St. Louis MO 63119. **Contact:** Personnel Director. **Description:** A commercial printing company. **Common positions:** Accountant; Customer Service Representative; Department Manager; Operations/Production Manager; Purchasing Agent; Quality Control; Sales Representative; Pressperson. **Special programs:** Internships. **Benefits:** medical insurance; dental insurance; life insurance; tuition assistance; disability coverage; profit sharing; 401K plan. **Corporate headquarters:** This location. **Other U.S. locations:** Darien, CT (sales office). **Operations at this facility:** manufacturing; administration; service; sales. **Employees:** 162.

ST. LOUIS LITHOGRAPHING COMPANY
6880 Heege Road, St. Louis MO 63123. 314/352-1300. **Contact:** Lou Briggs, Personnel Director. **Description:** A St. Louis lithography company, specializing in the manufacture of a variety of liquor labels.

JOHN STARK PRINTING COMPANY INC.
12969 Manchester Road, St. Louis MO 63131. 314/966-6800. **Contact:** Personnel Department. **Description:** A commercial lithographer, specializing in offset printing.

JOHN S. SWIFT COMPANY INC.
1248 Research Boulevard, St. Louis MO 63132-1714. 314/991-4300. **Contact:** Personnel Department. **Description:** A printing, lithography, and offsetting company.

UNIVERSAL PRINTING COMPANY
1701 Macklind Avenue, St. Louis MO 63110. 314/771-6900. **Contact:** Personnel Department. **Description:** A web offset printer and commercial bindery.

WESTERN LITHOTECH
3433 Tree Court Industrial Boulevard, St. Louis MO 63122. 314/225-5031. **Contact:** Homer May, Manager of Employee Relations. **Description:** Manufacturer of lithographic plates, chemicals, and high speed exposure/processing systems. **Common positions:** Accountant; Administrator; Advertising Worker; Blue-Collar Worker Supervisor; Buyer; Chemist; Computer Programmer; Credit Manager; Customer Service Representative; Draftsperson; Chemical Engineering; Civil Engineering; Electrical Engineering; Mechanical Engineering; Financial Analyst; Operations/Production Manager; Personnel and Labor Relations Specialist; Purchasing Agent; Sales Representative; Systems Analyst; Marketing. **Educational background sought:** Accounting; Business Administration; Chemistry; Computer Science; Engineering; Finance; Marketing. **Special programs:** Training programs and internships. **Benefits:** medical insurance; dental insurance; pension plan; life insurance; tuition assistance; disability coverage; profit sharing; savings plan. **Corporate headquarters:** This location. **Other U.S. locations:** Springfield, MO; Jacksonville, TX. **Parent company:** Mitsubishi Kasai America, Inc. **Operations at this facility:** manufacturing; research and development; administration; service; sales. **Revenues (1991):** $50 million. **Employees:** 340.

Additional large employers: 250+

COMMERCIAL PRINTING

Spartan Printing Co
2nd & Dickey St, Sparta IL 62286.
618/443-2154. Employs: 1,000+.

BOOKBINDING AND RELATED WORK

Sabregraphics
18102 Chesterfield Airport Rd,
Chesterfield MO 63005-1117.
314/537-3660. Employs: 500-999.

Small to medium sized employers: 50-249

COMMERCIAL PRINTING, LITHOGRAPHIC

Accu-Color Inc
11786 Westline Dr, St. Louis MO
63146-3402. 314/993-5669.
Employs: 50-99.

Ad-Sell Co
3333 Washington Ave, St. Louis
MO 63103-1118. 314/531-8100.
Employs: 50-99.

Butler Design Svcs
9 Wharf St, Lake St Louis MO
63367-1302. 314/441-4767.
Employs: 50-99.

Color Assocs Group
10818 Midwest Indl Blvd, St.
Louis MO 63132. 314/423-9300.
Employs: 100-249.

Fleming Printing Co
1550 Larkin Williams Rd, Fenton
MO 63026-3009. 314/343-8900.
Employs: 50-99.

Garlich Printing Co
5743 W Park Ave, St. Louis MO
63110-1834. 314/645-4211.
Employs: 50-99.

John H Harland Co Inc
15 Arrowhead Indl Blvd, Saint
Peters MO 63376. 314/441-6555.
Employs: 50-99.

Kohler & Sons Inc Printers
9800 Page Ave, St. Louis MO
63132-1429. 314/428-9800.
Employs: 50-99.

LBM Enterprises Inc
22025 Vandenter, St. Louis MO
63110. 314/773-1253. Employs:
50-99.

Marlo Graphic Inc
11550 Adie Rd, Maryland Hts MO
63043-3508. 314/997-3000.
Employs: 100-249.

Press Craft Co Inc
P O Box 3824, St. Louis MO
63122-0824. 314/965-0878.
Employs: 100-249.

Publication Printing Co Inc
2945 Washington Ave, St. Louis
MO 63103-1305. 314/652-6020.
Employs: 50-99.

Red Bud Litho
466 W Mill St, Red Bud IL 62278-
2708. 618/282-3491. Employs: 50-
99.

Skinner & Kennedy Co
9451 Natural Bridge, St. Louis MO
63134-3105. 314/426-2800.
Employs: 100-249.

St Louis Offset
1212 Dielman Indl Ct, St. Louis
MO 63132. 314/991-9400.
Employs: 100-249.

Suburban Business Products Inc
2290 Grissom Dr, St. Louis MO 63146-3309. 314/567-0087. Employs: 50-99.

Valuprint
2828 Brannon Ave, St. Louis MO 63139-1438. 314/776-1110. Employs: 50-99.

Von Hoffmann Press Inc
1000 Camera Ave, St. Louis MO 63126-1017. 314/966-0909. Employs: 100-249.

Wilkes Printing & Direct Mail
3401 Chouteau Ave, St. Louis MO 63103-2913. 314/776-5555. Employs: 50-99.

COMMERCIAL PRINTING

Decora
680 S Sturgeon, Montgomery Cy MO 63361-2708. 314/564-3783. Employs: 50-99.

Diversified Graphics Ltd
5433 Eagle Industrial Ct, Hazelwood MO 63042-2308. 314/895-4600. Employs: 50-99.

Jefferson Printing Co
1234 S Kingshighway Blvd, St. Louis MO 63110-2106. 314/533-8087. Employs: 100-249.

Louisiana Plastics Inc
13759 Rider Trl N, Earth City MO 63045-1205. 314/291-5759. Employs: 50-99.

Missouri Encom Inc
11945 Borman Dr, St. Louis MO 63146-4114. 314/994-1300. Employs: 100-249.

Perma-Graphics Inc
2470 Schuetz Rd, Maryland Hts MO 63043-3300. 314/567-4624. Employs: 50-99.

Scholin Bros Printing Co Inc
45 E Lockwood Ave, St. Louis MO 63119-3019. 314/968-2910. Employs: 50-99.

Screen Creations Ltd
804 Texas Ct, O Fallon MO 63366-1930. 314/272-2211. Employs: 50-99.

Sportsprint Inc
252 S Florissant Rd, St. Louis MO 63135-2786. 314/429-7979. Employs: 50-99.

St Louis Envelope Co
4257 Clayton Ave, St. Louis MO 63110-1719. 314/652-4110. Employs: 50-99.

The Color Process Co
710 N Tucker Blvd, St. Louis MO 63101-1150. 314/241-0777. Employs: 50-99.

Western Publishing Co Inc
510 Highway 175, O Fallon MO 63366. 314/272-7820. Employs: 100-249.

MANIFOLD BUSINESS FORMS

Hano Business Forms Inc
Old Rt 66, Mount Olive IL 62069-9703. 217/999-2311. Employs: 50-99.

M A R Business Forms Co
Mar Graphics Dr, Valmeyer IL 62295. 618/935-2111. Employs: 50-99.

Moore Business Forms Inc
16141 N Outer Forty Rd, Chesterfield MO 63017. 314/537-2427. Employs: 50-99.

BLANKBOOKS, LOOSELEAF BINDERS AND DEVICES

Enduro Binders Inc
300 Westlink Dr, Washington MO 63090-1106. 314/239-0140. Employs: 50-99.

Inter City Mfg Co Inc
7401 Alabama Ave, St. Louis MO 63111-3004. 314/351-3100. Employs: 50-99.

Quality Business Access Inc
159 Cassens Ct, Fenton MO 63026-2543. 314/349-0949. Employs: 100-249.

Blair Industries Inc
4 Roan Cir, Florissant MO 63033-3018. 314/921-9311. Employs: 50-99.

D L Binder Sales
117 Woods Mill Rd, Ballwin MO 63011-4339. 314/394-3312. Employs: 50-99.

Stationers Loose Leaf Co
300 Westlink Dr, Washington MO 63090-1106. 314/239-6922. Employs: 100-249.

BOOKBINDING AND RELATED WORK

Atchison Co
8300 Manchester Rd, St. Louis MO 63144-2806. 314/961-8585. Employs: 50-99.

San Val Inc
4127 Forest Pk Ave, St. Louis MO 63108-2808. 314/652-8495. Employs: 50-99.

TYPESETTING

Communitype
Stark Bros Bldg Hwy 54, Louisiana MO 63353. 314/754-4920. Employs: 50-99.

Datapage Technologies Intl Inc
222 Turner Blvd, Saint Peters MO 63376-1079. 314/278-8888. Employs: 100-249.

Graphic World Inc
2272 Grissom Dr, St. Louis MO 63146-3309. 314/567-9854. Employs: 50-99.

Publication Printing Co Inc
2911 Washington Ave, St. Louis MO 63103-1305. 314/534-5194. Employs: 50-99.

Suburban Photocomposition
2340 Hampton Av, St. Louis MO 63139-2909. 314/781-1112. Employs: 50-99.

T S I Graphics Inc
1035 Hanley Indl Ct, St. Louis MO 63144. 314/968-6800. Employs: 50-99.

PLATEMAKING AND RELATED SERVICES

Beaumont Graphics Ltd
2720 Market St, St. Louis MO 63103-2522. 314/534-4500. Employs: 50-99.

Lithocraft Studios Inc
5820 Fee Fee Rd, Hazelwood MO 63042-2428. 314/731-4041. Employs: 50-99.

Matthews Intl Corp
10866 Indian Head Indl Blvd, St. Louis MO 63132-1104. 314/423-9800. Employs: 50-99.

For more information on career opportunities in printing and graphic arts:

Associations

AMERICAN INSTITUTE OF GRAPHIC ARTS
1059 3rd Avenue, New York NY 10021. 212/752-0813.

ASSOCIATION OF GRAPHIC ARTS
330 7th Avenue, 9th Floor, New York NY 10001-5010. 212/279-2100.

BINDING INDUSTRIES OF AMERICA
70 East Lake Street, Suite 300, Chicago IL 60601-5905. 312/372-7606.

GRAPHIC ARTISTS GUILD
11 West 20th Street, New York NY 10011. 212/463-7730.

INTERNATIONAL GRAPHIC ARTS EDUCATION ASSOCIATION
4615 Forbes Avenue, Pittsburgh PA 15213. 412/682-5170.

NATIONAL ASSOCIATION OF PRINTERS AND LITHOGRAPHERS
780 Pallisade Avenue, Teaneck NJ 07666. 201/342-0700.

PRINTING INDUSTRIES OF AMERICA
100 Dangerfield Road, Arlington VA 22314. 703/519-8100.

TECHNICAL ASSOCIATION OF THE GRAPHIC ARTS
Box 9887, Rochester NY 14623. 716/272-0557.

Directories

GRAPHIC ARTISTS GUILD DIRECTORY
Madison Square Press, Ten East 23rd Street, New York NY 10010. 212/505-0950.

GRAPHIC ARTS BLUE BOOK
A.F. Lewis & Co., 79 Madison Avenue, New York NY 10016. 212/679-0770.

Magazines

AIGA JOURNAL
American Institute of Graphic Arts, 1059 Third Avenue, New York NY 10021. 212/752-0813.

GRAPHIC ARTS MONTHLY
249 West 49th Street, New York NY 10011. 212/463-6836.

GRAPHIS
141 Lexington Avenue, New York NY 10016. 212/532-9387.

PRINT
104 Fifth Avenue, New York NY 10011. 212/463-0600.

RESEARCH AND DEVELOPMENT

Science technicians with good technical skills should experience excellent employment opportunities in the next decade, largely due to the increased emphasis on research and development of technical products.

LAIDLAW WASTE SYSTEMS
1838 North Broadway, St. Louis MO 63102. 314/241-3721. **Contact:** Personnel Department. **Description:** A St. Louis research and development laboratory.

MIDWEST RESEARCH INSTITUTE
425 Volker Boulevard, Kansas City MO 64110. 816/753-7600. **Contact:** Personnel Department. **Description:** A scientific research and development firm.

SMITH-KLINE BEECHAM CLINICAL LABORATORIES INC.
11636 Administration Drive, St. Louis MO 63146. 314/567-3905. **Contact:** Rita Mohr, Senior Employee Relations Specialist. **Description:** A St. Louis clinical reference laboratory. **Common positions:** medical technologist; cytotechnologist. **Educational backgrounds sought:** Medical Technologist (BS, ASCP). **Benefits:** medical insurance; dental insurance; pension plan; life insurance; tuition assistance; disability coverage; daycare assistance; profit sharing; employee discounts; savings plan. **Other U.S. locations:** 24 locations. **Operations at this facility:** administration; service; sales; technical. **Listed on:** New York Stock Exchange. **Employees:** 648. **Corporate headquarters:** London and Philadelphia.

Additional large employers: 250+

TESTING LABORATORIES

Midcoast Aviation Inc
8 Archview Dr, E St. Louis IL 62206-1445. 618/337-2100. Employs: 500-999.

Small to medium sized employers: 50-249

COMMERCIAL PHYSICAL AND BIOLOGICAL RESEARCH

Alvey Laboratories
5004 Powell Dr, Red Bud IL 62278-2924. 618/282-2018. Employs: 50-99.

Pet Inc
101 Louis Latzer Dr, Greenville IL 62246-2153. 618/664-1554. Employs: 50-99.

Sherwood Medical Co Research Ctr
11802 Westline Industrial Dr, St. Louis MO 63146-3313. 314/567-1500. Employs: 50-99.

Asbestos Professional Svc Inc
501 N 2nd St, Breese IL 62230-1649. 618/526-2742. Employs: 50-99.

HBI International
Hwy 140, Moro IL 62067. 618/377-0203. Employs: 50-99.

Savvy Environmental Exchange
339 Westglen Dr, Glen Carbon IL 62034-1001. 618/288-5552. Employs: 50-99.

Radon Electronics
2327 Washington Ave, Granite City IL 62040-5433. 618/877-9007. Employs: 50-99.

TESTING LABORATORIES

Environmetrics Inc
2345 Millpark Dr, Maryland Hts MO 63043-3529. 314/427-0550. Employs: 50-99.

ISL Corp
1530 Page Indl Blvd, St. Louis MO 63132. 314/423-3141. Employs: 50-99.

TCT-St Louis
1908 Innerbelt Business Ctr Dr, St. Louis MO 63114-5760. 314/426-0880. Employs: 50-99.

RUBBER AND PLASTICS

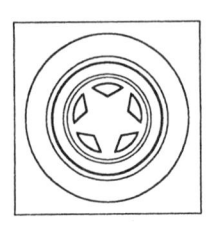

During the next five years, the demand for plastics is expected to be slow, and the U.S.' share of the world's plastics trade will continue to fall. The rubber industry, especially the synthetic rubber segment, will do much better. The highest growth rates will be for high-value, small-volume elastomers. In fabricated rubber, the big trend is toward customized production. Jobseekers with experience in Computer Aided Design and Manufacturing will reap the benefits of this trend.

CUPPLES COMPANY, MANUFACTURERS
9430 Page Avenue, St. Louis MO 63132. 314/426-7750. **Contact:** Mike Spaulding, Personnel Director. **Description:** Manufacturers of inner tubes, molded and extruded rubber products, charcoal, grocery bags and sacks. **Employees:** 400.

ICI ACRYLIC INC.
10091 Manchester Road, St. Louis MO 63122. 314/966-3111. **Contact:** Bailey C. Hurley, Director, Human Resources/Administration. **Description:** Manufacture and sale of extruded acrylic sheet, polymer, and monomer. **Common positions:** Accountant; Administrator; Customer Service Representative; Chemical Engineer; Marketing Specialist; Sales Representative. **Educational backgrounds sought:** Accounting; Business Administration; Engineering; Marketing. **Special programs:** Training programs. **Benefits:** medical, dental, and life insurance; pension plan; tuition assistance; disability coverage; savings plan. **Corporate headquarters:** This location. **Other U.S.**

locations: Los Angeles, Memphis, Toronto. **Parent company:** ICI (London). **Operations at this facility:** research and development; administration; service; sales. **Revenues (1991):** $160 million. **Employees:** 500. **Projected hires for the next 12 months:** 6. **Listed on:** New York Stock Exchange.

INTER-CITY MANUFACTURING COMPANY INC.
7401 Alabama Avenue, St. Louis MO 63111. 314/351-3100. **Contact:** Larry Werner, Plant Manager and Personnel Director. **Description:** Manufacture loose leaf catalog binders and plastic tab indexes.

MIDWEST RUBBER RECLAIMING COMPANY
Bos 2349, East St. Louis IL 62202. 618/337-6400. **Contact:** John Keseravskis, General Manager. **Description:** A St. Louis company engaged in the manufacture of reclaimed rubber.

MERAMEC GROUP
338 Ramsey Street, P.O. Box 279, Sullivan MO 63080. 314/468-3101. **Contact:** Karen Bazderesch, Personnel Manager. **Description:** A St. Louis company engaged in the manufacture of molded plastic heels and sole and heel combinations.

SEMCO PLASTIC COMPANY INC.
5301 Old Baumgartner, St. Louis MO 63129. 314/487-4557. **Contact:** Naomi Polite, Personnel Director. **Description:** Manufactures plastic injection and blow molders, plastic items, (boxes, wall anchors), packaging for hardware, electrical, and plumbing contractors.

SIEGLE-ROBERT INC.
8645 South Broadway, St. Louis MO 63111. 314/638-8300. **Contact:** Personnel Department. **Description:** Manufacture injection molding and electroplating of plastics along with decoration of plastics.

SINCLAIR & RUSH, INC.
6916 South Broadway, St. Louis MO 63111. 314/481-2450. **Contact:** Mrs. Hensley, Personnel Director. **Description:** A company engaged in the process of plastic dip molding and extruding for the manufacture of joint flange covers, plugs, and seals.

UNITED TECHNOLOGIES AUTOMOTIVE
1218 Central Industrial Drive, St. Louis MO 63110. 314/577-1100. **Contact:** Leon Gaddy, Personnel Manager. **Description:** Manufacturers of technical sealants, and expanded closed cell rubber products. **Common positions:** Chemist; Mechanical Engineer. **Educational backgrounds sought:** Chemistry; Engineering. **Special programs:** Training programs. **Benefits:** medical, dental, and life insurance; pension plan; disability coverage; savings plan. **Corporate headquarters:** Detroit, MI. **Operations at this facility:** manufacturing. **Listed on:** New York Stock Exchange.

Additional large employers: 250+

FABRICATED RUBBER PRODUCTS

Woodbridge Corp
11 Cermak Blvd, Saint Peters MO 63376-1019. 314/279-1002. Employs: 250-499.

PLASTICS PRODUCTS

Contico Intl Inc
1101 N Warson Rd, St. Louis MO 63132-1803. 314/997-5900. Employs: 500-999.

Cpc-Rexcel Inc
500 Washington Ave, St. Louis MO 63101-1261. 314/436-2822. Employs: 500-999.

Additional small to medium sized employers: 50-249

PLASTICS MATERIALS, SYNTHETIC RESINS AND NONVULCANIZABLE ELASTOMERS

A Schulman Inc
514 Earth City Plaza, Earth City MO 63045-1303. 314/291-8626. Employs: 50-99.

Akzo Resins
2904 Missouri Ave, E St. Louis IL 62205-1123. 618/271-6601. Employs: 50-99.

Anchor Inds Inc
737 Rudder, Fenton MO 63026-2014. 314/349-2900. Employs: 50-99.

Bruck Plastics Co
9920 Watson Rd, St. Louis MO 63126-1834. 314/966-5353. Employs: 50-99.

Bruck Plastics Co
9700 Watson Rd, St. Louis MO 63126-1831. 314/849-2479. Employs: 50-99.

M Holland Co
PO Box 1408, Ballwin MO 63022-1408. 314/227-5110. Employs: 50-99.

Marchem Corp
2500 Adie Rd, Maryland Hts MO 63043-3525. 314/872-8700. Employs: 100-249.

Reichhold Chemical Inc
3rd St & St Louis Ave, Valley Park MO 63088. 314/225-5226. Employs: 50-99.

The Resin Exchange
PO Box 4333, Chesterfield MO 63006-4333. 314/537-5203. Employs: 50-99.

CELLULOSIC MANMADE FIBERS

Mid America Fiber Co Inc
4193 Beck Ave, St. Louis MO 63116-2631. 314/772-2400. Employs: 50-99.

RUBBER AND PLASTICS FOOTWEAR

Western Textile Products Co
3400 Treecourt Industrial Blvd, St. Louis MO 63122-6618. 314/225-9400. Employs: 100-249.

RUBBER AND PLASTICS HOSE AND BELTING

Beltservice Corp
4143 Rider Trl N, Earth City MO 63045-1102. 314/344-8555. Employs: 100-249.

FABRICATED RUBBER PRODUCTS

Carlisle Syntec Systs
R R 4 Box 174-3 Bowman Indl, Greenville IL 62246-9458. 618/664-4540. Employs: 100-249.

Gencorp Automotive
R R 1 Box 135, Berger MO 63014-9700. 314/834-5287. Employs: 100-249.

Glazing Rubber Products
193 Woodcrest Dr, Highland IL 62249-1268. 618/654-1166. Employs: 50-99.

Reed Rubber Co Inc
5425 Manchester Ave, St. Louis MO 63110-1916. 314/645-5200. Employs: 50-99.

UNSUPPORTED PLASTICS FILM AND SHEET

Tetra Plastics Inc
620 Spirit Of St Louis Blvd, Chesterfield MO 63005. 314/532-3655. Employs: 50-99.

LAMINATED PLASTICS PLATE, SHEET AND PROFILE SHAPES

Dura Craft Industrial Inc
110 W Oak St, Gillespie IL 62033-1416. 217/839-2151. Employs: 50-99.

PLASTIC PIPE

Capco Pipe Co
475 Indl Pk, Litchfield IL 62056. 217/324-6515. Employs: 50-99.

PLASTIC FOAM PRODUCTS

Dow Chemical Co/Riverside Plant
500 Dow Indl Dr, Pevely MO 63070. 314/479-7111. Employs: 100-249.

PLASTIC PRODUCTS

American Stamp & Marking Products
500 Fee Fee Rd, Maryland Hts MO 63043-3206. 314/872-7840. Employs: 50-99.

Arundale Inc
900 S Highway Dr, Fenton MO 63026-2042. 314/343-5440. Employs: 100-249.

C P C-Rexcel Inc
625 W Columbian Blvd, Litchfield IL 62056-9572. 217/324-3921. Employs: 50-99.

Chris Kaye Plastics
715 W Park Rd Union Indl Pk, Union MO 63084-1097. 314/583-2583. Employs: 100-249.

Chris Kaye Plastics Corp
2343 Chaffe Dr, St. Louis MO 63146-3306. 314/872-9011. Employs: 100-249.

Clayton Corp
866 Horan Dr, Fenton MO 63026-2416. 314/349-5333. Employs: 50-99.

Continental Sprayers
27 Guenther Blvd, Saint Peters MO 63376-1013. 314/278-1600. Employs: 50-99.

Cope Plastics Inc
4441 Industrial Dr, Alton IL 62002-5939. 618/466-0221. Employs: 50-99.

D R G Plastics Inc
W Park Rd, Union MO 63084. 314/583-5550. Employs: 100-249.

G E T Plastics Inc
6540 M L King Dr, St. Louis MO 63133. 314/383-7225. Employs: 50-99.

J & K Enterprises
304 W Bway, Witt IL 62094. 217/594-7111. Employs: 50-99.

Koller Craft Plastic Products
1400 S Hwy 141, Fenton MO 63026. 314/343-9220. Employs: 50-99.

Louisiana Plastics Inc
3016 W Georgia St Hwy 54 W, Louisiana MO 63353-2516. 314/754-6201. Employs: 100-249.

Mac Molding Co Inc
12814 Gravois Rd, St. Louis MO 63127-1713. 314/849-0646. Employs: 50-99.

Magna Visual Inc
9400 Watson Rd, St. Louis MO 63126-1514. 314/843-9000. Employs: 100-249.

Missouri Knife Co Inc
2 Wagner Indl Ct, Saint Clair MO 63077. 314/629-1877. Employs: 50-99.

O' Brien Corp
6115 Eveline Ave, St. Louis MO 63139-3011. 314/645-8080. Employs: 50-99.

Owens Illinois Plastic Products
2122 Hereford St, St. Louis MO 63110-3106. 314/664-8390. Employs: 100-249.

Penn Corp
969 Executive Pkwy Dr #200, St. Louis MO 63141-6364. 314/434-9222. Employs: 100-249.

Pulsar Plastics Inc
26th & Franklin Sts, Carlyle IL 62231. 618/594-3692. Employs: 50-99.

Sonoco Products Co
13300 Interstate Dr, Maryland Hts MO 63043-4305. 314/344-2200. Employs: 100-249.

Spartech Corp
7777 Bonhomme Ave, St. Louis MO 63105-1911. 314/721-4242. Employs: 100-249.

Graham Packaging Co
8966 Latty Ave, St. Louis MO 63134-1025. 314/521-8302. Employs: 100-249.

The Plastics Molding Co
4211 N Broadway, St. Louis MO 63147-3323. 314/241-2479. Employs: 50-99.

For more information on career opportunities in the rubber and plastics industries:

Associations

SOCIETY OF PLASTICS
ENGINEERS
14 Fairfield Drive, Brookfield CT 06804. 203/775-0471.

SOCIETY OF PLASTICS
INDUSTRY
355 Lexington Avenue, New York NY 10017. 212/351-5410.

TRANSPORTATION

Aviation: The airlines are about as closely linked with the overall economy as any industry. Competition between airlines will remain brutal. Increasingly, the industry will be dominated by three companies - American, Delta, and United, with others at risk of falling by the wayside. With fewer major players, fewer jobs will be available. On a brighter note, according to the U.S. Labor Department, the hiring picture will improve over the long-term.

ABF FREIGHT SYSTEM INC.
P.O. Box 13928, St. Louis MO 63147. 314/869-3100. **Contact:** Personnel Department. **Description:** An over-the-road interstate trucking company. **Employees:** 200.

THE ALTON AND SOUTHERN RAILWAY COMPANY
1000 S. 22nd Street, East St. Louis IL 62207. 618/482-3232. **Contact:** F.E. Cooper, Superintendent. **Description:** A St. Louis-based railroad. **Employees:** 400.

AMERICAN AIRLINES
P.O. Box 10098, Lambert Airport, St. Louis MO 63145. 314/429-9606. **Contact:** Glenn Rutkowski, General Manager. **Description:** Metropolitan St. Louis office of the well-known airline. **Employees:** 100. For positions other than flight attendants and pilots, request an application from: American Airlines, Inc., P.O. Box 619040, MD4146, DFW Airport, TX 75261-9040. Send a self-addressed 9-by-12 inch envelope. The self-addressed envelope must contain .52 cents postage.

BE-MAC TRANSPORT COMPANY INC.
7400 North Broadway, St. Louis MO 63147. 314/382-1234. **Contact:** Personnel Department. **Description:** A St. Louis-area transportation company engaged in over-the-road trucking. **Employees:** 100.

BROWNING-FERRIS INDUSTRIES OF ST. LOUIS, INC.
11432 Bowling Green Drive, St. Louis MO 63146. 314/567-3330. **Contact:** Tracy Zahn, Personnel and Safety Manager. **Description:** A St. Louis-area corporation, engaged in local trucking, as well as refuse systems management. **Employees:** 100. **Common positions:** Blue-Collar Worker Supervisor; Claim Representative; Computer Programmer. **Benefits:** medical insurance; dental insurance; pension plan; life insurance; tuition assistance; disability coverage; profit sharing; savings plan. **Corporate headquarters:** Houston, TX. **Operations at this facility:** divisional headquarters; administration; service; sales. **Listed on:** New York Stock Exchange.

CASSENS TRANSPORT COMPANY, INC.
2000 Mraz Lane, Fenton MO 63026. 314/343-2161. **Contact:** Ron Risher, Terminal Manager. **Description:** Engaged in a variety of trucking services except local trucking. **Employees:** 600.

DELTA AIR LINES INC.
12770 Manchester Road, St. Louis MO 63131. 314/821-1600. **Contact:** Personnel Department. **Description:** Trunk carrier providing scheduled air transportation. **Corporate headquarters:** This location. **Listed on:** New York Stock Exchange.

THE HERTZ CORPORATION
Lambert Field, P.O. Box 10014, St. Louis MO 63145. 314/426-7555. **Contact:** Lynn Skelton, Personnel Director. **Description:** Transportation service organization. **Corporate headquarters:** New York, NY.

JIFFY DELIVERY
6744 Olive Blvd., University City MO 63130. 314/725-6365. **Contact:** Gina Zohner, Manager. **Description:** An area company engaged in the express package delivery service. **Common positions:** Delivery Drivers. **Operations at this facility:** service.

MADISON WAREHOUSE CORPORATION
4300 Planned Industrial Drive, St. Louis MO 63120. 314/382-3700. **Contact:** Jack Lipin, Assistant Comptroller. **Description:** A St. Louis general warehousing and storage company.

MIDCOAST AVIATION SERVICES INC.
Lambert Field, P.O. Box 10056, St. Louis MO 63145. 314/731-7111. **Contact:** Shawn Coonrod, Personnel Director. **Description:** A St. Louis airport terminal services company.

MANUFACTURERS RAILWAY COMPANY & ST. LOUIS REFRIGERATOR CAR COMPANY
2850 South Broadway, St. Louis MO 63118. 314/577-1700. **Contact:** Tom Buschman, Personnel Director. **Description:** A St. Louis switching railroad, commercial railcar repair shop and private car line company.

MOUND CITY YELLOW CAB COMPANY
6111 Delmar Boulevard, St. Louis MO 63112. 314/361-2345. **Contact:** John R. Siebert, Personnel Director. **Description:** A St. Louis taxi service.

PRESTON TRUCKING COMPANY INC.
150 Humbolt Avenue, St. Louis MO 63147. 314/385-2429. **Contact:** Personnel Department. **Description:** A long-distance trucking company.

ROADWAY EXPRESS INC.
205 Soccer Park Road, Fenton MO 63026. 314/349-5300. **Contact:** Personnel Department. **Description:** St. Louis office of the well-known over-the-road truck line.

RYDER TRUCK RENTAL
11447 Page Service Drive, St. Louis MO 63146. 314/567-6600. **Contact:** Personnel Department. **Description:** A St. Louis truck leasing and rental company.

SLAY INDUSTRIES
400 Mansion House Center, Suite 2210, St. Louis MO 63102. 314/231-8888. **Contact:** Personnel Department. **Description:** Transportation and distribution: liquid tank, dry hopper, van, reefer, flat bed and drayage trucking, warehousing and terminaling, river, rail and truck transfers, liquid and dry bulk storage, barge towing, fleeting and cleaning.

TRANS WORLD AIRLINES INC.
105 Northwest Plaza, St. Ann MO 63074. 314/291-7500. **Contact:** Personnel Department. **Description:** St. Louis office of the respected international airline.

TRI-STATE MOTOR TRANSIT COMPANY
P.O. Box 113, Joplin MO 64802. 417/624-3131, ext. 356. **Contact:** Beverly Clark, Asst. Director of Personnel. **Description:** A nationwide, specialized motor carrier with general commodity authority. **Common positions:** Accountant; Blue-Collar Worker Supervisor; Computer Programmer; Credit Manager; Customer Service Representative; Department Manager; Operations/Production Manager; Personnel and Labor Relations Specialist; Purchasing Agent; Sales Representative; Systems Analyst; Transportation and Traffic Specialist. **Educational backgrounds sought:** Accounting; Business Administration; Computer Science; Liberal Arts; Mathematics. **Benefits:** medical, dental, and life insurance; disability coverage; profit sharing; 401K. **Corporate headquarters:** This location. **Employees:** 2,529.

UNITED VAN LINES INC.
#1 United Drive, Fenton MO 63026. 314/343-3900. **Contact:** Human Resources. **Description:** Area offices of the international household goods moving service.

YELLOW FREIGHT SYSTEMS INC.
400 Barton Street, St. Louis MO 63104. 314/772-2905. **Contact:** Personnel Department. **Description:** A local and national trucking firm.

Additional large employers: 250+

RAILROAD EQUIPMENT

Union Pacific Railroad
491 N Main St, De Soto MO 63020-1537. 314/586-3950. Employs: 250-499.

RAILROADS, LINE-HAUL OPERATING

Burlington Northern Railroad
7059 Marquette Ave, St. Louis MO 63139-2106. 314/768-7021. Employs: 250-499.

RAILROAD SWITCHING AND TERMINAL ESTABLISHMENTS

Terminal RR Associate St Louis
2016 Madison Av, Granite City IL 62040-4617. 618/451-8300. Employs: 500-999.

TAXICABS

Laclede Cab Co
600 S Vandeventer Ave, St. Louis MO 63110-1240. 314/652-3456. Employs: 250-499.

INTERCITY AND RURAL BUS TRANSPORTATION

ATC Management Corp
1829 Belt Way Dr, St. Louis MO 63114-5815. 314/423-8800. Employs: 1,000+.

LOCAL TRUCKING WITHOUT STORAGE

Middlewest Freightways Inc
6810 Prescott Ave, St. Louis MO 63147-2706. 314/385-4700. Employs: 500-999.

TRUCKING, EXCEPT LOCAL

Truck Transport Incorporate
10825 Watson Rd, St. Louis MO 63127-1031. 314/965-2151. Employs: 250-499.

COURIER SERVICES, EXCEPT BY AIR

Missouri Pac Truck Lines Inc
210 N 13 St, St. Louis MO 63103-2357. 314/622-2918. Employs: 250-499.

WATER TRANSPORTATION OF FREIGHT

Consolidated Grain-Barge C
5100 Oakland Av, St. Louis MO 63110-1406. 314/658-9200. Employs: 250-499.

TRAVEL AGENCIES

Famous-Barr Co
Downtown, St. Louis MO 63101. 314/421-1295. Employs: 250-499.

Additional small to medium sized employers: 50-249

SHIP BUILDING AND REPAIRING

HBC Barge Inc
10 S Brentwood Blvd, St. Louis MO 63105-1694. 314/726-6670. Employs: 50-99.

Louisiana Dock Company
700 E Davis St, St. Louis MO 63111-3637. 314/544-7200. Employs: 100-249.

BOAT BUILDING AND REPAIRING

Quality Fiberglass Repair
2683 Highway 3, Granite City IL 62040. 618/451-0900. Employs: 50-99.

RAILROAD EQUIPMENT

St Louis Refrigerator Car Co
103 Cherokee St, St. Louis MO 63118-3301. 314/577-1759. Employs: 100-249.

ACF Industries Inc Techl Ctr
Technical Ctr, Saint Charles MO 63301. 314/723-9600. Employs: 50-99.

RAILROADS, LINE-HAUL OPERATING

East St Louis Junction RR Co
Exchange Bldg, Natl Stock Yd IL 62071. 618/274-6407. Employs: 100-249.

The Alton & Southern Ry Co
1000 S 22nd St, E St. Louis IL 62207-1943. 618/4823232. Employs: 100-249.

INTERCITY AND RURAL BUS TRANSPORTATION

Senior Citizens Shuttle Bus
125 S Center St, Collinsville IL 62234-2707. 618/344-2729. Employs: 50-99.

BUS CHARTER SERVICE, EXCEPT LOCAL

Ryder Student Transportation Svc
1300 Tom Ginnever Ave, O Fallon MO 63366-4408. 314/281-4433. Employs: 100-249.

LOCAL TRUCKING WITHOUT STORAGE

Barry Inc
2000 Saint Clair Av, E St. Louis IL 62205-1817. 618/274-0182. Employs: 50-99.

Creech Bro Trucke Lines Inc
100 Industrial Dr, Troy MO 63379-1367. 314/528-6001. Employs: 50-99.

Overnite Transportation Co
7455 Hall St, St. Louis MO 63147-2615. 314/679-3200. Employs: 100-249.

Rivers Two Trucking Inc
7401 Bunkum Rd, E St. Louis IL 62204-2300. 618/398-6753. Employs: 50-99.

Stahly Cartage Co
119 S Main St Box 486, Edwardsville IL 62025-1903. 618/656-5070. Employs: 50-99.

TRUCKING, EXCEPT LOCAL

Beaufort Transfer Company
PO Box 151, Gerald MO 63037-0151. 314/764-3376. Employs: 100-249.

Slay Transportation Co Inc
2001 S 7th St, St. Louis MO 63104-4031. 314/772-6666. Employs: 100-249.

COURIER SERVICES, EXCEPT BY AIR

Beelman Truck Co
PO Box 93, Saint Libory IL 62282-0093. 618/768-4411. Employs: 50-99.

J-C Hauling Co
PO Box 12, Millstadt IL 62260-0012. 618/397-5685. Employs: 50-99.

GENERAL WAREHOUSING AND STORAGE

Browning Arms Co
3005 Arnold Pembrook Rd, Arnold MO 63010-4728. 314/287-6800. Employs: 50-99.

Kilian Svcs
608 S Independence St, Mascoutah IL 62258-2607. 618/566-2312. Employs: 50-99.

Madison Warehouse Corporation
7275 Hazelwood Ave, Hazelwood MO 63042-2907. 314/522-8683. Employs: 50-99.

Red Arrow Corp
130 Byassee Dr, Hazelwood MO 63042-3125. 314/895-4121. Employs: 50-99.

Usco Distribution Services Inc
4327 Gustine Ave, St. Louis MO 63116-3416. 314/353-3000. Employs: 50-99.

Von Der Ahe Van Lines Inc
600 Rudder Rd, Fenton MO 63026-2013. 314/343-2200. Employs: 50-99.

SPECIAL WAREHOUSING AND STORAGE

Empire Hauling Service
7029 Bruno Ave, St. Louis MO 63143-2531. 314/644-5841. Employs: 50-99.

W & D Automotive Storage
5578 Martin Luther King Blvd, St. Louis MO 63140-1626. 314/361-2607. Employs: 50-99.

Record Masters
10720 Baur Blvd, St. Louis MO 63132-1615. 314/993-4575. Employs: 50-99.

The File Room
9889 Page Ave, St. Louis MO 63132-1428. 314/426-7800. Employs: 50-99.

DEEP SEA DOMESTIC TRANSPORTATION OF FREIGHT

CGM North America
222 S Bemiston Ave, St. Louis MO 63105-1900. 314/862-8001. Employs: 50-99.

Containership Agency Inc
1001 Craig Rd, St. Louis MO 63146-5277. 314/997-7403. Employs: 50-99.

Hanjin Shipping Co Ltd
734 Westport Plaza, St. Louis MO 63146-3000. 314/434-6668. Employs: 50-99.

Lloyd Hapag America Inc
7777 Bonhomme Ave, St. Louis MO 63105-1911. 314/726-9509. Employs: 50-99.

T F L Sales Inc
1810 Craig Rd, St. Louis MO 63146-4760. 314/469-5556. Employs: 50-99.

Valley Line Co
120 South Central Ave, St. Louis MO 63105-1705. 314/889-0100. Employs: 100-249.

WATER TRANSPORTATION OF FREIGHT

American Coml Barge Ln Co
730 E Davis St, St. Louis MO 63111-3637. 314/544-7224. Employs: 50-99.

American Commercial Trmnl Inc
5500 Hall St, St. Louis MO 63147-2902. 314/389-1500. Employs: 50-99.

Beelman River Terminals Inc
1 N Market St, St. Louis MO
63102-1415. 314/241-9600.
Employs: 50-99.

Cargo Carriers
2 Davis Street Ferry Rd, E
Carondelet IL 62240. 618/2864801.
Employs: 50-99.

Consolidated Grain & Barge
1750 S Wharf St, St. Louis MO
63104-4506. 314/421-3575.
Employs: 50-99.

Contlcarrlers and Trmnl Inc
1 Cargill Elevator Rd, E St. Louis
IL 62206. 618/332-0077. Employs:
50-99.

East Side River Tranportation Inc
6 Executive Woods Ct, Belleville
IL 62221-2016. 618/277-4481.
Employs: 50-99.

Huffman Towing Co
10 S Brentwood Blvd, St. Louis
MO 63105-1694. 314/726-2211.
Employs: 50-99.

Inland Oil & Transport Co
2510 S Brentwood Blvd, St. Louis
MO 63144-2328. 314/968-5280.
Employs: 50-99.

M C National T E & Repr Co
Ft W Hawthorne St, Hartford IL
62048. 618/254-7451. Employs:
100-249.

Marine Equipment Mgmt Corp
13523 Barrett Parkway Dr, Ballwin
MO 63021-3802. 314/821-8011.
Employs: 50-99.

McDonough Marine Service
2200 Westport Plaza Dr, St. Louis
MO 63146-3211. 314/469-0510.
Employs: 50-99.

Midwest Marine Management Co
13545 Barrett Parkway Dr, Ballwin
MO 63021-5896. 314/965-7550.
Employs: 50-99.

MVBL Terminal
1023 Rutger St, St. Louis MO
63104. 314/621-8587. Employs:
50-99.

Norman Brothers Inc
Mc Adams Hwy, Alton IL 62002.
618/466-8192. Employs: 50-99.

Nova Trading Co
1480 Woodstone Dr Ste 203, Saint
Charles MO 63304-6873. 314/928-
0011. Employs: 50-99.

Ohio River Co Traffic Division Inc
10733 Sunset Office Dr, St. Louis
MO 63127-1018. 314/821-7088.
Employs: 50-99.

Rrs Transportation Inc
109 Velma Av, South Roxana IL
62087. 618/254-8863. Employs:
50-99.

S C F Transportation Inc
11124 S Towne Sq, St. Louis MO
63123-7815. 314/894-6020.
Employs: 50-99.

Supply St Louis Inc
Gratiot, St. Louis MO 63102.
314/421-3962. Employs: 50-99.

AIR TRANSPORTATION, SCHEDULED

America West Airlines
Lambert-St Louis Intl Airport, St.
Louis MO 63145. 314/423-0700.
Employs: 100-249.

Japan Air Lines
7777 Bonhomme Ave, St. Louis
MO 63105-1911. 314/725-8522.
Employs: 100-249.

Lifeco Travel Management
8 Main, Belleville IL 62220.
618/746-2100. Employs: 50-99.

Northwest Airlines
Lambert-St Louis Intl Airport, St. Louis MO 63145. 314/427-7801. Employs: 50-99.

Trans World Airlines Inc
9825 Air Cargo Rd, St. Louis MO 63134-2044. 314/423-9550. Employs: 100-249.

Trans World Airlines Inc
4630 Lindell Blvd, St. Louis MO 63108-3702. 314/291-7500. Employs: 50-99.

USAir
Lambert-St Louis Intl Airport, St. Louis MO 63145. 314/428-8975. Employs: 100-249.

Action Express Inc
Carrollton Industrial Dr, Bridgeton MO 63044. 314/291-2362. Employs: 100-249.

Air Freight Forwarding Co
13761 Saint Charles Rock Rd, Bridgeton MO 63044-2458. 314/298-1566. Employs: 100-249.

Air Group Express
13761 Saint Charles Rock Rd, Bridgeton MO 63044-2458. 314/298-0811. Employs: 100-249.

Burlington Air Express
6115 McDonnell Blvd, St. Louis MO 63134-1936. 314/731-3338. Employs: 100-249.

Cargo Inc
4322 N Rider Trl, Earth City MO 63045-1104. 314/739-6171. Employs: 100-249.

Continental Airlines
Lambert-St Louis Airport, St. Louis MO 63145. 314/423-8983. Employs: 100-249.

Continental Quickpak Sm Pkg Svc
Lambert-St Louis Intl Airport, St. Louis MO 63145. 314/423-0338. Employs: 100-249.

Delta Air Lines Inc
Lambert International Airport, St. Louis MO 63145. 314/426-9258. Employs: 100-249.

Downtown Air Svc Inc
Bi-State Parks Airport, E St. Louis IL 62206. 618/337-7175. Employs: 50-99.

Kintetsu World Express
9420 Aero Space Dr, St. Louis MO 63134-3826. 314/427-2625. Employs: 100-249.

Land Air Express
9440 Aero Space Dr, St. Louis MO 63134-3826. 314/426-0999. Employs: 100-249.

LDI-Air Cargo
9420 Aero Space Dr, St. Louis MO 63134-3826. 314/427-5565. Employs: 100-249.

M B Freight Expediters Inc
4477 Woodson Rd, St. Louis MO 63134-3700. 314/429-4800. Employs: 100-249.

Mid West Express Co
4516 Woodson Rd, St. Louis MO 63134-3704. 314/428-1549. Employs: 100-249.

PJ Express Inc
4516 Woodson Rd, St. Louis MO 63134-3704. 314/428-7064. Employs: 100-249.

Profit Freight Systems
12755 Carrollton Industrial Ct, Bridgeton MO 63044-1202. 314/291-4499. Employs: 100-249.

Quincy Air Cargo Inc
9440 Aero Space Dr, St. Louis MO 63134-3826. 314/426-7000. Employs: 100-249.

Red Arrow Corp
4530 Woodson Rd, St. Louis MO 63134-3704. 314/426-3335. Employs: 100-249.

TMS Cargo Inc
9410 Aero Space Dr, St. Louis MO 63134-3826. 314/427-7667. Employs: 100-249.

Union Pacific Express Air
4516 Woodson Rd, St. Louis MO 63134-3704. 314/423-2299. Employs: 100-249.

Union Pacific Express Air
11789 Natural Bridge Rd, Bridgeton MO 63044-2299. 314/731-4944. Employs: 100-249.

Zantop International Airlines Incorp
6125 McDonnell Blvd, St. Louis MO 63134-1936. 314/731-5133. Employs: 100-249.

AIR COURIER SERVICES

Eden Air Freight
4530 Woodson Rd, St. Louis MO 63134-3704. 314/427-5595. Employs: 50-99.

AIRPORTS, FLYING FIELDS AND AIRPORT TERMINAL SERVICES

Aerotech Service Group
1173 Corporate Lake Dr, St. Louis MO 63132-1716. 314/997-2828. Employs: 50-99.

Aircare Aviation Ltd
3127 Creve Coeur Mill Rd, St. Louis MO 63146-2126. 314/542-0771. Employs: 50-99.

Airport Terminal Service Inc
Lambert-St Louis Intl Airport, St. Louis MO 63145. 314/423-4510. Employs: 50-99.

Dynair Tech
Lambert-St Louis Intl Airport, St. Louis MO 63145. 314/423-9320. Employs: 50-99.

Eagle's Nest
3127 Creve Coeur Mill Rd, St. Louis MO 63146-2126. 314/878-4128. Employs: 50-99.

Potosi Aviation Services Inc
3127 Creve Coeur Mill Rd, St. Louis MO 63146-2126. 314/434-4856. Employs: 50-99.

Sabreliner Corporation
Lambert International Airport, St. Louis MO 63145. 314/895-8788. Employs: 50-99.

Lambert St Louis International Airport
St. Louis Airport Authority, St. Louis MO 63145. 314/731-4100. Employs: 50-99.

St Louis General Avn Dev Corp
9024 Saint Charles Rock Rd, St. Louis MO 63114-4246. 314/426-3344. Employs: 50-99.

TRAVEL AGENCIES

Dillard's Travel
145 Crestwood Plaza, St. Louis MO 63126-1701. 314/962-4110. Employs: 100-249.

Intrav Inc
7711 Bonhomme Ave, St. Louis MO 63105-1908. 314/727-0500. Employs: 100-249.

Mid America Travel Svc Inc
222 W Main St, Washington MO 63090-2123. 314/239-5740.
Employs: 100-249.

ARRANGEMENT OF PASSENGER TRANSPORTATION

Greyhound Bus Lines
801 N Broadway, St. Louis MO 63102-2108. 314/231-8232.
Employs: 100-249.

ARRANGEMENT OF TRANSPORTATION OF FREIGHT AND CARGO

Circle Freight International
4711 Le Bourget Dr, St. Louis MO 63134-3117. 314/427-6030.
Employs: 100-249.

RENTAL OF RAILROAD CARS

Pacific Rail Leasing Corp
225 S Meramec Ave, St. Louis MO 63105-3511. 314/726-6767.
Employs: 50-99.

For more information on career opportunities in transportation:

Associations

AMERICAN BUREAU OF SHIPPING
2 World Trade Center, 106th Floor, New York NY 10048. 212/839-5000.

AMERICAN MARITIME ASSOCIATION
485 Madison Avenue, New York NY 10022. 212/319-9217.

AMERICAN SOCIETY OF TRAVEL AGENTS
1101 King Street, Alexandria VA 22314. 703/739-2782.

AMERICAN TRUCKING ASSOCIATION
2200 Mill Road, Alexandria VA 22314-4677. 703/838-1700.

ASSOCIATION OF AMERICAN RAILROADS
50 F Street NW, Washington DC 20001. 202/639-2100.

INSTITUTE OF TRANSPORTATION ENGINEERS
525 School Street SW, Suite 410, Washington DC 20024. 202/554-8050.

MARINE TECHNOLOGY SOCIETY
1828 L Street NW, Suite 906, Washington DC 20036. 202/775-5966.

NATIONAL ASSOCIATION OF MARINE SERVICES
5024-R Campbell Boulevard, Baltimore MD 21236. 410/931-8100.

NATIONAL MARINE MANUFACTURERS ASSOCIATION
401 North Michigan Avenue, Suite 1150, Chicago IL 60611. 312/836-4747.

NATIONAL MOTOR FREIGHT TRAFFIC ASSOCIATION
2200 Mill Road, Alexandria VA 22314. 703/838-1700.

NATIONAL TANK TRUCK CARRIERS
2200 Mill Road, Alexandria VA 22314. 703/838-1700.

SHIPBUILDERS COUNCIL OF AMERICA
4301 N. Fairfax Drive, Suite 330, Arlington VA 22203. 703/276-1700.

TRANSPORTATION INSTITUTE
5201 Authway Street, Camp Springs MD 20746. 301/423-3335.

Directories

MOODY'S TRANSPORTATION MANUAL
Moody's Investors Service, Inc., 99 Church Street, New York NY 10007. 212/553-0300.

NATIONAL TANK TRUCK CARRIER DIRECTORY
2200 Mill Road, Alexandria VA 22314. 703/838-1700.

OFFICIAL MOTOR FREIGHT GUIDE
1130 South Canal Street, Chicago IL 60607. 312/939-1434.

Magazines

AMERICAN SHIPPER
P.O. Box 4728, Jacksonville FL 32201. 904/355-2601.

DAILY TRAFFIC WORLD
The Traffic Service Corporation, 1325 G Street, Washington DC 20005. 202/626-4533.

FLEET OWNER
707 Westchester Avenue, White Plains NY 10604-3102. 914/949-8500.

HEAVY DUTY TRUCKING
Newport Communications, P.O. Box W, Newport Beach CA 92658. 714/261-1636.

MARINE DIGEST AND TRANSPORTATION NEWS
P.O. Box 3905, Seattle WA 98124. 206/682-3607.

OCEAN INDUSTRY
Gulf Publishing Co., P.O. Box 2608, Houston TX 77252. 713/529-4301.

SHIPPING DIGEST
51 Madison Avenue, New York NY 10010. 212/689-4411.

TRANSPORT TOPICS
2200 Mill Road, Alexandria VA 22314. 703/838-1772.

UTILITIES

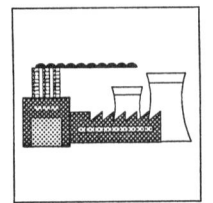

The major forces shaping the U.S. utilities industry are decreased regulation and competition from newly emerging alternative energy sources. Job prospects for those entering the utilities industry vary by sector; the best is electric, and at the bottom is the stagnant nuclear industry.

CENTRAL ILLINOIS PUBLIC SERVICE
607 East Adams Street, Springfield IL 62739. 217/523-3600. **Contact:** H.L. Gaffney, Employee Development Supervisor. **Description:** An electric and gas utility company serving the Central and Southern Illinois area.

ILLINOIS POWER
500 South 27th Street, Decator IL 62525. 217/424-6817. **Contact:** Robert Teel, Professional Recruiting Specialist. **Description:** An electric utilities company servicing approximately 1/4 of the state of Illinois. **Common positions:** Accountant; Chemist; Computer Programmer; Customer Service Representative; Economist; Civil Engineer; Electrical Engineer; Mechanical Engineer; Marketing Specialist; Public Relations Specialist; Statistician. **Educational backgrounds sought:** Accounting; Business Administration; Chemistry; Communications; Computer Science; Economics; Engineering; Finance; Marketing. **Benefits:** medical, and life insurance; pension plan; tuition assistance; disability coverage; 401 K. **Corporate headquarters:** This location. **Operations at this facility:** administration; sales. **Listed on:** New York Stock Exchange.

KANSAS CITY POWER AND LIGHT
P.O. Box 418679, Kansas City MO 64141-9679. 816/556-2200. **Contact:** George Crump, Personnel Representative. **Description:** Kansas City Power and Light, a Missouri Corporation incorporated in 1922, is a medium-sized public utility engaged in the generation, transmission, distribution and sale of electricity. Headquartered in downtown Kansas City, the company generates and distributes electricity to about 397,000 customers in a 4,700 square mile area located in all or portions of 23 counties in western Missouri and Eastern Kansas.

LACLEDE GAS COMPANY
720 Olive Street, St. Louis MO 63101. 314/342-0500. **Contact:** Jeff Mauer, Personnel Manager. **Description:** A gas utility serving the St. Louis area.

ST. LOUIS COUNTY WATER COMPANY
535 North New Ballas Road, St. Louis MO 63141. 314/991-3404. **Contact:** Mrs. Mitch, Manager of Personnel. **Description:** A water utility company.

UNION ELECTRIC COMPANY

P.O. Box 149, St. Louis MO 63166. **Contact:** Robert L. Moeller, Employment Supervisor. **Description:** Engaged in the generation and distribution of electricity. **Common positions:** Electrical Engineer; Mechanical Engineer. **Educational backgrounds sought:** Engineering. **Benefits:** medical, dental, and life insurance; tuition assistance; disability coverage; savings plan. **Corporate headquarters:** This location. **Operations at this facility:** service. **Listed on:** New York Stock Exchange. **Employees:** 6,600. **Projected hires for the next 12 months:** 6.

Additional large employers: 250+

SEWERAGE SYSTEMS

Metropolitan St Louis Sewer Dist
2000 Hampton Ave, St. Louis MO 63139-2934. 314/768-6211. Employs: 250-499.

Additional small to medium sized employers: 50-249

ELECTRIC, GAS AND SANITARY SERVICES

Illinois Power Co
140 N Main St, Edwardsville IL 62025-1902. 618/656-0940. Employs: 50-99.

Union Electric Co
122 E Broadway St, Alton IL 62002-6217. 618/463-4011. Employs: 50-99.

ELECTRIC SERVICES

Central Illinois Public Svc Co
200 E Spruce St, Jerseyville IL 62052-1749. 618/498-6421. Employs: 100-249.

Cuivre River Electrical Co Op Inc
1112 E Cherry St, Troy MO 63379-9705. 314/528-8261. Employs: 50-99.

Illinois Power Co
End Chessen La, Alton IL 62002. 618/462-9251. Employs: 100-249.

Illinois Power Co
1050 West Blvd, Belleville IL 62221-4169. 618/234-3400. Employs: 100-249.

Monroe County Electric Co Optv
901 N Market St, Waterloo IL 62298-1005. 618/939-7171. Employs: 50-99.

Southwestern Electric Coop Inc
Vadalabene Rd Rt 2, Maryville IL 62062. 618/288-6166. Employs: 100-249.

St Louis Thermal Energy Inc
1 Ashley St, St. Louis MO 63102-2233. 314/621-3550. Employs: 100-249.

Union Electric Co
200 Callahan Rd, Wentzville MO 63385-1999. 314/272-6203. Employs: 50-99.

Union Electric Power Co Plant
517 Main St, Venice IL 62090. 618/876-0181. Employs: 100-249.

NATURAL GAS DISTRIBUTION

Bishop Pipeline
401 N Lindbergh Blvd # 300, St. Louis MO 63141-7839. 314/991-4612. Employs: 50-99.

Center Oil Co
11605 Studt Ave, St. Louis MO 63141-7052. 314/993-3500. Employs: 50-99.

Clayton Gas Co
11862 Lackland Rd, St. Louis MO 63146-4206. 314/432-7008. Employs: 50-99.

Entrade Corporation
130 S Bemiston Ave, St. Louis MO 63105-1913. 314/862-4210. Employs: 50-99.

Illini Carrier Lp
4901 Lakeview Dr, Granite City IL 62040-3047. 618/931-6802. Employs: 50-99.

Illinois Power Co
Rt 159, Maryville IL 62062. 618/345-1130. Employs: 50-99.

Mississippi River Trans Corp
11839 Bluff Rd, Columbia IL 62236-3811. 618/281-7167. Employs: 50-99.

Union Electric Company
220 Kelly Ln, Louisiana MO 63353-2528. 314/754-5522. Employs: 50-99.

MIXED, MANUFACTURED OR LIQUEFIED PETROLEUM GAS PRODUCTION AND/OR DISTRIBUTION

Apex R E & T Inc
8182 Maryland Ave, St. Louis MO 63105-3786. 314/889-9600. Employs: 100-249.

COMBINATION UTILITIES

Mobile Power & Hydraulics
1721 S 7th St, St. Louis MO 63104-4025. 314/231-9522. Employs: 50-99.

WATER SUPPLY

Water Supply Districts Jefferson
Plant, Eureka MO 63025. 314/938-5909. Employs: 50-99.

Water Supply Districts Jefferson
Old Sugar Creek Rd, Fenton MO 63026. 314/326-0200. Employs: 50-99.

REFUSE SYSTEMS

Container Recovery Corp
10733 Sunset Office Dr, St. Louis MO 63127-1018. 314/821-2550. Employs: 50-99.

Laidlaw Waste Systems Inc
1838 N Broadway, St. Louis MO 63102-1203. 314/241-3710. Employs: 100-249.

For more information on career opportunities in the utilities industry:

Associations

AMERICAN WATER WORKS ASSOCIATION
6666 West Quincy Avenue, Denver CO 80235. 303/794-7711.

EMPLOYMENT AGENCIES AND TEMPORARY SERVICES OF ST. LOUIS

ABC EMPLOYMENT SERVICE
25 South Bemiston, Suite 214. Clayton MO 63105. 314/725-3140. **Contact:** C.J. Mills, General Manager. Employment agency. Appointment required. Founded 1959. **Specializes in:** Accounting; Architecture; Construction; Engineering; Industrial and Interior Design; Manufacturing; Sales and Marketing; Technical and Scientific. **Common positions filled:** Accountant; Actuary; Aerospace Engineer; Agricultural Engineer; Architect; Bank Officer/Manager; Biochemist/ Chemist; Biologist; Biomedical Engineer; Ceramics Engineer; Civil Engineer; Computer Programmer; Credit Manager; Electrical Engineer; Financial Analyst; General Manager; Industrial Designer; Industrial Engineer; Marketing Specialist; Mechanical Engineer; Metallurgical Engineer; Mining Engineer; Personnel Director; Petroleum Engineer; Physicist; Purchasing Agent; Systems Analyst. Company pays fee.

L.P. BANNING, INC.
212 South Central, Suite 302. Clayton MO 63105. 314/863-1770. **Contact:** John Speno, Vice President. Employment agency. Appointment requested. Founded 1975. Nonspecialized. **Common positions filled:** Accountant; Actuary; Administrative Assistant; Advertising Worker; Bookkeeper; Claim Representative; Clerk; Computer Operator; Computer Programmer; Credit Manager; Customer Service Representative; Data Entry Clerk; Draftsperson; Financial Analyst; Legal Secretary; Office Worker; Personnel and Labor Relations Specialist; Purchasing Agent; Receptionist; Sales Representative; Secretary; Statistician; Stenographer; Typist; Underwriter; Word Processing Specialist. Company pays fee. **Number of placements per year:** 201-500.

BEST PERSONNEL SERVICE/BESTEMPS
8901 State Line, Suite 242. Kansas City MO 64114. 816/361-3100. **Contact:** Louis Kram, President. Employment agency; temporary help agency. Founded 1966. Five locations in Metropolitan Kansas City and Kansas. **Specializes in:** Accounting; Insurance; Sales and Marketing; Secretarial and Clerical. **Common positions filled:** Accountant; Administrative Assistant; Bookkeeper; Claims Representative; Clerk; Credit Manager; Data Entry Clerk; Executive Secretary; Legal Secretary; Marketing Specialist; Medical Secretary; Personnel Director; Receptionist; Sales Representative; Secretary; Stenographer; Typist; Underwriter; Word Processor. Company pays fee. **Number of placements per year:** 51-100.

CAREER CONSULTANTS, INC.
8550 Holmes, Suite 120. Kansas City MO 64131. 816/941-8666. **Contact:** Dee Sesto, C.P.C., President. Employment agency. Appointment required. Founded 1981. **Specializes in:** Accounting; Banking and Finance; Insurance; Legal; Secretarial and Clerical. **Common positions filled:** Accountant; Actuary; Administrative Assistant; Attorney; Bank Officer/Manager; Bookkeeper; Claims Representative; Clerk; Customer Service Representative; Data Entry Clerk; Executive Secretary; Insurance Agent/Broker; Medical Secretary; Personnel Director; Receptionist; Secretary; Stenographer; Typist; Underwriter; Word Processor. Company pays fee. **Number of placements per year:** 51-100.

THE CHRISTIANSEN BROWN GROUP
2021 South Waverly, Suite 700. Springfield MO 65804. 417/883-9444. **Contact:** Scott R. Christiansen, President. Employment agency. Appointment requested. Founded 1983. **Specializes in:** Advertising; Engineering; Food Industry; Technical and Scientific. **Common positions filled:** Advertising Worker; Agricultural Engineer; Biomedical Engineer; Buyer; Chemical Engineer; Chemist; Civil Engineer; Electrical Engineer; Food Technologist; Industrial Engineer; Mechanical Engineer; Operations/Production Specialist; Personnel and Labor Relations Specialist; Purchasing Agent; Quality Control Supervisor. Company pays fee. **Number of placements per year:** 51-100.

COMPLETE HEALTH CARE, INC.
1869 Craigpark Court. St. Louis MO 63146. 314/576-4000. **Contact:** Helen Hagan, Personnel Manager. Temporary help agency. Appointment required. Founded 1983. In-home Health Care. Medicaid certified. Individual pays fee. **Number of placements per year:** 201-500.

CROWN TEMPORARY SERVICE OF MISSOURI
3316 Broadway Street. Kansas City MO 64111. 816/931-3380. **Contact:** Judy Mertz, Manager. Temporary help service. Appointment requested. Founded 1967. **Branch offices located in:** Cleveland, OH; Columbus, OH; Cincinnati, OH; Indianapolis, IN; Louisville, KY; Milwaukee, WI; Omaha, NE; Pittsburgh, PA. **Specializes in:** Accounting and Finance; Banking; Clerical; Engineering; Insurance; Legal; Manufacturing; Personnel and Human Resources. **Common positions filled:** Accountant; Administrative Assistant; Advertising Worker; Bookkeeper; Claim Representative; Clerk; Computer Operator; Computer Programmer; Construction Worker; Customer Service Representative; Data Entry Clerk; Demonstrator; Driver; Factory Worker; General Laborer; Legal Secretary; Light Industrial Worker; Marketing Specialist; Medical Secretary; Office Worker; Receptionist; Sales Representative; Secretary; Typist. Company pays fee. **Number of placements per year:** 1001+.

CROWN TEMPORARY SERVICE OF MISSOURI
9666 Olive Street, Suite 100. Olivette MO 63132. 314/993-5333. **Contact:** Brooke Colby, General Manager. Temporary help service. Appointment requested. Founded 1967. **Branch offices located in:** Cleveland, OH; Columbus, OH; Cincinnati, OH; Indianapolis, IN; Louisville, KY; Milwaukee, WI; Omaha, NE; Pittsburgh, PA. **Specializes in:** Accounting and Finance; Banking; Clerical; Engineering; Insurance; Legal; Manufacturing; Personnel and Human Resources. **Common positions filled:** Accountant; Administrative Assistant; Advertising Worker; Bookkeeper; Claim Representative; Clerk; Computer Operator; Computer Programmer; Construction Worker; Customer Service Representative; Data Entry Clerk; Demonstrator; Driver; Factory Worker; General Laborer; Legal Secretary; Light Industrial Worker; Marketing Specialist; Medical Secretary; Office Worker; Receptionist; Sales Representative; Secretary; Typist. Company pays fee. **Number of placements per year:** 1001+.

DECK AND DECKER EMPLOYMENT SERVICES
319 Kelly Plaza. Columbia MO 65202. 314/449-0876. Employment agency. Appointment requested. Founded 1971. Nonspecialized. **Common positions filled:** Accountant; Administrative Assistant; Bookkeeper; Buyer; Clerk; Computer Operator; Computer Programmer; Construction Worker; Credit Manager; Customer Service Representative; Data Entry Clerk; Draftsperson; Driver; EDP Specialist; Factory Worker; General Manager; Legal Secretary; Medical Secretary; Office Worker; Purchasing Agent; Quality Control Supervisor; Receptionist; Sales Representative; Secretary; Systems Analyst; Technician; Typist. Company pays fee; individual pays fee.

DECK AND DECKER EMPLOYMENT SERVICES
112 East Franklin. Jefferson City MO 65101. 314/636-2161. **Contact:** John Decker, Manager. Employment agency. Founded 1971. Nonspecialized. Full service agency. Company pays fee; individual pays fee.

DUNHILL OF JOPLIN
801 East 20th Street, Suite 1. Joplin MO 64804. 417/624-6552. **Contact:** Frank Wattelet, Owner. Employment agency. Founded 1976. **Specializes in:** Engineering; Technical and Scientific. **Common positions filled:** Chemical Engineer; Electrical Engineer; Industrial Engineer; Mechanical Engineer; Technician.

INTERIM PERSONNEL
111 Westport Plaza, Suite 271. St. Louis MO 63146. 314/878-6115. Temporary help service. Appointment requested. Founded 1954. Interim Personnel has over 100 offices throughout the United States. Nonspecialized. **Common positions filled:** Bookkeeper; Clerk; Computer Operator; Customer Service

Representative; Data Entry Clerk; Demonstrator; Draftsperson; Electronic Assembler; Factory Worker; General Laborer; Legal Secretary; Light Industrial Worker; Medical Secretary; Office Worker; Receptionist; Secretary; Stenographer; Technician; Typist; Word Processing Specialist. Company pays fee. **Number of placements per year: 1001+.**

LOEHR TEMPORARIES

P.O. Box 1388. St. Louis MO 63188. 314/421-1688. **Contact:** John Hayes, President. Temporary help service. Appointment requested. **Specializes in:** Clerical; Light Industrial; Technical. **Common positions filled:** Administrative Assistant; Bookkeeper; Chemist; Clerk; Customer Service Representative; Data Entry Clerk; Demonstrator; Draftsperson; Factory Worker; General Laborer; Legal Secretary; Light Industrial Worker; Medical Secretary; Office Worker; Receptionist; Secretary; Statistician; Stenographer; Technician; Typist; Word Processing Specialist.

B. LOEHR TEMPORARIES

500 Northwest Plaza, Suite 37. St. Louis MO 63074. 314/291-6397. **Contact:** John Hayes, President. Temporary help service. Appointment requested. **Specializes in:** Clerical; Light Industrial; Technical. **Common positions filled:** Administrative Assistant; Bookkeeper; Chemist; Clerk; Customer Service Representative; Data Entry Clerk; Demonstrator; Draftsperson; Factory Worker; General Laborer; Legal Secretary; Light Industrial Worker; Medical Secretary; Office Worker; Receptionist; Secretary; Statistician; Stenographer; Technician; Typist; Word Processing Specialist.

NICHOLS PERSONNEL

9201 Ward Parkway. Kansas City MO 64114. 816/444-5910. Employment agency. Appointment requested. Founded 1963. Nonspecialized. **Common positions filled:** Accountant; Actuary; Administrative Assistant; Bank Officer/Manager; Biochemist; Biomedical Engineer; Bookkeeper; Buyer; Chemical Engineer; Chemist; Civil Engineer; Claim Representative; Computer Operator; Credit Manager; Customer Service Representative; Economist; Electrical Engineer; Financial Analyst; Food Technologist; General Manager; Industrial Engineer; Insurance Agent/Broker; Legal Secretary; Marketing Specialist; Mechanical Engineer; Medical Secretary; Metallurgical Engineer; Operations/Production Specialist; Personnel and Labor Relations Specialist; Physicist; Purchasing Agent; Quality Control Supervisor; Sales Representative; Systems Analyst; Underwriter. Company pays fee; individual pays fee. **Number of placements per year: 51-100.**

OLSTEN SERVICES - HEADQUARTERS

2025 Craigshire Drive. P.O. Box 28369. St. Louis MO 63146. 314/434-2800. **Contact:** William C. Young, CEO. Temporary help agency. No appointment required. Founded 1950. **Operates as two main divisions:** Olsten Services and Olsten Healthcare Services, with separate management and usually separate facilities even in the same market. **Specializes in:** Accounting; Health and Medical; Legal; Manufacturing; MIS/EDP; Secretarial and Clerical. **Common positions filled:** Accountant; Administrative Assistant; Aerospace Engineer; Biomedical Engineer; Bookkeeper; Civil Engineer; Clerk; Data Entry Clerk; Draftsperson; EDP Specialist; Electrical Engineer; Executive Secretary; Factory Worker; General Laborer; Industrial Engineer; Legal Secretary; Light Industrial Worker; Medical Secretary; Metallurgical Engineer; Nurse; Personnel Director; Petroleum Engineer; Receptionist; Secretary; Stenographer; Technician; Typist; Word Processor. No fee. **Number of placements per year:** 1000+.

PERSONNEL POOL OF AMERICA, INC.
9738 Lackland. St. Louis MO 63114. 314/427-5555. **Contact:** Julie Tarkington, Office Manager. Temporary help service. No appointment required. Founded 1946. **Specializes in:** Clerical; Food Industry; Legal; Manufacturing. **Common positions filled:** Accountant; Administrative Assistant; Bookkeeper; Claim Representative; Clerk; Computer Operator; Computer Programmer; Construction Worker; Credit Manager; Customer Service Representative; Data Entry Clerk; Dietician; Demonstrator; Draftsperson; Driver; Factory Worker; Food Technologist; General Laborer; General Manager; Legal Secretary; Light Industrial Worker; Medical Secretary; Office Worker; Paralegal; Personnel and Labor Relations Specialist; Public Relations Worker; Receptionist; Secretary; Stenographer; Technical Writer/Editor; Typist; Underwriter; Word Processing Specialist. Company pays fee. **Number of placements per year:** 501-1000.

STATUS PRO
406 West 34th. Kansas City MO 64111. 816/931-8236. **Contact:** Landa Williams, Partner. Employment agency. Appointment required. Founded 1970. **Specializes in:** Advertising; Insurance; Printing and Publishing; Secretarial and Clerical. **Common positions filled:** Accountant; Administrative Assistant; Advertising Executive; Bookkeeper; Commercial Artist; Executive Secretary; Factory Worker; Marketing Specialist; Public Relations Worker; Receptionist; Sales Representative; Secretary; Technical Writer/Editor; Typist; Word Processor. Company pays fee; individual pays fee. **Number of placements per year:** 51-100.

STIVERS TEMPORARY PERSONNEL, INC.
500 Nichols Street, Suite 402. Kansas City MO 64112. 816/756-3377. **Contact:** Sharron Mayer, Office Manager. Temporary help service. Founded 1945. **Specializes in:** Clerical. **Common positions filled:** Accountant; Administrative Assistant; Assistant Manager; Bookkeeper; Clerk; Computer Operator; Computer Programmer; Customer Service Representative; Data Entry Clerk; Demonstrator; Driver; Factory Worker; General Laborer; General Manager; Legal Secretary; Light Industrial Worker; Medical Secretary; Office Worker;

Personnel and Labor Relations Specialist; Receptionist; Sales Representative; Secretary; Statistician; Stenographer; Switchboard Operator; Typist; Word Processing Specialist. Company pays fee. **Number of placements per year:** 501-1000.

TOBERSON GROUP
120 South Central Avenue, Suite 212. Clayton MO 63105. 314/726-0500. **Contact:** James C. Anderson, President. Employment agency. **Specializes in:** Food Industry; Health and Medical; Hotel and Restaurant Industry; Sales and Marketing; Supermarket Retail. Company pays fee. **Number of placements per year:** 51-100.

H.L. YOH COMPANY
14323 Outer Forty, Suite 484. Chesterfield MO 63017. 314/567-9660. **Contact:** Dennis Madden, Personnel Recruiters. Temporary help service. No appointment required. Founded 1940. **Specializes in:** Computer Hardware and Software; Engineering; Technical and Scientific. **Common positions filled:** Aerospace Engineer; Agricultural Engineer; Biochemist; Biologist; Chemical Engineer; Civil Engineer; Data Entry Clerk; Draftsperson; Electrical Engineer; Industrial Designer; Industrial Engineer; Loftsman; Mechanical Engineer; Mining Engineer; Nuclear Engineer; Petroleum Engineer; Planner; Purchasing Agent; Software Engineer; Systems Analyst; Technical Writer/Editor; Technician. Company pays fee; individual pays fee.

EXECUTIVE SEARCH FIRMS OF ST. LOUIS

THE ALEXANDER GROUP, INC.
1750 South Brentwood Boulevard, Suite 208. St. Louis MO 63144. 314/968-0100. **Contact:** David Rosen, President. Executive search firm. Appointment required; unsolicited resumes accepted. Founded 1983. Company seeks to remain small and work with a select client base in order to truly match the needs of the candidate with the client company. **Specializes in:** Construction. Contingency and retainer. **Number of searches conducted per year:** 51-100.

DUNHILL PERSONNEL SYSTEM OF MISSOURI
300 Chesterfield Center, Suite 260. Chesterfield MO 63017. 314/532-2243. **Contact:** Bill Eades, Owner. Executive search firm. **Specializes in:** Engineering; Metal Production and Fabrication.

DUNHILL PERSONNEL SYSTEM OF MISSOURI
4321 NE Vivion Street, Suite 305. Kansas City MO 64119. 816/452-0200. **Contact:** Elwyn Hays, President. Executive search firm. **Specializes in:** Accounting; Administration; Sales.

DUNHILL PERSONNEL SYSTEM OF MISSOURI
400 East Red Bridge Road, Suite 203. Kansas City MO 64131. 816/942-8620. **Contact:** Don Phillips, President. Executive search firm. **Specializes in:** Electronics; Engineering.

HASKELL ASSOCIATES, INC.
Post Office Box 31547. St. Louis MO 63131. 314/966-0745. **Contact:** Gerald C. (Jerry) Haskell, President/Owner. Executive search firm. Appointment requested; unsolicited resumes accepted. Founded 1973. **Specializes in:** Computer Hardware and Software; Engineering; Manufacturing; Sales and Marketing; Technical and Scientific. Contingency; noncontingency. **Number of searches conducted per year:** 26-50.

THE JOHNSON GROUP
8182 Maryland Avenue, Suite 200. Clayton MO 63105. 314/862-3000. **Contact:** David Johnson, President. A member of Abraham & London Ltd/Affluence International, "a cooperative executive placement network". The practice was founded in 1977 by the current Director, Richard London. It offers a cooperative placement system to its clients. The national headquarters are in Los Angeles, California. The practice has a nationwide network of offices and 400+ independent consultants to serve its national client list, and an international network of 100+ independent consultants serving other countries for its multinational clients. Abraham & London's practice concentrates on middle management to senior management placements. Affluence International's practice concentrates on executive level appointments. Both divisions work a wide spectrum of industries and commerce including Accounting, Banking, Data Processing, Engineering, Financial Services, Insurance, and many more. It prides itself on building a personal relationship with its clients and enjoys a high percentage of repeat business. Its attitudes in doing business are wisdom, integrity, and distinction. **The practice offers additional services to clients as follows:** Outplacement, Contract Services, Salary Evaluation, Career Planning, and Special Personnel Services. **Specializes in:** Accounting, Data Processing, and Retail.

KELLY AND ASSOCIATES
Mart Plaza Building, Suite L-8. 2921 North Belt Highway. St. Joseph MO 64506. 816/232-7735. **Contact:** John Kelly or Melrose Kelly, Co-Managers. Executive search firm. Appointment required; no phone calls; unsolicited resumes accepted. Specializes in mid-management/professional positions,

$25,000-75,000 per annum. **Specializes in:** Accounting; Administration, MIS/EDP; Advertising; Affirmative Action; Architecture; Banking and Finance; Chemicals and Pharmaceuticals; Communications; Computer Hardware and Software; Construction; Electrical; Engineering; Food Industry; General Management; Health and Medical; Human Resources; Industrial and Interior Design; Insurance; Legal; Manufacturing; Operations Management; Printing and Publishing; Procurement; Real Estate; Retailing; Sales and Marketing; Technical and Scientific; Textiles; Transportation. Contingency.

MR MEDICAL GROUP
Post Office Box 1197. Camdenton MO 65020-1197. 314/346-4833. **Contact:** Robert D. Hodgson, Manager. Executive search firm. Appointment required; no phone calls; unsolicited resumes accepted. Founded 1965. World's largest contingency search firm. Five hundred offices nationwide, doing business under the names "Management Recruiters", "Sales Consultants", "CompuSearch" and "OfficeMates5". Specializes in mid-management/professional positions, $25,000-75,000 per annum. **Specializes in:** Accounting; Administration, MIS/EDP; Advertising; Affirmative Action; Architecture; Banking and Finance; Chemicals and Pharmaceuticals; Communications; Computer Hardware and Software; Construction; Electrical; Engineering; Food Industry; General Management; Health and Medical; Human Resources; Industrial and Interior Design; Insurance; Legal; Manufacturing; Operations Management; Printing and Publishing; Procurement; Real Estate; Retailing; Sales and Marketing; Technical and Scientific; Textiles; Transportation. Contingency.

MANAGEMENT RECRUITERS OF COLUMBIA
1310 Business 63 South, Suite 1. Columbia MO 65201. **TEL:** 314/874-5698; **FAX:** 314/449-8200. **Contact:** David Dunn, Manager. Executive search firm. Appointment required; no phone calls; unsolicited resumes accepted. Founded 1965. World's largest contingency search firm. Five hundred offices nationwide, doing business under the names "Management Recruiters", "Sales Consultants", "CompuSearch" and "OfficeMates5". Specializes in mid-management/professional positions, $25,000-75,000 per annum. **Specializes in:** Accounting; Administration, MIS/EDP; Advertising; Affirmative Action; Architecture; Banking and Finance; Chemicals and Pharmaceuticals; Communications; Computer Hardware and Software; Construction; Electrical; Engineering; Food Industry; General Management; Health and Medical; Human Resources; Industrial and Interior Design; Insurance; Legal; Manufacturing; Operations Management; Printing and Publishing; Procurement; Real Estate; Retailing; Sales and Marketing; Technical and Scientific; Textiles; Transportation. Contingency.

MANAGEMENT RECRUITERS OF KANSAS CITY
Two Pershing Square. 2300 Main Street, Suite 1020. Kansas City MO 64108-2428. 816/221-2377. **Contact:** Steve Orr or Eileen Mason, Co-Managers.

Executive search firm. Appointment required; no phone calls; unsolicited resumes accepted. Founded 1965. World's largest contingency search firm. Five hundred offices nationwide, doing business under the names "Management Recruiters", "Sales Consultants", "CompuSearch" and "OfficeMates5". Specializes in mid-management/professional positions, $25,000-75,000 per annum. **Specializes in:** Accounting; Administration, MIS/EDP; Advertising; Affirmative Action; Architecture; Banking and Finance; Chemicals and Pharmaceuticals; Communications; Computer Hardware and Software; Construction; Electrical; Engineering; Food Industry; General Management; Health and Medical; Human Resources; Industrial and Interior Design; Insurance; Legal; Manufacturing; Operations Management; Printing and Publishing; Procurement; Real Estate; Retailing; Sales and Marketing; Technical and Scientific; Textiles; Transportation. Contingency.

MANAGEMENT RECRUITERS OF ST. LOUIS/AIRPORT
3301 Rider Trail South, Suite 100. Earth City MO 63045. 314/344-0959. **Contact:** Bob Keymer, Manager. Executive search firm. Appointment required; no phone calls; unsolicited resumes accepted. Founded 1965. World's largest contingency search firm. Five hundred offices nationwide, doing business under the names "Management Recruiters", "Sales Consultants", "CompuSearch" and "OfficeMates5". Specializes in mid-management/professional positions, $25,000-75,000 per annum. **Specializes in:** Accounting; Administration, MIS/EDP; Advertising; Affirmative Action; Architecture; Banking and Finance; Chemicals and Pharmaceuticals; Communications; Computer Hardware and Software; Construction; Electrical; Engineering; Food Industry; General Management; Health and Medical; Human Resources; Industrial and Interior Design; Insurance; Legal; Manufacturing; Operations Management; Printing and Publishing; Procurement; Real Estate; Retailing; Sales and Marketing; Technical and Scientific; Textiles; Transportation. Contingency.

MANAGEMENT RECRUITERS OF ST. LOUIS (CLAYTON)
11701 Borman Drive, Suite 250. St. Louis MO 63146. 314/991-4355. **Contact:** Phil Bertsch, Manager. Executive search firm. Appointment required; no phone calls; unsolicited resumes accepted. Founded 1965. World's largest contingency search firm. Five hundred offices nationwide, doing business under the names "Management Recruiters", "Sales Consultants", "CompuSearch" and "OfficeMates5". Specializes in mid-management/professional positions, $25,000-75,000 per annum. **Specializes in:** Accounting; Administration, MIS/EDP; Advertising; Affirmative Action; Architecture; Banking and Finance; Chemicals and Pharmaceuticals; Communications; Computer Hardware and Software; Construction; Electrical; Engineering; Food Industry; General Management; Health and Medical; Human Resources; Industrial and Interior Design; Insurance; Legal; Manufacturing; Operations Management; Printing and Publishing; Procurement; Real Estate; Retailing; Sales and Marketing; Technical and Scientific; Textiles; Transportation. Contingency.

MANAGEMENT RECRUITERS OF ST. LOUIS/WEST COUNTY
200 Fabricator Drive. Fenton MO 63026. 314/349-4455. **Contact:** J. Edward Travis, General Manager. Executive search firm. Appointment required; no phone calls; unsolicited resumes accepted. Founded 1965. World's largest contingency search firm. Five hundred offices nationwide, doing business under the names "Management Recruiters", "Sales Consultants", "CompuSearch" and "OfficeMates5". Specializes in mid-management/professional positions, $25,000-75,000 per annum. **Specializes in:** Accounting; Administration, MIS/EDP; Advertising; Affirmative Action; Architecture; Banking and Finance; Chemicals and Pharmaceuticals; Communications; Computer Hardware and Software; Construction; Electrical; Engineering; Food Industry; General Management; Health and Medical; Human Resources; Industrial and Interior Design; Insurance; Legal; Manufacturing; Operations Management; Printing and Publishing; Procurement; Real Estate; Retailing; Sales and Marketing; Technical and Scientific; Textiles; Transportation. Contingency.

OFFICEMATES5 OF ST. LOUIS (CLAYTON)
11701 Borman Drive, Suite 245. St. Louis MO 63146. 314/991-1433. **Contact:** Carol Zagarri, Manager. Executive search firm. Appointment required; no phone calls; unsolicited resumes accepted. Founded 1965. World's largest contingency search firm. Five hundred offices nationwide, doing business under the names "Management Recruiters", "Sales Consultants", "CompuSearch" and "OfficeMates5". Specializes in mid-management/professional positions, $25,000-75,000 per annum. **Specializes in:** Accounting; Administration, MIS/EDP; Advertising; Affirmative Action; Architecture; Banking and Finance; Chemicals and Pharmaceuticals; Communications; Computer Hardware and Software; Construction; Electrical; Engineering; Food Industry; General Management; Health and Medical; Human Resources; Industrial and Interior Design; Insurance; Legal; Manufacturing; Operations Management; Printing and Publishing; Procurement; Real Estate; Retailing; Sales and Marketing; Technical and Scientific; Textiles; Transportation. Contingency.

OFFICEMATES5 OF ST. LOUIS (DOWNTOWN)
100 North Broadway, Suite 1130. St. Louis MO 63102. 314/241-5866. **Contact:** Carol Zagarri, General Manager, or Georgia Reid, Manager. Executive search firm. Appointment required; no phone calls; unsolicited resumes accepted. Founded 1965. World's largest contingency search firm. Five hundred offices nationwide, doing business under the names "Management Recruiters", "Sales Consultants", "CompuSearch" and "OfficeMates5". Specializes in mid-management/professional positions, $25,000-75,000 per annum. **Specializes in:** Accounting; Administration, MIS/EDP; Advertising; Affirmative Action; Architecture; Banking and Finance; Chemicals and Pharmaceuticals; Communications; Computer Hardware and Software; Construction; Electrical; Engineering; Food Industry; General Management; Health and Medical; Human Resources; Industrial and Interior Design; Insurance; Legal; Manufacturing;

Operations Management; Printing and Publishing; Procurement; Real Estate; Retailing; Sales and Marketing; Technical and Scientific; Textiles; Transportation. Contingency.

MANAGEMENT RECRUITERS OF SPRINGFIELD
1807 East Edgewood, Suite B. Springfield MO 65804. 417/882-6220. **Contact:** J. Craig Rudolph or Arlyn B. Rudolph, Co-Managers. Executive search firm. Appointment required; no phone calls; unsolicited resumes accepted. Founded 1965. World's largest contingency search firm. Five hundred offices nationwide, doing business under the names "Management Recruiters", "Sales Consultants", "CompuSearch" and "OfficeMates5". Specializes in mid-management/professional positions, $25,000-75,000 per annum. **Specializes in:** Accounting; Administration, MIS/EDP; Advertising; Affirmative Action; Architecture; Banking and Finance; Chemicals and Pharmaceutlcals; Communications; Computer Hardware and Software; Construction; Electrical; Engineering; Food Industry; General Management; Health and Medical; Human Resources; Industrial and Interior Design; Insurance; Legal; Manufacturing; Operations Management; Printing and Publishing; Procurement; Real Estate; Retailing; Sales and Marketing; Technical and Scientific; Textiles; Transportation. Contingency.

INDEX TO PRIMARY EMPLOYERS

NOTE: Below is an alphabetical index of the St. Louis' primary employer listings included in this book. Those employers in each industry that fall under the headings "Additional large employers" or "Small to medium sized employers" are not indexed here.

A

AAA-AUTO CLUB OF MISSOURI, 79
ABF FREIGHT SYSTEM INC., 311
A.G.I.-DELHAVEN MANOR, INC., 219
AT&T NETWORK SYSTEMS, 127
THE ABSORBENT COTTON COMPANY, 259
ACKERMAN BUICK INC., 190
S.G. ADAMS PRINTING, 298
J.S. ALBERICI CONSTRUCTION CO., 66
ALEXANDER & ALEXANDER OF MISSOURI, 251
ALLEN FOODS INC., 177
ALLIED AFTERMARKET, 271
ALLSTATE INSURANCE COMPANY, 251
ALLTEL ILLINOIS, INC., 127
THE ALTON AND SOUTHERN RAILWAY COMPANY, 311
ALTON MEMORIAL HOSPITAL, 219
ALTON MENTAL HEALTH CENTER, 219
ALTON TELEGRAPH PRINTING COMPANY, 287
ALUMAX FOILS INC., 155
ALVEY INC., 271
AMERICAN AIRLINES, 311
AMERICAN INGREDIENTS COMPANY, 110
AMERICAN LOOSE-LEAF BUSINESS PRODUCTS, 298
AMERICAN NATIONAL CAN COMPANY, 155
AMERICAN TRADING & PRODUCTION CORP., 259
AMOCO PETROLEUM ADDITIVES COMPANY, 145
ARTHUR ANDERSEN AND COMPANY, 43
ANGELICA CORPORATION, 60
ANHEUSER-BUSCH COMPANIES INC., 177

ARBY'S ROAST BEEF RESTAURANTS, 241
ARCH MINERAL CORPORATION, 145
ARCHER DANIEL MIDLAND CO., 177
ARMSTRONG, TEASDALE, SCHAFLEY, DAVIS, DICUS, 257
ARROW GROUP INDUSTRIES, 66
ARTEX INTERNATIONAL INC., 60
ASCHINGER ELECTRIC COMPANY, 135
ASSOCIATED GROCERS' COMPANY OF ST. LOUIS, 66
AUTOMATIC DATA PROCESSING INC., 132
AUTOMATION INTERNATIONAL, INC., 259

B

B-LINE SYSTEMS INC., 155
BSI CONSTRUCTORS INC., 66
BALDOR ELECTRIC COMPANY, 135
BALLMAN ENGINEERING, 135
BANGERT BROTHERS CONSTRUCTION COMPANY, 67
BANJO IRON AND SUPPLY COMPANY, 155
BARNES HOSPITAL, 219
BARNES ST. PETER'S HOSPITAL, 220
BARNES WEST COUNTY HOSPITAL, 220
BARNHART INDUSTRIES INC., 260
BARRY-WEHMILLER COMPANY, 260
BASLER ELECTRIC, 135
BE-MAC TRANSPORT COMPANY INC., 311
BEALL MANUFACTURING DIVISION, 260
BECKITT & COLEMAN, 260
BELL SPORTS, 260
BELLEVILLE AREA COLLEGE, 115
BELLEVILLE SHOE MANUFACTURING COMPANY, 60
THE BENJAMIN ANSEHL COMPANY, 259
BERNADETTE BUSINESS FORMS INC., 298
BEST BEERS INC., 177
BETHESDA GENERAL HOSPITAL AND HOMES, 220
BEVERLY FARM FOUNDATION INC., 220
BIG RIVER ZINC CORPORATION, 155
THE BILTWELL COMPANY INC., 60
EDWARD L. BLAKEWELL, INC., 67
BLUE CROSS AND BLUE SHIELD OF MISSOURI, 251
BOATMEN'S NATIONAL BANK OF BELLEVILLE, 83
BOATMEN'S TRUST COMPANY, 170
BODINE ALUMINUM INC., 156
BOOKER ASSOCIATES, INC., 151
BORDEN PASTA, 177
BRASCH MANUFACTURING COMPANY INC., 135

BROD-DUGAN COMPANY, 111
BROWNING-FERRIS INDUSTRIES, 312
BRYAN AND CAVE, 257
BULL MOOSE TUBE COMPANY, 156
BURNS INTERNATIONAL, 281
BUSSMAN DIVISION/COOPER INDUSTRIES, 136

C

CBP PRESS, 100
CPI CORP., 260
CALGON VESTAL LABORATORIES, 220
CARDINAL GLENNON CHILDREN'S HOSPITAL, 220
CARDINAL RITTER INSTITUTE, 221
CARLE FOUNDATION HOSPITAL, 221
CARONDELET CORPORATION, 156
CARTER AUTOMOTIVE CO. INC., 80
CASHEX INC., 171
CASSENS TRANSPORT COMPANY, INC., 312
THE CATHOLIC HEALTH ASSOCIATION, 221
CEDARCREST MANOR INC., 221
CEDARCROFT NURSING CENTER INC., 221
CENTOCOR, INC., 221
CENTRAL COUNTER COMPANY, 261
CENTRAL HARDWARE COMPANY, 190
CENTRAL ILLINOIS PUBLIC SERVICE, 322
CENTRAL INSTITUTE FOR THE DEAF, 115
CENTRAL MEDICAL CENTER, 221
CENTRAL MICROFILM SERVICE, 261
CENTRAL MINE EQUIPMENT, 145
CENTRAL MISSOURI STATE UNIVERSITY, 115
CENTRAL STATES DIVERSIFIED INC., 298
CENTRAL STATES WIPING MATERIALS CO., 61
CENTREVILLE TOWNSHIP HOSPITAL, 222
CENTRIFUGAL AND MECHANICAL, 271
CHARLES F. VATTEROTT & CO., 71
CHILDREN'S HOSPITAL, 222
CHRYSLER CORPORATION/ST. LOUIS ASSEMBLY COMPLEX, 80
CITICORP, 171
CLARION HOTEL/ST. LOUIS, 241
CLARK OIL AND REFINING CORPORATION, 145
CLAYTON-DAVIS & ASSOCIATES, 46
CLEAN INDUSTRIAL SERVICE, 281
CLEAN-TECH COMPANY AND SUBSIDIARIES, 281
CLIMATE ENGINEERING CORPORATION, 67
COIN ACCEPTORS INC., 261

COLDWELL BANKER, 67
COLLINSVILLE HOLIDAY INN, 242
COLLINSVILLE MAC INC., 242
COLOR ART INC., 299
COLUMBIA QUARRY COMPANY, 145
COMFORT PRINTING AND STATIONERY COMPANY, 299
COMMERCE BANK OF ST. LOUIS, 84
CONAGRA FLOUR MILLING COMPANY, 177
CONCORDIA PUBLISHING HOUSE, 100
CONCORDIA SEMINARY, 116
CONDAIRE INC., 67
CONNECTOR CASTINGS INC., 136
CONTICO INTERNATIONAL, INC., 261
CONTINENTAL BAKING COMPANY, 177
CONTINENTAL FABRICATORS, 156
COOPERS AND LYBRAND, 43
CORRIGAN COMPANY, 67
COURION INDUSTRIES INC., 272
COVENANT THEOLOGICAL SEMINARY, 116
CHARLES L. CRANE AGENCY COMPANY, 251
CRANE NATIONAL VENDORS, 272
CUMMINS GATEWAY, 272
CUPPLES COMPANY, MANUFACTURERS, 306
CUPPLES PRODUCTS DIVISION, 156
CURTIS-TOLEDO/A WYLE COMPANY, 272

D

D'ARCY MASIUS BENTON & BOWLES, 46
THE DANIEL AND HENRY COMPANY, 252
DANVILLE METAL STAMPING COMPANY, INC., 156
DATAMAX OFFICE SYSTEMS, 190
DATAPAGE TECHNOLOGIES INTERNATIONAL INC., 136
DEACONESS HEALTH SYSTEM/CENTRAL CAMPUS, 222
DELOITTE & TOUCHE, 43
DELTA AIR LINES INC., 312
DELUXE CHECK PRINTERS, INC., 299
DEPARTMENT OF VETERANS AFFAIRS, 222
DEPAUL HEALTH CENTER, 222
THE DIAL CORPORATION, 261
DIDION AND SONS FOUNDRY COMPANY, 156
DIEMAKERS, INC., 272
DIERBERG'S MARKETS, 178
DIGITAL EQUIPMENT CORPORATION, 132
DIMAC DIRECT, 46
DIRECTORY DISTRIBUTING ASSOCIATION INC., 281

DIVERSIFIED INDUSTRIES INC., 156
DOW CHEMICAL USA, 111
DRUG PACKAGE INC., 290
DUKE MANUFACTURING COMPANY, 262

E

EG&G MISSOURI METAL SHAPING COMPANY, 157
EG&G VACTEC, 136
EAGLE BRAND SALES, 178
EAST CENTRAL COLLEGE, 116
EASTERN ILLINOIS UNIVERSITY, 116
EDISON BROTHERS STORE, INC., 190
ELDER MANUFACTURING COMPANY, 61
EMERSON ELECTRIC COMPANY, 136
EMPIRE STOVE COMPANY, 262
ENGINEERED AIR SYSTEMS INC., 51
EQUITABLE REAL ESTATE INVESTMENT MANAGEMENT, INC., 67
ERKER CATERING COMPANY INC., 242
ESSEX INDUSTRIES INC., 51
EXECUTIVE INTERNATIONAL INN, 242

F

JOHN FABICK TRACTOR COMPANY, 273
FACTORY MUTUAL ENGINEERING AND RESEARCH, 282
FAIRMONT RACE TRACK, 54
FALCON PRODUCTS INC., 262
FAMOUS-BARR COMPANY, 191
FEDERAL RESERVE BANK OF ST. LOUIS, 84
FERGUSON MACHINE COMPANY, 273
FINNINGER'S CATERING SERVICE INC., 242
FIREMAN'S FUND INSURANCE COMPANY, 252
FIRST BANK AND SAVINGS BANK, 84
FIRST FINANCIAL BANK, FSB, 84
1st FINANCIAL BUILDING CORP., 67
FIRST NATIONAL BANK OF BELLEVILLE, 84
FISCHER'S RESTAURANT, 242
FISHER SCIENTIFIC COMPANY, 191
FLOUR MILLS DIVISION, 178
FOLLMAN PROPERTIES, 68
FONTBONNE COLLEGE, 116
FOREST PHARMACEUTICALS, 222
FORESTER ENTERPRISES, INC., 299

FOX MEYER DRUG COMPANY, 191
FOX PHOTO, 299
FRAME FACTORY LTD., 191
FRITO-LAY INC./ROLD GOLD, 178
FRU-CON CONSTRUCTION CORPORATION, 68
FRUCON ENGINEERING/SUBSIDIARY OF FRU-CON CORP., 151

G

GANNETT OUTDOOR COMPANY OF ST. LOUIS, 47
GARRETT GENERAL AVIATION, 52
GAYLORD CONTAINER DIVISION, 290
GENERAL ELECTRIC COMPANY, 137
GENERAL INSTALLATION COMPANY, 68
GENERAL METAL PRODUCTS COMPANY, 157
GENERAL MOTORS CORPORATION, 80
GEORGIA PACIFIC, 290
GLASCO ELECTRIC COMPANY, 137
GRAMEX CORPORATION, 191
GRANITE CITY STEEL DIVISION, 157
GRAYBAR ELECTRIC COMPANY INC., 137
WARREN H. GREEN INC., 101
GREENSFELDER, HEMKER, AND GALE, 257
GREY EAGLE DISTRIBUTORS INC., 178
GROSS MECHANICAL COMPANY, 68
GROSSMAN IRON & STEEL, 157
GROW GROUP INC., 111
T.J. GUNDLACH MACHINE COMPANY, 273

H

H-R ELECTRONICS, 137
H.A. POPE & SONS INC., 244
H.B.D. CONTRACTING INC., 68
HBE CORPORATION, 68
HAAS BAKING COMPANY, 178
HAGER HINGE COMPANY, 262
H.H. HALL CONSTRUCTION COMPANY, 69
HARCROS PIGMENTS INC., 111
HARDEE'S INC., 242
HARTMAN-WALSH CORPORATION, 69
HARVARD INDUSTRIES, 157
HARVARD INTERIORS MANUFACTURING CO., 262
HELLMUTH OBATA & KASSABAUM INC., 151

JAY HENGES ENTERPRISES, INC., 69
HENRY VIII INN & LODGE, 243
THE HERTZ CORPORATION, 312
HEWLETT-PACKARD COMPANY, 191
HIGHLAND SUPPLY CORPORATION, 262
JEROME HIRSCH & ASSOCIATES, 47
HIT OR MISS, INC., 192
HITCHINER MANUFACTURING COMPANY INC., 157
HOLIDAY INN DOWNTOWN/CONVENTION CENTER, 243
HOLIDAY INNS INC./ST. LOUIS AREA, 243
P.J. HOLLORAN COMPANY, 282
HOME FEDERAL SAVINGS, 85
HOME NURSERY GREENHOUSES INC., 262
HOST INTERNATIONAL, INC., 243
HUDSON CHEMICAL COMPANY, 282
HUMANE SOCIETY OF MISSOURI, 106
HUNTER/KREY FOODS, 178
HUSSMANN CORPORATION, 273

I

ICI ACRYLIC INC., 306
IEA INC., 101
ISO COMMERCIAL RISK SERVICES, 252
ILLINOIS CONSOLIDATED TELEPHONE COMPANY, 127
ILLINOIS POWER, 322
INCARNATE WORD HOSPITAL, 223
INDUSTRIAL ENGINEERING, 137
INLAND CONTAINER CORPORATION, 290
INTER-CITY MANUFACTURING COMPANY INC., 307
INTERNATIONAL LUTHERAN LAYMEN'S LEAGUE, 103

J

JACKES-EVAN MANUFACTURING COMPANY, 263
JAKEL INCORPORATED, 263
JAMES RIVER CORPORATION, 290
JCPENNEY COMPANY INC., 192
JEFFERSON COUNTY JUNIOR COLLEGE DISTRICT, 116
JEFFERSON MEMORIAL HOSPITAL, 223
JEFFERSON PRODUCTS, 273
JEFFERSON SAVINGS & LOAN ASSOCIATION, 85
JEFFERSON SMURFIT, 290, 291
JEWISH CENTER FOR AGED, 223

JEWISH COMMUNITY CENTERS ASSOCIATION, 106
THE JEWISH HOSPITAL OF ST. LOUIS, 223
JIFFY DELIVERY, 312
JOHANSEN BROTHERS SHOE COMPANY INC., 61
GEORGE JOHNSON ADVERTISING, 47
JOURNAL NEWSPAPERS OF SOUTH COUNTY, 287

K

K MART DISCOUNT STORES, 192
K'S MERCHANDISE, 192
K-V PHARMACEUTICAL CO., 223
KMOX-RADIO/TV, 103
KPLR-TV, 103
KSDK-TV/MULTIMEDIA INC., 103
KTVI-TV/CHANNEL 2, 103
KAISER ELECTRIC INC., 137
KANSAS CITY POWER AND LIGHT, 322
KASCO CORPORATION, 273
CLIFF KELLEY INC., 46
KENRICK GLENNON SEMINARY, 116
KICKHAM BOILER & ENGINEERING COMPANY, 273
KILLARK ELECTRIC MANUFACTURING COMPANY, 138
KLEIN'S DEPARTMENT STORES INC., 192
KLOSTER COMPANY INC., 69
KRIBS FORD INC., 80
KRUPNICK & ASSOCIATES INC., 47
KUPPER PARKER COMMUNICATIONS, 47

L

LACLEDE GAS COMPANY, 322
LAIDLAW WASTE SYSTEMS, 305
LAMMERT FURNITURE COMPANY, 193
LANG & SMITH GROUP INC., 47
LAROUCHE INDUSTRIES, INC., 111
LEAF INC./DIVISION OF SWITZER CLARK, 178
LEE-ROWAN COMPANY, 263
LEGGETT & PLATT, INC., 263
LEMAY BANK & TRUST COMPANY, 85
LEONARD'S METAL, INC., 157
LEVER BROTHERS COMPANY, 111
LEWIS & CLARK COMMUNITY COLLEGE, 116
LINCOLN, 274

LINDELL TRUST COMPANY, 85
LINDENWOOD COLLEGE, 116
LION'S CHOICE, 243
JOSEPH LIPIC PEN COMPANY, 263
LOWELL MANUFACTURING COMPANY, 263
LOWY ENTERPRISES INC., 193
LUTHERAN ALTENHEIM SOCIETY OF MISSOURI, 107
LUTHERAN MEDICAL CENTER, 223
LYON SHEET METAL WORKS, 158

M

MCI TELECOMMUNICATIONS, 127
MFA INC., 179
MFG ASSOCIATED INC., 69
MACK ELECTRIC COMPANY, 138
MADISON WAREHOUSE CORPORATION, 312
MAGNA BANK, 85
MAGNABANK BRENTWOOD CENTER, 85
MAINTENANCE UNLIMITED JANITORIAL, 282
MANUFACTURERS RAILWAY COMPANY &, 312
MARK TWAIN BANCSHARES INC., 85
MARLO COIL NUCLEAR COOLING INC., 274
MARQUETTE TOOL & DIE COMPANY, 158
MARRIOTT AIRPORT HOTEL/ST. LOUIS, 243
MARRIOTT PAVILION HOTEL, 244
MARSH COMPANY, 263
MARSHALL-McLENNON INSURANCE AGENCY, 252
MARTIN INDUSTRIES, 264
MARYVILLE UNIVERSITY, 116
THE MAY DEPARTMENT STORES COMPANY, 193
McBRIDE & SON, 69
McDONALD'S CORPORATION, 244
McDONNELL DOUGLAS CORPORATION, 52
McDONNELL DOUGLAS ELECTRONICS COMPANY, 52
McKENDREE COLLEGE, 117
MELBOURNE MANUFACTURING COMPANY, 61
MEMORIAL HOSPITAL, 223
MERAMEC GROUP, 307
MERCANTILE BANCORPORATION INC., 86
MERCANTILE BANK OF ST. LOUIS, 86
MERCK & COMPANY INC., 179
MERRILL, LYNCH, PIERCE, FENNER & SMITH, 171
METAL GOODS, 158
THE MICHELSON ORGANIZATION, 69
MID-AMERICA DAIRYMEN INC., 179

MIDCOAST AVIATION SERVICES INC., 312
MIDWEST RESEARCH INSTITUTE, 305
MIDWEST RUBBER RECLAIMING COMPANY, 307
MIDWEST TELEVISION, INC., 103
MISS ELAINE, 61
MISS HULLING'S CAFETERIAS, 244
MISSISSIPPI LIME COMPANY, 146
MISSISSIPPI RIVER TRANSMISSION CORP., 146
MISSOURI ATHLETIC CLUB, 55
MISSOURI BAPTIST COLLEGE, 117
MISSOURI BAPTIST HOSPITAL OF SULLIVAN, 224
MISSOURI BAPTIST MEDICAL CENTER, 224
MISSOURI BOILER & TANK COMPANY, 158
MISSOURI BOTANICAL GARDEN, 55
MISSOURI GOODWILL INDUSTRIES INC., 107
MISSOURI MEDICAL SERVICE INC., 252
MONSANTO, 111
MOOG AUTOMOTIVE INC., 80
BENJAMIN MOORE & COMPANY, 112
MORGAN SYSTEMS INC., 282
MORGAN-WIGHTMAN SUPPLY COMPANY, 193
MOSBY-YEAR BOOK, INC., 101
MOUND CITY YELLOW CAB COMPANY, 313
MRS. ALLISON'S COOKIE CO., 179
MULTIPLEX COMPANY INC., 179
MULTIPLEX DISPLAY FIXTURE COMPANY, 193
MUNICIPAL THEATRE ASSOC. OF ST. LOUIS, 55

N

NCR CORPORATION, 132
NABISCO BRANDS INC., 180
NATIONAL CASUALTY COMPANY, 252
NATIONAL CLEANING, 282
NATIONAL GENERAL INSURANCE COMPANY, 253
NATIONAL HEALTH CARE, 224
NATIONAL INDUSTRIAL SECURITY CORPORATION, 282
NATIONAL LINEN SERVICE, 282
NATIONAL LOCK CORPORATION, 264
NATIONWIDE ADVERTISING SERVICE INC., 47
NEIMAN-MARCUS, 193
NESCO STEEL BARREL COMPANY, 158
NETTIE'S FLOWER GARDEN INC., 194
THE NEWS DEMOCRAT, 287
NIEHAUS CONSTRUCTION SERVICES INC., 70
NIES-KAISER PRINTING COMPANY, 299

NIXDORFF KREIN INDUSTRIES INC., 264
NOONEY KROMBACH COMPANY, 70
NOOTER CORPORATION, 158
NORTHWEST MISSOURI STATE UNIVERSITY, 117
NORWOOD SHOE CORPORATION, 61

O

OLIN CORPORATION, 264
ORCHARD CORPORATION OF AMERICA, 274
ORCHELN COMPANY, 80
OVERLAND MEDICAL CENTER, 224
OWENS-ILLINOIS INC., 291
OWENS-ILLINOIS INC., 291, 292

P

PACKAGING CORPORATION OF AMERICA, 292
PARAMONT LIQUOR COMPANY, 180
PAULO PRODUCTS COMPANY, 158
PAUWELS TRANSFORMERS INC., 138
PEA RIDGE IRON ORE CO., 158
PEABODY HOLDING COMPANY, INC., 146
PEAT MARWICK, 43
PETROLITE CORPORATION, 112
PEVELY DAIRY COMPANY, 180
PINKERTON SECURITY SERVICES, 283
PIZZA HUT OF ST. LOUIS INC., 244
POTTER ELECTRIC SIGNAL COMPANY, 138
PRAIRIE FARMS DAIRY INC., 180
PRESTON TRUCKING COMPANY INC., 313
PRINCE GARDNER, 61
PROGRESSIVE SERVICE COMPANY, 159

Q

QUAKER STATE CORPORATION, 112

R

RCA SERVICE COMPANY, 138
RADIO SHACK, 194
C. RALLO CONTRACTING COMPANY INC., 70
RALSTON PURINA, 48
RALSTON PURINA COMPANY, 180
RAX RESTAURANTS, INC., 244
THE RELIABLE LIFE INSURANCE CO., 253
RICHARDS BRICK COMPANY, 70
RITEPOINT CORPORATION, 264
ROADMASTER CORPORATION, 264
ROADWAY EXPRESS INC., 313
LT. ROBERT E. LEE RESTAURANT, 245
ROESCH INC., 159
ROOSEVELT BANK, 86
ROSS ADVERTISING, INC., 48
RYDER TRUCK RENTAL, 313
JOSEPH T. RYERSON & SON INC., 159

S

SSM REHABILITION INSTITUTE, 224
STI, 224
SABRELINER CORPORATION, 52
SACHS ELECTRIC COMPANY, 138
SAFECO INSURANCE GROUP, 253
ST. ANTHONY'S HOSPITAL, 225
ST. ANTHONY'S MEDICAL CENTER, 225
ST. CLAIR DIE CASTING COMPANY, 159
ST. CLEMENT HOSPITAL, 225
ST. ELIZABETH'S HOSPITAL, 225
ST. JOHN'S BANK & TRUST COMPANY, 86
ST. JOHN'S MERCY HOSPITAL, 225
ST. JOHN'S MERCY MEDICAL CENTER, 225
ST. JOSEPH HOSPITAL, 226
ST. LOUIS CHILDREN'S HOSPITAL, 226
ST. LOUIS CHRISTIAN COLLEGE, 117
ST. LOUIS COLLEGE OF PHARMACY, 117
ST. LOUIS COMMUNITY COLLEGE, 117
ST. LOUIS CONSERVATORY & SCHOOLS FOR THE ARTS, 118
ST. LOUIS COUNTY WATER COMPANY, 322
ST. LOUIS LITHOGRAPHING COMPANY, 300
ST. LOUIS NATIONAL STOCK YARDS COMPANY, 181
ST. LOUIS POST-DISPATCH, 287

ST. LOUIS REFRIGERATOR CAR CO., 274
ST. LOUIS REGIONAL MEDICAL CENTER, 226
ST. LOUIS STATE HOSPITAL, 226
ST. LOUIS STEEL, 159
ST. LOUIS STEEL CASTING INC., 159
ST. LOUIS SYMPHONY SOCIETY, 56
ST. LUKE'S HOSPITAL, 226
ST. MARY'S HEALTH CENTER, 227
ST. PAUL'S HOMES FOR THE AGED, 227
ST. PETER'S HOSPITAL, 227
SAKS FIFTH AVENUE, 194
L.E. SAUER MACHINE COMPANY, 274
SAYERS PRINTING COMPANY, 300
SCHNEITHORST'S, 245
SCHNUCK MARKETS INC., 180
SEMCO PLASTIC COMPANY INC., 307
SERVCO EQUIPMENT CO., 180
THE SEVEN-UP COMPANY, 180
SHADE TREE SERVICE COMPANY, 283
SHERATON WEST PORT INN, 245
SHERWOOD MEDICAL COMPANY, 225
SHONEY'S INC., 245
SHRINERS HOSPITAL FOR CRIPPLED CHILDREN, 225
SIEGLE-ROBERT INC., 307
SIGMA CHEMICAL COMPANY, 112
SINCLAIR & RUSH, INC., 307
SIX FLAGS OVER MID-AMERICA, 55
SLAY INDUSTRIES, 313
SMITH-KLINE BEECHAM CLINICAL LABORATORIES INC., 305
SMURFIT RECYCLING, 292
SOUTHEAST MISSOURI STATE UNIVERSITY, 117
SOUTHERN EQUIPMENT COMPANY, 274
SOUTHERN ILLINOIS UNIVERSITY AT CARBONDALE, 117
SOUTHERN ILLINOIS UNIVERSITY AT EDWARDSVILLE, 117
SOUTHERN MISSOURI STATE UNIVERSITY, 117
SOUTHSIDE NATIONAL BANK IN ST. LOUIS, 86
SOUTHWEST BANK OF ST. LOUIS, 86
SOUTHWEST STEEL SUPPLY COMPANY, 159
SOUTHWESTERN BELL CORPORATION, 128
SPANN BUILDING MAINTENANCE COMPANY, 283
SPORLAN VALVE COMPANY, 159
THE SPORTING NEWS, 287
STANDARD MACHINE & MANUFACTURING COMPANY, 274
STAR MANUFACTURING INTERNATIONAL, INC., 181
JOHN STARK PRINTING COMPANY INC., 300
STATE FARM INSURANCE COMPANIES, 253
STIFEL NICOLAUS, 171
STORZ INSTRUMENT COMPANY, 227

STOUT INDUSTRIES INC., 159
WILLIAM A. STRAUB INC., 194
J.D. STREETT & COMPANY INC., 146
STRUCTURAL SYSTEMS INC., 70
STUPP BROS. BRIDGE & IRON COMPANY, 159
SUBSURFACE CONSTRUCTORS, 70
SUNMARK, INC., 181
SUNNEN PRODUCTS COMPANY, 274
SVERDRUP CORPORATION CENTRAL GROUP, 70
SWANK AUDIO VISUALS INC., 194
JOHN S. SWIFT COMPANY INC., 300
SWING-A-WAY MANUFACTURING COMPANY, 265
SYLVANIA LIGHTING DIVISION U.S., 138

T

TBWA ADVERTISING INC., 48
TARACORP INDUSTRIES, 265
TARLTON CORPORATION, 71
TEMPMASTER CORPORATION, 274
THOMPSON & MITCHELL, 265
TITANIUM RESEARCH & DEVELOPMENT COMPANY, 275
TOBER INDUSTRIES INC., 61
TONY'S INC., 245
TRANS WORLD AIRLINES INC., 313
THE TRAVELERS INSURANCE COMPANY, 253
TRI-STATE MOTOR TRANSIT COMPANY, 313
TUBULAR STEEL INC., 159
TURLEY-MARTIN COMPANY, 71

U

U.S. PAINT CORP., 112
U.S. RINGBINDER, 160
UNION CAMP CORPORATION, 292
UNION ELECTRIC COMPANY, 323
UNITED MISSOURI BANK, 87
UNITED POSTAL SAVINGS ASSOCIATION, 87
UNITED TECHNOLOGIES AUTOMOTIVE, 307
UNITED VAN LINES INC., 313
UNIVERSAL PRINTING COMPANY, 300
UNIVERSITY HOSPITAL/ST. LOUIS, 227
UNIVERSITY OF MISSOURI-COLUMBIA, 118
UNIVERSITY OF MISSOURI/ST. LOUIS, 118

V

VALENTEC KISCO, 160
VALLEY FARM DAIRY COMPANY INC., 181
VELVET FOODS INC., 181
VENTURE STORES INC., 194
VI-JON LABORATORIES INC., 195
VISITING NURSE ASSOCIATION OF GREATER ST. LOUIS, 227

W

WALGREEN DRUG STORES INC., 195
WANG LABORATORIES, 133
WARNER-JENKINSON COMPANY, 181
WASHINGTON UNIVERSITY, 118
WATLOW ELECTRIC MANUFACTURING CO., 138
FRED WEBER INC., 71
WEBSTER UNIVERSITY, 118
WEHMUELLER JEWELERS, 195
WEISS & NEUMAN SHOE COMPANY, 195
WELSH COMPANY, 265
WESTERN LITHOTECH, 300
WESTERN SUPPLIES COMPANY, 275
WESTERN TEXTILE PRODUCTS COMPANY, 62
WESTERN UNION FINANCIAL SERVICES INC, 172
WESTINGHOUSE ELECTRIC CORPORATION, 139
WETTERAU INCORPORATED, 181
WEYERHAEUSER PAPER COMPANY, 292
WHELAN SECURITY COMPANY INC., 283
WHITE CASTLE SYSTEM INC., 246
THOMAS J. WHITE COMPANY, 71
WICKS ORGAN COMPANY, 265
WIESE PLANNING & ENGINEERING INC., 275
WILLERT HOME PRODUCTS INC., 266
WILLIAMS PATENT CRUSHER & PULVERIZER COMPANY, 275
WINCO VENTILATOR COMPANY, 71
WITTE HARDWARE CORPORATION, 195
WOHL SHOE COMPANY, 195
WOOD RIVER TOWNSHIP HOSPITAL, 227
F.W. WOOLWORTH COMPANY, 195
WORLD WIDE INSURANCE GROUP, 254

X

XEROX CORPORATION, 139

Y

YMCA OF GREATER ST. LOUIS, 107
YELLOW FREIGHT SYSTEMS INC., 313
YOUNG SALES CORPORATION, 71

Z

ZERO MANUFACTURING COMPANY, 275
ZURHEIDE-HERRMANN INC., 151

AVAILABLE AT YOUR LOCAL BOOKSTORE
Knock 'em Dead
The Ultimate Job Seeker's Handbook

The all-new 1993 edition of Martin Yate's classic now covers the entire job search. The new edition features sections on: Where the jobs are now and where they will be tomorrow, how best to approach companies; keeping the financial boat afloat; how to recharge a stalled job hunt; "safety networking" to protect your job regardless of the economy; why corporate resume databases and electronic bulletin boards are the new wave for the career savvy; and bridging the gender gap in salary negotiations. Of course, the new addition also includes Yate's famous great answers to tough interview questions. When it comes to proven tactics that give readers the competitive advantage, Martin Yate is the authority to turn to. 6x9 inches, 312 pages, $7.95.

Resumes that Knock 'em Dead

Martin Yate reviews the marks of a great resume: what type of resume is right for each applicant, what always goes in, what always stays out, and why. Every single resume in *Resumes that Knock 'em Dead* was actually used by a job hunter to successfully obtain a job. No other book provides the hard facts for producing an exemplary resume. 8-1/2x11 inches, 216 pages, $7.95.

Cover Letters that Knock 'em Dead

The final word on not just how to write a "correct" cover letter, but how to write a cover letter that offers a powerful competitive advantage in today's tough job market. *Cover Letters that Knock 'em Dead* gives the essential information on composing a cover that wins attention, interest, and job offers. 8-1/2x11 inches, 184 pages, $7.95.

ALSO OF INTEREST...
The JobBank Series

There are now 20 *JobBank* books, each providing extensive, up-to-date employment information on hundreds of the largest employers in each job market. Recommended as an excellent place to begin your job search by *The New York Times, The Los Angeles Times, The Boston Globe, The Chicago Tribune,* and many other publications, *JobBank* books have been used by hundreds of thousands of people to find jobs.

Books available: *The Atlanta JobBank--The Boston JobBank--The Carolina JobBank--The Chicago JobBank--The Dallas-Ft. Worth JobBank--The Denver JobBank--The Detroit JobBank--The Florida JobBank--The Houston JobBank--The Los Angeles JobBank--The Minneapolis JobBank--The New York JobBank--The Ohio JobBank--The Philadelphia JobBank--The Phoenix JobBank--The St. Louis JobBank--The San Francisco JobBank--The Seattle JobBank--The Tennessee JobBank--The Washington DC JobBank.* Each book is 6x9 inches, over 300 pages, paperback, $15.95.

If you cannot find a book at your local bookstore, order it directly from the publisher. Please send payment including $3.75 for shipping and handling (for the entire order) to: Bob Adams, Inc., 260 Center Street, Holbrook, MA 02343. Credit card holders may call 1-800-USA-JOBS (in Massachusetts, 617-767-8100). Please check first at your local bookstore.